Cybertraps for Educators 2.0

Frederick S. Lane

CYBERTRAPS

Other Books by Frederick S. Lane

Raising Cyberethical Kids
Cybertraps for Expecting Moms & Dads
Cybertraps for Educators
Cybertraps for the Young
The Court and the Cross
American Privacy
The Decency Wars
The Naked Employee
Obscene Profits

Dedication

This book is dedicated to the educator licensing professionals and investigators from around the United States who work tirelessly to protect our children and to raise the standards of the teaching profession.

It is an honor to have met and worked with so many of you.

Table of Contents

Frederick S. Lane

Introduction: From Slate to Tablet

For Educators, Administrators, and Parents

Few professions are as necessary, or as challenging, as teaching. I am fortunate to have several teachers in my family, and I am married to a professor of art history, so I have seen up close the day-to-day difficulty of educating students with variable interests, talents, challenges, and levels of maturity. My decade of service as a member of the Burlington, VT School Board further underscored for me the complexity of educating students in an era of near-constant funding crises, political debates, and changing standards for assessment.

Few things, however, present so profound a challenge to educators as digital technology. For the last twenty years or so, I have researched and written about the impact of technology on society. Nine years ago, I wrote *Cybertraps for the Young* [NTI Upstream 2011], which detailed the legal trouble that children can get into through the use and misuse of electronic devices, online services, and smartphone apps. While writing that book, it became clear that technology was creating similar issues for teachers, school administrators, and even school board members.

The goal of this book is to help prospective, new, and seasoned educators better understand the potential challenges raised by technology, as well as the genuine legal risks that can arise through its misuse and malicious application. To be clear, I am a big fan of digital technology, and I firmly believe that its myriad benefits vastly outweigh the negative consequences.

At the same time, however, we need to be realistic about the potential for abuse and do everything possible to prevent students (and educators themselves) from becoming victims of cyber abuse. I hope that this book will help educators reflect on their personal use (or misuse) of technology and advance the conversation about how best to offer students all of the advantages of technology while minimizing the potential risks.

Overview of the Contents

I have divided *Cybertraps for Educators v. 2.0* into five main sections. The following is a brief description of each section.

Technology Themes in Principles I-IV of the Model Code of Ethics for Educators

The Model Code of Ethics for Educators contains five core principles. Only one, Principle V, deals explicitly with an educator's ethical use of technology. However, as we are all well aware, technology and digital communications are woven into every aspect of our lives. It is not surprising, then, that your use of technology plays a role in your ability to adhere to many, if not most, of the ethical standards listed in the first four principles of the MCEE.

Besides discussing the possible implications of technology use to Principles I through IV in the chapters below, I also include potentially relevant standards from those initial Principles at the end of each cybertrap chapter.

Privacy Cybertraps for Educators

In the second section of the book, I review some specific cybertraps that educators and administrators face due to their private use of technology. In general, these cybertraps do not involve direct interaction with students, which is where the most serious concerns arise. Most of the privacy cybertraps occur because of choices educators make in their personal lives and their enthusiasm for documenting those choices with mobile devices or on social media.

The central point of this section of the book is that maintaining actual privacy (*i.e.*, the ability to control access to and use of personal information) is exceedingly difficult if you digitize that information. The phrase "information wants to be free" appears multiple times in this book for a good reason; once data is stored digitally, it has an almost organic compulsion to spread. Replication and distribution of information are at the very core of the internet's design, so this should not come as a surprise. But far too often, as these cybertraps illustrate, people get unpleasant reminders of just how easily private content can become public.

The easy spread of information is relevant to educators because it changes the dynamic of serving as a role model. Before social media, a school community would have minimal opportunity to sit in judgment of how a teacher behaved in the privacy of his or her home unless something unusual happened (like an arrest). Today, however, far too many educators live their lives in front of multiple tiny windows. It should not come as a shock when students and parents peer through those windows and react to what they see.

Cybertraps in the Classroom

When we leave the outside world and move into the classroom, the use of digital technology by educators immediately gets dicier. Now, you are no longer responsible merely for your privacy but that of your students as well. You are also spending hours each day interacting with large numbers of technically-skilled teens and pre-teens, many of whom lack the judgment and impulse control required by such powerful devices.

The level of community and administrator scrutiny rises as well. Parents understandably want educators to behave appropriately, set a good example, and treat their children well. Mobile technology makes it much, much more straightforward for parents and guardians to "observe" what is taking place in the classroom.

In a polarized nation undergoing several fraught crises, the proliferation of mobile devices among students is a persistent headache for administrators. Controversial actions by teachers (poorly thought-out homework assignments, for instance) can create a social media firestorm. No school board member wants large hostile crowds showing up for public comment, and no administrator wants the nightmare of fielding death threats at district headquarters. More than anything else, this section underscores the degree to which technology is a classic double-edged sword: a wonderfully powerful educational resource that can easily be misused.

Criminal Cybertraps

For obvious reasons, the Cautionary Tales in this section are the ones that garner the most headlines. That makes sense; anything that threatens the health and safety of students is inherently newsworthy. As much as possible, I have tried to avoid sensationalism and prurience when selecting these tales. While the substance of some of these stories is difficult to absorb, they are actual events, and we need to understand how and why they occurred.

Most readers will correctly reassure themselves that they would never engage in the types of conduct that I describe. Numerically, at least, that is correct. Only a tiny percentage of educators engage in behavior severe enough to merit criminal charges. But most of us can understand at least some of the feelings and emotions that contribute to these crimes: stress, depression, addiction, loneliness, desire, lust, *etc.* More importantly, virtually all of us use the devices and the communication tools that appear in the criminal cautionary tales. I refer collectively to these incidents as "cybertraps" for a particular reason: anyone who is incautious or unwary can find themselves snared. One of the main objectives of the Model Code of Ethics for Educators is to enhance our ethical muscle memory to make entrapment less likely.

Conclusion and Appendix

In the Conclusion, I offer some ideas and suggestions for how educators and administrators can address the issues that I discuss in this book. Each of us is responsible for how we use technology; if we commit crimes or act unethically, that is not the fault of our employer. However, school districts and individual schools have powerful incentives to help educators and staff avoid cybertraps. As you'll see repeated throughout this book, the goal is to create a culture of cybersafety that can protect both students and educators.

With the kind permission of the National Association of State Directors of Teacher Education and Certification, I have reproduced the Model Code of Ethics for Educators (MCEE) in the Appendix.

General Structure of Each Cybertrap Chapter

Overviews

Each substantive chapter begins with an overview of the cybertrap in question. Although the specific contents vary from chapter to chapter, each provides some social and legal context for the misconduct in question.

Cautionary Tales

I have illustrated each of the cybertraps in this book with incidents drawn from a variety of different news sources published in countries around the world. The bulk of the events occurred in the United States, but there are also stories of teachers who have run into trouble in Canada, the United Kingdom, Australia, China, and more. What I hope this will illustrate is that the cybertraps faced by educators are increasingly global, given the worldwide reach of the internet and the universality of both hardware and software. No educational system—and no educator—is entirely risk-free when it comes to the temptations and tribulations of our technological age.

To better illustrate and illuminate the changing nature of technology and social media, the cautionary tales I have added to this second edition focus on incidents mostly drawn from 2018 and 2019. For some cybertraps, however, I have included older cautionary tales that are particularly informative, or where the total number of incidents for that particular cybertrap is low.

Where possible, I also have chosen illustrative incidents where there has been a final resolution (typically a guilty plea, a conviction, or a dismissal). In some instances, however, I have included an unresolved case because it stems from unusual or even unique facts.

When a "cautionary tale" involves mere allegations rather than a final resolution, it is essential to remember the fundamental legal principle that an individual is ***innocent until proven guilty***. Teachers can be wrongly accused or maliciously targeted by students. Similarly, the final verdict may reflect a lower degree of culpability than was initially charged. One of the unfortunate byproducts of our hyperconnected age is an often precipitous rush to judgment, which can have a devastating impact on a teacher's professional and personal life. It cannot be reiterated often enough: ***mere allegation is not proof.*** Unfortunately, the reality is that this foundational precept increasingly has been eroded by the types of digital communications discussed in this book.

Provisions of the MCEE Relevant to Each Chapter

For each chapter discussing a specific cybertrap, I have listed the provisions of the Model Code of Ethics for Educators that I think are the most relevant for that topic. While I believe that each list of MCEE provisions is thorough, they are by no means dispositive. You should carefully review the MCEE and make your own assessment of which ethical standards might apply to the cybertrap in question.

Sources

Given the length of this book, I made the strategic decision to put the sources and citations for the various Cautionary Tales on a web page on my **cybertraps.com** web site. You can access that page by entering the following URL in your browser of choice:

https://link.cybertraps.com/C4E2_Sources

The Kindle edition of this book will contain all of the sources, organized by cautionary tale. If anyone has any questions or would like any additional information, please do not hesitate to contact me.

Foreword

The Model Code of Ethics for Educators: Cultivating Agency by Curating Conversations

By Troy R. Hutchings

Codes of Ethics and Codes of Conduct

Codes of Ethics are certainly not new to professions that have an obligation to act in the public's best interest—especially those that require licensure. The country's oldest professional organization, the American Medical Association, created its first Code of Medical Ethics in 1847. The American Bar Association created a code in 1908, the American Nursing Association adopted its first formal code in 1950, the American Psychological Association in 1953, and the American Counseling Association in 1961. For most professions, codes of ethics are incorporated into practitioners' preservice, licensure and inservice career continuums – and play a major role in how they go about their work. But what are codes of professional ethics, and how do they differ from codes of conduct?

But what are codes of professional ethics and how do they differ from codes of conduct? Codes of conduct (e.g., laws, certification statutes and employment policies) establish basic boundaries that, if crossed, may result in significant professional consequence. They contain enforceable standards that establish the lowest threshold of acceptable behavior for all practitioners. Codes of ethics, on the other hand, prompt, guide and inform the everyday decision-making that is untouched by law and policy. Ideally, these codes empower practitioners to work together to identify and address a broad range of challenging situations well before a legal line has been crossed. Codes of ethics, on the other hand, prompt, guide, and inform the everyday decision-making that is untouched by law and policy. Ideally, these codes empower practitioners in a given field to work together to identify and address a broad range of challenging situations well before he or she has violated a legal prohibition.

Codes of ethics and codes of conduct are both critically important tools for establishing the norms for professional practice – but there are major differences in their methodology and application.

Codes of conduct, for instance, require compliance by practitioners, whereas codes of ethics inform choice. Codes of conduct define punishment for transgressions, while a code of ethics aims for anticipation and prevention of misconduct. While codes of conduct impose universal rules and standardized outcomes for all members of a profession, a code of ethics allows for a contextualized response based on the unique variables inherent in every situation.

When used together, codes of ethics and codes of conduct can help ensure that the myriad choices made by practitioners on a day-to-day or hour-by-hour basis bear public scrutiny. Even more importantly, they assuredly reflect the highest levels of beneficence and public trust, signifying that the profession in question is acting in the best interest of those that it serves. Nursing ethicists Epstein and Turner (2015) clearly delineate the relationship between ethics codes and regulations in the following statement: "The choice to pursue a career in nursing, medicine, business, law, or other professions involves incorporating the obligations and virtues of that smaller 'society.' These obligations and virtues are added to our already assumed obligations as members of the larger society".[n.1]

But here is where it gets a bit tricky. Most states have a code of conduct that clearly defines unacceptable behavior justifying licensure sanctions – but often, such documents are called codes of ethics. The *Texas Educators Code of Ethics,* for example, contains 30 "enforceable standards"—28 of which start with the clause "an educator shall not ...."[n.2] Similarly, the *Georgia Code of Ethics for Educators* states that their code "... defines unethical conduct justifying disciplinary sanction."[n.3.] Both documents contain statutory language that is more consistent with the definition of a code of conduct. This mischaracterization is not unique to Texas and Georgia; many jurisdictions across the country conflate the two concepts. Understandably, this has caused confusion regarding the need for an actual code of ethics in the field of education.

The proposed code of ethics for the teaching profession, the *Model Code of Ethics for Educators (MCEE)*, is not meant to be used for practitioner sanctions, performance objectives or evaluations. It is not a set of rules that delineates right from wrong. It does not tell us what to do, or even what not to do. It is not meant to bind or constrain educators. Instead, the MCEE invites practitioners to collectively determine how to best navigate the intense demands of the overlapping roles and personal relationships they are expected to foster by using the profession's collectively agreed-upon standards as a guide. Key concepts that are present in all professional codes of ethics—transparency, risk, unintended consequences, equity, appearance of impropriety, communication, conflict of interest, confidentiality, multiple relationships, role ambiguity—are at the core of the standards contained within the MCEE.

Model Code of Ethics for Educators: History and Development

The Model Code of Ethics for Educators was unveiled at the historic National Press Club in Washington D.C. on June 25, 2015, with many of the professional organizations that participated in its development in attendance:

- the National Education Association (NEA);
- the American Federation of Teachers (AFT);
- the American Association of Colleges for Teacher Education (AACTE);
- the Association of Teacher Educators (ATE);
- the Council of Chief State School Officers (CCSSO);
- the Council for the Accreditation of Educator Preparation (CAEP);
- the National Association of Secondary School Principals (NASSP);
- the National Association of Elementary School Principals (NAESP);
- the National Board for Teaching Professional Standards (NBPTS);
- the National Network of State Teachers of the Year (NNSTOY); and
- the National Association of State Directors of Teacher Education and Certification (NASDTEC).

Yet, the discussions that led to the MCEE's creation started much earlier within one organization that historically has been active in the field of educator professional practices: the National Association of State Directors of Teacher Education and Certification (NASDTEC). Founded in 1928, NASDTEC represents state and provincial departments of education and professional standards boards that are responsible for the preparation, licensure, and, if necessary, the sanctioning of K-12 educational personnel.

In 1997, NASDTEC established the only annual conference in the country devoted solely to the topic of educator ethics, as well as the investigation and adjudication of educator misconduct. The Professional Practices Institute—a conference attended each year by attorneys, investigators, state directors, education preparation providers, and district officials—provided the setting for the initial conversations that eventually led to the development of the MCEE.

Several purposeful initiatives between 2012 and 2014—a national symposium, surveys, webinars, meetings with professional organization partners – affirmed the need and the professional organizational support for the development of a professional code of ethics. In the spring of 2014, a diverse and representative group of P-12 educational practitioners were selected by their professional organizations to serve on the MCEE Task Force. The task force members—practicing paraprofessionals, teachers, school administrators, district superintendents and state department of education officials from around the country—f irst gathered in Baltimore, Maryland in June of 2014 to start the year-long process of creating a code of ethics. Regular face-to-face meetings, along with numerous virtual meetings resulted in a draft edition of the code that was disseminated for public comment in February of 2015. After numerous revisions based on public comment, the final draft of the document was unveiled at the National Press Club in Washington D.C. on June 25, 2015.

Moving Forward

Numerous educational organizations have moved quickly to adopt the *Model Code of Ethics for Educators* since its introduction. These include state departments of education, county offices of education, school districts, educator preparation programs and professional organizations. As the promotion and implementation of the MCEE continue, we should ask ourselves this pertinent question: What impact will professional ethics have on the everyday working lives of educators?

In a series of articles that I wrote for *RealClear Politics* in 2016[n.4], I envisioned a future in which professional ethics was a natural part of the preparation and professional learning of educators – as it is in other professions:

> At first, the changes would be structural—teachers would receive training on professional ethics in preparation programs, have discussions involving ethical issues with mentors as they navigate the early years of their careers, and ideally, continue to get refreshers in the form of professional development in which teams of teachers revisit the principles of professional ethics … and discuss with each other how they apply to their own challenges in the classroom.
>
> All of this would go a long way toward helping individual teachers navigate the complexities of their role and become more aware of the unintended consequences of the thousands of decisions they make on a daily basis. But over time, once the idea of professional ethics has become engrained in the field as a whole—and as important to teaching as content and pedagogy—the impact could be transformative.

Educators would avoid falling into the trap of assuming that misconduct is a discrete event and something that only happens to teachers that lose sight of their personal moral compass. Instead, it would acknowledge the collective risk that all teachers face as a result of the demands of their overlapping roles and the intensely personal relationships they are expected to follow.

In turn, this understanding would give teachers permission to approach each other in candid, professional discussions about uncomfortable subjects. This kind of professional environment would allow teachers to self-regulate as a field. And the collective awareness of professional obligations fostered by this environment would allow many situations to be addressed before damage is done and the teachers' reputations—and students' lives—face irrevocable harm.

But that is just the beginning. If these kinds of conversations are brought to light in transparent ways, parents and the community as a whole also could understand the challenges that teachers face ... over time, this understanding could lead to a much deeper respect for teachers—and the profession as a whole. Perhaps more than anything, that's what professional ethics can bring to the field—a rethinking of teaching as a true profession, in the eyes of policymakers, the public, and most importantly, in the eyes of teachers themselves.

Let's be perfectly clear—the *Model Code of Ethics for Educators* is not the solution for every challenge facing teachers today. In the world of professional ethics, practitioners themselves are ultimately responsible for how they address those challenges. The effective application of professional ethics demands honest and transparent discussions about the complexities inherent within our profession, while working together to create appropriate solutions.

The real power comes from no longer having to go it alone - and that is the beauty of resources such as Frederick Lane's latest book, *Cypertraps for Educators 2.0.* By providing a rich application of the MCEE to authentic case studies involving the use of technology and digital media, educators are prompted to discuss a framework of decision-making that is based on collective professional norms – as opposed to simply following a personal code of morality.

And at its very core, that is exactly what professional ethics attempts to do – inspire and cultivate agency among practitioners.

Troy R. Hutchings, Ed.D.
Senior Policy Advisor, NASDTEC
Subject Matter Expert – *Model Code of Ethics for Educators*
Stockton, NJ, August 2020

Sources:

[n.1] Epstein, B. and Turner, M. (2015). "The nursing code of ethics: Its value and its history." *The Online Journal of Issues in Nursing.* Vol 20, No 2, May 2015.

[n.2] http://ritter.tea.state.tx.us/sbecrules/tac/chapter247/ch247.pdf

[n.3] https://www.gapsc.com/Rules/Current/Ethics/505-6-.01.pdf

[n.4] Hutchings, T. (2016). "Professional ethics and professionalizing education." *RealClear Politics.* October 21, 2016.

Section One

Technology Themes in Principles I-IV of the Model Code of Ethics for Educators

Logically, the bulk of this book will focus on the technology-related issues covered by Principle V of the MCEE and its subsidiary ethical standards. My background is in computers and law, so that is the area which best aligns with my experience and interests. My first exposure to computers occurred in 1972, when I took part in a summer computing class that gave me access to the card reader, paper tape drive, and shared workstations attached to a Digital Equipment Corporation mid-frame. I got my first personal computer in the fall of 1984 and have worked on various types of technology ever since.

As you'll see, technology is relevant to the first four principles of the MCEE, even though none of them reference it explicitly. But as we all are aware, technology is pervasive in our society. As a result, cyberethics should govern every aspect of an educator's professional and personal life. Looking forward, we cannot adequately prepare students to be successful teachers and positive role models in a school community without providing them with a solid understanding of the cyberethical issues that resonate throughout the MCEE.

Given the tremendous impact of technology on the education profession and the lives of educators in general, the MCEE Task Force deserves a lot of credit for devoting one of its five ethical principles entirely to the responsible and ethical use of technology. That decision makes the MCEE a remarkably forward-looking document. Very few, if any of the codes of ethics adopted by other professions make any mention of technology at all, let alone devote an entire section to it. As a result, those professions find themselves in the challenging and unenviable position of trying to apply often archaic language and concepts to today's hyper-accelerated social media environment.

It is both mete and just that educators should take the lead in addressing the unique ethical concerns raised by the use of technology (problems that are increasingly identified by the umbrella term "cyberethics"). No other professionals spend so much concentrated time with young people, the vast majority of whom are avid users of technology. Most educators realize that to be effective, they need to have a basic understanding of technology and incorporate it into their teaching practice.

Even if that is not a personal preference for a given educator, school administrators, school boards, state and federal regulators, and parents all expect teachers to incorporate technology into the classroom, from the earliest days of kindergarten to the last terminal days of senioritis.

Those professional and external expectations, combined with the myriad pressures that educators put on themselves, all heighten the potential for educators to stumble into cybertraps. One of the most significant contributions of the MCEE is to help educators develop a type of muscle memory that can help them navigate the ethically gray areas of their work. Another is to encourage frank and honest conversations among educators about how best to handle the seemingly endless decisions that must be made each day inside the classroom and out.

Chapter 1

Technology and Responsibility to the Profession

Principle I: Responsibility to the Profession

The professional educator is aware that trust in the profession depends upon a level of professional conduct and responsibility that may be higher than required by law. This entails holding one and other educators to the same ethical standards.

The Model Code of Ethics for Educators encourages educational professionals to show *responsibility to the profession of teaching* in three ways:

- By demonstrating responsibility to oneself as an ethical professional;

- By recognizing an obligation to address and attempt to resolve ethical issues in a manner consistent with the MCEE; and

- By promoting and advancing the profession both within and beyond the school community.

Subsection A of Principle I raises the most issues concerning educator use of technology. In broad strokes, that subsection underscores the fact that each educator is ultimately responsible for his or her ethical conduct. Moreover, he or she should be sufficiently self-aware to recognize when various aspects of his or her personal life might undercut ethical conduct inside or outside of the classroom. Self-awareness and self-care are especially necessary skills for educators who use social media and digital communications technology as many of the cybertraps I discuss are exacerbated by personal or professional turmoil.

As you will see, many of these initial ethical guidelines and performance indicators are broad enough that they will apply to many if not most of the cybertraps I discuss below. Nonetheless, it is worthwhile to provide a brief introduction so that you can start reflecting on the language of the MCEE and how it might apply to your use of technology.

MCEE I.A.2. Knowing and upholding the procedures, policies, laws and regulations relevant to professional practice regardless of personal views.

As a condition of obtaining and holding a teacher's license, there is a reasonable expectation that you will have a basic familiarity with the procedures, policies, regulations, and laws that pertain to your work in the classroom and the broader school community. These *codes of conduct* establish the bar for acceptable behavior by educators.

You don't have to have every single relevant provision memorized (no rational person would try to do so). However, you do need to have a working familiarity with them. It is reasonable to expect that your supervisors, your school district, and your union will help you prioritize what you need to know. Ultimately, however, it is your professional responsibility to educate yourself enough to avoid misconduct.

This ethical standard also includes an implied duty to keep yourself up to date on any changes to the codes that are relevant to your profession. You should pay particular attention to code provisions that regulate the use of technology. When it comes to technology, things tend to change very quickly. Laws and regulations don't keep pace with technology updates as well as they should, but they do typically change more rapidly than those dealing with other topics. Again, there should be structures in place in your district to help keep you updated.

MCEE I.A.3. Holding oneself responsible for ethical conduct.

MCEE I.A.3 is the beating, aspirational heart of the Model Code of Ethics for Educators. Regardless of the precise depth of your knowledge regarding specific policies, regulations, or laws, the MCEE makes it clear that your core responsibility to your profession is to conduct yourself ethically.

Through reflection and conversation with your colleagues, you can understand what the MCEE means for your professional work, the intersection of your personal and professional activities, and your role in the school community.

MCEE I.A.4. Monitoring and maintaining sound mental, physical, and emotional health necessary to perform duties and services of any professional assignment; and taking appropriate measures when personal or health-related issues may interfere with work-related duties.

In attempting to meet the objectives of the MCEE, there is probably nothing more important that you can do than to practice self-care and demonstrate self-awareness about your mental, emotional, and physical health. A significant number of the cybertraps discussed in this book either arise or are exacerbated by circumstances occurring in the educator's life.

The classic example, of course, is the educator who is having trouble in his or her marriage and, while feeling emotionally vulnerable, begins a seemingly innocuous electronic conversation with a student. In a remarkably short time, the potent combination of emotional fragility and tech-fueled intimacy can lead to an inappropriate and career-ending criminal violation.

Every teacher who is reading this book has worked for years to earn a teaching certificate and license. That's a considerable investment of time, money, and effort. It only makes sense to safeguard that investment by taking proactive steps to deal with any issues or vulnerabilities that might make you more vulnerable to the cybertraps discussed in this book.

MCEE I.A.5. Refraining from professional or personal activity that may lead to reduced effectiveness within the school community.

This admonition deserves particular attention because "effectiveness" is the ultimate yardstick by which administrators judge someone's fitness to teach. The term "effectiveness," of course, encompasses several different criteria: familiarity with your subject matter, your classroom management, your planning and preparation, your interpersonal skills, your collegiality, the respect you command, and so forth.

Your use of digital technology is relevant to several of these factors. Do you use digital technology to harass your colleagues or school parents? That will reduce your effectiveness. Do you post unhinged rants about politics, religion, vaccination, or other sensitive topics? Ditto. Are your middle or high school age students giggling over your online photos? Also a problem.

Inevitably, this provision of the MCEE raises concerns about First Amendment rights and self-censorship. Those are legitimate issues to consider, but it is always important to remember that under the best of circumstances, "free speech" rarely means "free from consequences." That is particularly true when you serve in a public-facing position where parents of the children for whom you are a role model pay your salary.

MCEE I.A.7. Taking responsibility and credit only for work actually performed or produced, and acknowledging the work and contributions made by others.

Ever since the widespread adoption of the World Wide Web in the early 1990s, far too many people have viewed the internet as an endless source of free content—music, movies, books, photos, text, etc. Taking and using copyrighted material without permission, of course, is intellectual property theft.

It took a long time for copyright owners to get their act together, but most music and movie companies now use a variety of sophisticated tools to prevent infringement. Penalties for intellectual property theft can include loss of access to the internet, civil fines, or even criminal prosecution (in extreme cases). It's also worth pointing out that if you use school equipment to download stolen content, there is a real possibility that your school or your district may also face penalties. Pay for content!

As a community role model, your handling of intellectual property has important ethical implications. Children, as we all know, are keen observers of adult behavior. If they see you using pirated videos in your class or using photos in your lectures without proper permission or attribution, their takeaway will be that they are allowed to do so as well.

MCEE I.B.2. Maintaining fidelity to the Code by taking proactive steps when having reason to believe that another educator may be approaching or involved in an ethically compromising situation.

One of the byproducts of the current digital era is that we know a lot more about our family members, our friends, and our colleagues than we did pre-Facebook, Instagram, or Pinterest. It is not an accident that the acronym TMI (Too Much Information) has become so popular.

The MCEE contains the reminder, however, that if you learn (online or off) that one of your colleagues is behaving in a way that might be unethical, you have an ethical obligation to take proactive steps to address the issue. If the ethically-compromising situation involves actual or suspected abuse of a child, then you may have not only an ethical but a legal obligation to take action. According to an April 2019 report prepared by ChildWelfare.gov, "[a]pproximately 47 States, the District of Columbia, American Samoa, Guam, the Northern Mariana Islands, Puerto Rico, and the Virgin Islands designate professions whose members are mandated by law to report child maltreatment." In all of those states, "educator" or "teacher" is one of the designated occupations. Three other states (Indiana, New Jersey, and Wyoming) require *everyone* to report suspected or actual child abuse regardless of their employment (or lack thereof).

Exactly what steps you should take will depend, of course, on the facts of the matter. And obviously, there is the potential that this can result in difficult conversations with your colleague or your supervisors. There is often strong institutional resistance to hanging dirty laundry out to dry. Ideally, ongoing discussion of the provisions and objectives of the MCEE will lessen the need for those conversations. But the overarching ethical obligation is clear: we are all responsible for the integrity and ethical conduct of our professions.

MCEE I.C.2. Engaging in respectful discourse regarding issues that impact the profession.

You can make a decent argument can that the most destructive impact of the internet is on the tone and tenor of our conversations with each other. The absence of face-to-face interaction, the speed, the apparent anonymity, the crowd *zeitgeist*—these factors all encourage people to communicate with each other in a remarkably rude and hostile fashion. Not everyone does so, of course, but there are very few internet users who have not been the recipient of some type of online abuse, from an insulting and dismissive reply to a full-on trolling.

Here again, your status as a role model in your community comes into play. If you find yourself online using language that is abusive or demeaning, then you should probably spend some time thinking about those choices. It's far too easy for students to see that their teacher is engaging in online fights; depending on the channel, you might be arguing with and cursing out a student without realizing it. It's an old-fashioned concept, but it is beneath the dignity of educators to act that way online.

The problem, of course, is that it is difficult to take the high road when all the action appears to be taking place on the low. But we all have complaints about online culture, and it won't start to improve until we each begin taking steps to improve our behavior. The MCEE offers the reminder that teachers have an ethical obligation to be among the first to do so.

MCEE I.C.5. Advocating for adequate resources and facilities to ensure equitable opportunities for all students.

From the release of the very first personal computer, a "digital divide" has existed among students. At its most basic, the digital divide referred to access to computing hardware—first computers, then tablets, and now most recently, smartphones. Over time, however, we have seen dramatic decreases in the costs of computing devices, so that particular divide is diminishing. Nonetheless, every educator has an ethical obligation to make sure that his or her school is addressing any technology-related resource and facility disparities that contribute to inequality in educational opportunities.

The digital divide is not the only one that exists, of course. Some of your students might be hindered by an "opportunity divide," which arises from the fact that not everyone has access to the internet or can pay for data plans that are fast enough to do homework. Others may experience a "comprehension divide," stemming from differences in literacy and critical thinking skills. And even if they can get online, some of your students may experience a "participation divide." They may discover that it is difficult to make their voices heard online, or that people cyberbully them when they try to participate in virtual discussions.

Educators should be sensitive to the different types of divides that can interfere with student achievement. When they see disparities of various kinds, educators have an ethical duty under the MCEE to alert their supervisors and to advocate for changes that will reduce such inequality.

Chapter 2

Technology and the Responsibility for Professional Competence

Principle II: Responsibility for Professional Competence

The professional educator is committed to the highest levels of professional and ethical practice, including demonstration of the knowledge, skills and dispositions required for professional competence.

The Model Code of Ethics for Educators encourages educational professionals to show **responsibility for professional competence** in three ways:

- By demonstrating a commitment to high standards of practice;

- By demonstrating responsible use of data, materials, research, and assessment; and

- By acting in the best interests of all students.

When it comes to the littlest tappers and swipers, most acceptable use concerns are alleviated by their inability to read and type, and by the fact that you can quickly put electronic devices out of reach. Nonetheless, you should use this opportunity to introduce some essential concepts.

At first glance, it might seem like Principle II has relatively little to do with technology. After all, only a small percentage of teachers teach technology or work in district information technology departments.

In actuality, though, familiarity with technology and competence in its use underlies many of the ethical standards that make up this principle. Like it or not, digital technology (and in particular, digital communication technology) is woven into virtually every aspect of a teacher's work. Logically, then, a duty of demonstrating professional competence carries with it an obligation to have basic competency regarding the use of technology.

MCEE II.A.3. Advocating for equitable educational opportunities for all students.

At the end of the previous chapter, I discussed MCEE I.C.5, which identifies an educator's ethical obligation to advocate for "adequate resources and facilities to ensure equitable opportunities for all students." MCEE II.A.3 is similar, but the emphasis is slightly broader.

The distinction is not insignificant. This ethical standard reflects the idea that a demonstration of professional competence goes beyond the more limited focus on purchase-order based "resources and facilities" discussed under Principle I. Instead, it requires that educators consider the systemic availability of educational opportunities and how those opportunities are allocated not only to specific groups of students but to individuals as well.

When you are considering your ethical obligation of advocacy regarding "resources and facilities," it's easy to understand how technology would be part of that advocacy, particularly in the higher grade levels. But any discussion of support for "equitable educational opportunities" in the broadest sense must consider technology as well. What disparities are there among students in their ability to use technology? Is there equity in exposure to digital skills and preparation for emerging jobs? Are there differences in necessary basic online skills, such as research, job searches, online citizenship, or forms of expression? Are efforts being made in your school or school district to help all students develop the critical thinking skills required to evaluate online information and distinguish what is real and what is fake?

MCEE II.A.5. Reflecting upon and assessing one's professional skills, content knowledge, and competency on an ongoing basis.

To meet your ethical duty of demonstrating professional competence, the MCEE contemplates that you will periodically conduct a self-assessment regarding your "professional skills, content knowledge, and competency." The primary focus of that self-assessment should be on the contents of the substantive areas that you teach. The next necessary topic for reflection is on the mechanics of teaching, from classroom management to record-keeping to curriculum preparation.

The final area that requires ongoing self-assessment is your familiarity with the technology that you use in all aspects of your teaching career. One important thing to remember here is that "professional competence" does not require that you be a technology expert. That's an unnecessary burden, particularly given everything else that a competent, professional educator needs to do.

What it does mean, however, is that if you use digital technology in the classroom, you have an ethical obligation to think about whether you are competent in its use. Do you know the essential functions? Are you aware of any potential pitfalls? Can you successfully explain how to use the technology to students and warn them about potential cybertraps? Do you know enough to protect yourself from any misbehavior by students?

One step that you should take to meet this ethical duty is to conduct a technology audit. Maintain a list of the hardware you use, including the type of the device, the manufacturer, and the model. (And while you're at it, jot down the serial number in a safe place for insurance purposes). Do the same thing for your most important software programs, both on your computer(s) and your mobile devices. It may seem daunting, but you will probably discover that you only use 15 or 20 programs or apps regularly. Prioritize your audit based on how often you use each device and application.

Once you've finished the audit, then go back and consider the questions above for each piece of hardware and software. The more time you think about these issues, the less likely it is that you will stumble into one or more of the cybertraps discussed in this book.

MCEE II.A.6. Committing to ongoing professional learning.

In conducting your self-assessment regarding your competence with technology, you may admit to yourself that it's not as good as it could be. If that's the case, then you should heed the terms of MCEE II.A.6, which states that educators have an ethical obligation to "commit to ongoing professional learning." Again, you should focus the bulk of that learning on your substantive area(s) of expertise and the mechanics of teaching, but you should not disregard the duty to stay up to speed on relevant hardware and software.

That can seem like a daunting task, but if you've done the audit discussed in the previous section, then the process is much more efficient. You don't have to try to understand *all* technology, just the tech that you regularly use (and in particular, the tech you use in the classroom).

Where can you learn about the tech you use? Answering that question can seem like a challenge, given how much material is written about technology every single day. It's far too easy to look at the flood of information and just throw up your hands. But meeting the ethical obligation for professional competence means finding a path forward. In this respect, search engines and filters are your friends. Using your narrowed list of most-used hardware and software, you can periodically search Google News for updates or create alerts to have relevant articles sent directly to your inbox.

In addition to your research, you should encourage your school and your school district to help with this ongoing professional learning. Your school or district IT department should be issuing periodic updates regarding the software and hardware that the school district itself requires you to use.

Keep in mind, however, that your district's IT department may not be able to track developments for all of the hardware and software used by educators in the building, so you have an independent obligation to keep your equipment and your software up to date. You should make it a priority to read any tech-related updates you receive. It's the information you are given and *don't* read that will make you most vulnerable to cybertraps. Engaging in ongoing professional learning regarding the tech you use is not just a good idea; it may save your career.

MCEE II.B.1. Appropriately recognizing others' work by citing data or materials from published, unpublished, or electronic sources when disseminating information.

To the untrained eye (say, for instance, the average 12-year-old), the internet looks like an endless buffet of Free Stuff. That's not entirely incorrect; there is, in fact, quite a large amount of free material online. If you like to read, you can get lost in Project Gutenberg (60,000 books and counting); if you need free images, you can find gorgeous and freely-shared photos on sites like Unsplash, Flickr, or Pexels; and you can even download free music from numerous websites.

Most adults, on the other hand, are at least nominally aware that downloading copyrighted content from the internet without paying for it is intellectual property theft. Civil courts typically handle claims of copyright infringement, but it is also a crime and, in particularly severe instances, has been prosecuted as such.

MCEE II.B.1 reminds educators that they have an ethical duty to go beyond the strict requirements of contract and criminal law. Teachers are required to avoid using anyone else's work as their own, regardless of the source.

Although all provisions of the MCEE are integral to an educator's obligation to be a good role model, this one is remarkably direct. If you are careless or cavalier in your use of other people's work, your students will be as well. That will damage their academic and professional careers and, more broadly, contribute to the further degradation of intellectual life online and off.

MCEE II.B.3. Conducting research in an ethical and responsible manner with appropriate permission and supervision.

One of the blessings (or curses, depending on your perspective) that digital technology has brought to our lives is the ability to quantify ridiculous amounts of our lives. How many steps have YOU taken today? How many flights of stairs have you climbed? Have you drunk all 64 ounces of your recommended daily water consumption? The list goes on and on.

Not surprisingly, researchers are making enthusiastic use of the data-collection capabilities of mobile devices (particularly fitness trackers and smartwatches). Shortly after I got my most recent smartwatch, I began getting requests to participate in medical research projects. Researchers wanted access to the data collected by my watch regarding heart rate, noise, falls, and so on. For each of the studies, researchers included multiple screens of information about the project's Institutional Review Board process, the privacy measures to protect my data, and my right to exit the study and delete my data at any time.

The ease with which you can harvest data from mobile devices (and their users) offers a powerful temptation to educators working in grades K-12. If you are teaching statistics in middle school, for instance, you might think it a good idea to use one of the many online survey tools to show how the students in your class respond to different questions. But depending on the specific topics you select, you might be asking for information that is private or potentially embarrassing. It is easy to get distracted by the many bells and whistles that software and app developers dangle in front of us. It is even easier still to overlook the potential ethical implications of those programs and the possible misuse of the data they collect.

The takeaway here should be obvious: Before you start collecting data from students about them or their families, regardless of the purpose or how trivial it might seem, you have an ethical obligation to discuss the exercise with your colleagues and your supervisors.

MCEE II.B.5. Creating, maintaining, disseminating, storing, retaining and disposing of records and data relating to one's research and practice, in accordance with district policy, state and federal laws.

In this ethical standard, the MCEE encourages you to reflect on the fact that it is not enough to make sure you ethically conduct your research. You also have an ongoing ethical obligation to make sure that you handle any data generated by your inquiry as required by all relevant policies and legal requirements.

There are two ways in which technology is particularly relevant to this performance indicator. The first reveals the ongoing tension between law and policy (the bare minimum of good conduct) and your ethical duty as an educator. Specifically, it may be perfectly legal to collect various types of information from your students, particularly if you have protocols in place to keep it safe after doing so. But the ethical question to ask is whether you should even gather the data in the first place. Put another way, has every effort been made to make sure the amount of data collected is as limited as possible? The amount of data generated by our use of technology and the ease of obtaining it heightens the ethical obligation to think carefully about how research is structured.

The second reason that technology is relevant to this ethical guideline is best summed up by the truism "information wants to be free." Once information has been collected or digitized, it can be next to impossible to keep that information from escaping out into the world. The nature of the data plays a role; a sexting photo is far more likely to be stolen or retransmitted than a survey of the brushing habits of your 6th graders. Still, as any cybersecurity specialist will tell you, it can be surprisingly challenging to make sure that data is not lost, stolen, mistakenly transmitted, left insecure online, and so on. Before engaging in any research, you have an ethical obligation to make sure that you have drawn up the best possible plan for protecting the data you collect and have included a full risk assessment of the consequences of unintended data disclosure.

MCEE II.C.1. Increasing students' access to the curriculum, activities, and resources in order to provide a quality and equitable educational experience.

This ethical standard is similar to both MCEE I.C.5 and II.A.3. The chief distinction here is that this underscores your obligation to consider the extent to which your students face access issues "to the curriculum, activities, and resources" necessary to obtain "a quality and equitable educational experience."

There are a lot of potential barriers to access in contemporary society, but without question, technology is at the forefront. While the digital divide has shrunk and continues to do so (particularly concerning smartphone use among high school students), we have not eliminated it. In particular, there are likely to be inequalities among students regarding the availability of computers (laptops or desktops), the speed of internet access (assuming it is available at all), and the types of paid resources online each student can access.

Neither districts nor individual educators can solve all of these national challenges. The text of the MCEE makes it clear, however, that educators have an ethical obligation to advocate for policies aimed at reducing technology disparities among students.

Even more importantly, the MCEE infuses the Hippocratic oath into the standards governing educator conduct: "First, do no harm." In the context of teaching, that standard suggests that your curriculum and classroom assignments should not rely on technology or online resources that are not readily available to all students. Similarly, you should try to avoid rewarding students whose work reflects better access to more sophisticated technology.

Technology is so thoroughly embedded in our culture these days that it is far too easy to assume that it is evenly distributed and equally accessible to all. The core ethical obligations of fairness and equality of opportunity reflected in the MCEE require each of us to scrutinize our assumptions.

MCEE II.C.2. Working to engage the school community to close achievement, opportunity, and attainment gaps.

As I have discussed throughout these first two chapters, there are myriad ways in which digital technology is relevant to or is a contributing factor to gaps in "achievement, opportunity, and attainment." No one is better positioned than an educator to observe the role that disparities in access to hardware, software, the internet, and online resources play in the relative opportunities enjoyed by their students.

Of equal importance is the fact that educators stand at the intersection of an essential social institution (schools), the people who support that institution (taxpayers), the children who attend, and their parents. To the extent that effective schools and successful students are a positive benefit for society as a whole, the MCEE instructs educators to use their position to raise policy issues concerning educational gaps with the community and to advocate for solutions.

MCEE II.C.3. Protecting students from any practice that harms or has the potential to harm students.

If there is one performance indicator that reflects the motivation for this book, it is this one. As role models, as individuals serving *in loco parentis*, and simply as decent fellow human beings, educators have a clear and unequivocal ethical obligation to avoid using technology in a way "that harms or has the potential to harm students."

The bulk of this book consists of examples of educators who forgot or ignored that fundamental ethical rule (and really, is there any other ethical precept that is more central to teaching?). Some of the cybertraps are a reflection of sociopathy or dishonesty, and others are the result of carelessness or even epic stupidity. You will likely read about some of these educators and say to yourself that there is no way that you would make THAT mistake. And hopefully, that's true. But don't forget that many of the former teachers discussed below would have said the same thing.

Again, Hippocrates was right: "First, do no harm."

Chapter 3

Technology and the Responsibility to Students

Principle III: Responsibility to Students

The professional educator has a primary obligation to treat students with dignity and respect. The professional educator promotes the health, safety and well being of students by establishing and maintaining appropriate verbal, physical, emotional and social boundaries.

The Model Code of Ethics for Educators encourages educational professionals to show *responsibility to students* in three ways:

- By respecting the rights and dignity of students;

- By demonstrating an ethic of care; and

- By maintaining student trust and confidentiality when interacting with students in a developmentally appropriate manner and within proper limits.

Principle III, Responsibility to Students, is at the core of each educator's ethical obligation. Teachers have the honor of serving *in loco parentis* for millions of students every single day, and this principle describes the solemn ethical duties associated with that responsibility. As we will see, technology is both central to the execution of those ethical duties and far too often, also the most significant temptation an educator will face.

MCEE III.A.2. Interacting with students with transparency and in appropriate settings.

Digital technology is wreaking profound change throughout our society. Few changes, however, are as consequential as the fact that virtually every high school student in the United States now carries a device that enables her or him to communicate directly with billions of people around the world at any time during the day or night.

That change has happened so quickly and has been so comprehensive that it is difficult for us fully to absorb the seismic quality of the shift. But that change lies at the core of virtually all of the student-related cybertraps this book will discuss.

The most obvious point is that just two decades ago, there were no smartphones and no communications apps (social media or otherwise). If someone was interested in speaking with a student by phone, they typically needed to call the landline associated with the student's house. A teacher could pre-arrange to have a private call with a student, aided by the fact that the percentage of households with both parents working grew steadily throughout the 1980s and 1990s. But even so, it would have been unthinkable that a teacher could safely call a student (or vice versa) in the wee hours of the night.

We now live in a very different world. Like most of us, students and teachers now take their global communication devices to bed with them. If a student messages a teacher late in the evening, there is an excellent chance that the messages are flowing directly from one bedroom to another. Even if the subject matter of the chat is utterly banal, the timing lends an implicit intimacy to the exchange that is inconsistent with professional boundaries. And the reality is that it doesn't take much for such conversations to shift to wildly inappropriate topics.

In the previous chapter, we discussed the ethical obligation of educators to know how the technology they use works. One of the most important things to understand is that text and app messages are generally not archived and are not readily reviewable by your school district. Districts should make it clear that educators will face disciplinary action if they engage in non-transparent communication with students except in extreme emergencies.

Fortunately, any communication tool can be made transparent by including other adults in the conversation, which should be standard practice (absent legitimate legal or privacy considerations). Having one-on-one electronic communication with a student is rarely an "appropriate setting," especially if done late at night and without the knowledge of the student's parents or guardians.

MCEE III.A.3. Communicating with students in a clear, respectful, and culturally sensitive manner.

The tone of both our public and private discourse has coarsened considerably over the past decade. People say things on social media today that would have been (or should have been) unthinkable just a few years ago. Unfortunately, educators have not fully resisted this national trend. Every few weeks, districts fire a teacher for posting something about his or her students (or a parent) that shouldn't be said face-to-face, let alone broadcast to the entire world. We are all at risk for inappropriate social media updates, but, fair or not, the scrutiny on educators is much more intense.

First, teachers are supposed to be role models to their students; when their public statements demonstrate hostility to a particular student or to that student's culture, they are failing one of the core missions of education. Second, disrespect towards a student or a student's culture reduces the effectiveness of the teacher in the classroom. Third, disrespectful public discourse by a teacher damages the profession in the eyes of the public. Educators, and public schools more broadly, face enough challenges without further erosion caused by intemperate and disrespectful posts and tweets.

To paraphrase the old saying, "Tweet in haste, repent at leisure." A core goal of the MCEE is to assist educators in slowing down and being more deliberate in their actions. That's true for life in general and especially for social media.

MCEE III.A.4. Taking into account how appearance and dress can affect one's interactions and relationships with students.

Until recently, this performance indicator would have applied almost entirely to the clothes you choose to wear at work. Before social media, the vast bulk of your interactions with students would take place in a school building and most of those in the classroom. Once school was over, teachers and students generally socialized in different environments, so teachers were able to let their hair down a bit without worrying that they might set a bad example. (Of course, teachers who worked in smaller communities had to be mindful of the fact that they might run into students and parents anywhere around town.)

With the advent of social media, however, teachers and students began to "socialize" in the same cyberplaces. And since social media is mostly a visual phenomenon, judgments are rendered every time teacher posts a selfie or a photograph online. How does he look? What is she wearing? Is she spending a holiday at the shore? Is he drinking with buddies at a dive bar? Ish she out clubbing with a bridesmaid's party? If there's anything comical, embarrassing, or risqué about the teacher's appearance, people inevitably will pass judgment and form opinion's about the teacher's character.

It's not fair in general, and it's intensely unfair for female educators, who tend to be judged more harshly for outfits and behavior deemed too provocative or overtly sexual. There is a possibility that as social media becomes a more and more regular part of our lives, we will become less judgmental about what teachers do and how they dress when they're not at work. Social attitudes, of course, can undergo dramatic change.

Female educators, unfortunately, are not the only ones who experience this type of Instashaming. A recent study published in the *Journal of Vascular Surgery* suggested that photos of doctors in bikinis or enjoying alcohol constituted "potentially unprofessional content." Female doctors responded by posting a veritable tidal wave of swimsuit and cocktail photos using the hashtag #MedBikini.

Clearly, we do not live in a judgment-free society yet, and perhaps we never will. The MCEE implicitly acknowledges that in this performance indicator by reminding educators that they have an ethical obligation to think about the choices they make about their appearance and their wardrobe. This book will serve as a reminder that those choices can be seen much farther and for far longer than most educators realize.

MCEE III.A.7. Avoiding multiple relationship with students which might impair objectivity and increase the risk of harm to student learning or well-being or decrease educator effectiveness.

An educator is supposed to have just *one* relationship with each person in her classroom: that of teacher and student. Of course, given the nature of human interaction, other relationships are always hovering around the edges: advisor, coach, counselor, confidant, friend, and so on. This ethical standard reminds educators that they have an ethical obligation to consider whether other types of interaction with a student will interfere with the educator's primary relationship.

Based on the research I've done over the last decade, there is no question that the widespread use of technology by both educators and students heightens the risk of multiple relationships developing. There is an implicit intimacy to electronic messaging that encourages emotionally-laden exchanges that are more consistent with a conversation between friends or confidants than teacher-student. The sheer speed of digital communication makes it harder to reflect on the direction the conversation is taking and whether there is a risk of an additional relationship forming.

One consistent theme in the cases I've seen is that educators ranked at the top of the profession—the ones most likely to be voted "Teacher of the Year," in fact—tend to be the most vulnerable to forming multiple relationships with students.

Our best teachers are empathetic, sympathetic, and driven by a desire to help every student reach his or her potential. The more an educator peers into a student's life through social media or chats electronically, the higher the likelihood that the teacher-student roles will be threatened or even overshadowed by an inappropriate and possibly career-ending relationship. I suspect that the growing reliance on remote teaching will exacerbate these issues.

The key term in this ethical standard is "objectivity." A certain amount of distance is required to maintain objectivity, and more than anything else, digital technology destroys barriers of time and space.

MCEE III.A.8. Acknowledging that there are no circumstances that allow for educators to engage in romantic or sexual relationships with students.

This performance indicator should be self-evident, but a few minutes reviewing the news each morning will make it clear that the reminder is necessary. The only adjustment I'd make in this statement would be to highlight the keyword: "there are *no* circumstances…"

If you read enough headlines and articles about educator assaults on students, you might conclude that technology or social media are responsible for these transgressions. But let's be clear: if an educator engages in a "romantic or sexual relationship" with a student, it was not technology that lured him or her into doing so. We know that educators assaulted students long before the invention of computers, let alone smartphones. Every inappropriate romantic or sexual relationship between a teacher and student is the product of a series of bad choices by the teacher that has nothing to do with technology *per se*.

It is undeniable, of course, that technology does play a significant role in many, if not most, teacher-student assaults. Educators most commonly use digital communication tools to facilitate private and inappropriate communication. But as you'll see, modern digital tools technology can be misused in a lot of creative—and disturbing—ways.

MCEE III.B.1. Seeking to understand students' educational, academic, personal and social needs as well as students' values, beliefs, and cultural background.

This performance indicator is closely related to the ethical obligation detailed in MCEE III.A.3., which requires educators to communicate with students in "a clear, respectful, and culturally sensitive manner." Thanks to the marvels of the internet, it has never been easier to learn about and understand the "values, beliefs, and cultural background" of your students. There are, for all practical purposes, unlimited resources online about virtually every topic under the sun, so there is simply no excuse for not knowing elementary about the culture and heritage of your students.

It is fair to point out, however, that this particular ethical precept asks educators to skate a fine line. The more that you know about a student's needs, the easier it is to be empathetic about the particular challenges he or she is facing. But excessive or unchecked empathy can all too easily lead a caring educator into one of the multiple relationships that violate the ethical principle of MCEE III.A.7. Put another way, the more that you know about a particular student's needs, the more careful you need to be about maintaining the appropriate teacher-student relationship.

There's a second potential problem raised by this particular ethical precept. It calls on educators to search for a better understanding of various aspects of each student's life. That's a noble and necessary admonition, but each educator should be careful about how they gain that understanding. You should not attempt to meet this ethical obligation by scouring a student's social media posts since doing so would probably violate the ethical precept regarding student privacy contained in MCEE III.C.1 (*see infra*).

MCEE III.B.2. Respecting the dignity, worth, and uniqueness of each individual student including, but not limited to, actual and perceived gender, gender expression, gender identity, civil status, family status, sexual orientation, religion, age, disability, race, ethnicity, socio-economic status, and culture.

It would be difficult to argue against the proposition that digital technology (particularly social media) has made us more politically polarized and more judgmental. The very structure of social media seems to demand it: We post curated snippets of our lives that reflect our values and our life choices; we opine on everything and nothing, and we all too often are the ones to cast judgment on others.

The ethical precept contained in MCEE III.B.2 calls on educators to reflect on how they view each of their students as individuals. It also invokes a broader philosophical dilemma: to what extent should educators leave their deeply-held religious, social, or political precepts at the threshold of the classroom? For instance, if you belong to a religion that teaches that homosexuality is a sin, can you meet this ethical duty to respect "the dignity, worth, and uniqueness" of a gay or trans student? It's easy to think of myriad other examples of potential conflicts between your views and one or more aspects of a student's identity.

Digital technology makes all of this more difficult. At the very least, it increases the number of potential flashpoints as we all learn more about each other online. As challenging as this ethical standard is (and it may be among the most challenging in the MCEE), it is also perhaps the most important. It encourages educators to model qualities of tolerance and respect for individual dignity that we all should apply to both our real and our virtual lives.

MCEE III.B.3. Establishing and maintaining an environment that promotes the emotional, intellectual, physical, and sexual safety of all students.

When students are in the classroom, each teacher serves *in loco parentis* for those children. The ethical obligation contained in this performance indicator is a vital part of that protective role since the first and highest responsibility of an educator is for a child's safety.

Like any other type of technology, digital technology can cause serious harm if misused. Educators should heed their ethical obligation to demonstrate professional competence in the use of technology to minimize the risks of mistakes and to understand how to prevent technology from being used to cause harm. For instance, a teacher should know if one student is using an otherwise innocuous program like Google Docs or SurveyMonkey to cyberbully or harass other students. The more you know about how your electronic teaching tools work, the less harm the miscreants can cause.

More directly, MCEE III.B.3 establishes an ethical duty that teachers avoid using technology in a manner that would threaten (or fail to promote) "the emotional, intellectual, physical, and sexual safety of all students." Many of the cybertraps I discuss in this book run afoul of this ethical duty. Among other things, it advises educators that they should refrain from using technology to bully, harass, stalk, solicit, and voyeuristically view their students.

MCEE III.C.1. Respecting the privacy of students and the need to hold in confidence certain forms of student communication, documents, or information obtained in the course of professional practice.

There are two different concepts of privacy implicated in this performance indicator. The first concept concerns the protection of information that students are required to provide to you or the district as part of attending school. The U.S. government and the various states have adopted numerous policies, regulations, and laws (*i.e.*, codes of conduct) that govern how you should handle that information, from collection to preservation to protection. Your ethical requirements concerning this first concept are essentially co-extensive with your legal obligations. If a student turns over information to you, you can only release it under proper circumstances and for specified purposes.

Where the ethical obligation of MCEE III.C.1 goes beyond the legal code is in its invocation of the broader concept of "student privacy." It was much easier to respect student privacy before social media; under normal circumstances, once the final bell rang, a teacher would not know much about what his or her students did outside of school. But thanks to the smartphone and endless social media apps, teachers now have ample opportunity to see what their students are doing when they are not in the classroom.

The ethical question here is the extent to which (or if at all) educators should avail themselves of that opportunity. There is no legal prohibition against looking at photos or other information that a student has posted publicly on a social media platform. But if you do that, are you "respecting the privacy of students"? Some will say that if students post something publicly, then they have voluntarily given up their right to privacy. And on one level, that is true: by posting publicly, a student gives up the ability to control who sees that data.

But one thing the MCEE should make clear to educators is that simply because they can do something does not necessarily mean that they should. In reflecting on this provision of the MCEE, educators may benefit from connecting it to MCEE III.A.7, which cautions against the formation of "multiple relationships." When you are looking at a student's social media posts, it is unlikely that you are doing so as part of the teacher-student relationship. Instead, you may be doing so as a social media "friend," a concerned adult, a proto-therapist, or something more sinister. Regardless, these are all types of multiple relationships that threaten your adherence to the ethical requirements of the teaching profession.

MCEE III.C.3. Protecting the confidentiality of student records and releasing personal data in accordance with prescribed state and federal laws and local policies.

Thanks to the Federal Educational Rights and Privacy Act (FERPA), a veritable industry has built up around the preservation and protection of student educational records. There is an endless number of companies offering a bewildering array of services and tools, and FERPA has become a regular part of the professional development rotation.

Not surprisingly, technology plays a central role in the FERPA landscape. In general, that's a good thing. Electronic storage of student information offers a lot of advantages in terms of analysis, data protection and durability, distribution, and so on. There are cybersecurity risks, of course, but in general, those are not the concern of classroom teachers.

What should be the concern of every classroom teacher, however, is the risk of accidentally disclosing student records through the careless use of smartphones. Many schools (and even more parents) encourage teachers to use their smartphones to take lots of photos of students and classroom activities. There are lots of good reasons for doing so: greater inclusiveness and involvement of parents, good publicity for the school, encouragement of students, *etc.*

Before uploading any photo taken in your classroom to social media, you should make sure that it does not accidentally contain information that could constitute a "student educational record." Does the photo show student grades on tests or quizzes? Is a transcript of grades visible on your desk or your laptop? Does the photo inadvertently reveal student addresses, phone numbers, or class schedules?

Fortunately, it is not your responsibility to sort out what constitutes a "student educational record." Legal counsel for your district should provide you with his or her interpretation of what the law covers. At the start of each school year, be sure to consult with your building or district supervisors and review what types of information you should exclude from photos and social media posts.

Chapter 4

Technology and the Responsibility to the School Community

Principle IV: Responsibility to the School Community

The professional educator promotes positive relationships and effective interactions with members of the school community, while maintaining professional boundaries.

The Model Code of Ethics for Educators encourages educational professionals to show *responsibility to the school community* in five ways:

- By promoting effective and appropriate relationships with parents/guardians;

- By promoting effective and appropriate relationships with colleagues;

- By promoting effective and appropriate relationships with the community and other stakeholders;

- By promoting effective and appropriate relationships with employers; and

- By understanding the problematic nature of multiple relationships.

When you simply list the subheadings for Principle IV, as I have here, one thing immediately becomes apparent. This ethical principle is focused almost entirely on the nature of your relationships with various groups and individuals in your school community. Although the language of those subheadings and the related performance indicators do not specifically reference technology, it should be self-evident to every reader that digital communication technology is an integral component of every one of those relationships.

One of the central goals, after all, of digital communication technology (and its trouble-making younger brother, social media) is to facilitate relationships. Regardless of the precise platform you use, digital communications can be banal, flirtatious, romantic, business-like, inane, teasing, remorseful, angry—in short, a distillation of all of the qualities of our real-life relationships. When it comes to relationships and digital communication technology, we can and should do better than we have so far. Principle IV of the MCEE offers us ample opportunity to reflect on how best to do that.

MCEE IV.A.1. Communicating with parents/guardians in a timely and respectful manner that represents the student's best interests.

When I was going through school, my parents had somewhat limited interactions with my teachers. Twice a year, they would go in for parent-teacher conferences, which generally lasted 15 minutes at most. On rare occasions, they exchanged notes with teachers on specific issues or made arrangements to have a brief conversation by phone, almost always while the teacher was still at school. They could call teachers at home (everyone was in the phone book), but it just wasn't something you did unless you were also friends with the teacher.

Digital communication technology has dramatically changed how parents and teachers communicate, the expectations governing those communications, and the risks of miscommunication. Both parents and schools have heightened expectations regarding how often and how quickly teachers respond to parent inquiries. In many, if not most schools, parents expect the teachers to provide them with their cellphone number, which implicitly creates an expectation among parents that teachers will respond to messages (or more infrequently, calls) at any time of the night or day. And closely related to that is the expectation that teachers will respond promptly, if not near-instantaneously.

The speed of digital communication is only one of its characteristics that heightens the potential for educator cybertraps. (Parents are absolutely at risk of cybertraps as well, but that's a different book.) Most of us, for instance, are aware that a recipient can easily misinterpret the meaning of a text message or social media post. We are also familiar with the fact that the absence of face-to-face reactions often encourages us to say things that we would never say in person. And of course, given the rapid-fire nature of instant messaging, a perfectly innocuous conversation can quickly get ugly thanks to the tiniest misunderstanding or perceived slight.

The key to fulfilling the ethical obligation in this performance indicator is two-fold. First, practice mindfulness and patience in your digital communications. If you have never written and then immediately deleted a hastily written message before sending, I highly recommend it.

Second, you should take the initiative to work with your building and district administrators to set up guidelines and procedures for teacher-parent communications. Schools should distribute these materials to parents at the start of each school year so that everyone knows what to expect.

MCEE IV.A.2. Demonstrating a commitment to equality, equity, and inclusion as well as respecting and accommodating diversity among members of the school community.

This performance indicator regarding your relationship with parents and guardians echoes the ethical obligation detailed in MCEE III.A.3., which calls for respectful and culturally sensitive interactions with students. The same principles apply: You should not talk about identifying characteristics of members of the school community (race, ethnicity, gender, sexual orientation, *etc.*) in ways that diminish your effectiveness in the classroom or the community as a whole. Doing so will unquestionably damage the reputation of your school and district and will harm the profession as a whole.

MCEE IV.A.2, however, goes beyond the scope of the earlier provision. It sets out an ethical obligation to "demonstrat[e] a commitment to equality, equity, and inclusion." There is no specific guidance on how you should do that, and given the breadth of those terms, the actual implementation is likely to vary from one school district to another. Admittedly, this raises complicated issues of the interplay among free speech, politics, religion, and ethics. Each school district and each educator will need to determine for themselves how best to meet this ethical standard.

However, I think that there is one thing upon which we can universally agree: At the very least, educators should not be using technology in ways that demonstrate their rejection of the principles of "equality, equity, and inclusion." Educators would do well to follow the Hippocratic Oath ("First, do no harm") or simply heed the old warning: "If you don't have anything nice to say, don't say anything at all."

MCEE IV.B.1. Respecting colleagues as fellow professionals and maintaining civility when differences arise.

In any workplace, there is a potential for conflict and disagreement. I've already listed several ways in which technology can foment or exacerbate those types of situations: misunderstanding, lack of reflection, misplaced humor, cyberbullying, cyberharassment, and so on. Many of these factors will play into the cybertraps discussed in this book. It is far too common for co-workers to use digital communication tools (even those that they know the district is archiving!) to carry on an electronic playground fight that should not have started in the first place.

This provision of the MCEE encourages you to follow the Golden Rule of Digital Communications: "*Post Unto Others as You Would Have Them Post Unto You.*"

We all experience highs and lows in the daily grind of work, and it is far too easy to dash off a sarcastic text message or take offense at someone's brusque tone in an email. As with so many of the ethical standards drafted for the MCEE, the main objective is to remain calm, take time to respond, and reflect on the impact of your actions before pressing "send." If everyone followed those basic precepts, we could significantly reduce the harm caused by digital conversations.

There's one other critical point: When educators do not treat each other as respected professionals, it is that much more challenging to get the public to do so. Unprofessional behavior is corrosive to the concept of professionalism, so each educator is, in effect, a trustee to his or her colleague's standing in the world. And since our society could benefit from higher levels of respect and civility in general, the teaching profession is an excellent place for that to start.

MCEE IV.B.2. Resolving conflicts, whenever possible, privately and respectfully and in accordance with district policy.

The two most important terms in this ethical standard are "privately" and "respectfully." Neither of those concepts should encourage you to use most forms of electronic communication to resolve conflicts that might arise between you and your colleagues.

In theory, of course, person-to-person forms of communication like email, instant messaging, and texting can and typically should be private. You could even argue that it is possible to have a personal and respectful conversation through the direct message capabilities of sites like Twitter and Instagram.

You should always remember, however, that there is the potential for your theoretically private conversations to become public in unexpected and destructive ways. And if you are conversing with someone on a social media platform, even directly, the chances that the conversation will stay private and respectful drop dramatically.

The best approach (and your district's policies should reflect this) is for educators to resolve conflicts in face-to-face conversations. If necessary, a colleague or supervisor can serve as a mediator or facilitator.

It is worth noting, however, that this ethical duty of privacy and respect is conditional. By using the phrase "whenever possible," the drafters of the MCEE acknowledged that some conflicts might require publicity. There is a perpetual tension between the generally desirable qualities of civility and politeness in the workplace and the discord that is sometimes necessary to call out inequity, injustice, and illegal behavior. (As recently-deceased U.S. Representative John R. Lewis put it, "Good trouble. Necessary trouble.") Put another way, ethical standards of equity and fairness may supersede an ethical standard that calls for private and respectful conversations.

MCEE IV.B.3. Keeping student safety, education, and health paramount by maintaining and sharing educational records appropriately and objectively in accordance with local policies and state and federal laws.

In the previous chapter, I discussed the ethical duties detailed in MCEE III.C.1 and MCEE. III.C.3, which describe your obligation to demonstrate a duty of care by preserving and protecting various student communications, records, *etc.* MCEE IV.B.3 reinforces that ethical obligation by making it clear that doing so is also integral to promoting an effective and appropriate relationship with your colleagues.

The most significant way in which technology can contribute to a violation of this ethical duty is through the use of digital communication technology to share educational records with your colleagues and to use that same technology to discuss students themselves.

Any time you share student records electronically, there is a possibility that you will send them to the wrong destination, possibly outside of the school district itself. And even you do not accidentally send them to the wrong person, there are legitimate security concerns about having multiple copies of student records floating around in cyberspace. Your district should have clear policies on this type of data exchange, and those policies should track state and federal law.

But even assuming you are not violating law or policy in your handling of student records, technology offers a powerful cybertrap for this ethical duty. It is all too tempting for colleagues to use supposedly private digital communication technology to indulge in gossip, mockery, complaints, or leering assessment of students. At the very least, such behavior is not civil or respectful. It runs the risk of embarrassing you, your colleagues, the school, and the profession. And most importantly, it is not conducive to the health and safety of your students. No one is naïve enough to think that teachers won't ever talk about their students.

But don't be lewd, crude, or cruel, and don't do it online.

MCEE IV.B.8. Working to ensure a workplace environment that is free from harassment.

This standard is related to the earlier ethical duty of respecting colleagues contained in MCEE IV.B.1, but it is slightly broader. Whereas the previous provision focused primarily on how you communicate with your colleagues, this performance indicator states that you have an ethical obligation to promote "a workplace environment that is free from harassment."

Since the passage of Title VII of the Civil Rights Act of 1964, it has been illegal for employers in the United States to discriminate against employees on the basis of "race, color, religion, sex or national origin." Over time, courts have extended the protections of Title VII to include situations in which an employer is aware of discriminatory harassment in the workplace (the so-called "hostile work environment") but fails to take action to prevent it. Those protections, however, sound broader than they are. As the United States Supreme Court said in *Oncale v. Sundowner Offshore Services, Inc.*, 523 U.S. 75 (1998), Title VII is not "a general civility code for the American workplace." On the other hand, the Court handed down that decision twenty years before the #MeToo movement started, so things have changed a bit.

One of the primary workplace challenges raised by digital technology is that it makes the creation and sharing of content so much faster and easier. If the distribution of offensive material and digital harassment is intentional, then the violation of this ethical standard is clear. But if the goal is to be funny and introduce some levity into the workplace, then MCEE IV.B.8 imposes an obligation to think not only about your intent but also about how your co-workers will view it.

As always, when you give yourself less time to think about whether reposting a "joke" is a good idea, the odds that you'll make a mistake rise substantially. Moreover, you should take into account the cumulative impact of the content you share. It can be harmful enough to send a dubious joke or image to a colleague; it's another thing altogether if the target of a joke also knows that dozens or even hundreds of colleagues also saw it.

As with so many of the MCEE performance indicators, your ethical duty is a buffer zone that surrounds the core legal principle. The Supreme Court might not rule that your latest meme is legally-actionable harassment, but that doesn't relieve you of the ethical responsibility for the damage that you cause to the workplace environment.

MCEE IV.D.1. Using property, facilities, materials, and resources in accordance with local policies and state and federal laws.

During your educational career, you will be provided with a variety of different technologies to assist with your work in the classroom. This provision of the MCEE simply states that your ethical duty is to know the "local policies and state and federal laws" that govern their use and to act accordingly.

A significant portion of this book is devoted to illustrating the many different ways that educators have violated policies and laws through the misuse of technology, so there will be ample opportunity to demonstrate breaches of this ethical standard. In most instances, it will be apparent that the educators in question were well aware of their legal and ethical obligations but forged ahead anyway.

If you are intent on committing a criminal act, the MCEE will not be much of an impediment. If you wish to avoid doing so, however, this ethical standard encourages you to know the laws and policies relevant to your use of technology and to advocate for ongoing professional development to help you stay abreast of any changes.

MCEE IV.D.2. Respecting intellectual property ownership rights (e.g. original lesson plans, district level curricula, syllabi, gradebooks, etc.) when sharing materials.

This provision echoes the ethical standard laid out in MCEE II.B.1, and all of the considerations discussed in Chapter Two apply here as well. The foremost thing to keep in mind with this standard is that your misuse of intellectual property can have significant consequences for your employer as well as for you personally. You can find additional details in Chapter 13, which deals specifically with intellectual property theft.

MCEE IV.D.3. Exhibiting personal and professional conduct that is in the best interest of the organization, learning community, school community, and profession.

As should be clear by now, technology has changed the meaning of the phrase "[e]xhibiting personal and professional conduct." Thanks to the dangerous combination of mobile devices and social media, you can now operate an ongoing, global exhibition of both your personal and professional conduct. This book will illustrate some of the reasons why that's neither necessary nor advisable.

A certain amount of public exhibition of your professional conduct may be unavoidable. Your school or district may actively encourage or even require you to incorporate social media into your teaching practice. Despite the risks (some of which I'll discuss below), there are many reasons why your school may be embracing social media: branding, interaction with the school community, transparency with parents, pressure from social media conscious students, *etc.* Is all school-related or mandated social media "in the best interest of the organization, learning community, school community, and profession"? That's a legitimate question and one that merits discussion with your colleagues and supervisors if you have concerns.

Your responsibility to adhere to this ethical precept is more apparent when you are using social media to exhibit aspects of your private life. That is the point at which your rights under the First Amendment bump up against practical and professional limitations. You certainly have the right to post whatever you wish to social media (subject to the platform's Terms and Conditions, which is another topic altogether). The reality, however, is that "free speech" has never meant "free from consequences." This ethical standard is a reminder that you should think about the potential consequences of your social media exhibitions not only for yourself but also for those in your larger professional circle.

MCEE IV.E.1. Considering the risks that multiple relationships might impair objectivity and increase the likelihood of harm to students' learning and well-being or diminish educator effectiveness.

This ethical standard is closely related to MCEE III.A.7, which cautions against having multiple relationships with students in the first place. MCEE IV.E.1 calls on educators to think not only about the impact of multiple relationships on the student involved but on the continued effectiveness of the educator within the workplace and the school community at large.

There are a variety of troubling community issues that are associated with these types of multiple relationships. For instance, bad publicity can harm a school's reputation and undermine public confidence in the teaching profession in general. And even the appearance of an inappropriate relationship—for instance, an observably close friendship with a student--can raise questions about your ability to assess the work of all your students fairly. The relationship may foster resentment, jealousy, and bullying in the classroom. And if there is, in fact, a sexual component to the relationship, it can cause untold emotional and psychological harm to not just the student involved but to classmates as well.

The types of bad decisions that lead to transgressive relationships are far too often made in vulnerability, in pain, in lust, or the throes of other emotions untethered from rational thought. One of the goals of each district's professional development should be to provide educators with exercises aimed at reflection, deliberation, and the slower use of technology. Everyone will benefit.

MCEE IV.E.3. Considering the implications and possible ramifications of engaging in a personal or professional relationship with parents and guardians, student teachers, colleagues, and supervisors.

The risks associated with multiple relationships with students trigger the most significant ethical obligations of the MCEE. Those risks—and the harms that can result—touch the core of your fundamental duty to protect the health and safety of your students.

MCEE IV.E.3, however, recognizes that other types of relationships raise ethical concerns as well. As always, communication technology is at the forefront of those concerns.

At the most superficial level, is your new relationship distracting you from your work? Mobile devices are tempting enough without the added lure of a flirty text, a shared joke, or a salacious photo. Is there a possibility that you will expose your students to inappropriate content? Will social media posts about your relationship create problems in your school or your classroom? Will technology be used to photograph or record you and your paramour *in flagrente delicto* (like the Canadian educators recorded by a student while having sex in a closed but poorly insulated office)?

One of the key themes of this book is that "Cameras Are Everywhere." If you enter into a relationship with someone who is part of your school community, you should devote some serious time and reflection to figuring out appropriate guidelines for discrete behavior. A frank and open discussion with your supervisor is probably a good idea.

Section Two

Privacy Cybertraps for Educators

1905 Teaching Contract for Story County, Iowa

- Teachers are expected to live in the community in which they are employed and to take residence with local citizens for room and board.

- Teachers will be required to spend weekends in the community unless permission is granted by the Chairman of the Board.

- It is understood that teachers will attend church each Sunday and take an active part, particularly in choir and Sunday School work.

- Dancing, card playing and the theatre are works of the Devil that lead to gambling, immoral climate, and influence and will not be tolerated.

- Community plays are given annually. Teachers are expected to participate.

- When laundering petticoats and unmentionables it is best to dry them in a flour sack or pillow case.

- Any teacher who smokes cigarettes, uses liquor in any form, frequents a pool or public hall, or gets shaved in a barber shop, bobbs [sic] her hair, has dyed hair, wears short skirts and has undue use of cosmetics will not be tolerated under any circumstances.

- Teachers will not marry or keep company with a man friend during the week except as an escort to church services.

- Loitering in ice cream parlors, drug stores, etc., is prohibited.

- Purchasing or reading the Sunday Supplement on the Sabbath will not be tolerated.

- Discussing political views or party choice is not advisable.

- Men teachers may take one evening each week for courting purposes or two evenings a week if they go to church regularly.

- After 10 hours in school, the teacher should spend the remaining time reading the Bible or other good books.

- Women teachers who marry or engage in other unseemly conduct will be dismissed.

- Every teacher should lay aside from his pay a goodly sum for his declining years so that he will not become a burden on society.

- The teacher who performs his labors faithfully and without fault for five years will be given an increase of 25 cents a week in his pay providing the Board of Education approves.

Do Educators Even Have a Right to Privacy?

The overarching question in this section of *Cybertraps for Educators 2.0* is whether the private conduct of teachers is relevant to their professional careers. For those educators who are active users of social media, the answer is unquestionably "yes."

To be fair, the conflict between a teacher's private life and public work predates social media. Educators may have the lowest inherent expectation of privacy of any professionals in American society. That stems in large part from the fact that parents expect educators to fill dual roles in the classroom, serving both content providers and as moral role models for their students.

Thanks in large part to social media, it is much easier these days for district administrators, school boards, parents, and the media to scrutinize the behavior and lifestyle choices of local teachers.

From the first days of the American public school system, local school boards placed as much if not more emphasis on a teacher's moral character as on his or her ability to teach. The primary objective was to make sure educators were setting a positive example for the students. Community leaders also wanted to be sure, however, that their teachers were focusing on their work and not on what they perceived as frivolous activities. As a local history guide to the Harn Homestead in Oklahoma put it, "School boards expected teachers to focus all their attention on teaching duties; strict standards of behavior were required from all teachers."

What should be evident from the cautionary tales in the chapters in this section is that there is still an enduring interest in the private lives of the nation's educators (especially those of women). Much of society has moved well beyond the days when school boards felt like they had the right to mandate church attendance and limit a teacher's courtin' and wooin' to just two nights a week.

But the expectation that teachers will serve as positive role models for their students not only while in the classroom but also in their private lives has not faded significantly. Post on Instagram accordingly.

Chapter 5
Revealing Too Much Personal Information

Our Phones Are Smarter But Are We?

Over the past decade, the cellphone and its supercharged offspring, the smartphone, have become the most popular and widely-adopted technology in contemporary American culture. According to a study published by the Pew Research Center in 2018, the digital conquest of millennials is complete: researchers found that **100%** of Americans ages 18-29 own a cellphone, and 94% of those devices are smartphones. The next older cohort (30-49) is similarly enamored: 98% own a cellphone, 89% of which are smartphones. All in all, only 5 out of 100 Americans manage to make it through the day without a cellular phone. The remarkably steep adoption curve of the smartphone attests to its popularity: ownership has more than doubled since 2011 when Pew Research first began asking about the devices.

People have been taking pictures of themselves and their friends in social situations for more than a century. It is only in the last couple of decades, however, that it has been possible to share those images instantaneously with the whole world. A series of technological developments—the personal computer, the World Wide Web, mobile devices, and social media—has made it much, much more difficult for educators to keep confidential or even intimate information private.

As we'll see, some of that is beyond the control of individual educators; powerful search engines like Google and Bing can resurrect information about educators that they might have thought was long dead and buried. Search engines are also highly effective at publicizing obscure opinions and creative literary works of educators that once would have remained hidden and mostly unread.

At the same time, however, it should be noted that a significant portion of the loss of privacy experienced by educators is selfie-inflicted. The digital communication revolution of the past forty years has given educators (and of course, everyone else) unprecedented opportunities to damage or even destroy their privacy with the click of a button. Remember, the "right to privacy" ultimately is the ability to control access to or the use of your personal information. If you choose to put information online in one form or another, then you have given up control of that data, regardless of the strength of your privacy settings.

A few statistics demonstrate the staggering popularity of posting photos online. On average, nearly 1,000 images are uploaded to Instagram *every second* of the day. In a white paper issued in 2013, Facebook reported that more than 250 *billion* photos had been uploaded by its users, which averages out to 350 million pictures per day. In an article for the photo storage service Mylio, journalist Eric Perret compiled a variety of different projections for digital photoactivity. Among his more remarkable predictions: 1) that we would take over 1.2 *trillion* digital photos in 2017; and 2) the total number of stored digital images would rise to 4.7 trillion.

People have been sharing photos on social media for about two decades. Nonetheless, users still struggle with two basic concepts: 1) If an online service has privacy settings, it is **not private**, and 2) if you digitize something (a document or photo), someone can and probably will copy it. The fundamental principle underlying the internet is that "*Information wants to be free.*"

There is an endless number of ways a teacher's supposedly private images can become public. In some instances, it's a combination of sheer bad luck and what Sacramento defense attorney Ken Rosenfeld once wittily described as "felony stupidity." In other cases, as we'll see, the disclosure results from the fact that someone—a student, a parent, a fellow teacher, a journalist—is actively looking for images of an educator to use for their own purposes.

In the end, of course, it doesn't matter precisely how your photos escape your social media feed. What matters is whether the images reveal some aspect of your life that you would prefer not to share with the public. The cold reality is that once you post something to social media, you almost certainly will lose some control over how someone might use the information.

You may believe that educators are held to unfair standards, particularly given how members of other professions often act online. That's not an unreasonable conclusion. But the reality is that higher standards for teachers do exist, and educators need to be particularly careful about how and when they use digital devices. The grim reality is that the margin of error for teachers, never large from the start, shrinks with every status update, tweet, or Instagram post.

Pregnancy and Sexual Orientation on Social Media

Job losses in the United States during the Great Depression were so severe that many school boards reached the dubious conclusion that married female teachers should not be allowed to work. By 1928, according to a survey conducted at the time by the National Education Association, nearly thirty percent of school districts with populations over 2,500 had adopted regulations that required a woman to resign as soon as she got married.

That trend was reversed during World War II when military mobilization caused huge vacancies in nearly every field. Faced with a rapidly growing shortage of educators, school districts dropped their prohibitions against married teachers. The baby boom that ensued when the soldiers came home kept the demand for teachers high, and for the most part, the marriage bars faded into history. In fact, for a variety of reasons—including growing suspicion of and prejudice against "spinsters"—by 1960, the percentage of married teachers was twice that of single women.

One restriction that lingered long after the disappearance of prohibitions against married teachers was the ban on visibly pregnant women in the classroom. In fact, according to the National Women's History Museum, a teacher named Peggy Whitley was the first to be allowed to teach children while pregnant—in 1968. There's no record of the first unmarried woman to teach while visibly pregnant, but not surprisingly, there are plenty of people who still don't think that's appropriate.

Fortunately, the prohibition against pregnant women teaching in public schools has substantially diminished. Forty years ago, Congress passed the Pregnancy Discrimination Act of 1978, which amended Title VII of the Civil Rights Act of 1964 to prohibit "sex discrimination on the basis of pregnancy." While pregnancy discrimination has not disappeared entirely, the prohibition against discrimination makes it relatively safe for public school teachers to share the news of their impending arrival on social media. Several online guides offer suggestions for teachers about how to turn their happy condition into a teachable moment for their students.

Educators should keep in mind, however, that communities and schools around the United States still have widely varying attitudes, as the endless debates over sex education demonstrate. Teachers can get into trouble for social media content that is too provocative, overtly sexual, or that simply contains "too much information" about a teacher's intimate activities. There are some religious schools (and politicians) who believe that evidence of merely shacking up is still sufficient to disqualify someone from teaching.

In 2010, for instance, then-Senator Jim DeMint (R-S.C.) told pastors at the Greater Freedom Rally in Spartanburg, South Caroline that "if someone is openly homosexual, they shouldn't be teaching in the classroom and he holds the same position on an unmarried woman who's sleeping with her boyfriend—she shouldn't be in the classroom."

As the case studies below make clear, however, the prohibition against teaching while pregnant has not entirely disappeared from the nation's religious schools. Educators who work at religious schools are not protected by the Privacy Discrimination Act (unless the school receives federal funds, which most do not), which makes pursuing a discrimination case more difficult. However, pregnant teachers have successfully sued religious schools for wrongful termination of a teaching contract and infliction of emotional distress. Most notably, a jury in 2018 awarded former science teacher Kourtney Liggins more than $3.5 million after the Los Angeles Archdiocese fired her for being pregnant and unwed.

Social media, not surprisingly, can play a role in a school's discovery that a teacher is pregnant. The pending arrival of a child is typically a pretty big deal, and couples are often eager to share the news on social media with families and friends. (For a discussion of some of the privacy risks in doing so, check out one of my recent books, *Cybertraps for Expecting Moms & Dads.*) But pregnancy does not need social media to announce itself, and none of the employment termination cases I have researched stemmed from the fact that school administrators accidentally saw a teacher's gender reveal online.

Unlike pregnancy, a person's sexual orientation does not inevitably announce itself to the world. You can make a decent argument that social media has played a significant role in accelerating the LGBTQ civil rights movement. At the same time, however, social media has also proven to be a particularly sticky cybertrap for this group of educators.

Not unreasonably, members of the LGBTQ community use social media for all of the same purposes as heterosexual and cisgender users: to share life events with family and friends, to comment on public affairs, to share funny memes, and so on. In the process, though, they may inadvertently reveal aspects of their lives that trigger homophobic colleagues, supervisors, students, or school parents. One consequence of that has been that until recently, notwithstanding the numerous strides that the LGBTQ community has made towards legal and social equality, employment discrimination (up to and including abrupt firings) was still a threat for many educators around the country.

In the summer of 2020, however, the United States Supreme Court ruled in *Bostock v. Clayton County*, 590 U.S. __, 140 S. Ct. 1731 (June 15, 2020) that Title VII of the 1964 Civil Rights Act prohibits employers from discriminating against workers based on sexual orientation or gender identity. For LBGTQ educators working in public or non-religious private schools in the United States, this was a significant expansion of their legal rights in the workplace.

LGBTQ educators who work in religious schools or organizations are in a more fraught position. In a 2014 case called *Hosanna-Tabor Evangelical Lutheran Church & School v. Equal Employment Opportunity Commission*, 565 U.S. 171, 132 S. Ct. 694 (2014), the Court established a "ministerial exception" to federal discrimination laws. Cheryl Perich, a teacher at the Lutheran School, spent a year on disability for narcolepsy. By the time doctors gave her the go-ahead to return to the classroom, the school had filled her position. Perich sued on the grounds of disability discrimination. The Court identified four criteria for determining whether a particular employee serves as a "minister" for a religious organization. Perich, the Court concluded, satisfied the criteria and thus fell within the exception to federal discrimination laws.

Three weeks after its ruling in *Bostock*, the Supreme Court handed down a decision in the case of *Our Lady of Guadalupe School v. Agnes Morrissey-Berru*, 591 U.S. ___, 140 S. Ct. 2049 (July 8, 2020). Morrissey-Beru sued her employer for age discrimination, and the school defended by raising the ministerial exception. The Ninth Circuit Court of Appeals determined that Morrisey-Berru's teaching position did not meet the "ministerial" criteria established in *Hosanna-Tabor* and held that she had the right to sue under federal law.

By a 7-2 vote, the Supreme Court disagreed. The Court said that the Ninth Circuit should have focused on the role that the position in question plays in furthering the goals of the religious organization. A teacher, the Court concluded, is generally central to the mission of a religious school in passing on the tenets of the faith. That makes teachers inherently ministerial, even if their subject matter is mostly secular.

In her dissent, Justice Sonia Sotomayor argued that this gave religious schools broad authority to discriminate against teachers "for reasons wholly divorced from religious beliefs." There is little doubt that the Court's ruling in *Our Lady of Guadalupe School* will make it harder for LGBTQ educators to challenge firings based on their sexual orientation or gender identity.

Cautionary Tales

Cautionary Tale 5-2019-US_New York

Sometimes, it's not the educator who posts the potentially damaging content online. In early January 2019, the West Genesee Central School District (near Syracuse, NY) announced that it had launched an investigation into the conduct of its superintendent, Dr. Christopher Brown. The investigation was triggered by a series of tweets from Brown's wife, in which she stated that her husband and another school employee had announced to her that they were in love and that Dr. Brown wanted a divorce.

When questioned by a reporter, Dr. Brown denied being in a romantic or sexual relationship, although he did admit to confiding in a "very close friend." He also refused to answer any questions about what was discussed in his kitchen, telling the reporter that "Unfortunately my private life made it into the public, but I need some privacy."

Notwithstanding Dr. Brown's categorical denial, the fall-out from the alleged relationship was both swift and uneven. After spending roughly $20,000 in fees on its investigation, the West Genesee school board agreed to pay Dr. Brown four months of salary ($120,000) and also cover his health insurance in exchange for his resignation.

At the time the deal was announced, several questions were raised "about the status of West Genesee High School Executive Principal Shannon Coholan," who was identified by Brown's wife as Brown's romantic partner. The board said that she was on administrative leave pending further investigation. Two months later, however, the board voted to terminate her employment. Since Coholan was part of the administrative bargaining unit and did not have tenure, she did not receive any severance package.

Top Three Takeaways:

- When it comes to the potential revelation of embarrassing or controversial personal information, don't overlook the fact that all of your family members have access to social media as well. Hell hath no social media posts like a spouse or partner scorned.

- Brown's plea for privacy, while not uncommon, was ultimately futile. Few horses escape from the barn more vigorously than salacious information.

- The disparity in the treatment of male and female educators is a constant theme in this book. This case is an excellent example of that. One person got a golden parachute, and the other received a pink slip.

Cautionary Tale 5-2018-US_California

The experience of California middle school teacher Amy Estes is a cautionary tale that helps illustrate two potential cybertraps: first, the risk associated with putting lifestyle content on social media and second, the potential for cyberbullying by students.

Before the events of this cautionary tale, Amy Estes had taught English at Spring View Middle School in the Racklin Unified School District for five years. In the summer of 2018, she posted a message on Facebook explaining why she had been on mental health leave for five months:

> At the start of the [2017] school year, some students found out that I am gay—a fact I had never shared with my students. They posted photos online and it became the talk of the campus. While it is dehumanizing and painful to be outed, my hope was that it would die down. Instead, it escalated to the point that I was being harassed in and out of the classroom.

According to news reports, the problems started when a former student followed Estes on Instagram and saw a photo showing Estes and her female partner. The former student told some current RUSD students about the picture, and Estes began receiving a variety of homophobic comments in her Instagram feed.

As the fall progressed, Estes tightened up the privacy settings on her Instagram and Facebook accounts. Some RUSD students, however, connected Estes to a YouTube channel that she had launched as part of her work towards a master's degree. Several followed her, and one unknown individual posted a comment that read, "Don't be stupid, be a smarty. You can join the Nazi Party. Now accepting dykes."

In an interview with reporter Liz Kreutz, Estes said that there was no identifying information in her YouTube profile, and she never discussed her sexuality in them.

"I presented that [comment] to my administrators and said, you know, again, 'I really think we need to look into this, this is feeling more serious.'" The administration, however, declined to take any specific action.

Eventually, the anti-gay rhetoric spilled over into the classroom. One eighth-grade student responded to an assignment about how to create a utopian society by titling it "No Homos" and saying that she would ban gay marriage because it was immoral. Estes again asked her supervisors to help respond to the situation. When they declined to do so, she went on mental health leave and later that year, took a new teaching position in the San Juan Unified School District.

Top Three Takeaways:

- The endless admonition: It is next to impossible to keep anything "private" that you post on social media. Your ability to control who views the information and how they use it is negligible.

- Moreover, if kids are motivated, they can be relentless in finding **all** of your online accounts. Be aware of your community, be open with your colleagues and supervisors in advance, and think through the possible implications of certain information becoming known throughout the school community.

- Given the high expectation that teachers will not only serve as role models but as enforcers of community values, each educator needs to be realistic about the potential consequences of sharing personal content online. Be aware of your community, be open with your colleagues and supervisors in advance, and think through the possible implications of certain information becoming known to a wide swath of the public. You may be willing to be an activist in your social postings, but that is not always a comfortable role.

Cautionary Tale 5-2018-US_Florida

For Miami couple Jocelyn Morffi and Natasha Hess, it was an idyllic weekend: in early February 2018, they stood before family and friends in Key Largo and celebrated their marriage. After enjoying a brief honeymoon, they returned home to Miami.

The next day, Morffi went back to her job at Sts. Peter and Paul Catholic School, where she had taught first grade for nearly seven years. According to the *Miami Herald*, Morffi also coached basketball and ran a successful charitable organization called #teachHope70x7, in which student volunteers spend time on weekends distributing meals to the homeless in Miami.

At the end of the school day, Principal Carlota E. Morales asked Morffi to meet with her, the school's HR director, and a priest from the Miami Archdiocese. They told Morffi that her gay marriage and the related posts on Facebook violated the "moral turpitude" clause of her teaching contract. Morales then asked Morffi to resign. Morffi refused to do so and was fired by the school the next day.

In a letter to parents, Morales said that "[t]oday a difficult and necessary decision has been made regarding Ms. Jocelyn Morffi, our first-grade teacher. She is no longer teaching at our school."

Morales did not offer parents any specific reason for the firing, but Morffi offered her thoughts in an Instagram post:

> This weekend I married the love of my life and unfortunately I was terminated from my job as a result. In their eyes I'm not the right kind of Catholic for my choice of partner. However, I will CONTINUE with #teachHope and will inform you of the new location for the February 25th outing very soon. Also THANK YOU for the outpour of love and support.

The reaction from parents was vigorous. The day after Morales fired Morffi, nearly two dozen parents went to the school to protest her termination and demand her reinstatement. Samantha Mills told the *Miami Herald* that "[Morffi] never imposes her personal beliefs on others. She just does everything in love. She has a way of teaching that is so amazing." Another parent, Valentina Simon, toyed with the idea of removing her child from the school and complained that "This is really bad. It can't be that in 2018 … they still do this type of thing."

This case serves as a good reminder that religious and private schools are often not subject to the same legal rules and regulations that govern public schools. Educators should always think carefully about the culture and values of a school and the surrounding community before accepting an offer to work in a given district or school. That culture and those values are integral to how an educator's social media activity and lifestyle choices will be perceived.

Top Three Takeaways:

- This cautionary tale is yet another reminder: The environment in which you work is a critical factor to consider when you are posting on social media.

- Social media makes it far too easy for all of us to post text and images frequently without stopping to think about what might happen if we do. We need to continually remind ourselves that "free speech" does not mean "free from consequences."

- It may be gratifying to have vocal and enthusiastic support from parents (and sometimes students), but don't expect that to save your job. I have seen very few instances in which school administrators reversed an employment decision due to public protest.

Cautionary Tale 5-2017-Australia

As you might expect, religiously-oriented schools pose particular problems for LGBTQ educators. The experience of Australian Craig Campbell, a former teacher at South Coast Baptist College in Waikiki, Australia, offers an excellent example of what can happen. (Despite the use of the term "college," SCBC is a PK-12 school and, as the name implies, is aligned with the Baptist religion.)

Campbell's problems began when he posted a photo to Facebook in which he parodied a solo album cover by Belinda Carlisle, a former member of "The Go-Gos." The cover of her pseudonymous album "Belinda" shows the singer straddling a chair while dressed in a black leotard, black nylons, and black spike heels. For his recreation of Carlisle's photo, Campbell substituted a polo shirt, shorts, and sneakers, but in pose and aesthetic, his homage was pretty much spot-on.

As so often happens, the students in Campbell's class discovered the photo. "A couple of kids thought it was funny and shared it," Campbell told *News.com.au.* "It's nothing that's not happened to me before," he said. "Sometimes kids find your Facebook profile picture."

Unfortunately, however, not everyone was amused; one student started openly mocking Campbell during class. "He was laughing at me" Campbell said, "and then I was trying to get him to do his work and he said to me, 'I'm not going to be taking orders from a gay teacher,' he said. I said, 'OK, you need to leave then.'"

A typical social engagement further complicated Campbell's situation. A short time after the Facebook incident, he and his boyfriend went together to a family wedding, and three students from the school were there as well. After those incidents, and knowing that some students in the school were grappling with similar issues, Campbell decided to come out to his colleagues and the broader school community.

While there is a diversity of opinion regarding homosexuality and same-sex marriage among Baptists, the administration at SCBC informed Campbell that he would not be utilized further as a substitute teacher. The school's principal, Des Mitchell, specifically referenced Campbell's social media post in an interview with *The West Australian*:

> Young people are naturally inquisitive. The image he posted created interest in his personal life, including his sexuality. I shared with him that, at present, there is an inconsistency with his beliefs on sexuality and the college's beliefs.

Following his dismissal from SCBC, Campbell found a job teaching in the WA state school system. In an interview with ABC (the Australian Broadcast Company), he expressed concern about a government proposal to formalize rules allowing religious institutions to discriminate against gay students and teachers.

> I think what this looks like is a deliberate attack on some of the most vulnerable people in our community for the sake of winning political points. I don't think there's a place for it in our world today. It denies religious diversity. My experience of working in these schools is that there are multiple views on the subject anyway.

Top Three Takeaways:

- This cautionary tale helps to illustrate the importance of adhering to the ethical standard that calls for separate personal and professional lives. In practical terms, that can be difficult to do on social media, particularly with Facebook, which has long had a "real name" policy. Nonetheless, it is an important goal.

- Every school administration should swiftly and firmly respond to any bullying that occurs in the school environment. That can include social media if the school is aware of the bullying and the identities of the people involved.

- While Campbell's desire to serve as a role model for gay students in the school was admirable, the circumstances of this cautionary tale illustrate why the MCEE warns against "multiple relationships" between educators and students.

Cautionary Tale 5-2016-Wales

Dating apps have created a variety of challenges for educators and school administrators. The profiles created on the sites are by definition public (if they weren't, you'd be dating yourself), so the contents can cause issues of propriety and morality. And what if minors either see the dating profiles or respond to them? Dating apps, in general, do a miserable job of policing their supposed age restrictions, and numerous teachers have tried to defend a sexual relationship with a minor by arguing that he or she pretended to be an adult on a dating app.

This issue arose during a spring 2016 investigation of 39-year-old Matthew Aplin, the headteacher at Tywyn Primary School in Sandfields, West Glamorgan (located in southern Wales). The inquiry was sparked by a report that Aplin had a consensual three-way sexual encounter with two 17-year-old young men he met on the gay dating app Grindr.

Since the age of consent in the United Kingdom is 16, and neither of the young men was a student in Aplin's school, the local police and social services concluded that nothing illegal had occurred. Dissatisfied with that outcome, however, the governors of the school conducted a separate investigation and then held a disciplinary hearing, at which they decided to fire the 19-year educator.

Aplin filed an appeal but resigned before the hearing took place. He then filed an employment tribunal claim in which he alleged that the governors had effectively terminated him for being gay. A labor tribunal agreed that he had been discriminated against by the investigating officer and ruled in his favor. As part of its decree, the tribunal assessed nearly £700,000 (roughly $915,000) in damages against the school. The school appealed, but an appellate tribunal upheld the judgment in favor of Aplin in November 2019.

Top Three Takeaways:

- Of all the types of social media, dating apps may be the most dangerous for educators. If students find your dating profile, they may learn much more about you than you would like, which can make it challenging to maintain your authority in the classroom. And if you wind up dating someone who is the same age as some of your students (or not much older), then that may raise concerns about your judgment with your supervisors and parents in the school community.

- Discrimination laws vary from jurisdiction to jurisdiction. But where discrimination against LGBTQ educators is prohibited, administrators and school boards should make sure that they handle any disciplinary actions without regard to the sexual orientation of the people involved.

- It is equally important for teachers to use their collective power to stand up for colleagues who are discriminated against (or worse) based on their sexual orientation or gender expression and to push for the elimination of unjust policies.

Relevant MCEE Provisions for Chapter 5

Principle I: Responsibility to the Profession

Standards I.A.2, I.A.3, I.A.4, I.A.5, and I.C.2

Principle III: Responsibility to Students

Standards III.A.2, III.A.8, and III.A.9

Principle IV: Responsibility to the School Community

Standards IV.A.3, IV.B.2, IV.C.3, IV.D.3, IV.E.1, IV.E.2, and IV.E.3

Principle V: Responsible and Ethical Use of Technology

Standard V.A.1, V.A.5, and V.A.7

Sources

The sources for the Cautionary Tales in this chapter can be viewed at the following URL:

https://link.cybertraps.com/C4E2-Sources-Chap5

Chapter 6
Setting A Bad Example for Students

Overview

Almost a decade ago, Cameron Diaz starred in a movie called "Bad Teacher," in which she played a young woman who returns to teaching after being dumped by her wealthy boyfriend. Critic Roger Ebert aptly summarized the point of the movie—and its primary source of "humor":

> [Teaching was] an occupation she had no talent for or interest in; she passes the time showing DVDs to her students while she naps, drinks and does drugs at her desk.

It's vaguely encouraging, for those of us who admire the teaching profession, that the film has a well-deserved and anemic 44% rating on Rotten Tomatoes.

Most people, it is fair to say, believe that teachers should be role models for students, and indeed, the Model Code of Ethics for Educators actively promotes that objective. But the concept of "role model" can be complicated; in any community, parents may have competing ideas about the roles they want teachers to model and those they don't.

Moreover, the expectation that teachers will be role models (which is often a factor in evaluations, promotions, and pay raises) can very quickly raise difficult issues regarding the line between the professional and the personal. If a teacher is tossing back shots of whiskey at his or her desk at 10 in the morning, most of us will file that under "bad role model." But if that same teacher enjoys a dram or two in the evening while grading papers, is he or she still being a flawed role model?

As is the case with so many other cybertraps, this is only an issue because of social media. Today, careless or carefree teachers actively invite not just the school board but administrators, parents, and students into their private lives whenever they post anything online. And as this book attempts to point out repeatedly, even if a teacher is meticulous with his or her privacy settings, there are an endless number of ways to capture and reproduce anything that shows up on a computer screen. As a result, there is a much higher potential for a conflict to develop between an educator's "private" behavior and the sensibilities of district officials or the broader school community.

Districts and schools that take disciplinary action against teachers for social media posts that show legal but perhaps inappropriate behavior may be entering a tricky area. Take, for instance, a Facebook post that shows a teacher having a drink. As long as the teacher is over the age of 21, the mere consumption of alcohol is non-criminal behavior. (Obviously, if the use of alcohol leads to negligent or criminal conduct, that's a different story.) Nonetheless, many school boards or administrators often feel justified in taking disciplinary action in such situations. They believe that by sharing such images, a teacher is not being a good role model for students or has violated a morals clause included in his or her contract.

There is a fair amount of social hypocrisy in all of this, of course. Virtually every major sporting event in the United States is sponsored to one degree or another by liquor companies, and Americans consume staggering amounts of alcohol every year. It is fair to assume that the vast majority of teachers have a drink now and then (insert your joke here), as do the majority of parents. So the operative question is whether censorious districts are holding teachers to an unreasonable standard.

And of course, broad social changes can affect our expectations regarding the behavior of teachers. If districts and schools, for instance, discover that a teacher is using illegal drugs, they are quick to take action. But as we all know, that bright line is getting fuzzier as state laws have changed.

As of June 2019, eleven states (plus the District of Columbia) have legalized the recreational use of marijuana, and another twenty-two states (plus the Virgin Islands) have decriminalized its use for medical purposes. In those thirty-five jurisdictions, marijuana is now the functional equivalent of alcohol, which raises the question of how school supervisors should react if educators create social media posts that show their use of marijuana. And how should districts handle the situation of educators from non-pot-friendly jurisdictions who share the "high"-lights of their vacations in more mellow states?

As the cautionary tales below should make clear, the concept of "role model" is a malleable one. The expectation that you will serve as a role model is not likely to go away, but what that role entails will change from one community to the next and from one year to the next. It is incumbent upon school districts and administrators to adopt clear guidelines regarding the types of behavior that constitute positive role-modeling and those that do not. School districts should be particularly clear about how they will view social media posts in the context of an educator's duty to be a good role model.

Cautionary Tales

Cautionary Tale 6-2019-US_Missouri

"With friends like these…" One of the challenges of social media is that it is, well, social. Since the majority of your friends likely have smartphones and social media accounts, there's always a risk that one of them will take a photo of you doing something that is not consistent with your status as a role model and share it with the world.

Here's a classic example. In January 2019, a friend of Dr. Dennis Carpenter, then the superintendent of the Lee's Summit School District, posted a photo to social media. Media reports did not specify which channel he used, but it was most likely Facebook.

The photo was taken at a football game in Atlanta between Georgia Southern and Georgia State on November 24, 2018. It shows three people enjoying the tailgate scene. Dr. Carpenter, the middle of the three, has a big grin on his face and is sticking up his middle finger at the photographer.

Carpenter acknowledged that the photo did not set a good example for students in the district:

> As the leader of the Lee's Summit R-7 School District, I care deeply about representing our district and our community responsibly. I am aware of and concerned about an image of me enjoying time with family and friends that has been brought into the public light. It's unfortunate that this photograph has surfaced. As such, I'm committed to discussing the image with the Board of Education and moving forward.

The Lee's Summit Board of Education put out one of the more reasonable statements that I've seen in situations like this:

> The ubiquity of social media and the inability to control what people post on social media can have ramifications beyond our control and is a problem we are all wrestling with in both the public and private sector. The Board of Education will look into the circumstances and visit with Dr. Carpenter to seek his perspective just like we would anyone else.

Top Three Takeaways:

- So, what can you do about your friends? Well, first, choose wisely. In an ideal world, you are not regularly hanging out with people who will embarrass you online. Of course, anyone can make a mistake, but if you surround yourself with people who are thoughtless about what they post online, there's a good chance that it will cause problems for you sooner or later.

- Second, your friends should understand your obligation to serve as a role model in the community. They should also know that you trust them to respect that position and to help you fulfill it by keeping certain activities—and gestures—private.

- And finally, you should actively monitor your presence on social media. The sooner you see something that might be problematic, the quicker you can ask your "friend" to take it down. That may not prevent controversy, given how easy it is to copy information online, but when you're dealing with social media, vigilance is your best option.

Cautionary Tale 6-2018-US_Oregon

There are a lot of different ways in which educators can get themselves in trouble online, but you wouldn't think that a community "Buy and Sell" Facebook page would be one of them. And yet, even an otherwise bog-standard car ad proved to be a cybertrap capable of snaring a careless educator.

In 2011, a Facebook group called "CoosVille Buy & Sell" was started for people living in and around Coos Bay, Oregon. In September 2018, an unnamed woman posted an ad for a car she was trying to sell.

Jeff Collier, a math teacher at Winter Lakes High School in nearby Coquille, was doing some car shopping one Sunday afternoon. He saw the woman's car ad and, for reasons unknown, decided to offer multiple editorial comments regarding her profile photo (expletives deleted during re-publication):

> I don't want to think of her doing dirty deeds when looking for a car to buy…where is her dignity?" Your profile pic looks like you are giving the gesture of eating (expletive)… nothing wrong with eating (expletive), it's just not very lady like to have it as a profile pic lol.

Collier's comments were quickly flagged by "multiple members" of the Coquille community and forwarded to Coquille School District Superintendent Tim Sweeney. He convened a meeting Monday at 7 a.m. with the principal of Winter Lakes High School, Tony Jones, and Special Programs Director Wayne Gallagher to discuss the posts. By the end of the day, Collier had submitted his resignation from the district.

"We found the posts to be disturbing," Sweeney said to a reporter, "and do not find that to be the professional behavior we expect."

Part of the reason for Collier's quick resignation may have had something to do with the fact that he interacted with at least one student during the online discussion that was sparked by his original comment. The media did not report the contents of her post, but regardless of what she wrote, Collier's response was inappropriate (again, expletive deleted during re-publication): "And the (explicit) unite ... again, you know I'm right, slutzzz..."

Left unexplained is why Collier decided to post his critical comments in the first place, but it doesn't matter. There is a range of possible reasons, but it's not useful to speculate without more information. What can be learned from this incident, however, is just how quickly the decision to post inappropriate content can end an educator's career.

Top Three Takeaways:

- If you hold a position of public prominence (for instance, as an educator), you should anticipate that other members of your community will flag anything stupid, cruel, or offensive that you say online.

- Always take time to do humor or simple decency check before pressing "send." Seriously, it's hard to think of many situations where it is essential that post something online at that precise moment. If Collier had stopped even long enough to walk to the fridge for another beer (I'm just speculating here), he might have had second thoughts about insulting a stranger in such a crude fashion.

- It's not clear from the coverage whether Collier knew that he had directed his second off-color post at a student. Ultimately, it doesn't matter; given the public nature of Facebook conversations, every educator should assume that students might read or respond to their comments. Post accordingly.

Cautionary Tale 6-2017-US_Georgia

At the end of January 2017, Strong Rock Christian School in Locust Grove, GA, announced that it had hired a new high school football coach. It was quite a catch for the school: Their choice was Fernando Bryant, a first-round pick in the 1999 National Football League draft. Bryant played for ten seasons and won the Super Bowl in 2009 as a member of the Pittsburgh Steelers. He retired from professional football a few months later.

Just three weeks into his new job, however, Bryant was called into the principal's office and abruptly asked to resign. When Bryant asked why, the principal said that a school parent had raised concerns about his past social media activity. Bryant, however, refused to resign. The principal then terminated Bryant's contract.

The letter of termination that Bryant later received from the school specifically referenced on-line content:

This letter will confirm that Strong Rock Christian School has made a decision not to move forward with your employment in the position of head coach of the football team and physical education teacher. As we discussed, after we made the offer to you, some within our parent community raised concerns regarding your family's public presence on social media and the internet and questioned whether the postings and information were consistent with our Christian values. We're sorry that our relationship had to end before it started. We wish you the best.

In an interview with Alec McQuade, a reporter for Atlanta-area television station *11Alive*, Bryant said that the school did not show him any particular posts. However, he said that he "was led to believe that it was something his wife posted a few years earlier."

McQuade, however, obtained a copy of the photo that a parent sent to the school. Bryant told him that it was a promotional photo that his wife posted to her private Instagram account three years earlier. In the picture, Bryant and his wife are standing side-by-side, holding a closed bottle of clear liquid, which Bryant acknowledged was alcohol. He told McQuade that he and his wife were doing sponsor photos for the on-line publication BEMagazine

Bryant also explained to McQuade that during his eight-week hiring process, the school had made a point of reviewing not just his social media history but that of his wife as well. McQuade's source in the Strong Rock football program reportedly said that before they hired Bryant, school administrators had seen the photo in question. Nonetheless, the objection by the parent was sufficiently strenuous to persuade the school to fire their new coach.

He understood from the start, Bryant said during his interview with *11Alive*, that the school expected him to be a born-again Christian and to promote the values of the school as a coach. But no one told him, Bryant said, that there was a prohibition against alcohol. He also did not receive any guidelines regarding acceptable or unacceptable use of social media (which wouldn't have made much difference in this case, given how long ago his wife posted the photo).

The entire incident, Bryant said, left him feeling discouraged:

If one parent or one part of a school can control it that much as far as Christianity, it makes you wonder what times we're in. I am a Christian, that's the one thing that gives Christianity a bad name, when we start passing judgment on each other. The only problem I had, and I told them this, the only problem I had is nothing about me changed from the day they started interviewing me, to the day they hired me, to the day they fired me. So it's hard for me to understand why, what happened?

In May 2017, Bryant filed a discrimination complaint with the Equal Employment Opportunity Commission, alleging that Strong Rock unfairly terminated him over the old social media post. The matter is still under review.

Top Three Takeaways:

- How well do you remember everything that you've post online? Can you be entirely sure that nothing is lurking in your Facebook or Twitter feed that you might wish you hadn't posted, five or ten years later? There's a growing number of businesses offering products and services designed to help people clean up their social media history. If you take a job in a school or community with particularly strong views on specific social or moral issues, you might want to give it some thought.

- The school's treatment of Bryant certainly seems capricious. Still, it is a good reminder that private schools—and in particular, private religious schools—have far more latitude in enforcing standards of moral behavior. Apply for jobs accordingly.

- Never underestimate the energy that some parents or moral activists may put into reviewing your publicly-available social media posts. Some people are motivated by legitimate concerns about who is teaching their children. Others, unfortunately, are far more interested in advancing a moral or political agenda and look for opportunities to make you an unwilling participant in that project.

Cautionary Tale 17-2016-Mexico

We now have proof that what happens in Cabo San Lucas doesn't stay in Cabo San Lucas. Thanks to the ubiquity of camera-equipped smartphones, teachers can no longer be confident that vacation activities will remain private, even if they completely abstain from using social media themselves.

Consider, for instance, what happened to Carla Clarissa, a 24-year-old elementary school teacher in Ciudad Obregón, a city of roughly 400,000 people in the northern Mexican state of Sonora. Clarissa decided to spend her 2016 spring break in Cabo San Lucas, a resort town at the very tip of Baja California Sur. It's fair to say that she wanted to get away from her day-to-day routine: It's about a 15-hour drive from Ciudad Obregón to Cabo San Lucas, including an eight-hour ride on a ferry across the Gulf of California.

During her stay at the resort, she and her friends went to a beach bar called Mango Deck Restaurant Bar & Beach Club, which was hosting a dance competition. Egged on by her buddies, Clarissa not only entered the contest but took home the top prize of $260 for her energetic twerking to the Daddy Yankee reggaeton hit, 'Rompe.'

The remainder of the story is a well-trod path. A video recording of Clarissa's winning performance (one of many, no doubt) found its way onto the internet and, of course, onto the screens of students and parents at the Instituto Cumbre del Norestre, the private school in Ciudad Obregón at which she taught. Outraged parents complained to the school's administration, and when Clarissa returned from vacation, her supervisors forced her to resign.

According to the Daily Mail, Clarissa offered a spirited defense in an interview with the Mexican newspaper Reforma. She raises several valid points:

> The situation got out of control and even before I got back from holiday it was becoming a problem on social media.

> They didn't give me any other option at my school than to resign. I felt I was being attacked and put under pressure. I didn't know what else to do apart from leave as quickly as I could. I knew there were mobile phones but I never imagined this would go viral and anyway, I'm not doing anything bad. It was a dance competition, something like this doesn't define me as a person, it was my free time and we're in the 21st century. It's not something to be afraid of, I'm not naked, I'm not having sex or taking drugs or disrespecting anyone.

An online petition was launched on Change.org, praising Clarissa for her work and demanding that the school rehire her. Within a couple of weeks of her firing, nearly 1,000 people had signed the petition, but there is no indication that she got her job back.

Top Three Takeaways:

- Clarissa's experience underscores the speed with which digital material can spread. It only took a few clicks of a button for the video of her dance routine to travel several hundred miles back to her school community.

- It also underscores the fundamental question of whether teachers are ever "off-duty" when they are in public. It would be one thing if Clarissa had performed her dance wearing an Instituto Cumbre del Norestre t-shirt (she didn't) or had even publicly identified herself as a teacher beforehand. Should the mere potential for irate parents be enough to regulate teacher off-duty behavior?

- Regardless of your personal views of booze-fueled, highly-sexualized dancing at a beach bar, there is no question that there is a vast difference between the pre-social media world and the world in which we live today.

Cautionary Tale 6-2015-Canada

One of the things that I have discovered during my work on this project is that sometimes, a seemingly insignificant incident can help illuminate many of the themes that I think are important for educators and administrators to consider. A good example occurred about five years ago in Markham, Ontario (a suburb of Toronto). It's got a little bit of everything: silly teacher behavior, student misbehavior, parental overreaction, an alleged cover-up, a digital trail of evidence, and impressive investigative reporting. Sadly, there are actual crimes that don't get this level of scrutiny. Nonetheless, this cautionary tale offers some useful lessons.

This story begins in March 2015 with a visit by a group of Markham High School teachers to one of the hot new trends in after-work entertainment: an indoor ax-throwing arena (the first of which, incidentally, was established in Toronto in 2011). Afterward, the teachers posed for a group photo that shows each of them grinning broadly and giving the finger to the photographer. (Some sources suggest that is a "tradition" for participants in this newly-created sport.) And predictably, for reasons unexplained, one of the teachers thought it would be fun to post the photo to a personal Facebook page. A minor flap occurred, and the teacher quickly deleted it.

That should have been the end of the matter. The teacher's second thoughts, however, didn't occur quickly enough. During the brief time that the photo was publicly available, a student made a copy and then reposted it nearly a year later. The republished image was seen by several parents who banded together to form a group called "Concerned Markham." The group then began an email campaign aimed at getting the district to take action against the teachers."

The *Toronto Sun* experienced some difficulty getting any answers from school officials about what was going on in the district, so it filed a Freedom of Information request. The school district disclosed a stash of 35 emails exchanged by various officials on April 8, 2016, discussing the student's repost. As *Toronto Sun* reporter Jenny Yuen summarized the exchange, "[e]ffectively, everyone involved attempted to sweep the whole matter under the proverbial carpet."

Among the steps taken by district officials: 1) using a private Twitter account to ask the student to remove the photo; 2) suggesting possible talking points for the student to minimize the publicity and the impact of the picture; 3) trying to figure out whether the student had talked to the media (and specifically, the *Toronto Sun*); and instructing a trustee of the district not to speak to the press.

Top Three Takeaways:

- Ultimately, all of this seems like a tempest in a teapot. Sure, the photo may depict inappropriate behavior by teachers, but compared to most of the other incidents in this book, it's pretty thin beer. It's rather remarkable that the student's republication (which itself only lasted three days) caused so much angst in district headquarters.

- Of more significance is the fact that the district put so much effort into figuring out a coordinated response (although the school district denied trying to limit what the student could say). Under different circumstances, you could construe some of the emails reviewed by the *Toronto Sun* as evidence of either spoliation or even obstruction of justice. While neither concept came into play in this case, it is an excellent example of how easily concern for the reputation of a district or individual teachers can lead to potentially unethical conduct.

- If you post **anything** online, you should simply assume that someone has made a copy of it, and you no longer have any control over how that person might use the content. Of course, you do retain legal ownership of the material that you post online, but enforcing that ownership may be more expensive, more time-consuming, and far less satisfying than you might like. I am no fan of self-censorship, but self-censorship and discretion are not precisely the same thing; the only content that can't be misused is the content you **don't** post online.

Cautionary Tale 6-2012-US_Colorado

In the category of "posting inappropriate content," few educators, if any, can top the efforts of Colorado's Carly McKinney. The 23-year-old was a math teacher at Overland High School in Aurora, Colorado, when a local television station received a tip that McKinney was posting questionable material on Twitter under the handle "@CrunkBear." The Twitter ID itself was arguably inappropriate for a high school teacher; the Urban Dictionary defines the word "crunk" variously as "crazy drunk" or "high AND drunk."

Regardless, it was the content of McKinney's posts and the attached photos that raised administrator concerns. Here are a few samples of McKinney's contributions to contemporary literature, which were captured by Denver's 9News before the Twitter account was made private and then shut down altogether:

- @SpliffMeister All day every day... unless you're a teacher like me. Then you just wait for after school.

- #SpliffManiac Nothing better than medical marijuana.

- My favorite ▫ http://t.co/C3Dd7dQ5 " (the attached photo showed McKinney smoking some substance in her car)

- Sleep naked. Good night twitter. Sweet muthafuckin dreamzzzzz http://t.co/oRjAoCQi (the attached photo showed McKinney lying face down on her bed, apparently nude, with a blanket just barely covering her rear end)

- Just got called Ms. McCutie. Points for being clever, however you are still jailbait.

- Naked. Wet. Stoned

- Watching a drug bust go down in the parking lot. It's funny cuz I have weed in my car in the staff parking lot.

- Such an easy day ... Can't wait to roll up after school.

- @DaveyCiar I do that, but I don't make a big deal out of it. Maybe someday I'll teach high just to see what happens!

McKinney illustrated several of her tweets with provocative photos showing her in various states of undress and near-nudity.

In response to the reports about McKinney's Twitter feed, Overland High School administrators put her on paid leave while they conducted an investigation. McKinney told school officials that she intended the Twitter account to be a parody and that she shared its administration with a "friend." McKinney said her friend was the one responsible for the more salacious posts. (Left unexplained was how the "friend" obtained the selfies showing McKinney in various stages of undress).

To be fair, none of McKinney's tweets were technically illegal (the pictures are at most PG-13), and recreational marijuana use was legal in Colorado at the time she was tweeting. Nonetheless, Overland administrators called in the Aurora police to determine whether McKinney had brought pot onto the school campus, which is still prohibited. The results of the investigation were inconclusive, and local law enforcement did not charge McKinney for any drug-related offenses. As of March 2013, McKinney was no longer an employee of the Cherry Creek School District, either through resignation or termination (the exact terms of her departure are unclear).

As an expression of solidarity with McKinney, many students at Overland (as well as "CrunkBear" fans around the world) began tweeting the hashtag "#FreeCrunkBear" and wearing t-shirts protesting her firing. The campaign enjoyed a brief flurry of media attention in early 2013 but subsided rather quickly. It had no discernible impact on the school district's position regarding McKinney's fitness to teach.

Top Three Takeaways:

- This particular cautionary tale is a little bit like shooting fish in a barrel. For starters, there's the role-modeling. Even if recreational marijuana use is legal in Colorado, that doesn't mean that administrators and parents are likely to be comfortable with a teacher so brazenly discussing his or her smoking habits on social media.

- Equally problematic were the numerous photos of McKinney in skimpy clothing or poses that suggested nudity. The images undercut McKinney's ability to maintain authority in the classroom and to be taken seriously by her students. Her claim that her Twitter feed was a "parody" was frankly ridiculous.

- The suggestion in some of her tweets that she was breaking the law (by bringing marijuana onto school property) was more than enough justification to fire her. Even if she did not break the law, the fact that she suggested that she did on a public forum gave the district ample grounds to take action. Some cautionary tales are a close call. This is not one of them.

Cautionary Tale 6-2009-GA

Although this is one of the older cautionary tales in this book, it remains a classic example of potentially negative consequences of oversharing online. Ashley Payne, a teacher at Appalachee High School in Barrow County, Georgia, spent the summer of 2009 on an enjoyable trip to various places in Europe. When she returned home, she created an album on Facebook of about 700 photos, precisely ten of which showed Payne drinking alcohol. One showed her sipping from a foaming glass of Guinness, and another showed her holding a half-empty glass of wine in one hand and a glass of beer in her other.

Sometime after returning home that summer, she also posted on Facebook that she was heading out to play "Crazy Bitch Bingo," a game popular with several restaurants and bars in the area in which she lived. Payne had set her Facebook privacy settings to a very high level, and her posts and album were only available to a small group of her friends and acquaintances.

On the morning of August 27, 2009, Payne's superintendent, Dr. Ron Saunders, received an anonymous email informing him of the contents of Payne's Facebook page and alleging that the writer's daughter had started using the slang term "bitches" (as in "female friends") because of Payne's Facebook posts. Attached to the email was a copy of the photo showing Payne holding up two glasses of alcohol.

The email concluded: "I am repulsed by Ms. Payne's profane use of language and how she conducts herself as an example to my teenage daughter. Her behavior is intolerable. I have a question to the Barrow County School System. Is it too hard for our educators to lack [sic] discipline online and offline? I have chosen to remain anonymous regarding this matter for the sake of my daughter."

As *Atlanta Journal-Constitution* reporter Maureen Downey noted, the email criticizing Payme was grammatically perfect and used with proper business memo formatting to boot. It also contained one significant factual error: none of Payne's students were friends with her on Facebook, and Payne insisted there were no errors in her privacy settings. Downey tried to contact the writer, but the email was from a temporary anonymous email account that was no longer active.

Regardless of the source of the email (Downey speculated that it was a hostile co-worker), the outcome for Payne was draconian. Just two hours after the email was received, Superintendent Saunders confronted Payne and told her that the combination of photos showing alcohol use and foul language on her Facebook page made it impossible for her to keep her job. Saunders gave her the option of resigning on the spot or receiving a suspension that would be on her permanent teaching record.

Payne agreed to resign but later filed a lawsuit in Georgia state court, alleging that Saunders had unlawfully terminated her. The Piedmont Circuit Court, however, issued summary judgment in favor of the school district in April 2013. Multiple news sources reported that Payne, by then a graduate student at the University of Georgia, was planning to appeal the lower court's decision.

The coverage of Payne's case largely faded after that, so it is not clear if she did, in fact, appeal. However, things appear to have worked out for her nonetheless: Payne is currently working as an English and social studies teacher at Decatur High School in Decatur, Georgia. Notwithstanding the relatively positive outcome, Payne's case should serve as a warning that even relatively innocuous content can get an educator in trouble, depending on the sensitivity of the district in question and the trustworthiness of your social media "friends." It also illustrates how difficult it can be, even with international media support, to overturn a disciplinary action or termination.

Top Three Takeaways:

- Notwithstanding the relatively positive outcome of Payne's case, this cautionary tale illustrates that there are risks if you share too much information online. To be fair, of course, none of the photos she shared depicted any illegal activity; instead, just a young woman having a pleasant time on a great summer vacation. But the reality is that the more content you share with the world, the more potential there is for someone to take offense and try to use it against you.

- Another thing to consider is that you may not even know the identity of the person who uses your social media post to get you in trouble. Although it is challenging to be entirely anonymous online, there are plenty of tools available (like anonymizing email accounts) that can make it very difficult and time-consuming to figure who is behind an anonymous report. The sad truth is that digital technology makes it far too easy to be malicious these days.

- Lastly, just how well do you know (and trust) all of your social media "friends"? Since the report was anonymous, there is no way to know precisely how the instigator got access to Payne's social media account, but it is not unreasonable to think that it was someone Payne thought she could trust. Far too many educators have discovered to their dismay that social media "friends" have their back solely to figure out where best to insert the knife.

Relevant MCEE Provisions for Chapter 6

Principle I: Responsibility to the Profession

Standards I.A.2, I.A.3, I.A.4, I.A.5, and I.C.2

Principle III: Responsibility to Students

Standards III.A.2, III.A.8, and III.A.9

Principle IV: Responsibility to the School Community

Standards IV.A.3, IV.B.2, IV.C.3, IV.D.3, IV.E.1, IV.E.2, IV.E.3

Principle V: Responsible and Ethical Use of Technology

Standard V.A.1, V.A.5, and V.A.7

Sources

The sources for the Cautionary Tales in this chapter can be viewed at the following URL:

https://link.cybertraps.com/C4E2-Sources-Chap6

Chapter 7

Criticizing or Mocking Students and Parents

Overview

Just about everyone has had at least one bad day at work, or a day when some combination of illness, depression, and interpersonal dyspepsia leave them out of sorts and just plain grumpy. Educators might once have offered snarky and even off-color student assessments in the privacy of the teacher's lounge, or on a long phone chat with a friend, or maybe over a consoling drink at a bar.

But thanks to Mark Zuckerberg (and others, to be fair), teachers now have the option of grousing in very public ways. Social media platforms like Facebook and Instagram have been designed to encourage us to share thoughts and impressions that we once would have kept to ourselves (and still should). These platforms give us an audience for all of our impolitic, inane, mean-spirited, or petty thoughts.

Most educators are aware (or at least should be) that if they post something publicly, even by accident, then they need to deal with the consequences of doing so. But what if you have double-checked the privacy settings and triple-checked to make sure that only your "friends" can see your latest bitter summary of life? An old German proverb sums it up best: ***Behüte mich Gott vor meinen Freunden, mit den Feinden will ich schon fertig werden*** ("God preserve me from my friends, I can deal with my enemies"). And all too often overlooked is the fact that Facebook has severely diluted the meaning of the word "friend." Is the 200th person on your Facebook friend list a "friend," or just someone you hope to impress with jealousy-inducing vacation photos?

Not surprisingly, when educators publicly ridicule or grouse about their students, their parents typically take offense and frequently demand that school officials discipline or fire the indiscreet educator. In some instances, they may go so far as to file a lawsuit against the offending teacher, building or district administrators, the school district, and anyone else their lawyer can credibly put in the complaint.

"But I intended the comments to be private," an aggrieved educator will no doubt will protest. "I had my 'privacy' settings at the highest level!'

That's terrific. But in the digital era, it's also basically meaningless. The following grim reality cannot be reiterated often enough: if you post something online, the odds are excellent that it WILL get out, one way or the other.

Here's a trivial but telling example: The photo-sharing website **Flickr** allows its users to disable downloading for any or all photos stored on the site. That feature prevents websurfers from simply right-clicking and saving a restricted image to their computer. It's a feature frequently used by photographers to protect their commercial work. But it's a relatively simple matter to perform a screen capture of any photo on the web, regardless of the download setting. The same is true for virtually every other type of information online.

It is entirely possible that over the next few years, societal attitudes towards online temper tantrums may ease. Even better, social media privacy controls will grow sufficiently sophisticated to allow educators to carefully limit access to what they post to a small, trusted group of real "friends."

In the interim, however, every educator should think long and hard about what they post online, and never forget that what is digital is easily copied. If it's not something that can be said or shown at a PTA or school board meeting, then maybe it's not fit for social media.

Cautionary Tales

Cautionary Tale 7-2018-US_Ohio

We all have things that drive us nuts for no particularly good reason. For example, I can't stand the Beatles song "Hey Jude," which puts me in a tiny minority of people, particularly in my generation (it's only the most popular song ever released by the Fab Four...). And for what do we have social media if not to rant about the songs, movies, tv characters, or dance fads that annoy us?

But for educational professionals, some lines should be observed, regardless of how many people may agree with your hot cultural take. That was a painful (and expensive) lesson learned by Amy Vajdich, a 3rd-grade social studies teacher in Aurora, OH, when she decided to share her caustic thoughts about the so-called "floss dance."

For those of you, like me, who don't have the pleasure of currently living with teens or tweens right now, here's a quick primer on the already-passé "floss dance." In the spring of 2017, an Instagram-famous 15year-old named Russell Horning (aka "Russell Got Barzz" or, more commonly, "The Backpack Kid") invented the dance moves and posted a video of the routine to his Instagram account. Horning's expressionless face and mesmerizing swinging backpack helped make the video a social media sensation, one that eventually attracted the attention of celebrity singers like Rihanna (who shared it on her massively popular Instagram account) and Katie Perry.

A few months later, Perry invited Horning to dance the "floss" during her appearance in the 2017 finale of "Saturday Night Live." The national TV exposure cranked Horning's follower count into the millions (he currently has 2.3 million followers on Instagram). It also made the "floss dance" a cultural phenomenon, particularly with tweens and pre-tweens.

The dance moves were a big hit among Aurora kids or at least a big enough hit for the "floss dance" to get on Vajdich's nerves. In an ill-advised post on Facebook on April 23, 2018, Vajdich made her feelings abundantly clear:

> ...Parents – Shut that shit down. I can't take it. Why can't kids hold the fuck still for one minute anymore? ... If you have seen this dance at home, then your child is probably one of the jerks who is currently driving his/her teacher crazy. More importantly, know that early intervention is the key, and it is OK to smack them just this once. Thanks

The line-crossing here should be pretty evident: It's never a smart move for an educator to publicly post profanity, call kids jerks, or advocate corporal punishment. Although it's not clear from media reports exactly how the post came to the attention of Aurora administrators, they didn't waste any time taking action. Less than a month after her post, the Aurora school district fired Vajdich for "inappropriate" social media posts that it characterized as "misconduct." The district's letter also flagged two other posts that were considered inappropriate: one that referenced a woman pulling something from her cleavage and another that talked about "how men view women and included a sexually explicit hashtag."

Top Three Takeaways:

- I shouldn't need to say this, but it's never a smart move for an educator to publicly post profanity, call kids jerks, or advocate corporal punishment. Those are the types of statements that tend to upset parents, and few school districts will put much effort into defending them (or the educator who made them).

- Pay careful attention to the fact that once Vajdich's initial offensive post came to light, someone at the Aurora School District headquarters took the time to go through all of her publicly-available Facebook posts and found at least two others that raised concerns. It's a good reminder: a school district may ignore social media posts when they first go online, but then view them in a much more negative light when it is looking for evidence of alleged misconduct.

- Both administrators and educators should take the time to review district and building policies regarding social media activity regularly. Remarkably, when local reporters examined the policies and procedures of the Aurora School District, they did not find any that specifically applied to social media. District Superintendent Pat Ciccantelli told reporters that the district has "several policies that speak to employee conduct and related areas," but that's not a great answer. Both the school district and its employees would have benefited from a greater focus on this issue.

Cautionary Tale 7-2018-US_Texas

"I'm mad as hell and I'm not going to take this anymore!" is one of the iconic and evergreen lines in American cinema. It was delivered with passion and bug-eyed verve by newscaster Howard Beale, played by Peter Bennett, in the 1975 classic Network. The film, a deeply cynical look at what was happening to the news business in the era of television, remains painfully relevant nearly forty-five years later.

Undoubtedly, more than one teacher has said something similar at various points in her or his career. Only recently, however, have teachers had access to a national (or international) network on which to vent their frustration and rage. Sometimes, the worldwide distribution educator spleen is an accident; in a handful of cases (like this one), it's an intentional act of outrage and disapproval.

In the spring of 2018, Julie Marburger -- a sixth-grade teacher at Cedar Creek Intermediate School -- sat down at her computer and had her Howard Beale moment on the global network known as Facebook:

> I left work early today after an incident with a parent left me unable emotionally to continue for the day. I have already made the decision to leave teaching at the end of this year, and today, I don't know if I will make it even that long. Parents have become far too disrespectful, and their children are even worse. Administration always seems to err on the side of keeping the parent happy, which leaves me with no way to do the job I was hired to do...teach kids.

Along with her rant, Marburger posted several photos that she said illustrated the damage her students had caused in her classroom, including gum stuck on windowsills, damaged classroom decorations, a dirty floor, and a half-destroyed bookcase with books cascading onto the floor. (Marburger long ago deleted her Facebook post, but her photos are readily discoverable if you search for her name and read the articles about her online diatribe.)

Top Three Takeaways:

- It is a good thing that Marburger had decided to quit because it would have been tough for her to continue in her position after sharing her thoughts on Facebook. To be fair, what she wrote was not particularly outrageous, and I'm confident that many other educators have had similar views. Still, there is a significant difference between a private rant over drinks and publishing something for the whole world to read.

- It is also necessary to consider the impact that this will have on Marburger's career going forward. What if she changes her mind and decides that she wants to return to teaching? The odds are excellent that someone in her new school district will do an internet search, and all of these articles will come flooding back. At the very least, Marburger will have some explaining to do, and there's a decent possibility that some districts would simply decide not to interview her at all.

- There are a lot of reasons to think once, twice, or three times about posting something to social media. The top contender, however, is the fact that once something goes online (particularly if it becomes a news story!), it can be virtually impossible to get rid of it. As the not-so-old saying goes, "Post in haste, repent at leisure."

Cautionary Tale 7-2017-US_New York

Given the immediacy of social media and the ease of adding content, it shouldn't come as a shock that people sometimes overshare. Most of us, I suspect, have been guilty of oversharing at one time or another. Typically, the oversharing involves something that is happening at that moment; former baseball player Jose Canseco, for instance, once tweeted, "I'm on the toilet thinking about writing a third book." Did we need to know what he was doing at that exact moment? But beware: you can get in trouble today for oversharing something that happened to you a long time ago.

An excellent example of this occurred in Uniondale, NY in the fall of 2017, when high school health teacher Steven Solomon posted the following story to his Facebook feed (NB: misspellings and punctuation errors in original):

> Tom,
>
> Your going to love this story.I had a class I was teaching where I also had home room where I required all my students to at least stand for the pledge.Two of my students refused to stand and went to the principal complaining I couldn't legally make then stand. The principal told me not to make them stand. I told the students standing for the flag was showing respect for the men of our military who risked their lives to protect our freedoms. They said "we didn't ask them to"The next day they refused to stand saying "they didn't have to" I told them that is true and what makes this country great is "that I didn't have to pass them either"
>
> Well I know God has a sense of humor because both of these un patriotic kids both ended up with a 63 avg, and under ordinary circumstances I would have passed them both, instead I failed them both.

Well the next year miraculously I had them both back in my home room class and when I asked the class to stand, these two suckers were the first up! True story!

As word of Solomon's post spread, several parents lodged complaints with the school district. Superintendent William Lloyd issued a statement announcing that Solomon was re-assigned to "out of classroom duties" while the District investigated the incident. Superintendent Lloyd noted that the situation occurred "more than a decade ago."

In an interview with WABC-TV in New York, the 30-year veteran teacher defended what he did, saying that "[t]hese kids failed themselves." He also complained that members of the school community were taking his Facebook comments out of context:

> This was 10 years later, in a Facebook post, goofing off to a friend. I thought this just went to him. ... That was meant for one person to read. Not everyone. ... To say that they failed because they didn't stand for the pledge is untrue. I could see people misconstruing that. It was poorly written, and you know what, if I had written that for the public, I'd have written it differently.

Solomon later told Newsday that he did understand that students have a right not to stand [a Supreme Court precedent for 75 years] and denied that he required the failed students to stand. Nonetheless, Solomon said, the district placed him on indefinite suspension with pay as of November 8, and the union removed him as a representative.

Top Three Takeaways:

- As I've repeatedly pointed out, parents pay close attention to the attitudes and conduct of teachers. The rise of social media and its widespread use by educators has given parents much more opportunity to form judgments about the people teaching their children and to raise concerns with school administrators. This cautionary tale is a perfect example. There was no need for Solomon to use Facebook to tell a potentially upsetting story to his friend; it would have been much better if he had done so in person and preferably out the hearing of anyone else. Once it was on social media, however, it could easily be reproduced and redistributed.

- Solomon said that "if I had written that for the public, I'd have written it differently." I'm not sure what he could have written that would have made his conduct less offensive and unconstitutional. Still, the main point is simple: You should anticipate that everything you post on social media is public and draft accordingly.

- The "taken out of context" defense rarely works, especially if parents or reporters are quoting you in full. Anytime you post something on social media, you should take a few seconds (or longer) to think about whether someone could genuinely take your comments out of context or whether they are simply offensive as written.

Cautionary Tale 7-2017-US_Ohio

Like so many other social functions in American society—weddings, engagement parties, Sweet Sixteen celebrations, etc.—senior proms have gotten fancier and fancier. In 2015, the average cost of prom for students in the United States was just under $1,000 per person. Increasingly, a significant portion of the budget is devoted to elaborate "promposals," a trend undoubtedly influenced by the implicit one-upmanship of social media. Ashley Prendable, a teacher in Maryland, expressed a little frustration with that new trend:

> I am getting a little annoyed by the number of students who are asking to be excused from class to take part in others' promposals. Some of these get a small army of a hundred or more students together. Thoughtful? Yes. Cute? Sure. Too much hype? Absolutely. The amount of planning that goes into promposals is getting to be a little ridiculous – or maybe I'm just jealous because my marriage proposal wasn't as elaborate as some of these promposals!

Prendable is undoubtedly not the only teacher to have misgivings about over-the-top prom expenditures, but once again, using social media to express those feelings and opinions can create unanticipated problems. In the town of Bedford, Ohio (a suburb of Cleveland), administrators asked middle school teacher Caitlin Cormack to help chaperone the 2017 high school prom. Sometime over the following weekend, she posted a selfie on Snapchat with a tart caption:

> These damn kids and parents...not enough money for school supplies or passing grades but out here renting horses

As one parent elaborated, Cormack's Snap referred to the fact that two students rode to the Bedford High School prom in a horse and carriage.

It is not clear from media reports exactly who saw Cormack's Snap and captured it. Regardless, her comments quickly started making the rounds of the relatively small community (further proof that the auto-delete function of Snapchat is a dubious protector of privacy). Bedford School superintendent Andrea Celico said that the district was "disappointed" by Cormack's statement but added (somewhat naively) that she was surprised that the post was circulating online. Celico said that she had received several calls from parents, both critical and supportive of Cormack.

Cormack, a popular teacher and coach, was briefly put on administrative leave but is still employed at the Heskett Middle School in Bedford.

Top Three Takeaways:

- Lots and lots of people are sure that anything they put on Snapchat quickly disappears and can't be retrieved. Lots and lots of people are incorrect. There are multiple methods for capturing and saving Snapchat content, so users (especially educators) should treat it just like any other social media app. If you don't want to see your comments printed in the paper, don't post them in the app.

- The fact that someone in the Bedford community was able to capture Cormack's Snap raises questions about her list of followers. It would not be appropriate for her to have student followers at all, since that immediately raises the ethical concern of multiple relationships with the people she is supposed to be educating. That ethical concern is lower concerning her adult followers, but it does not go away altogether. At the very least, every additional follower who is a member of her school community increases the likelihood that an ill-considered post or Snap will create problems.

- Cormack's experience is a helpful reminder that not every social media mistake is career-ending. It might have been different if she had name-checked the horse-renting teens, but her somewhat grumpy Snap op-ed was not enough to cost Cormack her job.

Cautionary Tale 7-2017-US_North Dakota

In early April 2017, someone delivered a packet containing more than twenty pages of tweets to administrators at the Liberty Middle School in West Fargo, North Dakota. Local media outlets received similar material at about the same time to local media. The sender, "an anonymous group of self-described concerned parents," objected to many of the Twitter comments made by Sheridan Tihista, a young special education teacher at the school.

In 2013, Tihista (then Sheridan Pope) was crowned Miss Montana in part based on her platform of "Possibilities for Disabilities: Inclusion Education." As she told the website Autism Speaks, her personal experience led to her desire to advocate for those students:

> Growing up, I saw a lot of problems in the educational system. Granted, I grew up 15 years ago just starting school in a rural small town. My sister has autism and she had experienced a lot of difficulties in school. We'd both ride the special needs school bus. All the special needs aids would wear gloves because they thought they might catch her autism. It was nuts. I was in 1st or 2nd grade when this happened. People were not understanding of my sister. They weren't understanding of her autism and I wanted to do right by my sister and help make everyone feel like they were included in the schools, disability or not.

As a result, Tihista said that her Scholastic Ambition was "To receive a Bachelor's Degree in Elementary Inclusive Education and then to pursue a Master's Degree in Applied Behavior Analysis Therapy."

Working in the field of inclusive education, however, apparently proved more frustrating than Tihista anticipated. For several months in late 2016 and early 2017, Tihista used Twitter to vent about the challenges of her job and to make immature and mocking comments about her students. She deleted her account within a few hours of the discovery of her tweets, but you can find examples and screenshots of her comments scattered around the web. Among her more incendiary remarks:

- Writing a research paper about parenting struggles of kids with autism and instead of writing "mothers" I wrote "monsters." (laughing emojis) #samething [April 5, 2017]

- I yelled at my student today but accidentally called him by my cat's name.... not even ashamed bc that's how annoying he was. (stare emoji) [January 21, 2017]

- YOU. GUYS. I have a student that I've not been able to figure out who she reminds me of & NOW I KNOW. She is Tina Belcher. Not even lyin. [October 19, 2016]

- 5 weeks into school and my students are just now figuring out my name isn't "Mistie." Even though "Miss T" is everywhere in my room. [September 22, 2016]

- I'm going to start a blog under a pseudonym called "Shit My Students Say." [August 23, 2016]

Interestingly, Tihista's Twitter bio suggested that she was aware that she might be crossing a line: "just a teacher trying to hide from her students on social media. If you're a student, go away." But a bio like that, of course, is about as effective as the porn site warning pages that tell kids, "If you are under the age of 18, don't click here!" The reality, of course, is that there is nowhere teachers can hide from students on social media.

Following receipt of the printouts, school officials announced that they would undertake an investigation. Later that same day, Tihista texted a local TV station and said that "My tweets may have been distasteful but don't illustrate what kind of educator I am."

The West Fargo school district disagreed with Tihista's view of the matter and placed her on administrative leave. Following the district's decision, Tihista issued the following somewhat defensive and only partially apologetic statement:

I attended basketball games, bought my kids lunch when their accounts were negative, attended adoption events, and stayed after school daily with any child that needed it. I differentiated all academic and behavior plans and I always made sure to send a photo of a student posing with an A+ assignment or their classroom reward home as often as I could. I made a mistake and let my humor and venting become inappropriate which then was misconstrued.

I am devastated that this media attention still means another day that my students have to suffer this horrible situation. Of course if I could change this, I would. I hope however you run your story, that you add a positive light out there for any adult or child that life continues after a mistake. You can be hated across the country and people will still love you. You can get death threats, and people will still love you. What I did was wrong and I hope it can be used to teach and inspire others, because its done just that for me. Best of luck on your story. I hope it brings peace to kids and families and maybe someone whose [sic] in my boat right now.

Notwithstanding her statement to the press, Tihista decided the next day that it would be best if she resigned from her position.

Top Three Takeaways:

- At first blush, it's difficult to understand why someone with Tihista's background would be mocking students with special needs on social media. I think that there are a couple of different explanations. First, teaching is difficult under the best of circumstances, and I believe that Tihista found it challenging to work full-time with special needs students. It's not unreasonable for a first-year teacher to need to vent now and then. Second, Tihista was 23 or 24 when she began teaching in 2016, which means that she was probably born sometime around 1993. Like my eldest son, she grew up with the World Wide Web and is part of the first generation for whom social media was a significant part of their adolescent and college life. For that generation and for the ones that follow, sharing on social media is the default form of communication. Older generations have not done a great job explaining the potential risks of all that.

- Tihista may have thought she was clever using a fake name and profile photo on Twitter, but she was just kidding herself. There's no clear explanation about how the "concerned parents" made the connection between "Sher" and Tihista, but however it happened, they were correct.

- It is pretty common for people in Tihista's situation to try to minimize the damage by deleting their social media accounts. It's an exercise in futility. First, it is far too easy for people to preserve copies of your offensive social media posts. Second, if you are for some reason newsworthy, there is an excellent chance that media outlets will include copies of your thoughtless social media comments, and search engines will permanently index them. And worse, even if the articles eventually are deleted by media outlets (as sometimes happens), there is a better than even chance that the Internet Archive will preserve copies for the foreseeable future, if not eternity. So, think carefully about the potential consequences before venting on social media.

Cautionary Tale 7-2017-US_Florida

One of the significant problems with social media services like Facebook is that they misuse the word "private" in ways that lull users into thinking that they have more control than they do. In early 2017, a Florida teacher named Susan Creamer stumbled into precisely this cybertrap.

Creamer, a teacher at the Merritt Brown Middle School in Panama City, belonged to a "private" Facebook group called "Atheists of Bay County." The word "private" is used by Facebook in this instance to indicate that the group's moderators can control who belongs to the group and who can see information posted to the group. (There are two types of "private" groups on Facebook: "Visible," which can be discovered by non-members, who can then ask for permission to join, and "Hidden," which only be seen by people who are already members or those invited to participate.)

What the word "private" does not mean, however, is the ability to control the spread of information posted to the group (which, of course, is true for any information posted online). At the end of what seems like a stressful day, Creamer shared the following post with her fellow atheists:

> There is a bevy of boys in one of my classes (middle school) who are taking turns either inviting me to their church or leaving (anonymously) flyers inviting me to church events. Today, I found one on the A/V cart I use for a podium. Every time any child sneezes, they loudly say "God bless you!" and look in my direction. I have complained twice to my principal—once last month and once today. She has spoken privately to one or two of the little cretins, but it seems to do NO GOOD. I am feeling bullied and harassed. It has become intolerable. I don't feel like talking with the parents will stop the inappropriate behavior because, for all I know, the parents are encouraging them. Any suggestions?

Creamer's post to the "private" Facebook group did not stay private very long; someone in the group took a screenshot (or photo) of her post and sent it to Bay District school officials. As district spokesperson Karen Tucker pointed out to the press, it is a violation of Bay District policy to criticize students or parents "either in person or on an Internet page." She added that the private nature of the group makes no difference:

> I don't think it matters (if the page is closed), because eventually someone else is going to see it posted, which is what happened. People were re-posting. If you said things on there, which she did, about students, no, I don't think it matters.

Jeromy Henderson, a fellow member of the Atheists of Bay Area group, staunchly defended Creamer:

> It has turned into a modern-day witchhunt. The group is closed. It was never meant for public consumption. She was just looking for advice from the group on how to deal with students she felt were harassing her. Yes, her terminology was off-putting, but she was just looking for advice about how to deal with them. She'd already been to her principal and was not getting results.

On February 16, Merritt Brown Middle School Principal Charlotte Marshall formally reprimanded Creamer in a letter placed in her HR file. Marshall acknowledged that Creamer had accepted responsibility for her actions and had apologized in Marshall's presence to each of her classes, which Marshall described as "an awesome display of ownership." Nonetheless, Marshall said, the fact that Creamer referred to a small group of her students as "cretins" constituted "a clear violation of our Employee Code of Conduct for Social Media." She also underscored the difficulty of keeping material private online:

> I know that you thought you were posting to a private group, but as you can see from the following policy language, we must always assume our posts are public: "Employees should closely monitor their privacy settings, remembering that such settings are subject to change and may not fully protect their content, and that even anonymously posted content may be traced back to them. When posting, even under the strictest privacy settings, employees should act on the assumption that all postings are in the public domain.

Top Three Takeaways:

- The statement that Principal Marshall included in her letter to Creamer is one of the more concise and accurate summations of educator responsibility that I have seen in this area. Every educator should memorize her final sentence: "act on the assumption that all postings are in the public domain."

- Think carefully about how once-familiar words are taking on new and sometimes deceptive meanings. How does the contemporary definition of "friend" differ from how we used it twenty years ago? How can a written comment be "private" if you can no longer control who reads it and how others may use it? For your protection, it is essential to examine regularly whether your assumptions about language remain accurate.

- Periodically review your district's policies regarding the acceptable use of online services and, in particular, those governing the use of social media. There is an ethical duty to abide by such policies and an overarching obligation to consider how your use of social media may affect your interactions with students, parents, and other members of the school community.

Cautionary Tale 7-2015-Sweden

It is only fair to point out that not every teacher criticism of parents or their parenting results in disciplinary proceedings. In late August 2015, Jonas Harrysson, a teacher at the Thoren Framtid school in Ronneby, Sweden, offered some parenting suggestions in a Facebook post. His prescription for parents received global attention and generated thousands of positive responses. Here's what he recommended (as translated by someone a few days after Harrysson's initial post):

> I have worked with kids for almost 16 years and there are several things that I've noticed children getting worse and worse at.

> No.1. Children find it very difficult to be bored! There constantly needs to be something going on.

> Please stop spoiling and servicing your children. It's not dangerous for them to be bored sometimes.

> No 2. I've met many parents who are soooo proud that their kids can read and count before starting preschool.

> Well, I hate to break it to you, but reading and counting, they'll learn to do soon enough. Teach them instead to play, to be a good friend, and to share.

My third point is that many children find it difficult to show gratitude, both to other kids and towards adults. Can they get an "another one" is unfortunately often a first question – and "we only get one!?" is a common complaint I hear. What happened to PLEASE!? And thanks for dinner, and thanks for the ride, and so on? I have no children at the moment, but if I do sometime in the future I plan to teach them to play, to be good friends, to show gratitude and to be bored from time to time. Once they've learned those things, then I'll teach them to read and count :)

As of January 2018, Facebook users had shared Harrysson's post nearly 18,000 times. The comment section is a veritable United Nations of languages (which says something as well about the global reach of Facebook). Harrysson's advice to parents did not cause him any employment difficulties. What is interesting, however, is that media outlets used such grim terms to describe his relatively mild Facebook post. Here are just a few examples:

- "Swedish teacher launches attack on parents ..."

- "This Teacher Has Had It! ..."

- "Fed Up With Children's Attitudes, Teacher Tells Parents 3 Things ..."

- "Teacher lays into parents who pamper ..."

- "This Teacher's Had It Up to Here with Kids Today, So He Posted ..."

- "This Teacher Got So Fed Up With Kids' Behavior That He Wrote ..."

I was able to find Harrysson on Facebook, and he graciously agreed to do a brief Q&A with me (I have reproduced his replies as written):

Q: What prompted you to write your Facebook post about parenting?

A: Actully I had none bigger thougts when I wrote it. In the first it was to my freinds on Facebook. But just in a few days it became very big and alot of poeple start to share it.

Q: Did the post cause you any problems in your school community? For instance, with your administrators, colleagues, parents, or students?

A: No not any. More the opisite, some offer me Jobs and more.. Everyone near me has been very happy and proud when they saw me on tv, in the papers and so on. I have got alot of mail from all over the world but 9 of 10 support me.

Q: Have your views changed since you wrote the post?

A: No, not really. Not on that I wrote. I still think that many kids needs that I wrote and that some parents (not all) need to step up. But I know now how big and fast a post can go viral. That I didnt knew earlier.

Q: Do you have any advice or suggestions for teachers who might be thinking of writing similar posts?

A: Think one more time so it is something you stand for beacouse it can go very fast viral.

Q: Is there anything else you would like to add?

A: It was never my thought to blame some parents. I Know it must be very hard to be a parent this times. But if all adults help each other to change focus on whats importend when your kid is 5-8 years it wuld be alot better. The kids is our future and we need them to be good and kindful in this hard world.

Top Three Takeaways:

- So yes, as this cautionary tale demonstrates, it is possible to make critical comments online about parents and the choices they make without necessarily losing your job. There may be some cultural differences involved here, as the Swedes seem more tolerant of this type of statement than is often the case in the United States.

- At the same time, however, it is necessary to remember that if your post attracts significant attention in your community (or under the right circumstances, in much of the developed world), you will have no control over how the media portrays your comments. While the odds of receiving the level of global attention Harrysson experienced may be quite low, it is yet another good reason to think, as he said, "one more time" before clicking "post."

- On Facebook, you can prevent your post from being shared with the click of a button by marking it "Friends Only." That will reduce the likelihood that your comments will bring you global fame (or disgrace). Never forget, however, that if just one of your "friends" disagrees with or is outraged by something you've said, all it takes is a single screenshot, printout, or photo to turn your carefully-restricted post into a public document. "Information wants to be free."

Relevant MCEE Provisions for Chapter 7

Principle I: Responsibility to the Profession

Standards I.A.3, I.A.4, I.A.5, I.C.2

Principle II: Responsibility for Professional Competence

Standard II.C.3

Principle III: Responsibility to Students

Standards III.A.1, III.B.1, III.B.2, III.B.3

Principle IV: Responsibility to the School Community

Standards IV.A.1, IV.A.2, IV.C.3

Principle V: Responsible and Ethical Use of Technology

Standards V.A.1, V.A.5, V.A.6, V.A.7, V.C.1, V.C.2, V.C.3

Sources

The sources for the Cautionary Tales in this chapter can be viewed at the following URL:

https://link.cybertraps.com/C4E2-Sources-Chap7

Chapter 8

Using Social Media as a Political Soapbox

Does the First Amendment Protect Educators?

That may be one of the most common (and plaintive) questions that educators pose during my professional development lectures. On the surface, the answer is straightforward: any United States citizen on American soil should reasonably expect that he or she has the right to freedom of speech, especially when that speech is made away from the workplace and on personal time. But as is so often the case, things are a little more complicated, particularly for educators.

First, let me provide a little bit of legal history. In 1964, an Illinois teacher named Marvin Pickering wrote a letter to the editor of his local newspaper, in which he alleged that the local Board of Education had botched efforts to pass necessary tax bonds. He also asserted that the Board inappropriately cut funds for education to boost athletics and that the district superintendent tried to suppress commentary by district teachers. The Board promptly fired Pickering, and he sued, alleging violation of his First Amendment rights.

In June 1968, the United States Supreme Court upheld Pickering's claim of First Amendment protection. "[I]n a case such as this," the Court said, "absent proof of false statements knowingly or recklessly made by him, a teacher's exercise of his right to speak on issues of public importance may not furnish the basis for his dismissal from public employment."

Over the next four decades, the Supreme Court issued several different rulings regarding the First Amendment speech rights of public employees, including teachers. The most recent of these decisions was *Garcetti v. Ceballos* (2006), in which the Court announced a two-part test for determining whether statements by a public employee are entitled to First Amendment protection:

1. Was the statement made as a private citizen about a matter of public concern, or as an employee about issues within the scope of his or her employment?

2. Did the state employer have an "adequate" reason for treating the employee differently than a member of the general public? Put another way, did the speech unduly interfere with the ability of the state employer to operate effectively?

Taken together, these cases (and dozens of lower court decisions like them) raise the legitimate question of whether teachers are ever entitled to First Amendment protection for the things they say. As Professor Leora Harpaz points out, the test for determining if a public employee's speech is protected now actually has five parts:

1. Is the employee speaking pursuant to his or her "official duties"? If the answer is "yes," then the employee is not protected by the First Amendment;

2. If the employee is speaking as a private citizen, is he or she speaking about an issue of public concern? If the answer to that question is "no," then the employee is not protected by the First Amendment;

3. Even if the employee is speaking as a private citizen about a matter of public concern, does the employee's interest in commenting outweigh "the interest of the state as the employer"? (In the education context, this question typically focuses on whether the speech causes "disruption" in the school or classroom.) If the answer is "no," then the employee is not protected by the First Amendment;

4. Even if the employee's interests in the speech are more significant than the employer's interests in the efficient operation of the workplace, the employee must still demonstrate that the challenged statement was a "substantial factor" in an adverse employment action. If not, then the employee is not entitled to prevail; and

5. Finally, a state employer can still prevent recovery by a plaintiff employee if the employer (a school district, for instance) can demonstrate that it would have taken the same employment action "even in the absence of the protected speech."

You don't have to be a law school graduate to see that the chief consequence of the Court's decisions in this area has been a steady weakening of educator First Amendment protection. It is a classic Catch-22: if you talk publicly about something that is within the scope of your employment, or if you comment on something deemed not to be of public concern, then you don't have First Amendment protection.

But commenting on a significant public issue (immigration, for instance, or Black Lives Matter) is no guarantee of First Amendment protection. If your supervisors decide that your comments are too disruptive to the school environment or the operation of the district, they can still take disciplinary action.

The net effect, then, is that First Amendment protection can only reliably be enjoyed by public school teachers who make non-controversial statements about subjects that have nothing to do with their professional responsibilities.

We are all aware (or should be) that the nation currently is grappling with a large number of challenging, contentious issues, and a hotly contested national election is only a few months away. Administrators and school boards are eager to avoid controversy, and they will not look favorably on educators who make provocative statements on social media that undercut their effectiveness in the classroom.

I don't know how the 2020 national elections will turn out, but I do know this: between now and early November 2020, several teachers will lose their jobs because of their political posts on social media.

Cautionary Tales

Cautionary Tale 8-2019-US_Iowa

Just five words posted to Facebook.

That's all it took to trash a 26-year teaching career. It brings to mind the old game show, "Name That Tune": I can lose my job with just *three* words, Tom….

Matt Baish was a long-time science teacher at West High School in Waterloo, Iowa. In late September 2019, a man named Mason Severson posted a link on Facebook to an article on LittleVillageMag.com. The story discussed an upcoming visit to Iowa City by 16-year-old Swedish climate activist Greta Thunberg; alongside the link to the report, Severson asked, "Who's all going?"

According to a screenshot republished in the *Des Moines Register*, Baish clicked on the "Angry" emoji and wrote: "Don't have my sniper rifle."

Baish's response shocked Severson and several other people who read it, including parents of students in Baish's classes. One mother shared his post throughout the school community and said that she was concerned for the safety of any of his students who agree with Thunberg about climate change.

A week after he posted his comment, Baish was put on administrative leave while the District prepared to conduct an investigation. When it announced Baish's suspension, the school district reminded the public that it has social media guidelines for its employees. Among other things, the guidelines prohibit content that "would be defined by a reasonable person as obscene, racist, or sexist," "promotes illicit, illegal, or unethical activity," or "violates the district's affirmative action and/or bullying and harassment policies."

Later that same day, Baish resigned from his position in the Waterloo School District. He declined all press requests for comment.

Top Three Takeaways:

- Given the amplifying power of the global megaphone that is social media, you can do a lot of damage to your career in a small amount of space. Still, losing your teaching job for just five ill-chosen words might be some kind of dubious record. It's not one that you should try to top.

- One thing you should pay close attention to is how social media companies attempt to use your emotions to drive engagement with their sites. They all do it to one degree or another, but Facebook is particularly egregious. Facebook specifically designs its emojis to serve both as emotional shorthand and as tools for pushing your buttons, whatever they may be. Would Baish have posted his comment if there weren't an "Angry" emoji ready and waiting right below Severson's post? Quite possibly, but there is at least a chance that the tone of what he wrote might have been different.

- Educators should keep in mind that an acceptable use policy is not a pre-condition for district action if you post something offensive or threatening on social media. The primary purpose of an AUP should be to educate teachers and staff about the guidelines for appropriate behavior and to encourage conversation and debate about those guidelines. Both technology and social mores are continually evolving, so every AUP should be regularly reviewed to make sure that its provisions still provide the best guidance possible for a complex world. Every educator should understand, however, that a school district can discipline you for social media misconduct even if it has never drafted an AUP.

Cautionary Tale 8-2019-US_Texas

One of the longer-running educator cybertraps cases helps underscore just how important it is for teachers to understand the technology that they are using. In the late winter and spring of 2019, Georgia Carter, an English teacher at Carter-Riverside High School in Fort Worth, Texas, posted a series of tweets about illegal immigration. Most of the tweets were addressed directly to President Donald Trump, who made immigration one of the core issues of his candidacy and subsequent presidency. Here are some samples of what Clark wrote:

- [May 17, 2019] @realDonaldTrump Mr. President, Fort Worth Independent School District is loaded with illegal students from Mexico. Carter-Riverdale High School has been taken over by them. Drug dealers are on our campus and nothing was done to them when the drug dogs found the evidence.

- [May 17, 2019] @realDonaldTrump I need protection from recrimination should I report it to the authorities but I do not know where to turn. I contacted the Texas Education Association and then my teacher organization. Texas will not protect whistleblowers. The Mexicans refuse to honor our flag.

- [May 17, 2019] @realDonaldTrump I do not know what to do. Anything you can do to remove the illegals from Fort Worth would be greatly appreciated. My phone number is 817-862-7923 and my cell is 817-781-4814. Georgia Clark is my real name. Thank you.

- [May 17, 2019] @realDonaldTrump Mr. President, I asked for assistance in reporting illegal immigrants in the FWISD public school system and what I received was an alarming tweet from someone identifying himself as one of your assistants followed by a second tweet from the same person -cont

- [May 17, 2019] @realDonaldTrump with the f word used in the dot com. I promptly deleted both tweets and sent a message to Twitter about it. I really do need a contact here in Fort Worth who should be actively investigating and removing the illegals that are in the public school system. Thank you.

Once copies of her tweets began circulating in cyberspace, a significant backlash began forming. After an investigation, the Fort Worth school board met on June 4, 2019, and voted 8-0 to terminate Clark's contract, finding that she had violated the District's social media policy. Clark had told investigators that she did not realize that everyone could see the tweets she addressed to Trump; she thought that only he or his staff would be able to read them.

Clark's firing has turned into a significant battle over the First Amendment rights of teachers. Texas law requires that the FWISD hire an independent examiner to evaluate its decision to fire Clark. The examiner concluded that the school board had violated Clark's First Amendment rights and that her tweets were not "racially insensitive and/or discriminatory." In September, however, the school board overruled the examiner's conclusion and affirmed its termination of Clark. (It is worth pointing out that there is an additional context here; Clark has a long history of disciplinary actions related to her attitudes towards minority students.)

Clark appealed the board's decision to the Texas Education Commissioner, who agreed that her tweets were protected speech. The Commissioner ordered FWISD to either reinstate Clark or provide her with one year's salary as compensation for her termination. Instead, the District promptly issued a statement saying that the Commissioner had made a critical factual error and that it would be appealing the decision.

Superintendent Kent P. Scribner offered a single terse comment: "We stand by our decision because we firmly believe this is in the best interests of all students."

Top Three Takeaways:

- It will be interesting to see how this plays out. There are significant constitutional issues, and in general, I believe that teachers should have the ability to speak their minds on important public issues. On the other hand, the concept of "free speech" has never meant "free from consequences." If your public comments suggest bias against specific groups of students or are so inflammatory that it makes it difficult, if not impossible, to do your job, then you should not be surprised when your district decides to take action.

- It may be that Clark would have made her comments on Twitter regardless, but it is certainly true that her difficulties arose in part because she did not fully understand how the software works.

- The Texas Education Commissioner takes a pretty expansive view of educator First Amendment rights, and that is good news for educators working in Texas. Those who work in other states, however, should bear in mind that the U.S. Supreme Court would probably uphold the district's right to fire Clark or any other teacher who made similar comments about a significant portion of the district's student body.

Cautionary Tale 8-2018-US_Idaho

Every year, a handful of teachers around the country get into trouble when insensitive Halloween costumes and social media combine to form a toxic mix of bad publicity for them and their school districts. The Middleton School District in Idaho may have set some sort of dubious record, however, by placing 14 elementary school educators (13 teachers and the school principal) on administrative leave following fierce criticism of two poor group costume choices.

To be fair, it doesn't appear that the educators involved intended to use social media to make a political statement with their costumes. Nonetheless, this serves as an excellent example of how, in this era of ubiquitous recording devices and global distribution, even a small district in a remote state can find itself in the center of a viral vortex.

During a week-long staff team-building exercise that culminated with an after-school party on Halloween, the district challenged groups of teachers to come up with costumes that best depicted various nations. The U.S. and Mexico teams were declared the winners; the six U.S. team members collectively formed a wall with the slogan "Make America Great Again," while the seven members of the Mexican team all donned mariachi style garb. (It is worth noting that there were some reports that the teachers wore their costumes during the school day before the staff party began.)

The balance of the story is entirely predictable. Someone (it's unclear exactly who) uploaded photos of the winning costume designs to the school Facebook page. Within a few hours, members of the community began redistributing and commenting on the posts. Parents and activists posted the school district phone number and links to the U.S. Department of Education Office of Civil Rights and the ACLU of Idaho. Middleton residents also launched an online petition, demanding disciplinary action for the educators.

Even though someone quickly removed the photos from the elementary school Facebook page, the images had already been shared thousands of times. The story soon became both a national and an international sensation; one of the outlets that picked up the account was the global Spanish language outlet *Univision News*, which described the incident as "racismo."

The morning after the images first appeared, Middleton School District Superintendent Josh Middleton (seriously; I checked) posted a Facebook Live video in which he apologized on behalf of the District for what he called "clearly insensitive and inappropriate" costumes. On the morning of Saturday, November 3, Middleton announced that he had placed the thirteen teachers who were pictured and the school principal on administrative leave pending an investigation.

After a very brief investigation, district administrators announced on November 7 that they would be reintegrating the people involved in the incident (except for school principal Kim Atkinson) into the school community over the next few days. In another public statement, Superintendent Middleton said that "[i]t is important to note that after the district's review, it has been validated that there is nothing more than love and commitment in the hearts of these teachers and aides."

"Our focus," he said, "is now one of healing with an opportunity for all of us to grow together as a community. Today we begin the re-entry process with training on cultural sensitivity and correspondence with parents, the staff and community."

Presumably, part of the investigation and re-entry process involved determining who posted the photos to the school Facebook page. At the very least, the Middleton School District (like every district across the country) should pay careful attention to who has access to district and school social media feeds, establish criteria for posting content, adopt procedures for posting (including appropriate prior review), and so on. If there is one clear takeaway from this incident, it's that there is nothing that happens in a school that social media can't make worse.

Subsequent comments from Latinx residents in the area offer a good reminder of the damage that can occur when social media amplifies educator actions. A week after Superintendent Middleton testified to the "love and commitment" of his staff, local deejay Gustavo Acosta told the *Idaho Statesman* that the incident was upsetting for him and other members of the Latinx community.

I would expect it from a group of young people. I would expect it in a private home or business. But I wouldn't expect it, first, from adults, and second, people with professional ethics.

Margie Gonzalez, the executive director of the Idaho Commission of Hispanic Affairs, echoed Acosta's assessment: "We're trying to take one step forward and when something like this happens, I feel like it's taking us three steps back."

Despite pressure from a group of Middleton Heights Elementary school parents, the school board declined to reinstate Atkinson to her position as an elementary school principal. She announced that she was resigning from the district at the end of the 2018-2019 school year.

At the beginning of April 2019, the kids in the Middleton schools got a pleasant surprise: a visit from NASA astronaut José Hernández. The son of Mexican farmworkers, Hernández devoted his life to becoming an astronaut and was finally selected (after a dozen rejections) in 2004. He traveled on the Space Shuttle Discovery to the International Space Station in 2009.

When Hernández read about the controversy in Middleton, he sent out a tweet with the photo of the wall costume with the following generous offer:

I think I will call the Middleton School District & offer to tell my story of reaching the American dream. Only requirement is that those teachers sit in the front row! What do you say Superintendant Dr. Josh Middleton? It's free sensitivity training! I will pay my way!!

The Middleton School District took Hernández up on his offer, and he spent much of April 2, 2019, traveling around to different schools in the district, including Middleton Heights Elementary. During an informal photo session with kids and parents afterward, he explained why he made the trip:

I wanted to be a role model and an example that, hey, not every Latino wears a sombrero, has a big, long mustache and is under a cactus taking a siesta—which is how we're portrayed. That's what really got to me. I said no, we're better than this, and the best way to counteract things like this is through example.

Top Three Takeaways:

- When it comes to the distribution of questionable social media content, no holiday quite matches Halloween. At the start of the school year each fall, administrators should require educators and staff to review the district's acceptable use policy concerning social media posts. The school district should remind every educator that what may seem humorous at a party with friends may not necessarily be well-received if you share it with the whole world.

- It does not appear that the educators in this cautionary tale were trying to make a political statement with their costumes. Nonetheless, this serves as an excellent example of how, in this era of ubiquitous recording devices and global distribution, even a small district in a remote state can find itself in the center of a viral vortex. All it takes is one person with a camera and a social media account, which these days are pretty close to everyone.

- District and building administrators should pay close attention to who can add content to school social media feeds. Anyone with access should receive periodic training and reminders regarding what types of content are appropriate for sharing. It is also important to remember to change passwords if a previously authorized person is fired or leaves the district.

Cautionary Tale 8-2018-US_Louisiana

In September 2018, Nike released an advertisement called "Dream Crazy." The narrator was former NFL quarterback Colin Kaepernik, best known for kneeling during the National Anthem as a protest against police violence.

On September 5, 2018, two days after Nike launched its ad campaign, Slidell High School math teacher (and 2003 Slidell graduate) Valerie Scogin was reading posts on Facebook from other Slidell alums. One of them posted a confrontational image. It showed an angry-looking man with his middle finger raised, with a caption that read, "If you're upset about Nike choosing Kaepernick for the 'Just Do It' campaign, 'Just Ignore It' like you do police brutality and racial injustice."

Scogin had the option to let the comment slide or to respond in a way that engaged her fellow alum in a legitimate debate. But she decided to go in a different direction altogether with her response:

> They don't have to live in that country. They could go back. But it was their own people selling them into slavery to begin with and tearing them even worse in those countries of origin.

Want a better neighborhood? Move. You don't have to choose to live in those zip codes. Want to not be stereotyped, tell people of that color to quit acting like animals and perpetuating the stereotype. Many are average people; the few ruin it.

Want to be in better neighborhoods, quit voting for handouts and pay taxes. They are what helps the neighborhoods/schools/services provided for the community. There is a reason for taxes.

The fallout was predictable. Other members of the Slidell alumni community made screenshots of her comments and circulated them around multiple corners of the internet. Parents began contacting the St. Tammany Parish Public School District and demanding that district leaders take action against Scogin.

As the controversy heated up, Scogin removed her post and tried to apologize with a follow-up post on Facebook:

To my friends and family, both personal and professional:

Recently, I posted a comment that may have been hurtful to some of you. In my reaction out of frustration at another facebook post, I made some remarks that were against my better judgement and sensibilities. I now wish I hadn't. Any one who has known me for any time should know that the last thing I want to do is to hurt anyone. I apologize for what I said and sincerely wish to avoid this in the future.

Scogin's apology, however, was not sufficient for her to keep her job. On September 11, 2018, the school district announced that she was no longer employed, although it declined to say whether she resigned or the district fired her. In a statement, the school district said that "[t]his incident does not reflect our district's values, mission and vision, and we remain committed to providing a school culture that is inclusive and meets the needs of all our students, employees and community."

Top Three Takeaways:

- Every educator should take the time to reflect on the "values, mission, and vision" of the district in which they work. How are those values articulated? Are they included in a faculty handbook or the district's acceptable use policy? School boards and administrators should help guide educators' use of social media by making it as clear as possible what is acceptable and what is not.

- This cautionary tale is a pretty clear example of the difference between expressing one's views around the dinner table or over drinks at a bar and making the same statements on a global communication service. The farther the reach of your voice, the more likely it is that there will be consequences if your comments raise concerns about your ability to provide an equitable education to all students.

- The internet does not easily forget. Like many of the other educators discussed in this book, the top search results for Scogin are almost entirely links to stories about her controversial post and the fallout from it. In the heat of the moment, it can be challenging to remember this crucial lesson, but the potential for long-lasting internet ignominy is real.

Cautionary Tale 8-2018-US_Minnesota

In 2015, Education Minnesota, the state teachers union, selected Dr. Amy Hewett-Olatunde, a teacher of English Language Learning at the LEAP High School in St. Paul, Minnesota, as its "Minnesota Teacher of the Year." Eighteen months later, the Minnesota legislature reorganized the state's system of teacher licensing and established the Minnesota Professional Educator Licensing and Standards Board (PELSB). Hewett-Olatunde was named as one of the original 11 members and appointed interim chair of the new board.

On January 12, 2018, CNN reported that President Trump had referred to Haiti and various African nations as "shithole countries" in a private meeting. Hewett-Olatunde is a staunch critic of President Trump and an educator whose students are primarily immigrants and non-native English speakers. She wrote an angry response on her personal Facebook feed: "He is not worthy, nor are his puppet masters, of human dignity. He is the s***hole, and we should line up to take a dump on him." Hewett-Olatunde deleted her post at some point during the controversy, so it's not clear whether Hewett-Olatunde spelled out the epithet or self-censored. Nonetheless, the import of her comments was crystal clear.

A short time later, Hewett-Olatunde's appointment to a full four-year term on the PELSB came before the Minnesota State Senate. She was initially confirmed on May 20 by a 34-33 vote, with one Republican, Senator Carla Nelson, voting with Democratic Senators. However, Senator Nelson told her GOP colleagues that she had voted "aye" by mistake because she was distracted, so she moved to reconsider the appointment. The second time, Hewett-Olatunde's re-appointment failed 33-34 on a straight party-line vote.

Minnesota State Senators Eric Pratt and Paul Utke, who led the charge against Hewett-Olatunde, said that they were offended by her remarks but had broader concerns. In particular, the senators noted that HewettOlatunde had frequently criticized a new licensing law the PELSB is responsible for implementing. Senator Pratt told a local paper that "When you look at the body of some of the things she's said and done, I find it hard to believe that she in fact could execute the law as intended."

The day after the Senate's vote, Hewett-Olatunde once again took to Facebook, and her tone remained defiant:

> The GOP voted me off last night in a second round of voting when Senator Nelson flipped her vote. Senator Pratt and Senator Utke were at the forefront of this. This may be the first time this has happened, and it was all based on posts you have all read about 45. Not about Republican or Democrat. Not about my credentials or two decades spent in the classroom. About a man who calls undocumented immigrants animals and deems certain countries as inferior to this one. I can and will never stay silent, because silence enables. A true advocate stands up and stands with, even in the face of adversaries. To educate. To advocate. To elevate. Thank you to the senators who saw me for who I am and not the narrative that was created about me. Your votes are enough for me to hold my head high.
>
> And by the way, Senator Pratt, my name is Dr. Amy Hewett-Olatunde, not Ms. Olatunde.

Top Three Takeaways:

- I am sure that I do not need to remind anyone reading this book that politics in the United States are more polarized than they have been in decades. This polarization makes the use of social media by educators that much more risky, as there is an increased likelihood that someone (or several people) may take offense to any politically-oriented comments you make on social media. Educators unquestionably have a right to free speech under the First Amendment, but that does not mean (and has never meant) "speech free from consequences."

- Educators should remember, regardless of the language used by the President, that they are still expected to serve as role models for children and should speak and write accordingly. In some instances, I think that people react more negatively to an educator's use of coarse language on social media than they do the actual opinion that the educator is expressing.

- The media coverage of this controversy repeatedly noted that Hewett-Olatunde made her comments about the President on "her personal Facebook page." As should be crystal clear by now, you may have a "personal" Facebook page, but you don't have a private one.

Relevant MCEE Provisions for Chapter 8

Principle I: Responsibility to the Profession

Standards I.A.3, I.A.5, and I.C.2

Principle III: Responsibility to Students

Standards III.A.1, III.B.1, III.B.2, and III.B.3

Principle IV: Responsibility to the School Community

Standard IV.A.2

Principle V: Responsible and Ethical Use of Technology

Standards V.A.1, V.A.5, and V.A.7

Sources

The sources for the Cautionary Tales in this chapter can be viewed at the following URL:

https://link.cybertraps.com/C4E2-Sources-Chap8

Chapter 9
Posting Overly Revealing Content Online

Overview

From a technological perspective, there isn't much that is complicated about this chapter. Some tech gurus figured out how to jam a camera and a phone together, and others designed software that lets us share those photos to the rest of the world with the press of a button. Since we are innately social creatures, it was an easy sell. Add in the fact that it is a fast and cheap way to share photos with family and friends, and social media had us hooked. Our online distribution of pictures and videos is staggering. As of June 2019, users uploaded an estimated 300 million photos to Facebook and 300 hours of video to YouTube *every single day*. From a content production perspective, the past decade or so has been the most active in human history, by several orders of magnitude.

Predictably, these new technologies and social behaviors have led to some unforeseen consequences. Nobody predicted, for instance, that kids would start taking and sharing nude photos of themselves. We didn't anticipate the rise of horrifically hostile trolls. No one realized back in 2007, when Steve Jobs held up the first iPhone, that just nine years later, the data generated by the descendants of that device would upend elections around the globe. And we failed to anticipate how easy it would be for people to use these devices in ways that would damage or end their teaching careers.

So what, then, is the point of the cautionary tales listed below? First, they are a reminder that educators need to continually think about the standards of the communities in which they teach. As I've discussed in earlier chapters, there is a deep-seated and not unreasonable expectation that teachers serve as role models for their students. What it means to be a "role model," however, is dependent on the underlying values of the district in which you teach. If you have any doubts or concerns about whether your social media presence might be a problem in your community, the MCEE encourages you to discuss those concerns with a colleague or supervisor before a problem arises.

The second point of these cautionary tales, unfortunately, is to serve as a reminder that a deep-seated double standard is applied to male and female educators, particularly when it comes to public displays of clothing and potentially risqué activities.

Over nearly a decade of research, I have yet to find an example of a single male teacher who was criticized or disciplined for social media content. Instead, it's more common to see gushing reviews like the one published in the Femail section of the *Daily Mail* in February 2018 that was headlined: "He's just so hand-SUM! The Dutch maths teacher turned Instagram star who juggles lesson planning with jet-set modeling trips, extreme sports, and shirtless ice fishing." Robert Ligtvoet shares Instagram-worthy photos of his adventures, many of which feature him standing in just his bathing trunks in some exotic location. I'm certainly not saying he should be fired, but it does seem unfair that many female teachers have been.

One other quick point: the double standard goes well beyond the reaction of supervisors and other community members to what educators post online. When a problem does arise (for instance, a sexual assault) involving a female teacher, journalists will scour her public social media posts and invariably republish any that are the least bit salacious or revealing. It's wildly unfair and entirely predictable.

Cautionary Tales

Cautionary Tale 9-2019-US_Oregon

Three years ago, Wendy Myers signed up with an outside staffing contractor to be a part-time substitute in the Dallas School District in Oregon. About a year ago, she also decided to train as a competitive bodybuilder and work towards earning a personal trainer's license. She uses Instagram as a training and competition diary and as an advertisement for her training services. In addition to her training and competition shots, many of the photos in Myers's Instagram feed depict her modeling dresses, athletic wear, and swimsuits in a variety of provocative poses. None of them are explicit *per se,* but on the other hand, they leave relatively little to the imagination.

In mid-November 2019, Myers received a message from the human resources department at EDUStaff, the temp agency with which she works. EDUStaff told her that a couple of school districts, including Dallas, had raised concerns about her Instagram feed. The company asked her to make her photos "private," but Myers said that would make it difficult for her to attract new training customers and would violate sponsorship contracts she has signed.

EDUStaff did not continue to insist that Myers make her photos private. A short time later, however, Myers learned that she would no longer be offered substitute slots at Dallas High School, although she is still eligible to sub in the district's middle and elementary schools. Superintendent Andy Bellando declined to say the school district changed Myers's eligibility.

Myers told a reporter for the *Polk County Itemizer-Observer* that "she always kept in mind that she was a teacher when posting photos."

I make sure that my quotes and everything that I say on my Instagram is not about what I look like; it's always about, 'Have the right attitude for life, make sure you apply what you are learning in the gym to your life and be strong.'

To be fair to the district, it's not her captions that are problematic. If disruption was occurring in her classroom, it undoubtedly was a result of the photos and not the text that accompanies them. But there is no way to know, given the District's silence, whether Myers's Instagram account was actually causing problems or whether someone in the school community simply objected to the types of photos she posted. And it should be noted that if the administration somehow thinks that middle school-aged kids haven't found her feed yet, they're kidding themselves.

Top Three Takeaways:

- This cautionary tale presents something of a hybrid situation. From one perspective, this is the story of how an educator damaged her teaching career through the use of social media, even though her posts were about personal achievement and body positivity. But to the extent that Myers is using her Instagram account to satisfy modeling or sponsorship requirements, then it's more like having a risqué second job. (*See* Chapter 11 for more examples.) However, most districts are much more concerned about what you've posted as opposed to your reason for doing so.

- Myers was somewhat naive to suggest that the upbeat, affirming nature of her Instagram captions would offset the potential disrupting impact of her photos. If kids were seeking out her Instagram feed, I feel pretty confident in saying that it wasn' to read her cheerful messages. But there is no way to know, given the District's silence on the issue, whether Myers's Instagram account was actually causing problems or whether someone in the school community simply objected to the types of photos she posted.

- This cautionary tale is a good reminder that educators who work for temp agencies have even fewer protections than educators who work directly for a school district. Third-party substitute jobs generally are at-will, which means that the employer can fire you for a good reason or no reason at all. In theory, an at-will employer still can't fire you for a "bad" (*i.e.*, discriminatory) reason, but that can be difficult to prove.

Cautionary Tale 9-2019-US_Connecticut

In October 2016, a week before the presidential election, a young woman named Chelsy Zelasko agreed to do an interview and semi-nude photoshoot for a now-defunct entertainment website called "Better than the Weekend." Zelasko, 25 at the time and a registered Democrat in Pennsylvania, answered several questions about the campaign, her goals, her decision to pose for the website, and her plan to vote for Donald Trump for President. The interview was illustrated by several semi-nude photos of Zelasko, with her modesty protected (mostly) by strategically placed flags and firearms.

Two and a half years later, the Grove School, a private boarding school located in Madison, Connecticut, hired Zelasko as an art teacher and counselor. Within just a few weeks, however, someone found Zelasko's photoshoot online, and the link to her interview began circulating in the school community. Parents complained to the school's executive director, Peter Chorney, and in April, he told Zelasko that she would have to resign or he would fire her.

In an interview with local news channel WTNH, Zelasko complained that the school was violating her First Amendment rights. "I don't feel like they should have let me go or fired me because of my political beliefs and what I believe in," Zelasko said. "I would never ever bring that into a classroom or nor would it affect my teaching skills at all."

It was a little ironic for Zelasko to argue that the photo shoot would not affect her ability to serve as a role model in the classroom, given a statement she made in her earlier interview. When asked if she thought "Donald Trump is a good role model for America," she replied that "I don't think Donald Trump or Hillary Clinton should have the burden of being someone's role model. That's a parents job to guide a person and be a role model until they're old enough to make their own decisions. The president's job isn't to be our role model."

Regardless of whether the U.S. President should be a positive role model, the Grove School administration expects its teachers to be. Chorney allegedly told Zelasko that "The issue is about role-modeling for emotionally fragile kids and holding oneself to a higher standard as an educator. Your credibility is now a major concern."

Zelasko filed a wrongful termination suit in June 2019, alleging that her termination was the result of discrimination over her political beliefs. That certainly does not appear to be the case here, however. In any event, it is unlikely that Zelasko will prevail, given the fact that private institutions can terminate employees without violating the First Amendment.

Top Three Takeaways:

- The internet rarely forgets, thanks to the vast data storage resources and stunning algorithmic tools used Google, Bing, and dozens of other web search engines. An impressively thorough review of someone's background can be conducted now with just a computer, an internet connection, and the patience to click on link after link. Of course, if your name is a little unusual (like, for instance, "Chelsy Zelasko"), the process can speed up dramatically.

- If you are breathing a sigh of relief because your long-ago risqué interview or photo shoot was for a website that has long since disappeared, don't get too comfortable. Thanks to the so-called "Wayback Machine," which is part of the Internet Archive, it is often (but not always) possible to retrieve long-deleted content. That's what happened in this case. The site that interviewed Zelasko is defunct, but her remarks live on in the Internet Archive.

- In this case, it appears that the school was more concerned about the fact that Zelasko posed with an assault rifle than the fact that students might see her naked rear end in a couple of photos. I suspect that over time, school communities will grow less shocked about the fact that an educator might once have posed nude or semi-nude (particularly given the percentage of upcoming educators who have taken and send nude selfies). But for a school that works with emotionally troubled kids in a community about an hour away from Sandy Hook, overlooking Zelasko's ostentatious display of an assault rifle was undoubtedly more problematic. The problem for Zelasko, of course, is that she can't go back and undo the photo shoot. It now indelibly in that category of things that have unintended and unforeseeable consequences.

Cautionary Tale 09-2018-Russia

The Russian city of Omsk lies deep in the middle of the Siberian forest, just north of the border of the neighboring country of Kazakhstan. Notwithstanding its remote location, Omsk is a significant transportation hub and has a surprisingly large population of more than a million people.

In summer 2018, an Instagram controversy arose that perfectly illustrates many of the issues in this book. An Omsk history teacher named Viktoria Popova signed a contract to do a photoshoot with a local modeling agency. She posed in a relatively conservative one-piece swimsuit, although it is fair to say that the pin-up poses she chose highlighted her cleavage.

In an interview with the news agency NGS Omsk, Popova said that she was not trying to launch a modeling career but posed "to lift my self-esteem." She also said that she did not intend for the photos to become public. "I just wanted to store them in my album," she told NGS Omsk.

If her wishes had been honored, of course, this wouldn't be a cautionary tale. Someone at either the agency or the swimsuit shop, however, decided to post the photos on Instagram. The pictures upset some of the parents of her students, who complained to the school. Omsk city officials declared that Popova "had caused 'irreversible damage' to the reputation of the teacher."

"By spreading frivolous images on the internet in order to promote a commercial project," officials added, "she also hurt the image of the school."

Concluding that Popova had violated a "morals and ethics" clause of her contract, the school terminated her contract.

This being 2018, however, neither Popova nor her fellow teachers took the decision lying down. As Popova put it:

> I do not understand why I am getting the blame. I wasn't posing in underwear or stockings. I said to them: "Don't you know about about American 1950s pin up style?" I'm sorry but this was not promoting some men's saloon. People do take pictures nowadays. They pose on holidays and post pictures online. This was just an advert for a shop.

Across Russia, teachers and supporters posted photos on Instagram, showing themselves in swimsuits, bikinis, and other casual clothes. Each of them tagged their picture with a Russian phrase, "учителятожелюди," that translates as "teachers are people too."

Within a day, the hashtag was used in over 4,000 Instagram posts (as of 10 May 2020, the number is over 32,000). In many cases, the Instagram posts also included statements of strong support for Popova. One of the most widely-quoted messages at the time was written by Instagram user Yulia Makarova (@julijamakarova1984), who posted a photo of herself standing beside a lake in a much-skimpier two-piece (translation by Google):

> This summer, I have not bathed in open reservoirs, so I decided to upload this photo of past years to support the national flashmob #teachersarepeopletoo. I consider the dismissal of a teacher from Omsk for a photo in a swimsuit an outrageous example of hypocrisy, hypocrisy, stupidity, lawlessness and insanity prevailing in various organizations in our country, and in the educational system especially! We are teachers, but we are also people, therefore we have the right to look differently outside of school and in our social networks.

Of course, not all of the reaction was positive. Some people argued that Popova was merely indulging in exhibitionism and that school districts should hold teachers to a higher standard. Still, the outpouring of support was sufficiently strong that the school reversed course and told Popova that she could have her job back if she wanted. The notoriety from her firing, however, expanded Popova's professional options—she received job offers from NGS Omsk and from another modeling agency called Plus Size Omsk.

Popova's supporters overlook, of course, the fact that there used to be a much clearer distinction between "inside school" and "outside of school." While the internet may be a physical entity, the "Cloud" is not. When you post something to social media, there is no distinction between the personal and the professional. "Information wants to be free."

Top Three Takeaways:

- If you are an educator and you decide to do a photo shoot of any kind, whether it's for a company or an individual, make sure that there is a contract and that the contract spells out how who has control of the images and how they can use them. I understand that it may seem unnecessarily formal. However, if there is any possibility that someone could use your photos could in ways you do not intend, you owe it to yourself (and your teaching career) to make sure that you protect yourself as much as possible.

- Of course, you should be aware by now that your ability to control what happens to digital images is limited. "Information wants to be free." As soon as you create a digital image, it takes on a life of its own, and you may not necessarily be able to prevent its use or misuse. You can, of course, attempt to sue for any damages you suffer, but that can be expensive and may be of little consolation if you need to find a new job. Think before you pose.

- The rise of an organic movement in support of Popova may offer a clue as to where things are going. I think that more and more educators are speaking up for the right to post unobjectionable content on social media without suffering employment consequences. As the hashtag campaign illustrates, there is strength in numbers. Moreover, as society grows more familiar and comfortable with the use of social media, I think it is less likely that members of the school community will single out educators for criticism about what they post. Every educator should keep in mind that shifts in social attitudes are often slower than we would like and do not play out evenly across the country. Think carefully about the community in which you teach.

Cautionary Tale 09-2017-England

Bathing suits are not the only items of clothing that can get an educator in trouble. The case of former English schoolteacher Lydia Ferguson helps to illustrate the perils of oversharing on social media, even if the bulk of your clothing choices show far less skin than the average bikini. (And yes, yet again, it is essential to underscore the persistent and destructive double standard that exists in these types of situations; the vast majority of educators disciplined for this type of social media post are women.)

In the spring of 2017, Ferguson was working at the Ousedale School, an academy in the United Kingdom town of Newport Bagnell that caters to students age 11-18. One day in March, students at the school heard a loud argument (8 minutes of which they recorded on their phones), and then local law enforcement escorting Ferguson off school grounds.

Ferguson triggered the incident by posting a selfie to Facebook before going out one evening. Her photo shows Ferguson sitting on the edge of a bed, wearing a sleeveless white dress, black spike heels, and holding a small purse. School officials were upset by the fact that Ferguson was sitting with her legs slightly spread, and her dress rucked up towards her waist, exposing a generous portion of her inner thigh. While it doesn't exactly qualify as a "wardrobe malfunction," it's definitely in the same zip code. In the exchange recorded by the students, administrators accused Ferguson of posting a "sultry" photo.

When they learned that the school had suspended Ferguson, some students in the school launched a petition drive to "Get Miss Ferguson Back," which quickly garnered the support of several hundred members of the school community. In the comments section of the petition (which was ultimately futile), the kids offered their support for Ferguson:

> "There is nothing wrong with the photo at all. We think Miss looks lovely."

> "She is a brilliant teacher. She is there to help students who have problems like bullying and stuff. She does so much to help us and we're so upset she's been suspended. Not a single person thinks there is anything inappropriate about it."

> "All it was showing was a bit of leg."

In a comment thread posted underneath her "sultry" photo, Ferguson and her friend Julie Perridge discussed the situation:

> [Julie]: Love this pic, so natural

> [Lydia]: Thank you Julie! I wouldn't class this as inappropriate would you? Xxxx

> [Julie]: Err what? No of course not xx

> [Lydia]: Thank you for that, I don't think it's seductive or inappropriate either! I've always stuck to a rule on FB and Insta that if my Grandad [sic] bless his heart would look at any of my pictures in disgust then I would never post them. I think he would agree with you on this one Julie [that the photo is not inappropriate] xxx

> [Julie]: I can totally understand that, and I think your grandad [sic] would love this pic. I certainly don't think it looks seductive either, I'm hoping everthing's ok? Your [sic] not normally worried about your pics xxxx

[Lydia]: Thanks Hun! I'm not worried about my pics but it seems some people are! Xxx

[Julie]: Yeah well those ppl need to get a life xx

It is essential to point out that there is no suggestion that Ferguson misbehaved toward any student or posted anything that the BBC (or ABC, for that matter) would feel uncomfortable broadcasting. Nonetheless, the school district Ferguson from teaching. After contesting the disciplinary action for two months, Ferguson elected to resign her post.

Top Three Takeaways:

- Yet again, it is essential to underscore the persistent and destructive double standard that exists in these types of situations; the vast majority of educators disciplined for this type of social media post are women. The conversation between Ferguson and her friend raises a couple of issues that every educator should consider. First, what are your standards for the photos you post to social media? How well do your guidelines square with either the explicit or implicit rules of your school district or the broader school community? Are you a conformist or an activist?

- Second, have your guidelines shifted over time? Are photos that you posted months or even years ago ones that you would be comfortable having administrators, parents, or students view today? The coverage of Ferguson's suspension included several other photos from her social media accounts. As is so often the case, editors and reporters chose photos showing the single mother-of-three in tight or cleavage-baring outfits.

- It is also clear from the coverage of this cautionary tale once parents raised concerns, the school administrators did a deep dive into her social media feeds and used the material it found. Unfortunately, it is typical behavior for administrators to do this, and again, tends to happen more with women than men. It is not surprising that many companies are offering services to delete old social media posts in bulk.

Cautionary Tale 09-2014-UT

In an all-too-rare victory for common sense over prurience, a Utah middle school teacher avoided termination despite her slightly risqué Instagram photo gallery.

Mindi Jensen, a teacher at the North Sanpete Middle School in Moroni, Utah, used the pseudonym "minscakes" to post photos of herself working out, posing in front of mirrors, and competing at a bodybuilding competition. In many of the pictures, Jensen shows herself dressed in a bikini or revealing workout clothes. [Sometime before May 2020, the account was set to "private."]

According to a report by local television station ABC 4 Utah, Jensen's Instagram account was (of course) discovered by students at her school, who showed the photos to their parents. The reaction in the tiny town (pop. 1,280), located 60 miles south of Provo, was predictable. In an interview, Jensen described the local response:

> These kids found it and the parents were appalled by the pictures, they called it immodest. They called it pornographic. They called the pictures inappropriate and these are my fitness and show pictures in my sport, in my uniform in my bodybuilding sport.

Jensen, who was recently divorced and is a single mother of four, told the station that she took up fitness and bodybuilding to help cope with depression and improve her health. She said that she receives lots of positive feedback from other women and single mothers.

> I get women, single woman, single mommas that message me, even on Instagram they will message me and tell me that what they read and what they see that I'm doing has inspired them to be healthier, has inspired them to leave a bad situation, to build strength.

Initially, the North Sanpete School District told Jensen that she had three choices: make her Instagram feed private, remove any objectionable photos, or accept her termination. She did make her account private for a short while but then changed her mind, believing that her positive message of fitness and personal strength was too important to shut down.

Following a query to the school district by ABC 4 Utah and a meeting of the local school board, administrators dropped their threat. They decided instead to focus on better educating parents about student internet use. District Superintendent Dr. Sam Ray said in a statement that "The district has cleared up any misconceptions with employees." Jensen added that she received an apology for the threat from the district.

It's not entirely clear that this remained a happy ending for Jensen, at least concerning the North Sanpete School District. As I noted earlier, her Instagram account is now private, and the school district website does not list her as an employee. Efforts to contact her through Instagram have so far been unsuccessful.

Top Three Takeaways:

- One of the great things about social media is that it is a classic blank slate. You can use it for whatever purpose suits your fancy. But the most significant drawback that it is *social*, which means that it is inherently public. You can't control how people will react to what you post online. Far too often, one person's empowerment is another person's pornography.

- Educators need to think about their audience. In this case, Jensen aimed her Instagram feed at a national, if not global audience. The values of the people viewing her content beyond the borders of Utah were not necessarily those of the people in her state, let alone the much smaller rural community in which she taught.

- In general, it would be better if district administrators and building supervisors could approach situations like this as teachable moments, rather than reflexively issuing employment threats. I seriously doubt that Jensen's Instagram feed was the most explicit thing that the kids of Moroni have seen on the internet. There is a role for both parents and schools in providing children with the appropriate context for the material they see online.

Relevant MCEE Provisions for Chapter 9

Principle I: Responsibility to the Profession

Standard I.A.5

Principle III: Responsibility to Students

Standard III.A.4

Principle IV: Responsibility to the School Community

Standard IV.D.3

Principle V: Responsible and Ethical Use of Technology

Standards V.A.1, V.A.5, and V.A.7

Sources

The sources for the Cautionary Tales in this chapter can be viewed at the following URL:

https://link.cybertraps.com/C4E2-Sources-Chap9

Chapter 10

Publishing or Promoting Provocative Works of Art Online

Overview

If you type the question "What is art?" into Google, you'll get just under 18 million answers, beginning with a dictionary definition, a link to Wikipedia, and then a quick descent into collections of quotations, scholarly articles, and a series of newspaper articles with that title. For instance, in 1997, at the height of the funding controversy over the National Endowment for the Arts, the *New York Times* ran a piece entitled "ART; Is It Art? Is It Good? And Who Says So?" Art critic Amei Wallach posed those questions to several different people in public life, both in and out of the art world, and got back a wide array of answers.

One reply, in particular, was a striking foreshadow of our contemporary debates. Philippe de Montebello, then the Director of the Metropolitan Museum of Art in New York City, said in part:

> There's no consensus about anything today; even the notion of standards are in question. But I don't think art matters less to our lives than it did in past; it probably matters more. Look at the millions who go to museums today. Art has landed in many more households and in the awareness of many more people than ever before. You could argue that because art is so ubiquitous it is even harder to make judgments.

Like any other category of people, some educators do creative work in addition to their full-time teaching careers. It is difficult to think of anything more squarely within the parameters of the First Amendment than the creation of art, whether it is a painting, a book, a photograph, or a video. But as we've seen with other types of educator speech, there are legal, social, and political considerations that arise when a teacher is doing the creating.

Here too, we see the amplifying effects of the internet in general and social media in particular. If you decide to turn your basement into a studio and art gallery that only your family can visit, the chances of potential problems are low. But the minute your work goes online—a painting shared on Instagram, for instance, or a book for sale on Amazon—then you not only expose yourself and your work to the public but, more importantly, to members of your school community. Inevitably, then, your artistic creations will not be judged solely on their merit but also on how they square with your position as a role model in the community.

Among your foremost critics, of course, will be your administrators and school board members. Mexican poet Carlos A. Cruz may have been correct when he said that "[a]rt should comfort the disturbed, and disturb the comfortable." If your art is causing disturbance and disruption in the classroom, however, then it doesn't matter how objectively fantastic it may be. Put another way, if your creativity is damaging your ability to be an effective educator, don't be surprised to receive bad reviews.

Cautionary Tales

Cautionary Tale 10-2018-US_West Virginia

Imagine that you are a novelist looking for inspiration. Imagine also that you are a civics teacher in a high school, filled with students constantly roiled by the daily drama of teenage lives. How tempting would it be to dip into that vast well of material? I'm kind of amazed that more aspiring educator novelists don't avail themselves of the "opportunity."

One aspiring author who apparently couldn't resist that temptation was J. David Crosby, a member of the social studies department at Lincoln High School in Shinnston, West Virginia. At the beginning of 2018, Crosby self-published a novel on Amazon called *Untouchable* [which is no longer available]. In an interview on February 1, 2018, Harrison County Superintendent Dr. Mark Manchin offered a preliminary assessment of the book:

> From what I can gather, it was supposed to be fictional. But it ended up very specific with specific names of students, interaction with students that apparently really happened, things of that nature. I think there's real concerns of the parents, there's real concerns of the students, there's concerns of the Administration, and there's the concern on my end.

Manchin said that investigators had not concluded yet whether Cosby broke the law by using some of his students as book characters. Using real students as characters, for instance, might be a violation of local district policy, state and federal law, individual privacy rights, and the Family Educational Rights and Privacy Act (FERPA). But he added that the first excerpts he had seen were enough to justify Crosby's suspension.

Before investigators concluded their work, however, Crosby chose to resign from the district. The school board accepted his resignation.

Top Three Takeaways:

- If you are an educator and an aspiring novelist, think long and hard about your choice of genre. There is no question that the Young Adult sector of the publishing industry, for instance, can be extraordinarily lucrative (you may have heard of J.K. Rowling or Susan Cooper). But the temptation to write what you know (which is, of course, the classic advice for writers) may lead you to delve more deeply into the lives of your students than is appropriate.

- There are a lot of different ways that you could violate FERPA in this situation, and using the actual names of your students as characters in a novel is merely the first and most obvious step. In the process, you will inevitably ascribe characteristics and qualities to your characters/students, and the more detailed your descriptions, the more likely a FERPA violation will occur. It is a total minefield for an educator/novelist and one that you should carefully avoid.

- It might be tempting to think that you can successfully hide your literary endeavors under a pseudonym. Don't kid yourself. It takes extraordinary discipline to maintain an alias under the best of circumstances successfully, and the more details you include in your book, the less likely it is that the ruse will succeed. In this case, of course, it does not appear that Crosby even attempted to do so.

Cautionary Tale 10-2017-US_Texas

Contemporary politics, art, and intellectual property rights collided in the pages of a recent children's book. The self-published book, entitled *The Adventures of Pepe and Pede,* was written by Texas middle school assistant principal Eric Hauser and illustrated by Nina Khalova. It follows the adventures of two best friends, a frog and a centipede, and their adventures on Wishington Farms.

As the *Dallas Observer* noted, "[w]ithout context, *The Adventures of Pepe and Pede* looks like a fairly standard children's book." But art is never produced in a vacuum, and a closer examination of the artistic choices made by Hauser raised many deeply troubling issues.

First, Hauser's choice of Pepe as his main character was intentionally provocative. "Pepe the Frog" is an animated character created by cartoonist Matt Furie, who has described Pepe as merely a "blissfully stoned frog."

Much to Furie's dismay, over the past decade, the alt-right movement has adopted Pepe as an informal mascot. In particular, users on the websites Reddit, 4Chan, and Twitter have made extensive use of the character to promote Donald Trump and white nationalist policies. There is very little chance that Hauser was not aware of that when he chose to include Pepe in his book, given the fact that his book included numerous phrases that are common on right-wing websites.

Second, Hauser made the creative decision to have Pepe and Pede "impose law and order on a bearded alligator character named Alkah," and to surround Alka with "pink creatures covered in mud that look similar to women in burqas." None of this is particularly subtle. In an interview, Hauser told the *Dallas Observer* that he wrote the book "as an attempt to break down the barriers of political correctness," an argument that is increasingly popular among right-wing activists as a justification for engaging in hate speech and harmful stereotypes.

Following the book's publication, Furie contacted Hauser and threatened to sue him for intellectual property theft if he did not stop sales of the book. Khalova, Hauser's illustrator, produced correspondence that made it clear that Hauser specifically asked her to base the book's frog character on Furie's Pepe. Khalova, who lives (ironically) in Ukraine, said that she was unaware of the political controversy surrounding the Pepe character.

Hauser admitted his copyright infringement and agreed to donate the proceeds of the book (just over $1,500) to the "Council on American-Islamic Relations (CAIR), the nation's largest Muslim civil rights and advocacy organization." He also agreed to stop all future sales of the book.

Not long after his book was first published, the Denton Independent School District said that it was reassigning Hauser to an "unannounced role" because of the "implied message" in his book. Superintendent Jamie Wilson offered the following explanation:

> We pride ourselves on providing a welcoming and nurturing environment to all students. Our staff is reflective of the community we serve, where all individuals are respected. We encourage our staff and students to be free-thinking and express their ideas; however, when these ideas interrupt the ability to learn, work or create divisiveness, each of us is held accountable.

Rather than accept reassignment, Hauser elected to resign from the district.

Top Three Takeaways:

- This story could have served as a cautionary tale in the chapter on intellectual property theft. Overall, however, it seemed more illustrative of the potential consequences flowing from the creation of a provocative and even disturbing literary work. There is a perpetual tension between your First Amendment rights and the legitimate pedagogical concerns of your district or school. If your creative work damages your ability to teach effectively or causes a disruption in the educational environment, then your free speech rights may be overridden.

- Putting aside the copyright issues for a moment, let's talk about memes. This cautionary tale demonstrates that while memes can be very amusing (do a search, for instance, for "Ryan Gosling hey girl meme"), they also can be dangerous things. You can get caught up in the subversive humor and mockery inherent in so many memes, without necessarily stopping to think about who might be hurt or insulted by the words or images that you are distributing. Perhaps the most significant risk of memes is that they are an intellectual shortcut; they encourage people to spread concepts depicted in the memes without really thinking about the content or the underlying message. Re-share with care!

- There is ample room in our educational system for legitimate debate, both public and private, about ideologies, politics, history, *etc.* There is even room (or should be) for a robust discussion of where to draw the line between the free speech rights of educators and the right of students to an education free from bias, bigotry, and discrimination. But there shouldn’t be any room for hurtful stereotypes wrapped in a thin cloak of aggrieved libertarianism.

Cautionary Tale 10-2014-US_Utah

Even a casual observer of America's political scene is aware that Utah is a very conservative state. It is also a highly reliable supporter of Republican presidential candidates; no Republican has failed to win the state by less than 19 percentage points since 1964. Much of the state's approach to social issues, predictably, is driven by Mormon Church, since 62 percent of the state's residents (and 75 percent of its voters) identify as Mormons.

Among other things, the Mormon Church has an unequivocal position on homosexuality: "sexual relations are proper only between a man and a woman who are legally and lawfully wedded as husband and wife." As a result, the Church has been particularly active in lobbying against legislation to permit same-sex marriage. (That position that was rendered moot by the decision of the U.S Supreme Court in *Obergefell v. Hodges* [June 26, 2015], that required states to treat same-sex couples the same as opposite-sex couples).

This background regarding the attitudes of the Mormon Church toward homosexuality may be useful in helping to explain the firing of Tim Torkildson, a social media specialist at the Nomen Global Language Centers in Provo. It is relevant in the context of this cautionary tale to understand that Provo is a notably conservative community in what is a deeply conservative state.

Nomen Global Language Centers opened in 1997. According to its website, it "substantially helps students from all cultures and walks of life to excel in each aspect of their English acquisition and to obtain their goals for the future."

As part of his job as a social media specialist, Torkildson was responsible for writing articles for the company's blog. It was not a particularly onerous obligation. Torkildson also had time to blog frequently on a personal site called IWritetheBlogggs.com, covering topics from Agriculture to Welfare, with stops along the way for Book of Mormon, DNA, Global Warming, John McCain, Pluto, and Sex, to name just a few of his many categories. Torkildson's blog is now defunct, but you can still view many of his posts on the so-called Wayback Machine, where the website Archive.org stores snapshots of webpages.

On July 2, 2014, Torkildson wrote a blog post for the Nomen Global blog entitled "Help with Homophones," in which he explained a concept that can sometimes be tricky for English language learners. On July 24, he described on his blog what happened next:

> This week I was fired for writing a blog about homophones for an educational website.
>
> "I'm letting you go because I can't trust you" said Clarke Woodger, my boss and the owner of Nomen Global Language Center. "This blog about homophones was the last straw. Now our school is going to be associated with homosexuality." I said nothing, stunned into silence.
>
> "I had to look up the word" he continued, "because I didn't know what the hell you were talking about. We don't teach this kind of advanced stuff to our students, and it's extremely inappropriate. Can you have your desk cleaned out by eleven this morning? I'll have your check ready."
>
> I nodded, mute.

Not surprisingly, Torkildson's firing attracted a fair amount of media attention, ranging from *The Salt Lake Tribune* to New York's *Daily News* to *Newsweek*. A paper in his hometown, the Minneapolis *City Pages*, helpfully reprinted the 184-word blog post that led to Torkildson's firing, which Nomen Global had deleted from its blog. In the interests of combatting the scourge of "homophonia," I have done the same:

> Help with Homophones.
>
> In English a homophone is a word that has several different meanings and spellings, but always sounds the same. The best way to learn these tricky words is to memorize them little by little. Today we will begin with homophones that start with the letter A:
>
> - Ad is an advertisement. Add is a mathematical function.
> - Ail is to be sick. Ale is an alcoholic beverage.
> - Aye means yes. Eye is what you see with.

- Air is what you breathe. Err is to make a mistake. Heir is someone who inherits.

- Ate is the past tense for eat. Eight is how you spell out the number 8.

- Allowed is to do something with permission. Aloud is to vocalize, to speak.

- Ant is an insect. Aunt is your mother or father's sister.

- Assistance is help. Assistants are helpers.

Nomen Global Language Center, in Provo, Utah, has the most up-to-date teaching curriculum to help you succeed in using the English language to succeed in school, in business, and in every other important endeavor in your life.

It is worth noting that a Google search for "Nomen Global Language" does not produce any hits that contain words with the prefix "homo-." In contrast, the search results for "Clarke Woodger" start with his LinkedIn profile and continue with a couple of dozen articles from around the country mocking his decision to fire Torkildson (including an op-ed in *The Baltimore Sun* entitled "You Can't Fix Stupid"). The school may have dodged any unwanted association with homosexuality, but Woodger has solidified a place for himself in language lore.

For readers who enjoy discussions of language or snarky commentary about word usage, I recommend the coverage by the *Language Log* and the ensuing comments.

Top Three Takeaways:

- This cautionary tale helps to illustrate the simple truth that administrators are as much at risk for internet ignominy as educators. It is precisely the kind of story that will inevitably go viral, and the more broadly it does so, the harder it will be for someone like Woodger to live it down.

- From an employment perspective, Torkildson had no recourse. It's a safe guess that he was an at-will employee for a private educational company, and I've said before, businesses can fire at-will employees for a good reason or no reason at all. The only limitation is that a company can't fire an at-will employee for a bad, *i.e.*, discriminatory reason. Unfortunately, being smarter than your boss or administrator does not count as a protected category.

- If Torkildson had thought this through, could he have anticipated that his conservative boss might misunderstand a blog post on "homophones"? Unfortunately, it apparently did not occur to him that someone *in the business of teaching English* would misconstrue his post. Fair enough. But still, it's worth asking whether Torkildson might yet have his job if he had thought about the surrounding community environment and had run his blog post past his supervisor before putting it on the Nomen Global website. That's a worthwhile exercise for every educator thinking of posting something online.

Cautionary Tale 10-2014-US_Texas

In the fall of 1995, Houston artist Bill Davenport published a brief review of a young artist named Scott Burns in his biweekly self-published *Art Letter*:

> It's a great visual party. Humorous regurgitations of the 70's with a Lost in Space/retro feel and a dash of folk art reference. Takes objects from childhood (at least mine) and floats them back at you. A potpourri of techniques: glitter, old bedsheets, cake icing. Each painting has little failures which add to its liveliness. Most artists would tighten it up and ruin it. He openly steals from a lot of different people: Rachel Hecker, Carroll Dunham, Donald Baechler, and the big daddy Sigmar Polke. The camp quality makes me feel as if I'm in Provincetown for the Drag Ball. One of the most alive shows in Houston in a long time.

Two decades later, Burns was working as an art teacher at the Alvin Independent School District just south of Houston, Texas. In the spring of 2014, reports surfaced that Burns had been using former students, all female, as models for a series of risqué photographs and paintings. An investigation by district administrators determined that none of the models were current students, and none were underage; nonetheless, Burns was quickly removed from campus and placed on administrative leave.

It is unlikely that Burns would have kept his job in any case, but the news of his art hobby helped accelerate much more severe legal problems. Roughly two years earlier, someone brought an abandoned briefcase containing child pornography to the Brazoria County Sheriff's Office. Law enforcement officials believed that the contents of the briefcase were part of an ongoing child pornography investigation into Burns and his online activity. Following his suspension by the Alvin ISD, officers executed a search warrant at Burns's home. Agents uncovered "418 images and 15 videos of child pornography, including pictures of prepubescent minors, acts of sadism, masochism, bestiality and/or bondage."

In an interview the following day, Burns admitted to investigators that he did use the internet to locate child pornography, but only "to report it to website administrators."

That defense did Burns little good. A grand jury indicted Burns on multiple counts of receiving and possessing child pornography on December 20, 2014. After pleading guilty six months later, Burns was sentenced by U.S. District Court Judge Lynn N. Hughes on December 21, 2015, to 97 months in prison, followed by 12 years of supervised release. Once he leaves prison, Burns will be required to register as a sex offender.

Top Three Takeaways:

- If you are an educator who takes photos as a hobby or even as a side job, think long and hard about using student-aged models. Even if they are all over the age of 18, as was the case here, it still creates a massive appearance of impropriety. It also inevitably will complicate your relationship with your current students and their parents. All of them will inevitably wonder whether you are dealing with them as students or assessing them as possible models.

- The existence of an ongoing child pornography investigation into Burns is something of a coincidence. Still, it helps illustrate the point that in the area of educator misconduct (particularly anything involving sex or suggesting sexual activity with students), things can snowball very quickly. If another administrator or a law enforcement agency has any prior or ongoing concerns about your actions, they will bump you up to the top of a very undesirable list of investigative priorities.

- Every so often, someone will futilely try to defend against child pornography charges by playing the vigilante card (an idea encouraged, I think, by shows like "To Catch a Predator"). Suspects argue that child pornography terms are in their search history and contraband on their computer only because they were doing undercover research, the results of which they planned to turn over to the police. (One of the more notorious attempts to use this defense occurred when David Malakoff, a former National Public Radio science editor, was arrested after NPR repair techs found child pornography on his work computer. He ultimately pleaded guilty to possession.) It's pretty straightforward: there is no private investigator exception to federal or state child pornography statutes.

Cautionary Tale 10-2012-US_Illinois

In the summer of 2012, Illinois high school guidance counselor and basketball coach Bryan Craig published a book entitled *It's Her Fault.* The book, which is still available on Amazon.com, purports to offer pickup advice to men, advice to women on how to behave with men, and comparisons of the bodies and sexual organs of different races of students. Over half the reviews gave it just a single star, with review titles that ranged from "Reading this book will deplete your brain cells" to "Vile, sexist, almost amusingly ridiculous trash" to "Absolute Filth!" As one reviewer observed, "this was a real waste of money, it seems to have been written by a horney [*sic*] high school boy who never grew up[.]"

Word of Craig's debut book quickly spread through the Rich Central High School school community in Olympia Fields, Illinois. Almost immediately, school officials launched an investigation into the book and its impact on Craig's teaching and coaching. Almost immediately, Craig submitted his resignation as a basketball coach, but the school still placed him on administrative leave.

After concluding its investigation, the administration recommended that the district fire Craig and the school board unanimously agreed. Board President Betty Owens issued a statement that read in part:

> Mr. Craig's conduct in this matter fell far short of our expectations and evoked outrage from me, members of this board and many others in our district who have come to expect the highest level of professionalism and sound judgment from the people they entrust with their children each day. Our actions tonight bring a swift conclusion to this matter and to Mr. Craig's employment with the district and allow us to return to our priorities of preparing District 227 students for success in school and in life.

Almost immediately after his firing, Craig filed a lawsuit against the school district seeking $1 million in damages for violations of his First Amendment rights. He alleged that his firing caused "humiliation, mental anguish, and emotional distress," and that his book should not have been considered in the assessment of his job performance because it had nothing to do with his work responsibilities.

The U.S. District Court dismissed Craig's lawsuit in March 2013. According to Franczek Radelet, writing for the law blog Lexology, "The court found that the book was 'actually little more than a lurid account of plaintiff's own sexual preferences and exploits,' and therefore not a matter of public concern." The court also concluded, Radelet said, that Craig's speech was unquestionably "detrimental to the mission and functions of the employer[.]" Finally, the court rejected Craig's claim of a due process violation.

Eighteen months later, the United States Court of Appeals for the Seventh Circuit affirmed the District Court's decision, albeit on different grounds. Significantly, it disagreed with the District Court regarding its assessment of the "public importance" of Craig's book. "The court explained," Radelet said, "that 'while full of objectionable content, Craig's book deals with adult relationship dynamics, an issue with which a large segment of the public is concerned.'"

However, the Appeals Court said, simply because the book discussed an issue of public concern is not the end of the analysis. It agreed with the school district's argument that the book would likely cause significant disruption in the school and make some students (chiefly women) reluctant to ask for his assistance. Accordingly, the Appeals Court upheld the District Court's conclusion that the school district did not violate Craig's First Amendment rights.

Top Three Takeaways:

- For many of the cautionary tales in this book, the most immediate response is, "What was he (or she) thinking?" This particular incident is right at the front of that line. It is challenging to come up with a reasonable explanation for why a guidance counselor and a girl's basketball coach would think it was acceptable to write a sexually-explicit book about pickup lines, the value of stripping as a source of female empowerment, and other intimate topics. There's judgment, there's bad judgment, and there's whatever this was.

- The debate over his First Amendment rights is interesting. My initial inclination is to disagree with the Seventh Circuit on the "public importance" issue. It appears, however, the Court felt it could take an expansive view of Craig's First Amendment claim given the "significant disruption" issue. Courts will generally be very respectful to school districts on that point, provided that the district can produce any credible support for its position (which can include reports of misbehavior in the classroom, student protests, complaints from parents, *etc.*).

- One obvious question here is why Craig did not publish his book under a pseudonym. To be fair, as I've said repeatedly, it is challenging to maintain anonymity online, and members of the school community might have discovered Craig's authorship in half a dozen different ways. Nonetheless, using a pseudonym would have demonstrated at least some sensitivity to the gulf between his position and his artistic creation.

Cautionary Tale 10-2012-US_Ohio

"How far will you go for an A?"

> The horrifying shock of witnessing her husband banging his skank-whore secretary spurred this ever-wholesome and rule-following teacher to seek some new lessons of her own. A young teacher learns about sexuality, pleasure, and satisfaction from rather unlikely and forbidden teachers, her former students, now recent college graduates.
>
> Not only does she get SCHOOLED by the beautifully-built, all-American football player who struggled to pass her class, but she also learns a few tricks from the innocent, well-read, and thoroughly sexy bookworm.
>
> Both men teach her that not all curricula worth learning comes from a book.

That's the salacious description in the iTunes bookstore for a four-book series called *Schooled*, by author Deena Bright. On Amazon.com, the latest installment of her series has a solid 4.5 stars (out of 5) rating, with reviews like "An awesome read!", "A must read," and "Sexy, fun, down and dirty. Great read!"

But of course, if you are this far into *Cybertraps for Educators*, you can see the plot twist coming: Deena Bright is the pen name of Carol Ann Albright Eastman, a popular teacher of English at Hoover High School in North Canton, Ohio. At some point in the fall of 2012, students at Hoover High somehow figured out the connection between Eastman and Bright. Gossip about the salacious and explicit sex scenes "spread like wildfire among the students," and administrators began fielding complaints from parents.

After learning of Eastman's extra-curricular activities, North Canton school district officials pulled Eastman from her classroom and placed her on paid administrative leave while they investigated. She returned to her class three weeks later, on December 3, 2012.

There are a couple of different ways that the news might have emerged. The first is that Eastman had set up an author's website using the domain name "deenabright.com" (now defunct). Someone might have stumbled across her real name through a WHOIS search on that domain name.

A somewhat more likely scenario, however, is that Eastman offered one too many clues in an author interview she did in October 2012 with a site called *Lisa's Book Review* (also now defunct). For instance, she admitted to the website that she is a teacher and that she had tried to get permission from her school's curriculum director to publish *Schooled*. She held off when she was told not to do it, but then added: "A year later, erotica really did take off and my friend, Kelli Maine's book, 'Taken,' just topped the chart… Kelli told me to do it anyway. So, I did.

It wouldn't take a Hercule Poirot or a Perry Mason to figure out which of Kelli Maine's friends might be the teacher in question. Given her position, it is fair to question some of the statements that she made in her author interview. For instance, here is one troubling passage that was quoted by *HuffPost*:

The storyline was easy, so easy. I'm the teacher that every student, boy or girl, goes to with his/her problems. I'm the friend every person goes to with his/her problems. I know their stories, their secrets, their flaws. Many times, especially with the boys, I think, "Dude, you're playing this all wrong; I could have you in her panties by 9th period." Being a teacher, I'd never SAY those things, but I know what girls want. I know what boys want. I know what I want, in bed, in a man, in life. People who don't know what they ultimately want are those who are flailing in and out of relationships, not forcing their relationships to work.

At a meeting of the North Canton Schools Board of Education on December 19, several parents sat through the full session to express their concerns during public comment. Here's a sample:

- "[B]ecause I am a mother and a proud North Canton resident I cannot stand by and be quiet that a teacher in our community has a reaction of shock, disappointment, disgust and embarrassment. I don't see any room for vulgarity and insubordination."—Devina Streb

- "It poses a conflict of interest since she is a teacher of children and not adults."—Joanna Polis

- "[T]here's an element of free speech there. [However,] [t]hose comments are in direct opposition to what I'm trying to teach my children. I really think that if he were placed in her class I would have to ask that she be removed."—Matt Sutter

- "I do agree that I would have to take my daughter out of that teacher's class. I understand first amendment rights, but I also know rights don't exist separate from responsibilities."—Karen Dhyanchand

- "I cannot understand what this educator was thinking sharing these inappropriate statements with the media."—Holly Pierpont

Notwithstanding the parental concerns, Eastman continued to teach at Hoover for another four years. In the spring of 2017, she and her family moved to South Carolina. Eastman now teaches at Cane Bay High School in Summerville, South Carolina.

Top Three Takeaways:

- So here's the counterfactual to Bryan Craig's case: Eastman published her books using a pseudonym and still was outed as the author of wildly inappropriate content for a school setting. What's an aspiring erotica author (and an educator) to do? It's a fair question, but it proves my overarching point: it is tough to remain anonymous online, especially when motivated investigators (*i.e.,* students) surround you.

- Every educator should understand, with every fiber of their being, that titillated middle and high school students, and their "bulldozer" parents, are the two most relentless groups of digital investigators in existence. It's not clear who actually "outed" Eastman, but it could have been any number of people in her school community, given the background details she provided in her interview. Had she been just a little more circumspect, this might not have been a controversy.

- This cautionary tale is unusual in that neither the administration nor the school board overreacted to the initial reports. The details are a little sketchy, but it does not appear—apart from the parental complaints—that Eastman's unmasking caused much disruption in the classroom or the district. The other salient point is that it does not appear that Eastman included any identifiable details about her students. Still, given the relatively explicit nature of her text and her interviews, it is a little surprising that Eastman was allowed to keep teaching for another four years.

Cautionary Tale 9-2011-US_Pennsylvania

Author Judy Mays has one of the livelier author bios on Amazon.com:

Sexier than a Hollywood starlet! More buxom than a Vegas show girl. Able to split infinitives with a single key stroke!

Look! At the computer!

It's a programmer!

It's a computer nerd!

No! It's - Judy Mays!

Yes, Judy Mays - romantica writer extraordinaire who came to Earth with powers and abilities beyond those of mortal authors. Judy Mays! Who can write wild, wanton werewolves; adorable, alluring aliens; vexing, vivacious vamps; and cagey, cuddly kitty cats; and, who, disguised as a mild-mannered English teacher in a small public high school, fights a never ending battle for Hot Hunks, Hip Heroines, and Sexy Sensuality!

Unfortunately, like most superheroes, her secret identity was eventually unmasked. In 2011, Wendy Apple, a parent of a student at Midd-West High School in Middleburg, Pennsylvania, began hearing rumors that a teacher at the school was writing erotic novels in her spare time. She did some research and discovered that Mays—the author of luridly-covered books with titles like "Perfumed Heat," "Undercover Heat," and "Nibbles and Bits"—was, in reality, Judy Buranich, an English teacher with more than 30 years of experience at Midd-West.

Led by Apple (who was a former student of Buranich), some parents complained to the superintendent, demanded an investigation, and suggested that Buranich should either stop writing erotic novels or stop teaching. Deanna Stepp, another outraged parent, told a local television station that "She is teaching children that are under the age of 18 and definitely the books that she is writing are adult books. I think she needs to make a decision as to what she wants to do. Either be a school teacher or author."

As news of the parental protests against Buranich began to spread, a counter-protest movement quickly sprang up. A "Support Judy Mays (Mrs. Buranich)" Facebook page was created, which was swiftly "liked" by more than 7,000 people. Less-offended parents and students spoke up, defending not only Buranich's teaching ability but also her right to engage in a perfectly legal hobby in her spare time. Not surprisingly, her case struck a chord with free speech advocates and other writers of erotic fiction (there's a considerable overlap of the two groups, as you might expect), many of whom penned outraged and sarcastic diatribes against the school district and the prudish parents.

In contrast to the extensive coverage sparked by the WNEP segment revealing Buranich's alter-ego, there was no follow-up regarding action by the school district or its administrators. Buranich herself, however, was gracious enough to fill me in:

> Everything ended well for me, though there were members of the school board and the superintendent who wanted to fire me. They reported me to the PA Department of Education and even sent copies of my books. PDA replied with even if it were true that the material in my novels was pornographic, they would not pursue it.

That was my thirty-third year of teaching so how things worked out for me would not necessarily be the same for someone with fewer years of experience. Many of my former students came out of the woodwork to support me. Most were thrilled to have a published, award winning author teaching their children how to write. They didn't care about the content of my novels.

I never discussed my writing in class, nor did I ever tell my students I was published because of the content. Midd-West is a very conservative school district. I'm pretty sure one of the other teachers let slip the fact that I wrote romance novels. Until I was outed on WNEP, however, the superintendent didn't know about my writing though I always kept the building administrator informed.

In an interesting display of karma, that superintendent was later fired by the board. I retired at the end of my thirty-fifth year, and more than a few parents were sorry to see me go because their children wouldn't have me for 10/11th English. (In my letter of resignation, I offered to autograph the novels they'd sent to PDE if they'd been returned.)

Top Three Takeaways:

- You can't be enormously surprised if your efforts at anonymity fall apart because you use your actual first name as part of your pseudonym. You need to put a little more effort into it, particularly if your bio references the fact that you are a "mild-mannered English teacher."

- Like Eastman, Buranich's cautionary tale presents a straightforward question: Should an educator be able to engage in a hobby, even one that is a little risqué, if he or she takes reasonable steps to limit or minimize student awareness of that activity? What more should Buranich have done here? Or is any involvement in erotic material off-limits for an educator of children? An educator can write erotica on the side and be a great teacher or a terrible teacher, but the sideline writing is not the core issue.

- Even though Buranich's case occurred almost a decade ago, it offers a great preview of where we are today: the rapid mobilization of outrage. Modern communication technology provides activists up and down the political spectrum with a robust set of tools to marshal and deploy public opinion. Woe unto the school district that finds itself on the receiving end of digitized outrage. The best prophylactic measures are swift investigations, aggressive transparency, and reasonably rational outcomes.

Cautionary Tale 10-2009-Wales

It's one thing to write erotic novels that feature vampires, werewolves, and other mythical creatures. It's another thing altogether to write an edgy story, featuring both sex and drug use, that contains characters named after actual students and the school's headmaster.

In August 2008, Leonora Rustamova—a teacher of English at Calder High School in the village of Mytholmroyd (located roughly between Manchester and Leeds)—published a novel entitled *Stop! Don't Read This* that did just that. Among other things, her book includes scenes depicting children skipping classes, flirting with their teacher (known affectionately as Miss Rusty), stealing cellphones, stealing cocaine, and lighting themselves on fire.

Rustamova's husband Denis formatted the book for her and printed copies on the self-publishing website Lulu.com so that she could print out copies for the students who had worked on the story with her in class, as well as other members of the school community. Unbeknownst to her, however, the book was available to the general public as well. Once she learned the book could be freely purchased, she removed it from the site.

In January 2009, several months after Rustamov's book was unintentionally released, the Board of Governors for Calder High School suspended her and began an investigation. Following a disciplinary hearing in May, the school formally dismissed her.

Both her suspension and termination sparked vigorous protests by parents and students, who praised Rustamova as an innovative and inspiring educator. More than 250 students walked out of the high school, "holding banners and chanting slogans in support of Leonara Rustomova." The protest did not end until local police came to the school and threatened the students with truancy charges.

Rustamova appealed her termination to the Leeds Employment Tribunal in West Yorkshire, and the tribunal heard the appeal in February 2011. After describing the devastating financial and emotional impact of her firing (which included the dissolution of her marriage), Rustamova's attorney told the tribunal that the controversial book emerged as a teaching tool for a challenging group of students known as the "Commy Boys." To better engage the students and keep them in school, Rustamova began writing a story that featured herself and five of the students. During the school year, she read drafts to the students and solicited their input. The boys began suggesting new content, which "ratcheted up the tally of swear words and risqué episodes[.]"

Despite her travails, Rustamova refused to second-guess her decision to work on the project with her students:

> I don't wish I had not written it. I think it is a terrible shame that something so positive has ended up in this terrible mess. It was a groundbreaking project that could have formed the basis of some really useful work with other children.

Top Three Takeaways:

- Educators have an ongoing obligation to make sure that they (or their spouses) fully understand the operation of the software and online services they use. Rustamova may have been genuinely surprised to learn that something her husband uploaded to Lulu.com was publicly available. However, she is ultimately responsible for what she distributes online.

- As for the content of the book itself, it seems clear that Rustamova employed a novel (pun intended) and dynamic writing technique to engage her students. Should she have resisted their more salacious or profane suggestions? Perhaps. But clearly, she saw this as an opportunity for the students to use their authentic voices in the creative process. No educators nor parents should have any illusions about the language teenagers use either online or off. A problem, of course, is how the school administration should respond to the general tone of the book or apparent confessions of illegal or inappropriate behavior.

- While the unfolding of her case was painful (termination, divorce, hearings, *etc.*), the outcome offers some insight into the changing social and moral landscape of our time. Not only did the General Teaching Council dismiss the case against her, but she eventually landed a teaching position at the university level. The Calder High School administration arguably overreacted in this matter. You can make a good argument, however, that Rustamova should have discussed her creative writing project with colleagues before incorporating the dialogue and scene suggestions of her young Hunter S. Thompsons.

Cautionary Tale 10-2006-US_Virginia

Sometimes, it's not the content of the art that bothers school administrators but how the educator makes it. After all, you wouldn't expect that even the stuffiest school district would have a problem with a teacher who specialized in painting tulips, sunflowers, and other floral themes.

But in 2006, school officials in Chesterfield County in Virginia first suspended and then fired art teacher Stephen Murmur because of his cheeky painting shtick: stripping down to a thong, sitting in paint, and then using his buttocks as his brush.

Murmur was probably one of the earliest victims of the unforeseen spread of information online. As a teacher at Monacan High School in central Virginia (a little southwest of Richmond), he understood that his unusual technique might cause problems. With somewhat less originality than his artwork, he used the name "Stan Murmur" to promote his paintings and donned disguises (a fake nose and glasses) when he demonstrated his painting technique in public.

In 2003, a now-long-defunct cable show entitled "Unscrewed with Martin Sargent" invited Murmur to appear as a guest. When asked why he showed up wearing a disguise, he explained that "I do have a real job, where I do have real clients. I don't think they'd be too understanding if I was also the guy that painted with my [rear]."

Murmur's words were prophetic. Not long after the show aired, someone filed a complaint with the school district, but it did not take any action at the time (perhaps because the low viewership for "Unscrewed" made it unlikely that many students had seen it). But three years later, in December 2006, the district abruptly placed Murmur on administrative leave and then fired him the following month.

What changed during those three years to make Murmur's butt painting a problem? In a word, technology. The video-sharing website YouTube (or as all of the papers called it back then, YouTube.com) was founded in 2005. It was almost immediately popular but took off when Google purchased it in November 2006 for $1.65 billion, a transaction that vastly boosted YouTube's profile with the public in general and students in particular.

One of the early clips available on YouTube, it turned out, was Murmur's butt-painting demo on "Unscrewed." As *USA Today* reported following Murmur's suspension, "[t]hat video has made the rounds at Monacan High, where the mere mention of Murmer's name was enough to elicit grins from students Tuesday. Most appeared to support their teacher, describing his suspension as 'stupid,' 'ignorant' and 'kinda retarded.'"

The American Civil Liberties Union agreed and filed suit on Murmur's behalf in July 2007. Eight months later, the Chesterfield County School Board agreed to settle the case by paying Murmur $65,000. In an amusing coda to the affair, Murmur used his unusual painting technique to create a portrait of Stephen Colbert and donated it to a fundraising-auction on behalf of Virginia public schools.

Top Three Takeaways:

- When I describe this case in my lectures, it's always good for a laugh. What isn't amusing, after all, about a teacher who ran into difficulties because administrators discovered that he was proficient in the art of gluteal impressionism? The jokes write themselves. But Murmur unquestionably had a legitimate legal beef: there was nothing indecent about the art he created, merely discomfort with how he did it. Hence the lawsuit.

- A more sobering aspect of this case for educators is the fact that it arose from the digitization of pre-internet content. As we'll see in later chapters, this is an issue that has tripped up other educators. It is highly unlikely that Murmur anticipated that his brief appearance on a cable television show would end up on the internet. It must also have been especially frustrating given the fact that he wore a disguise when he did so. Nonetheless, the internet has the potential to frost heave up old content; every educator should prepare for the possibility that previously-undigitized content may emerge from your analog past.

- Any educator who is concerned that his or her creative endeavors might cause problems with district administrators would be well-advised to make an annual contribution to the ACLU. Few things are quite as comforting as having the assistance of experienced First Amendment legal experts when you are struggling to keep your job.

Relevant MCEE Provisions for Chapter 10

Principle I: Responsibility to the Profession

Standard I.A.5

Principle IV: Responsibility to the School Community

Standard IV.A.3

Sources

The sources for the Cautionary Tales in this chapter can be viewed at the following URL:

https://link.cybertraps.com/C4E2-Sources-Chap10

Chapter 11
Risqué Second Jobs

Overview

One of the painful realities of teaching is that it frequently doesn't pay very well, particularly when you are first starting. The Great Recession made things significantly more difficult, as have austerity policies aimed at shrinking public education budgets. It's not uncommon, then, for teachers and administrators to pick up a second job over the summer (or even at night during the school year) to help make ends meet. When my older son was in fifth grade, for instance, we would occasionally see his teacher at the Italian restaurant where she worked two or three nights a week. My son liked the food but was less enthusiastic about the bonus parent-teacher conferences.

Unfortunately, she was not the only one pulling extra duty. According to the National Center for Educational Statistics, nearly twenty percent of the nation's teachers were working two or more jobs in the 2015-2016 school year (the last year for which data is available). The Bureau of Labor Standards reports that teachers are about *three times* more likely than other U.S. workers to be holding down multiple jobs.

But as this chapter illustrates, not all second jobs are viewed with equal favor by administrators or other members of the school community. The temptation, of course, is that the risqué jobs discussed below generally pay better than more socially acceptable options, like waitressing, tutoring, driving for Lyft, proctoring exams, working as a mystery shopper, and so on. But even though all of the jobs in the cautionary tales below are entirely legal, you'll see that they created problems for the educators with school administrators and parents in the school community. As always, it comes back to the expectation that teachers serve as positive role models for their students.

That expectation, of course, has not changed significantly over the past fifty years or more. For educators, picking up some extra money as a topless waitress or lingerie model today is just as frowned upon today as it would have been to work evenings as a Playboy Bunny 50 years ago or prance around selling cigarettes in a 1920s jazz club. And once again, it is necessary to point out the massive double standard at play here; members of a school community are much more like to scrutinize the part-time job choices of female educators than those of their male counterparts.

The internet has exacerbated the odds that this will be a cybertrap for educators in two different ways. First, the internet has made it much more tempting for educators to test the old maxim that "sex sells," or at least pays well. Second, the internet has also made it much harder to do these types of jobs secretly or anonymously. What the web giveth, the web taketh away.

The practical outcome is that this type of news is now much more likely to erode a teacher's moral authority and effectiveness with students and cause disruption in the classroom. When salacious information emerges, it now spreads at the speed of light. Once the internet echo chamber fires up, it is tough for district administrators or school board members to ignore the noise and defend an educator who's making a few extra bucks on the wild side.

My research in this area over the last decade suggests that if anything, school districts and school boards are much quicker these days to take disciplinary action against a teacher who is "outed" online for risqué or explicit activity for one simple reason: kids now have easy access to all of the same information, websites, Twitter feeds, and other electronic resources that adults do. Most kids are far more attuned to the buzz of the internet than adults and generally much more adept at locating information.

In the digital world in which we live, an educator's zone of privacy is microscopically small and steadily shrinking. It raises the question, not quickly answered, of just how risqué can a second job be before it's a problem in the classroom. It is ultimately up to you whether you want to run the professional risk of working a risqué second job. You should not be surprised, however, if it quickly leads to an uncomfortable conversation with the school principal or district administrators.

Cautionary Tales

Cautionary Tale 11-2018-US_North Carolina

Pole dancing is most commonly associated with strippers, but it has a long and respected history. The use of poles in athletic performances originated over 1,200 years ago in India and quickly spread eastward to China. It wasn't until the rise of the American traveling sideshows in the late 19th century that pole dancing became associated first with burlesque shows and then with strippers.

Pole dancing swung its way out of strip clubs and became something of a fitness fad in the mid-1990s. It's proven incredibly popular, so popular that there are now national and international pole dancing competitions. In 2017, the International Olympic Committee awarded pole dancing "special observer" status, which means that the IOC now considers "pole dancing" to be a sport. Activists hope that it will become part of the Olympics in the next 8-12 years (and for those of you who might scoff, spend some time watching rhythmic gymnastics or synchronous swimming).

In the summer of 2018, Kandice Mason, a widowed mother-of-two, was hired by the Hoke County Schools in Raeford, North Carolina, to teach sixth grade in one of the district's middle schools. During her orientation, however, Mason was stunned to learn that she suddenly had been suspended by the school district.

Four years earlier, Mason had taken up pole dancing as a form of exercise and personal relaxation. Her husband bought her a pole and had it installed in their house, and over time, Mason began teaching pole dancing part-time. Using a different name, Mason published videos of her dancing routines to a "private" Facebook page. Most of the videos showed Mason performing pole routines in lingerie or a sports bra and panties.

Despite the "private" status of Mason's Facebook page, someone managed to copy or share one of her videos (anonymously) with school officials, which led to her suspension. Mason acknowledged that the social media policy of the Hoke County Schools states that teachers are held to the same standards online as in public. However, as she told a local television station, "It's just an art for me. I just don't see it as a negative."

Notwithstanding Mason's personal view of her hobby, the district disagreed and made the suspension permanent. In a subsequent interview with the website PoletryinMotion.com, Mason said that she was uncertain what would happen next:

> This could be a stretch, but if out of all of this I was able to find an investor who could help me to open my own pole studio, that would be amazing. I would love to be able to have my own studio and teach other women. I would love to start a pole apparel clothing line. I don't know.
>
> Maybe this is all a huge sign from the universe that I need to start using my artistic side more.

Top Three Takeaways:

- By definition, "social" networks are not private. They have been specifically designed to encourage people to interact with each other. The cold hard reality is that once you digitize something and put it on the internet, even in a so-called "private" group, you lose some of your control over who might use that content and for what purpose. Mason could control who could join her "private" group, but she had little ability to prevent any member from copying and redistributing the content available to the whole group.

- More and more districts are adopting acceptable use policies that make it clear that educators can be disciplined for purely online activity, even if they take all available steps to minimize public access and block students altogether. I think that many school district administrators believe that inappropriate online conduct can cause more classroom disruption and harm to a teacher's authority than misconduct IRL ("in real life"). Given how far and wide digital content can be redistributed, they are not necessarily wrong.

- This cautionary tale reflects yet another clash of technology and public mores. The residents of Raeford may disapprove of pole dancing, but there are plenty of public practitioners of the art in strip clubs in Fayetteville, just 40 minutes to the east, so it's hardly unheard-of in the area. And if pole dancing meets with the approval of the IOC, should Mason have been penalized for posting videos of herself to promote her side gig? Assuming no discriminatory motive, that's a decision for each district to make. But just as educators need to think about the values of the community in which they teach, districts and schools likewise need to realize that the educational ecosystem is no longer entirely as local as it once was.

Cautionary Tale 11-2016-England

In the spring of 2016, Bloemfontein Primary School in Craghead, County Durham hired 21-year-old Gemma Laird to work as a teaching assistant. Craghead is a small village just south of Newcastle-on-Tyne near the coast of the North Sea in the northeast of England.

In addition to her part-time teaching, Laird also earned income as a fashion model for Lexi Fashions. She told the school about her side job before being hired and assumed that administrators were okay with it.

Laird was called into the office of the headmistress a week after school started. She told Laird that a parent had done a search of her name online and had seen her lingerie modeling photos. Laird summarized the conversation with the headmistress for *The Daily Mail*:

> They had reported me for it. I was told that they didn't want to damage the school's reputation and that people would lose respect for the school if they found out I was a model. She said she doesn't want her year-six pupils thinking it is acceptable to be a model. She made me feel dirty and like I was a prostitute. It's ridiculous.

Given the brevity of Laird's employment, legal experts said, she would have a hard time recovering damages from the school for unfair dismissal.

Top Three Takeaways:

- If an educator or prospective educator freely and frankly discloses his or her side gigs and is still hired, then the school district should show a little backbone. Administrators should not cave the instant some self-appointed moralist makes a complaint. As a former school board member, I know that there is a need to be responsive to the community, but if someone is a good hire, even though he or she works part-time as a lingerie model, then stand by your decision.

- This cautionary tale is a good reminder for educators: The members of your school community will always scrutinize your online presence and activities. The parents of the children in your classroom will pay especially close attention to what you say and do online. The more you share on the internet, the easier it will be for someone to pass judgment and criticize the choices you've made. The use of social media is a constant balancing between principle (your right to have a side job and promote it) and practicality (the fact that school officials and members of the school community may dislike what you do).

- There is a fundamental question lurking in this case. The complaining parent was worried about the possibility that her elementary-age child might learn that her teacher is a lingerie model. The child could only do so, of course, if she had unsupervised access to the internet, which doesn't seem like it would be Laird's fault. There is a real need for parents to accept some responsibility for what their children see on the internet.

Cautionary Tale 11-2015-Italy

Many people noticed that just a few months before Bloemfontein Primary fired Laird for her modeling work, media outlets around the world were running articles calling a maths lecturer at University College London (UCL) "the world's hottest math teacher."

In the spring of 2015, UCL student Arief Azli wrote a post on Facebook that read, "That moment when you realized your maths lecturer is one of the top designer model." Azli attached two photos to his post: a candid photo he took of his maths lecturer, Pietro Boselli, conducting a class, and a professional photo of Boselli posing with his shirt off. Azli's post set off a wave of other live-action posts of Boselli teaching, which in turn sparked the widespread media attention. Over the following year, Boselli's Instagram feed gained nearly 900,000 followers (it's since ballooned to 2.7 million).

There is a difference between teaching university-age students and those who are just 10 or 11 years old and presumably more impressionable. Likewise, there is a higher expectation that a primary school teacher will serve as a role model for students than those teaching people who are already adults. Still, it is jarring to see the stark disparity in the treatment of Boselli and Laird. The phrase "double standard" appeared quite often in the comments sections of the media reports and social media posts.

Boselli, who started modeling when he was just 6, conceded that his new notoriety had provided a lot of upsides. However, as Boselli told the *Daily Mail,* he did not mention his modeling when he applied to the UCL mechanical engineering Ph.D. program, because he was worried that the school would not take him seriously. The newly-minted Dr. Boselli also said that as his fame has grown, it has been increasingly common for women to touch and grope him:

> If a guy did to a girl some of the things I've been subjected too, everyone would agree how out of line they were - yet it's often accepted the other way around.

Top Three Takeaways:

- The double standard regarding male and female educators is relentless, pervasive, and wide-ranging. Education is not the only profession confronting systemic sexism, of course, but given its often-complicated history with female educators, it may need to conduct a particularly thorough self-examination.

- Some might argue that the different treatment accorded Laird and Boselli has more to do with the ages of their students than their genders. I think that's a little disingenuous. At best, one could say that our disparate attitudes towards male and female sexuality are more of a societal problem than one unique to education. And frankly, it's not much of an excuse. A profession with such a high percentage of female employees should take the lead in ensuring that women are not unfairly punished for the monetization of their looks or sexuality when male colleagues are congratulated for doing so.

- Interestingly, Boselli alluded to a reverse double standard that arises in the context of sexual assault. Later in this book, there are some disturbing examples of how this reverse double standard affects the handling of female-on-male sexual assault cases. Too often, our ability to protect young men from sexual assault by female educators is gravely hampered by outmoded social attitudes that suggest the young man should be grateful, should celebrate, or should be congratulated. As Boselli makes clear, assault is assault, regardless of the gender of the perpetrator and victim.

Cautionary Tale 11-2015-US_New York

In many ways, it's a classic New York story: a young, attractive subway rider is randomly spotted on a Bronx subway train by someone working in the fashion industry. A photo is snapped, and a few weeks later, the young woman (or in this case, the young man) is whisked off to a runway show in London, Paris, Milan, or some sun-bleached Caribbean island. It's New York's equivalent of discovering the next movie starlet waiting tables in Beverly Hills or Westwood.

But in this story, there's a twist. The newly-discovered model, Sam Pearce, already had a day job as an 8th-grade teacher of English in Bushwick, a neighborhood in the east-central area of Brooklyn, NY.

Nonetheless, after mulling over the chance encounter, Pearce decided to go to an open casting call at RED NYC in late summer 2014, just before the start of the school year. Several of the leading contemporary fashion designers, including Alexander Wang, DKNY, Alexander McQueen, and (ironically), one named Public School, quickly hired him to model their clothes at upcoming fashion shows.

Pearce decided to keep his modeling career separate from his day job by using his mother's maiden name, Worthen, as his professional name. But as inevitably happens, his very public night job was linked to his work as a teacher, and Pearce received a flurry of press coverage in the spring of 2015.

But unlike most of the other teachers discussed in this chapter, Pearce does not appear to have suffered any adverse job consequences as a result of moonlighting as a model. That is probably due in large part to the fact that the high-end clothes designed for men are not particularly revealing or controversial. (Although based on the show photos on Pearce/Worthen's Models.com page, some other adjectives do come to mind: bizarre, outre, challenging, even uncomfortable.)

Another factor, however, is that Pearce was particularly conscientious about putting his teaching work ahead of his modeling. He only took part in fashion shows that occurred on weekends or school vacations and made it clear to potential clients that his teaching job came first. In addition to prioritizing his teaching,

Pearce also chose to use some of his modeling earnings to buy books for the library of his school and set up a GoFundMe campaign called "The Right Book" that raised an additional $5,255 for books and school supplies. As RED NYC president Neil Mautone told the *Daily News*, Pearce is "a dedicated teacher who has a real, genuine, love for what he does."

In a later interview, Pearce told *HuffPost* that he was uncomfortable with the idea of his students learning about his side job. He also struggled with how best to make good use of his heightened profile.

I didn't see how my students knowing that I'm a model could possibly benefit them. I called my agent, George Brown, who at some point said the phrase "public cause." That sparked the connection in my head: to accept publicity and use it to raise money for my kids.

Top Three Takeaways:

- This a sweet, heartwarming story: "kid gets discovered on the 6 train in New York and makes it big as a fashion model." Eighty years ago, the Hollywood glitter mill would have made it into a hit starring Jimmy Stewart. You never know what will happen on the subways of New York.

- That being said, this cautionary tale also underscores the profound challenge of keeping one's personal and professional lives separate in this digital era. It seems evident that Pearce hoped to keep his modeling as distinct as possible from his teaching work and took reasonable steps to do so. However, the cautionary part of his tale lies in the fact that it just wasn't possible. In an era of almost infinite digital information, it is far too easy for interested individuals to connect seemingly disparate dots.

- Pearce's cautionary tale is yet another opportunity to discuss the double standards that male and female educators experience. The disparity is ultimately more a function of deep-seated social biases than any inherent flaw in the educational system. The bulk of male modeling jobs, after all, are for outfits that are not particularly revealing. Some men, like David Beckham or Cristiano Rinaldo, do receive ridiculous amounts of money to pose in revealing underwear. Overall, however, the number of men hired to do intimate advertisement photo shoots is quite small. The market for attractive women to do lingerie ads, of course, is vastly greater and even more relentless in its search for the fresh young face. In a world where such opportunities exist, and educators are consistently underpaid and overworked, is it reasonable to criticize or discipline female educators for availing themselves of opportunities that their male colleagues can take with so much less criticism?

Cautionary Tale 11-2014-US_Massachusetts

In early 2014, administrators in the Fitchburg School District in Massachusetts received a package from an anonymous individual. Inside were fifty-plus printouts of online modeling photos of Kaitlin Pearson, who worked as a teacher's aide in the special education program at the South Street Elementary School. The images showed Pearson posing semi-nude or in revealing lingerie for a variety of products and organizations.

The photos appeared to have been printed from Pearson's profile (since deleted) on a job board for models called ModelMayhem.com. In her profile, Pearson stated that she is willing to do shoots with "implied nudity" but not fully nude shoots. She also elaborated on her professional goals:

> I am energetic, creative, feisty, passionate about modeling, and I bring my love of life to every shoot! I have a background in graphics and business and as such I am as reliable and responsible as a model could be. I'm balancing modeling with a full time job, so my time is very precious. I am here to expand my modeling horizons and am interested in serious opportunities.

The next day, the same package was delivered—again anonymously—to the Fitchburg *Sentinel & Enterprise*, this time with a note that read: "Can you believe that this girl was hired to work with special education children in the Fitchburg schools?!!"

The school district placed Pearson on administrative leave on January 17, 2014, while it conducted an investigation. In the meantime, a debate raged among Fitchburg residents (and others farther afield) about the propriety of Pearson's side job. Here is just a sampling of the comments posted at the time, most of which fit into pretty predictable categories:

- Why didn't any of my teachers look like this?

- Finally, a teacher that'll make a kid ignore his phone and pay attention.

- "I think she should be able to keep her job," said every dad whose kid goes to this school. To each his/her own, I suppose, and she is just an aide. However...pick one occupation: nude model or educator of young children.

- Somebody had it in for her. If she does her job well, leave her be !

- Thats stupid. If she doesnt come to school naked why does it matter? People are allowed to have more than one career/hobby. People are just bored. I went to school with this girl, she is very smart and very beautiful. If she is professional while at school I dont see how her modeling is relevant to anything?

- If this was a man most of you would be all over this story demanding he be fired. Just put a pole in the damn school and be done with it. Teachers used to have morals... now some of them even watch porn on the schools dime. She may be beautiful, she is not teacher material. Someone should put the kids first.

The last comment was clearly among the minority; an informal review of the responses showed overwhelming support for Pearson. Whether that played a role in the district's handling of the case is unclear, but ten days after her suspension, the district told Pearson she could go back to work. Superintendent of Schools Andre Ravenelle issued a statement that read:

> After reviewing all relevant information, Ms. Kaitlin Pearson was notified Monday afternoon that she could return to work, effective immediately. She resumed her original duties at South Street Elementary School on Tuesday morning. We are confident that she will bring the same level of commitment to her job and her students that she always has.

One interesting aspect of this story is that the local Fitchburg paper a need to explain (and to some degree, justify) its decision to run a story about Pearson, notwithstanding the anonymous nature of the tip and the fact that she was not engaged in any illegal activity. The paper's editorial board explained that they had not decided to run a story until they learned that the superintendent had already placed Pearson on administrative leave. The latter part of the editorial is worth quoting in full:

> We decided the story on the teacher's leave was warranted because the Fitchburg Public Schools at that point had to make an important decision about what kind of conduct by a School Department employee outside the classroom would be considered inappropriate. We felt it was important to tell our readers—many of them parents of children in the district as well as school employees—what was happening so they could give Ravenelle feedback as he decided what to do. We also considered the fact that Pearson made no effort to hide her modeling work— she used her given name with her profile—and that we would not be ruining her reputation by reporting the story.

> We believe Ravenelle took appropriate action in placing Pearson on paid leave while he and school officials investigated the matter. Ravenelle is an outstanding educator who has impressed us with his handling of several crises during his administration, as well as his efforts to be as transparent as possible—with the media, his staff, parents and students. He is an asset to the city and its people.

We also believe he made the right call to reinstate Pearson on Tuesday. If we have any quibble with Ravenelle in this case, it's that he offered little explanation for his decision, other than expressing confidence that Pearson would continue with the professionalism she had demonstrated since the district hired her in November. By reinstating Pearson, he has set a tolerance level for employees who work part time in professions of a sexual nature, and he should explain what went into his decision. Not everyone who sends a child to the Fitchburg Public Schools will agree with Ravenelle's call. Nonetheless, we are confident that he made his decision only after a thorough review of the facts and careful consideration of the impact that decision might have going forward.

As for Pearson, she seems to have weathered the controversy well, even commenting on social media that she hopes the controversy will get her more work as a model. She appears to have a bright future as both educator and model, and we wish her well.

It appears that Pearson agreed with the *Sentinel & Enterprise*. In a radio interview with *The TJ Show*, a local Fitchburg radio program, Pearson said that she was grateful for the worldwide publicity:

I really right now would just go up to them and shake their hand. I couldn't even pay for this. ... If it is the person I think it is, I'm just going to go in with a smile on my face and I'm going bring them cookies and be like: 'Thank You!'

Top Three Takeaways:

- For administrators and building leaders, this is an excellent example of the importance of developing and maintaining credibility with the public, local leaders, and the press. It is inevitable, in our hyper-connected and emotional-trigger-happy world, that someone will see an educator saying or doing something online that upsets them. How you handle the unavoidable complaint and the reaction you get from the school community as a whole will depend to a large extent on the groundwork you've laid ahead of time.

- No educator should ever underestimate the enthusiasm and dedication some people will display in critiquing your life choices if they don't match that person's view of how a teacher should behave. Never forget that any material you post to the web can be reproduced in a variety of ways (including old-school printouts) and used in an attempt to damage or derail your career.

- Cautionary tales like this raise numerous challenging questions for districts and educators. Was Pearson's modeling work inherently immoral? Is it immoral for someone who works as a teacher? Is there evidence of disruption in the classroom or the school environment, or mere speculation that there might be? With public mores changing so quickly, how should districts and schools handle these situations? There are no easy answers to any of these questions, but every school district in the country should regularly consider them. The one thing about which school leaders can be confident is that new and upcoming teachers will continuously press the boundaries of what has long been thought acceptable.

Cautionary Tale 11-2012-Italy

Castello di Serravalle is a small Italian town located roughly 25 miles west of Bologna in north-central Italy. Sometime in the early 2000s, an American named Michela Roth moved to Italy and wound up teaching in a nursery school located in the picturesque community. During school holidays and summer vacations, Roth worked as a model and competed in beauty contests (including *Miss Cultetto D'Oro* [Miss Golden Bum] and *Miss Mamma Italiana*).

For five or six years, Roth's outside activity did not attract any attention in Castello di Serravalle. But at some point after September 2006 (when Facebook opened its doors to the entire world), Roth set up a Facebook account and began posting photos of herself. While none of the images show Roth nude, she did include a photo taken for a 2008 Harley Davidson calendar shoot, for which she posed in transparent lingerie.

Not long afterward (the exact timeline is a little vague), her Facebook gallery was discovered. Outraged by Roth's photos, some of the mothers of her kindergarten students pulled their children from the school. Not everyone disapproved; the *International Business Times* reported that a local newspaper, *il Resto del Carlino*, ran an online poll regarding the incident and found that 82% of respondents supported Roth, with just 14% disapproving of her out-of-school activities. Thanks to the extensive publicity, Roth's Facebook page received over 25,000 friend requests from new fans around the world in the following month.

In an interview with the Italian weekly newsmagazine *OGGI* [translated by Google], Roth strongly defended her right to be a model in the face of some aggressive questioning:

> *OGGI*: Michela, come on, you must be a naïve person if you really thought you were not provoking a hornet's nest. One who is a kindergarten teacher and puts photos of this kind on the Internet ...
> Roth: "What kind, excuse me? To me they seem only artistic photographs."
> *OGGI*: It does not seem very artistic with cowboy boots and micro shorts, riding a Harley Davidson.

Roth: "This picture is the difference of a calendar I made some time ago. With the asylum I earn 400 euros a month and in the summer I do the model to round up. In fact, I want to clarify that I put my photos on the Internet just to advertise with the agencies. As a model I can bring home up to 2 thousand euros for a photo shoot, all money to invest in the nest. That is my dream and my goal."

OGGI: If she had wanted to throw water on the fire of this whole affair, given that she declared herself 'terrified' by notoriety, would not it have been better to avoid participation in TV programs? Her sexy photos ended up on a big screen ...

Roth: "I think I have to be judged for my work as a teacher and not for what I do in my private life and I wanted to talk about it on television. And then, all these stories for some photos where I appear in costume: but these thinkers have never seen women on the beach in Milano Marittima?"

The town's mayor, Milena Zanna (whom *OGGI* somewhat unprofessionally observed is "a beautiful woman as well"), said that "[T]he only thing that matters to us is this: that she is a good teacher. The rest is just gossip."

Top Three Takeaways:

- This cautionary tale is not significantly different from Pearson's, but it helps to illustrate the global impact of the internet and the commonality of the issues now facing educators around the world. There is no question that cultural differences remain strong—certainly, Europeans are more easy-going about sexual matters than Americans, at least in terms of media—but those differences shrink when it comes to the educator of children.

- Roth's situation also offers a particularly clear illustration of being an educator both pre- and post-social media. Her modeling career was not a problem until Facebook became available, and Roth decided to use it to promote her modeling. As with Pearson, nothing Roth posted was in any way illegal. However, some members of the community did not think that her photos were consistent with how an educator should behave.

- Mayor Zanna's response to the controversy was delightfully concise, and it is tempting to suggest that every school and civic leader should take a similarly pragmatic approach. But her statement, of course, raises a fundamental question: what does it mean to be a "good teacher," particularly in our hyper-connected and socially-networked world? As this cautionary tale (and others throughout the book) should make clear, when an educator shares a "private" aspect of their life on social media, someone somewhere will nominate themselves to pass moral judgment. Yes, people should spend more time reflecting on Matthew 7:1-3, but the practical reality is that when you post on social media, you give people a window into your world, and you can't predict how they will react.

Cautionary Tale 10-2008-US_Florida

One particularly notorious case of a risqué second job involved Tiffany Shepherd, a single mother of three boys and a well-liked biology teacher at Port St. Lucie High School in the St. Lucie County School District in Florida. In 2008, needing some extra income after a painful divorce, Shepherd took a part-time job as a "bikini hostess" for the now-defunct Smokin' Em Charters. The company advertised full and half-day fishing trips accompanied by bikini-clad and occasionally topless waitresses. The company's website featured photos of some of its hostesses, including Shepherd, wearing bikinis. One image on the site also showed Shepherd lying face down and apparently topless on the deck of the charter boat.

In an interview with ABC News, Shepherd (a self-described life-long angler) strenuously denied ever working topless, although she admitted that she would occasionally go topless on private trips. She said it as an ideal second job:

> I wasn't making enough money. This was perfect because I could get paid to fish.
> It was easy money. In two days fishing, I make more than I do in a week teaching.

Shepherd worked her first trip for Smokin' Em Charters on April 19, 2008, and four days later, the St. Lucie County School District fired her. The district alleged that Shepherd had excessive absences and that it was unaware of her working as a bikini hostess when it let her go. Shepherd told *ABC News*, however, that rumors about her new gig had begun to circulate among school board members and even students even before the district fired her. She blamed the notoriety accompanying her online photos for her termination.

If the school district or board members viewed her topless waitressing as pornographic, then they helped to create a self-fulfilling prophecy. After 18 months of looking for a new teaching job, Shepherd adopted the stage name "Leah Lust" and began making adult videos (partly at the urging of the Smokin' Em Charters boat captain, who just so happened to run an adult website with his wife on the side).

Shepherd told the *Palm Beach Post* that she only agreed to make the adult videos after she had sent out 2,500 resumes but was unable to find even a minimum wage job. Her decision to do so probably ensures that she will never teach again (*see* Chapter 12), but the real nail in the coffin is that one of her first videos was entitled "My First Sex Teacher." That'll raise some flags in an HR department.

Top Three Takeaways:

- It is, of course, typical for the school district and the educator to disagree about the facts that led to the teacher's dismissal. In this case, I'm not sure I wholeheartedly believe either side. The timing is too coincidental for the district to be able to argue that Shepherd's part-time gig had no impact on the decision. At the same time, Shepherd does not appear to have been the most dedicated employee. Even if Shepherd were an exemplary teacher, the school district probably would have been within its rights to release Shepherd because her topless topside activities were causing too much distraction and disruption in her classes.

- For educators considering a part-time job that may be a little risqué, it is critically important to have an explicit agreement with your employer about what images and videos of you can be created and shared. It's not clear whether Shepherd was aware that the fishing charter website would feature photos of her. Given the fact that the captain had pictures of other hostesses on his charter boat website, it would have been naïve of Shepherd not to anticipate that she would be featured as well.

- It doesn't take a Cape Canaveral rocket scientist to realize that if you replace your teaching job with a foray, however brief, into the world of adult films, it's going to be very difficult to reverse course. Given the charter captain's web activities, it's not possible to say whether Shepherd would have gone down this path if the district hadn't fired her. But what if the St. Lucie County School District had been just a little less straight-laced and severe? Might she still be teaching? And of course, one can always wonder if this would have unfolded in the same way had Shepherd been male.

Relevant MCEE Provisions for Chapter 11

Principle I: Responsibility to the Profession

Standard I.A.5

Principle III: Responsibility to Students

Standard III.A.4

Principle IV: Responsibility to the School Community

Standard IV.D.3

Sources

The sources for the Cautionary Tales in this chapter can be viewed at the following URL:

https://link.cybertraps.com/C4E2-Sources-Chap11

Chapter 12

Past or Present Work in the Adult Entertainment Industry

Overview

In much of American society, the adult industry has lost a significant chunk of the social stigma that it once had. What was once a collection of underground enterprises rarely discussed in polite society is now a source of sitcom plots, fashion ideas (so-called "porn chic"), and technological innovation (streaming video, online credit card processing, website optimization, among others).

This social change is reflected, among other places, in our politics. Our current president was featured on the cover of *Playboy Magazine* and made a cameo appearance in at least three different Playboy videos. And only a few years ago, Massachusetts elected a U.S. Senator (Republican and Tea Party-darling Scott Brown) who once reproduced Burt Reynold's famous *Playgirl* pose after being named "America's Sexiest Man" by *Cosmopolitan* in June 1982.

Adult film stars are finding it increasingly easy to cross over to the mainstream: Sibel Kikelli appeared in the smash hit "Game of Thrones"; James Deen had a highly-touted cameo in "The Canyons"; and Sasha Gray appeared in "The Girlfriend Experience." And not surprisingly, tech companies are happy to hire engineers and programmers with experience working on large, high-traffic porn websites.

Given all that, should someone once affiliated with the adult industry be permanently barred from working as an educator? After all, not only is it a legal activity, but it's constitutionally protected as well; thanks to a 1988 decision by the California Supreme Court, porn stars have a clear First Amendment right to engage in on-screen sexual activity.

It is fair to say that things haven't completely changed; relatively few school communities would be comfortable with hiring a teacher who is actively working in the adult industry while simultaneously teaching children. Still, there seems to be a steady stream of educators who think that they can get away with moonlighting in adult entertainment or who believe that their explicit work is sufficiently in the past or adequately hidden.

Time and time again, however, the internet is proving them wrong. Until the mid-1990s, what happened in the adult industry tended to stay in the adult industry. If a young person posed nude or even made one or two adult films and then sometime later decided to become a teacher, particularly in a different part of the country, the chances were reasonably low that anyone would uncover the X-rated materials.

Increasingly, however, all of the flotsam and jetsam of our lives trails behind us online, like our own personal Great Pacific Garbage Patch. We have Google, in particular, to thank for that: The headline on the company's overview page states that the company's express "mission is to organize the world's information and make it universally accessible and useful." The information that Google is trying to make "universally accessible and useful" comes from an almost infinite variety of sources: media outlets, professional websites, historical archives of one kind or another, databases, social media sites, and of course, whatever individuals and organizations decide to put on the web.

Any teacher who thinks that he or she can keep contemporary involvement in the adult industry secret is, of course, remarkably naïve. Many educators are shocked, however, to discover that even long-forgotten adult entertainment jobs can suddenly re-emerge from the depths of the past. The internet's demand for data is insatiable, and it is always looking for new content, which sometimes means that it regurgitates old material once safely locked away in other media, like film reels or videotapes. Invariably, once that content goes online, it gets hoovered up by search engines and potentially exposed to the world. As you can see in the cautionary tales below, recently unearthed material can range from nude photos from a modeling session someone did to earn some extra cash while putting himself or herself through school, or a long-forgotten but brief foray into adult films.

We're entering the third decade of the widely-adopted web, so all of us need to think back to all the people, organizations, groups, and businesses with whom we've interacted or had dealings with over the last twenty-plus years. Any or all of them might have information—text, photos, videos—that they conceivably could post somewhere on the internet for search engines to index and make accessible. And if any of the information that someone has about you involves sex, the odds of that information finding its way online increase significantly. This is one of the reasons I recommend that people routinely Google themselves. It's not narcissism; it's just good sense to know what is associated with your name online.

The stark reality is that regardless of the growing tolerance for porn work in tech, film, and Congress, there is no statute of limitations when it comes to educators and their ongoing responsibility and ethical duty to serve as role models for their students. From a school district's perspective, it doesn't make much difference how long ago the adult industry work occurred; old nude photos or porn film clips can be just as disruptive today as they would have been when they were first created.

Cautionary Tales

Cautionary Tale 12-2017-US_California

Typically, when a teacher's involvement in the adult entertainment industry is discovered, he or she exhibits some sense of shame or embarrassment. If the work is ongoing, the educator typically leaves the school or district quietly and, more often than not, changes careers altogether. Even if the adult industry work is something the educator has been trying to put in the rearview, there is generally a recognition that the news will upset a portion of the school community.

And then there's "Nina Skye."

Skye (who, it need hardly be said, is not using the name that her parents gave her), was a kindergarten teacher at a Christian school in Los Angeles who decided that she would try to launch an adult video career. It is a complete understatement to say that apart from using a fake name, Skye did very little to conceal her identity or her profession. Around the time she decided to join the adult industry, she launched a now-deleted Twitter feed to chronicle her exploits and to promote her videos. (Unlike Instagram, Facebook, *etc.*, Twitter does not prohibit sexually explicit content.)

On March 18, she traveled to Phoenix to shoot her first online adult video for the company Amateur Allure and, on March 31, tweeted: "What if your school teacher was secretly a porn star? [emojis]" In what was either a publicity stunt or a dubious declaration of independence, Skye invited Fox 11, a local Los Angeles television station, to accompany her on the video shoot. In a piece that aired on May 15, 2017, the station used a few clips from the beginning of the video shoot (before the clothes started flying) and gave Skye several minutes of screen time to explain her decision to start doing adult films.

As the transcript shows, Skye was wholly unapologetic and saw no problem with her new part-time job:

> I have a genuine interest in children. I know what I'm doing when it comes to teaching. I'm a really good teacher.

> I love teaching. I love sex. If I can get away with doing both, then I will.

> I guess some people are really tied by that moral code. There's a really big stigma associated with it, and how our society views it, but that's not how I am. I'm really open-minded. Super open-minded. Not judgmental. I don't get why people don't understand that they're against people being porn stars but they watch it, all the time. It doesn't make sense to me.

> I was really nervous. It had been on my mind for a really long time and then I finally went with it. I put an ad up online and then I was contacted right away. I was really nervous but really excited. It's been really exciting. I've been having a lot of fun, making money, and I've met a lot of cool people.

It is easy money, so for my very first scene, I just did a regular boy-girl scene and I got paid $2,500 on the spot. I'd never had that much money like, just handed to me in my life. It doesn't make me an incompetent teacher that I do porn. That's probably how [parents and colleagues] will see it but it's not true.

[Q. And if she's fired?] I think I'll still be shocked no matter what. I can't really prepare for that as much as I would like to. I will probably just find another school to work at that's more accepting in that sense.

There are times, like emotionally, I guess, I never thought I would be a porn star growing up. I just seemed different. I always felt like I was the innocent, good girl, sweet girl-type, but then when you start doing porn and people don't see you as that innocent girl any more, so it's like part of my identity is gone in that sense and people see who you really are.

If Skye thought that her openness about her new line of work would earn her the respect of her employer, she was sadly mistaken. On June 13, 2017, she tweeted: "Got fired from a religious school just because I do porn smh [puzzled emoji]." In a follow-up story by *Fox 11*, however, Skye conceded that the school did not summarily fire her. In fact, the school offered to help Skye with housing and offered her a raise on one condition: that she stop making adult films. Skye declined the proffered assistance.

I couldn't work [at the school] because it goes against their statement of faith that it goes against their views of fornication, like sex before marriage and that's what I'm doing. They say it goes against the paper I signed, saying I wouldn't do that. … They were really trying to pull me away from staying in the industry, they just really wanted me out. They offered help and advice, but I don't really want out of the industry."

Skye has not given up all hope on teaching. During her post-termination interview, Skey told *Fox 11* that while it is unlikely that she can get a job in a private or religious school, she thinks that a public school might be willing to hire her someday. Of course, tweets like this probably won't help her job prospects: "[June 18, 2017] Happy fathers day to all the daddies I use to flirt with when I was a teacher and then some [whistling emoji]."

It's possible that despite her initial defiance, Skye had second thoughts after all: she has deleted all of her social media accounts, and there is no indication that she has been active in the adult entertainment industry recently.

But this particular cautionary tale raises an important question: is a shift underway in the attitudes of new teachers towards not just pornography but involvement in the adult video industry? And if so, will school districts, administrators, and parents change with them? I have long argued that we don't fully understand how the ready availability of pornography is affecting our children, and therefore our society; this cautionary tale may offer a partial answer. We should be prepared to have some challenging but frank conversations going forward.

Top Three Takeaways:

- Here's something upon which district administrators and school boards should reflect: Every teacher candidate today (in June 2020) who is 25 years old or younger has grown up in a world in which children have had virtually unlimited access to online adult content. There are certainly gender, familial, cultural, and regional variations, but they are not as extensive as people might think. Arguably, the members of Gen-Z have had more exposure to adult content than any generation in history—and they're just the start. That does not make them bad people, but it does mean that they will have different attitudes towards sex and online sexual content than their predecessors. These attitudinal changes will present a variety of administrative and pedagogical challenges for school districts.

- To be fair, by any measure, Skye's approach to her side gig was remarkably brazen. The open promotion of her adult video work would have been remarkable enough in a public school environment, but to bare all like that as a Catholic school kindergarten teacher is gobsmacking. It's tempting to read Skye's bewilderment over her employer's reaction as yet more evidence of her generation's deep-seated self-absorption. As my Gen-Z sons remind me, however, it's not necessarily fair to generalize from one particularly egregious example.

- Skye was an enthusiastic self-promoter and generated a large quantity of digital content to promote her new career. The school had ample material on which to base its employment decision.

Cautionary Tale 12-2016-US_Texas

Can having a past in the adult film industry serve as an example of female empowerment? That's the question raised by Texas middle school teacher Resa Woodward, who taught science in the Young Women's STEAM Academy at Belch Springs Middle School until Thanksgiving 2016. Earlier in the year, school officials received a tip that Woodward (who also goes by the name "Resa Willis") once worked as an adult film actress. Woodward initially denied the report but then admitted that from 2001 to 2004, she had appeared in a about a dozen adult films under the stage name "Robyn Foster" (compilations containing scenes in which Woodward appeared were released after she left the industry, including one as recently as 2013).

Following an investigation, school officials told Woodward that since she was no longer working in the industry, she could keep her teaching job so long as the news did not become public. Woodward's cover was blown, however, thanks in part to the country's contentious political environment. After her move to Texas, Woodward joined the Libertarian Party and quickly became an active member of the organization. She got elected as a district representative from her area and served as the state party's membership coordinator. She also contributed frequently to various libertarian websites and publications.

At some point in the fall of 2016, Woodward wrote a post on Facebook in which she revealed that she had recently called the police to report a drunk driver. Most people, of course, would consider that a noncontroversial and even socially responsible thing to do. But it turns out that drunk driving is a surprisingly divisive issue among libertarians. While most libertarians recognize the danger posed by drunk drivers, there is a segment of the libertarian community (more commonly referred to as anarchists) who oppose **any** interference by the government (or the state) in an individual's behavior until that behavior causes harm to another individual. As someone who was nearly killed by a drunk driver when I was 18, I have quite strong opinions about this. Some actions can cause irreparable harm to other individuals, even if the perpetrator freely accepts his or her financial responsibility or any criminal consequences.

One of the people who saw Woodward's post about drunk driving was David Javier Blodgett, a libertarian/anarchist from Michigan and a member of a small group known as the Anarchy Roundtable, which produces periodic YouTube videos and podcasts on politics and anarchy. He took offense at Woodward's action, which he described as "statist," and "decided it would be fun to take her down a notch." Blodgett somehow discovered Woodward's adult film work and dumped the information on Facebook.

When Woodward saw what Blodgett had published, she reported the incident to her supervisors. Notwithstanding her recent teacher ratings by the Dallas ISD of "distinguished" and "exemplary," the district placed her on administrative leave and then terminated her employment. Woodward summarized her disappointment with the district's action in an interview with the *Dallas News* website:

> I taught in an all-girls STEAM academy that was all about empowerment for women. The sad thing is that if these girls find out that I'm being punished for something that I did nearly 20 years ago and had no control of and fought to get out of, well, what does that say about empowerment?

In a subsequent interview with a local television station following her termination, Woodward talked about the fact that she had been teaching for fifteen years and had been nominated for teacher of the year eleven times. She explained that her brief career in the adult industry occurred because her then-husband was both physically and emotionally abusive. Woodward said that he first coerced her into doing photo shoots for some quick cash and then adult videos. Once she graduated from college, Woodward said, she divorced her husband, earned her master's degree, and began teaching.

"It was always hanging over me somewhere in the distance, but it all came and hit me in the face that day," Woodward concluded.

Top Three Takeaways:

- Should there be a statute of limitations on involvement with the adult entertainment industry, or is any involvement at any time disqualifying for a teacher? As this cautionary tale illustrates (and others in this chapter), the internet is a remarkably powerful tool for resurfacing decades-old films, videos, and photos. Are there—or should there be—any extenuating circumstances that would save a teacher's job? I believe that school boards and administrators should take a less binary approach to these cases. I think the motivations for someone's involvement in the adult entertainment industry are often complicated. If handled appropriately, these kinds of incidents can serve as powerful teachable moments for educators, students, and the broader school community.

- Should school boards and administrators consider the circumstances that led to the disclosure of negative information about a teacher? This cautionary tale raises that issue. It is evident that Woodward was not flaunting her adult entertainment past in any way. If anything, this is a fairly classic case of cyberbullying and cyberharassment, which women experience online far more often than men. Moreover, Blodgett disclosed the information about Woodward's past in retaliation for her opposition to behavior that all educators should oppose: drunk driving.

- The global scope of the internet and social media should give educators pause. It has always been true that members of the community in which you teach will have opinions about your behavior, your teaching methods, your politics, *etc.* But now, every time you use social media, you open yourself up to those same types of judgments from anyone in the world who has access to what you post. If you are comfortable exposing yourself to those types of reports, more power to you, but you may want to think about the potential consequences before you post.

Cautionary Tale 12-2016-Wales

In April 2016, David Phillips, the health and safety officer at Grŵp Llandrillo Menai (GLM) in north Wales, received some startling news from two staff members. The pair had heard reports that one of the GLM's popular teaching assistants, Dr. Robyn-Jane Williams, had posed for pornographic photos and appeared in an explicit video. The rumors started flying because someone posted the pictures and a link to the video to Twitter. The staff members verified the information and provided Phillips with the Twitter links.

GLM, which oversees the education of 34,000 students, promptly suspended Williams and referred the matter to the Education Workforce Panel in Ewloe, a small village in northeast Wales about twenty miles south of Liverpool.

The British tabloid *The Sun* noted that Williams was facing "three counts of unacceptable professional conduct": "posing for photographs of a pornographic nature and knowing they were to appear in an adult magazine [and] appear[ing] in a pornographic video."

At some time before her EWC hearing on September 12, 2017, Dr. Williams wrote a blog post in which she expressed disappointment in the way that GLM handled her situation:

> Some time ago, I had to leave my previous job when a man outed me as a porn model to my employer. I had never connected my two separate roles. I worked with adults and not children. I had little choice, either I faced disciplinary action or left.

Williams recognized that "privacy will always be a problem" for someone who moonlights in the adult industry but added that the work was "validating." She went to say that her departure from teaching would give her the opportunity of pursuing a new career in event catering.

As news of her departure and disciplinary hearing spread, there was an outpouring of support for Williams, including a particularly impassioned defense from a student named Tyler Turner. Ms. Turner, who is the daughter of Welsh actor Spencer Wilding, has dyslexia and credits Williams with helping her graduate:

> With being dyslexic, I relied on teaching assistants to help me through my course. During my second year, Jane was assigned to me and we got on like a house on fire, we just clicked straight away. We used to meet up for an hour every week but quite often, she'd go the extra mile to help, not just me but any student that needed it.
>
> I have nothing against the college, they were brilliant with me, I know they have their reasons and have a reputation to protect, I understand that, but from a student's perspective, it doesn't matter. What a person does in their personal life shouldn't interfere with their job. Jane's teaching ability is the only thing that matters and she was brilliant, it's such a loss to other students like me. She helped me, not only with my work but as a person and without her, I wouldn't have passed. I think it's a shame that all this has overshadowed the fantastic teacher she was. I honestly think she was one of the college's greatest assets.

Turner's endorsement had little impact on GLM or the Education Workforce Council. After suspending its initial proceeding to consider new evidence, the panel reconvened in July 2018. Phillips provided blunt testimony to the panel:

> I thought [the images were] pretty grim. I recall viewing images of Robyn Williams, who was naked, and there was graphic text. I recognized Robyn Williams' face and I have no doubt it was her.

Williams did not appear at the hearing, but she did exchange emails with the EWC in which she denied uploading the photos or the video link. Without specifying who did upload the content, Williams argued that she did not intend for the pictures to become public and took steps to prevent open access as soon as she learned that they were online. She also told the panel that the photos were "erotic, not pornographic" and were intended for a "top-shelf magazine."

The EWC rejected all of her arguments, especially since investigators found that the change in the Twitter privacy settings did not occur until after GLM began investigating the rumors about the photos. Panel chair Steve Powell announced that Williams would lose her license for a minimum of five years:

> A prohibition order is proportionate given the seriousness of Dr Williams' conduct, which was a serious departure from the standards expected of a professional person.

Dr Williams' responses demonstrated a lack of insight and she has shown no remorse. The committee could not be confident there would be no repetition.

Williams is eligible to re-apply for her license after five years, but she must first satisfy a restoration committee that "she is a fit and proper person" to teach.

Top Three Takeaways:

- "Erotica" and "pornography" are two different but overlapping categories of sexual imagery. This book is not the place for a detailed discussion of the precise parameters of each class of image; in brief, erotica aspires to be "art," while pornography is considered immoral. Administrators and school boards, however, are not interested in such hairsplitting. If you decide to pose in the nude, be prepared; your employer will not care if the world's leading art photographer is the one behind the camera if it turns out that kids have access to the photos. The "it's art, not pornography" defense is a tough sell.

- Be diligent in supervising the publication and distribution of photos that might trash your career. Assuming you are over the age of 18, you have the right to pose in whatever stages of dress or undress you like. But if you don't intend to torch your teaching career purposely, then you need to make sure you control the images or that you can completely trust the person who does.

- Investigators have a wealth of digital data available to them. There is generally a record of when you make changes to things like online privacy settings. Ideally, this is not a situation you will confront, but if you do, it is crucial to understand that just a few lines in a network log file can undermine your credibility.

Cautionary Tale 12-2015-US_Ohio

For eight years, Kristin Sundman worked as an assistant band director at Theodore Roosevelt High School in Kent, Ohio. At the beginning of the school year in 2015, however, an "unidentified web user" contacted officials at the Kent City Schools to alert them to the fact that Sundman was moonlighting as an adult webcam performer under the name "melodyXXXtune." After a brief investigation, the school district placed Sundman on administrative leave. Rather than contest the job action, Sundman tendered her resignation the following weekend.

Kent City Schools Assistant Superintendent Tom Larkin told a local *Record-Courier* reporter that the revelation was "a shock for many of us." "(She) has done an outstanding job," he added. "Parents and students have been very supportive of (her)."

The Record-Courier also reported that two former students and their friends were the ones who discovered Sundman's online adult performances. As the gossip spread through the school community, parents of students contacted the newspaper as well. Kent City Schools Superintendent George Joseph said that the district did not take any disciplinary action against any students. He added that "[i]f any students had any of these images on their phones, they were just asked to remove them."

Sundman's performed much of her webcam work for an adult website called ITSCleoLive.com (utterly NSFW, of course). Although Sundman was careful to use her alias in connection with any of her online performances, anyone who knew her stage name could easily find sexually explicit images and videos of Sundman online. It was also easy to find videos of Sundman appearing as a model at various adult entertainment expos around the country.

Cleo, the operator of the pseudonymous ITSCleoLive.com site, told the adult trade journal *AVN* that the school district was mistreating Sundman:

> Kristin and I shot a number of live camshows in March of this year on VNALive.com,
>
> MFC.com and we also did an on air appearance for BTLSRadio.com with radio host 25 Cent. It was a lot of fun and fans loved her. She did nothing wrong, broke no laws and at all times performed using her alias. Kristin does not deserve the backlash and I feel badly for her. A lot of girls have 'normal' jobs and cam on the side. It's sad that in 2015, girls still can't do cam shows without society judging and shaming them.

Top Three Takeaways:

- Educators who were involved in the adult industry at some point in the past can make a credible argument that their school district should not hold that against them. But educators who are currently working in the adult industry will find that a much more difficult case to make. Even though such conduct is generally legally, it raises legitimate concerns about the educator's ability to maintain authority in the classroom, serve as a role model, and ultimately, about his or her judgment.

- Complicating matters is the fact that nowadays, children are as likely, if not more so, to be the ones who discover the educator's side gig.

- Sundman's efforts to keep her professional career separate and apart from her xxx-tracurricular activities were utterly unsuccessful. An educator's ability to do so will get harder and harder in the not-too-distant future, as facial recognition software grows increasingly sophisticated and more widely used both online and off. It is not difficult to imagine, for instance, some overly-aggressive hiring firm offering to cross-reference the face of each prospective hire with faces linked to a variety of supposedly undesirable activities. The potential for abuse and lifestyle discrimination will be profound.

Cautionary Tale 12-2014-Canada

One of the unfortunate truths of the current era is that it is getting harder and harder these days to make a fresh start in the world. Every day, our past is relentlessly resurrected by multiple websites and indexed by search engines. Google, of course, is the most significant player of this game; it is an explicit goal of the company, after all, to "[o]rganize the world's information and make it universally accessible and useful."

In theory, that's a noble goal. In reality, however, Google's idealism can impose painful and unwanted consequences on the blithely unsuspecting. That is one of the main reasons that the European Union is adopting a "right to be forgotten," under which news sites can publish information, but search engines are prohibited from indexing it.

A particularly striking example of this phenomenon is former Quebec educator Jaqueline Laurent-Auger. In 2014, she was working as a drama teacher Collège Jean-de-Brébeuf, an all-boys Christian academy in Montreal, a position she had held for 15 years. During the school year, some of her students discovered that Laurent-Auger had an entry in the Internet Movie Database. The 73-year-old educator, who did most of her screen work between 1969 and 1978, was quite surprised by this, as she was unaware that IMDB even existed.

The sharp-eyed students scrolled down her list of film credits and found such titillating entries as *Sinner: The Secret Diary of a Nymphomaniac* (1973), *Hot and Naked* (1974), and *Swedish Sex Games* (1975). The films, like many of their European counterparts from the 1970s, feature ample nudity (including Laurent-Auger).

In the wake of the discovery, the Collège Jean-de-Brébeuf announced in July 2014 that it would not renew Laurent-Auger's contract. Michel April, the general manager of the school, told Radio-Canada that the student discovery of Laurent-Auger's early work had created "an element of distraction" within the classroom. He added that the classroom should be "conducive to learning" and that Laurent-Auger's authority as a teacher "was broken."

Not surprisingly, Laurent-Auger was upset by the school's decision. "I did it as a young actress to make a little money," she told *The Globe and Mail*. "The idea of throwing someone out the door for something they did almost 50 years ago is idiotic. It makes me angry."

Laurent-Auger also argued that her film work contributed to society more broadly:

> If young people have so much freedom of expression nowadays, that's probably because there were men and women like me who once paved the way towards a creative space that allows great freedom of expression."

In a statement, the school defended its action:

> The fact that these films were shot 40 years ago doesn't change their bold and suggestive – even explicit – character. The availability on the Internet of erotic films in which she acted created an entirely new context that was not ideal for our students. After discussion and reflection, we concluded that adult films must remain just that, a product for adults. That's why we decided not to renew Mrs. Laurent-Auger's contract.

The decision by the elite school (which educated both Pierre Trudeau and his son Justin) to fire LaurentAuger sparked widespread outrage, with one local blogger describing the action as "retroactive slutshaming." Collège Jean-de-Brébeuf grads Marc-Antoine Audette and Sebastien Trudel—who form the comedy duo "Les Justiciers Masques"—began organizing a group letter from other alums to protest the drama teacher's firing.

"It's a retrograde and deplorable decision that goes against what we are taught in Brébeuf, freedom of mind," Trudel said. The two comedians praised general manager April for his leadership but suggested that this was "a very bad decision."

Following a week of criticism on social media, the Collège Jean-de-Brébeuf issued a statement that said the matter "could have been handled differently" and announcing that negotiations were underway with Laurent-Auger to return to the school "in new roles." The school also said that it would be leading a community-wide discussion on "sexuality, digital platforms and social networks in educational settings":

> This exercise is part of the role that the College has played in education in Quebec and is part of a public debate that clearly needs to be had... College management wants Ms. Laurent-Auger to have a stake in this debate, if desired.

Top Three Takeaways:

- Ultimately, Laurent-Auger decided that she did not want to return to the school. Instead, her lawyers negotiated a settlement of the dispute, and Laurent-Auger began work on a book detailing the lives of her mother, herself, and her daughter. Few of the cautionary tales in this book illustrate the unpredictable consequences of the internet as this one. According to IMDB.com, Laurent-Auger's acting career began, coincidentally, the same year the internet was invented (1969) and ended in 1978, about twelve years before the launch of the International Movie Database. (Between 1990 and

2006, Laurent-Auger made a handful of minor guest appearances in non-sexual roles.) If there was ever an educator who might reasonably have believed that her nude film work was well and truly in the past, it was Laurent-Auger. But everything is grist to the internet's relentless mill.

- It is a little surprising that this cautionary tale unfolded as it did, since Canadians in general and in particular, the French-leaning Quebecois tend to be more easy-going about matters of sex and nudity than their neighbors to the south. But of course, Laurent-Auger was teaching at a former Jesuit private school that retains strong religious influence. It is also possible, as can happen even at public schools, that the desire to protect the reputation of the school influenced its action against Laurent-Auger. Administrators and school boards should not miss the lesson, however, that the school's handling of this matter undoubtedly did more reputation harm than it would have suffered from association with Laurent-Auger's film career.

- It is worth noting that the school's conclusion that Laurent-Auger's "adult films" should remain "a product for adults" is regrettably naive in this day and age. Not only was Laurent-Auger's entire film catalog readily available to any student who could discover her IMDB.com entry (not precisely a Sherlockian task), but so too are bootleg copies of those long-forgotten movies. Given the utter lack of an effective means of age filtering on the internet, there is simply no way that any "adult content" can remain "a product for adults." Administrators, educators, and parents all need to come to terms with that fact and adjust their expectations accordingly.

Relevant MCEE Provisions for Chapter 12

Principle I: Responsibility to the Profession

Standard I.A.5

Principle III: Responsibility to Students

Standard III.A.4

Principle IV: Responsibility to the School Community

Standard IV.D.3

Sources

The sources for the Cautionary Tales in this chapter can be viewed at the following URL:

https://link.cybertraps.com/C4E2-Sources-Chap12

Section Three
Cybertraps in the Classroom

Chapter 13

Intellectual Dishonesty: Copyright Infringement, Plagiarism, and Cheating

Overview

One of the themes that run through the Model Code of Ethics for Educators, as you might expect, is intellectual and professional honesty. There is a clear expectation that educators will hold themselves (and each other) to high standards and model those standards for their students. After all, it's just a little hypocritical to punish students for plagiarism if you fill your class lessons with "borrowed" and unsourced material that you've downloaded from the internet.

The concept of "intellectual honesty" covers a lot of ground, but there are three specific categories that present potential cybertraps for educators: copyright infringement, plagiarism, and cheating. In each instance, digital technology and the internet make it much easier to be intellectually dishonest. While these cybertraps tend not to grab headlines (except for large-scale cheating cases, as we'll see), they can nonetheless have a profoundly negative or even terminal impact on your career.

Copyright Infringement

The concept of copyright is generally pretty well understood, but a review is useful. When an individual creates a work in a fixed medium (book, movie, song, diary, software program, *etc.*), that person automatically owns the copyright to that work and has certain legal rights regarding its use and the creation of derivative works. If you use that person's creative work without permission or a legitimate defense, then you may be liable for civil damages or, in rare instances, subject to criminal prosecution.

The primary cybertrap in this area arises from the fact that the internet, as many people have observed, is one gigantic copyright infringement machine. Despite the best efforts of copyright owners like movie studios and record labels, it is still incredibly easy to download copyrighted material from the internet without paying for it. For most images, little more is required than right-clicking and choosing "Save As."

It takes a bit more effort to effectively pirate movies or music. Some familiarity with BitTorrent is helpful or the ability to access and navigate the dark web. You can teach yourself the necessary tricks by doing some brief searches on Google or Bing (although I don't recommend doing so.

> **Necessary Reminder:** Mucking about on piracy sites or the dark web not only raises significant legal and ethical issues, but doing so is also risky to the health of your computer. It is far too easy to stumble across various types of malware that will damage your computer and threaten the security of your personal information. There is also a non-trivial likelihood that contraband material (like child pornography) will wind up on your computer, which can result in serious legal consequences.

If you use copyrighted materials without permission, there are a variety of potential consequences. At the very least, the copyright holder can ask a court to order that the infringement stop and that any infringing works be seized. The copyright owner can also try to recover lost profits or other damages resulting from the infringement. If the copyright owner properly registered his or her work with the U.S. Copyright Office, it may be possible for the copyright owner to recover what are called statutory damages, which range from $200 to $150,000 *per infringement,* depending on the circumstances of the case. Finally, if the court determines that infringement has occurred, the infringer can be ordered to pay the costs and attorney fees that the copyright owner incurred in bringing the lawsuit.

It is possible to prosecute someone for copyright infringement, but the circumstances are relatively rare and typically involve activities that are not common in the classroom.

The practice of digital piracy deserves some special attention. "Digital piracy" is the downloading of copyrighted electronic content—software, movies, music, books, *etc.*—without paying for it. Digital piracy costs online content providers billions every year.

Teachers who pirate movies or music for use in their class are subject to all of the infringement penalties listed above. Also, if you download and install pirated software, you run a substantial risk of causing damage to your classroom computer and potentially your district network as well. If your district's IT department is on the ball, they won't let you randomly download and install unauthorized software, but mistakes do happen.

Fortunately, educators have several options for finding copyright-free content for use in the classroom. The Internet Archive (archive.org) has enormous quantities of public domain and copyright-free materials in every medium; it's a fabulous resource. Numerous websites offer images that are available for re-use. Some have no restrictions on usage at all, while others permit users to use their photos for non-commercial purposes. My favorites include Flickr.com, Pexels.com, and Unsplash.com. Another useful tip is to do a Google Image search, click on the "Tools" menu, and filter for images "Labeled for Reuse."

If you are determined to use a copyrighted work in your classroom (and haven't obtained a license to do so), you may still be able to argue that it falls under the doctrine of 'fair use,' which is one of the recognized defenses to a copyright infringement claim.

In deciding whether your use of copyrighted material without a license is "fair," a judge or jury will consider the following four factors:

1. What was the nature and purpose of your use of the copyrighted material? Was the use transformative in some way, or was it merely a verbatim copy? Education is generally considered a transformative use, because of the interaction with students.

2. What is the nature of the copyrighted material? As an educator, you have more latitude in copying from non-fiction books than you do creative works like novels or poems. The exception, of course, would be English or literature teachers who are providing their students with relevant examples of style or structure.

3. How much of the copyrighted work did you use, and how substantial was it? Some people say that you can safely claim "fair use" if you use ten percent or less of a copyrighted work, but there is no statutory or case law support for that rule. Instead, a court or jury will focus on whether the infringement uses the "heart" of the copied work. Again, educators have a little more latitude here because the pedagogical goal is often to illustrate the central and most noteworthy aspects of a copyrighted work.

4. What impact does the infringement have on the copyrighted work's potential market? If your infringement damages the ability of the copyright owner to market his or her work, then it will be difficult to argue that your use of the work is "fair." The limited use of a creative work for educational purposes in a classroom is not likely to have a significant impact on the market of a copyrighted work. However, teachers should consider that issue before handing copyrighted material out to smartphone-equipped teenagers.

Plagiarism

As with copyright infringement, the concept of plagiarism is generally well-understood by educators and administrators. For those who need a quick refresher, however, here is the definition used by Oxford University in its guidance to students on study skills:

> Plagiarism is presenting someone else's work or ideas as your own, with or without their consent, by incorporating it into your work without full acknowledgement. All published and unpublished material, whether in manuscript, printed or electronic form, is covered under this definition. Plagiarism may be intentional or reckless, or unintentional. Under the regulations for examinations, intentional or reckless plagiarism is a disciplinary offence.

K-12 educators and administrators most typically deal with this particular cybertrap in the context of educating students about their ethical obligations. The goal, of course, is to help students understand why it is intellectually dishonest to simply copy resources verbatim, forget to reference sources, or suppose that a little light paraphrasing is sufficient to take credit for someone else's ideas and text.

However, as you can see below, there are circumstances in which plagiarism has tripped up educators and administrators. In most cases, digital technology is not the main reason that the plagiarism occurred, but as with students, technology makes it much easier to detect.

Cheating

I wrote an entire section of my book *Cybertraps for the Young* on the innovative ways in which students use technology to try to cheat on tests and exams. The phrase "fiendishly clever" comes to mind. A quick online search will turn up dozens of tutorials by 'generous' students explaining their preferred techniques.

That's not the type of cheating cybertrap that snares educators. Instead, the tremendous surge in standardized testing over the past few decades underlies most educator cheating cases. As a general policy matter, I think that the rise of standardized testing has been an enormously destructive trend. Academic standards are necessary, of course, but there is growing evidence that standardized tests are arbitrary, socially and racially discriminatory, and damaging to the broader goal of developing critical thinking skills in students. It is not remotely clear that we can reduce education to a series of bubble answers.

The most corrosive aspect of standardized testing is the outsized importance placed on test scores by administrators, education officials, and legislators. In many U.S. school districts (and in the UK and Canada as well), standardized test results now play a role in determining teacher raises, promotions, and even employment. Collectively, standardized test results can also play a role in determining whether a school should remain open or undergo substantial reorganization. It is not surprising that teachers feel an enormous amount of pressure to make sure that their students score well (which, of course, is a slightly different thing than "test well").

Unfortunately, some teachers have responded to the intense emphasis on standardized test scores by helping their students to cheat during the test or by altering student answers. Such conduct is not merely unethical, but depending on the circumstances, illegal as well.

The most infamous case of cheating in the United States emerged out the Atlanta Public Schools after the *Atlanta Constitution-Journal* ran a series of articles in 2009 that raised questions about remarkable increases in test score results. The stories led to a state-led investigation and, ultimately, to the indictment of Atlanta schools superintendent Beverly Hall and thirty-four teachers and school officials. Eventually, 11 teachers were convicted of racketeering.

No one was under any illusions that Atlanta Public Schools was the only district grappling with cheating. As many as 40 different states reported cheating cases around the same time, and it remains an ongoing concern in the education community.

Cautionary Tales

Cautionary Tale 13-2019-West Virginia

In the spring of 2013, actor Ashton Kutcher received the "Ultimate Choice" award during the Teen Choice Awards. The 35-year-old actor opened his speech by saying, "What up? Oh wow! Okay, okay, let's be brutally honest, this is the old guy award, this like—this is like the grandpa award, and after this, I get to go to the geriatric home."

Kutcher then went on to give a widely-praised speech about what he had learned during his years in Hollywood, which he boiled down to three things: "The first thing is about opportunity, the second thing is about being sexy and the third thing is about living life."

Squealing teens were not the only ones who were inspired by Kutcher's gracious speech. Six years later, Kenny DeMoss, principal of Parkersburg High School in West Virginia, gave a speech to the Class of 2019 that leaned heavily on Kutcher's speech. Given the fact that Kutcher's speech already had been viewed millions of times by the time of the Parkersburg graduation, the chances that one or more of the students would recognize the language and structure of Kutcher's acceptance were remarkably high.

And in fact, that's what happened. One of the graduates, Abby Smith, thought she recognized the speech and did a little research. Convinced that DeMoss had replicated much of Kutcher's text, she created a video that cut back and forth between DeMoss's speech and Kutcher's, showing the similarities. (If you search for "Abby Smith" and "Ashton Kutcher," you'll quickly find a copy of her video.)

In an interview with a local news affiliate, Smith said that Moss should acknowledge his error:

> Originally I just uploaded it because I think that if his students and his other teachers are held to a standard of a zero tolerance policy for plagiarism that's written in our school code of conduct, that he should be held to that same [standard].

DeMoss defended himself in part by saying that the video created by Smith did not include his opening lines, in which he described how he had been influenced by "many great ideas and thoughts ...." But he conceded that "[i]n hindsight, I wish I would have cited more."

Ashton Kutcher himself caught wind of the incident and offered this pithy comment on Twitter:

> "Imitation is the sincerest form of flattery that mediocrity can pay to greatness."– Oscar Wilde.

* cite your sources kids and faculty [Emoji: Smiling face with smiling eyes]

According to a subsequent report in *The Washington Post*, DeMoss tried to engage in some damage control when Smith's video started to go viral. He emailed Smith to ask her to take the video down (using the spurious "ideas are meant to be free" defense). Smith declined, so DeMoss "blocked her on social media and instead asked a teacher to persuade her to remove it[.]" That didn't work either.

Although DeMoss wrote an apology to parents and then apologized in person to the Wood County Board of Education, the Board nonetheless voted on June 11, 2019, to suspend him for five days without pay.

DeMoss declined to comment on the Board's decision.

Top Three Takeaways:

- If you are going to rip off someone's speech, maybe it would make sense to choose an address that wasn't seen (most likely) by a significant percentage of your audience. It might also make sense to avoid choosing comments that are archived on the favorite distribution medium of your audience (in this, YouTube.com). Of course, the best course of action is to write your own speech.

- These darn kids today, they have amazing tech skills. Not only did Smith do the research necessary to find the source of the speech, but she also put together an amusing video that made DeMoss's plagiarism crystal clear. Educators and administrators should never forget that their media- and tech-savvy students have worldwide broadcast capabilities at the tips of their fingers. It is a profound shift in the traditional power dynamic, and it's not going away anytime soon.

- The worst part of this cautionary tale, I think, is DeMoss's effort to squelch Smith's report and his petulant response when she refused to do so. We should applaud her support of intellectual integrity and academic honesty.

Cautionary Tale 13-2018-US_Florida

In the summer of 1990, the state of Florida entered into a consent decree to resolve litigation filed by the League of United Latin American Citizens (LULAC) and numerous other plaintiffs against the Florida Board of Education, the Florida Department of Education, and various other defendants. The lawsuit filed by LULAC alleged that Florida was not "doing enough to provide educational resources to meet the needs of students with limited English skills."

The parties entered into a consent decree in the summer of 1990 to resolve the litigation. As part of that decree, people who are hired from other professions to become teachers must take between 60 and 300 credit hours of coursework on how to teach English for Speakers of Other Languages (ESOL). As the *Tampa Bay Times* noted, "[t]he assignments are substantial. [Teachers] must design lessons, summarize academic readings, show how they reach out to families from diverse cultures, and reflect on their practices and experiences.

For new teachers, the ESOL course requirements can create a substantial burden, one that unfortunately encourages some to look for shortcuts. In early 2018, *Tampa Bay Times* reporter Marlene Sokol analyzed ESOL-related disciplinary proceedings in Hillsborough County Public Schools. Her story led off with an account of two sisters, Claudette Wilson and Annella Fender, who were flagged by a sophisticated anti-plagiarism algorithm for allegedly copying each other's work. The paper illustrated its story by reproducing an assignment completed by each sister that did appear to contain some very similar text.

The alleged plagiarism by Wilson and Fender (which Fender denied) was not the main point of Sokol's story. Her primary focus was on the "unusually sophisticated system" that Hillsborough County uses to detect possible plagiarism in ESOL course work. Sokol reported that over the last few years, the algorithm flagged the work of over 60 teachers.

Before starting their ESOL training, each new teacher is required to sign an academic integrity statement. If teachers are caught violating integrity requirements, they are typically are assessed "a one-year suspension, a $750 fine and a requirement that the teacher earns at least a B in a college course on educational ethics."

Gretchen Brantley, the executive director of the Florida Education Practices Commission, praised Hillsborough for its rigorous monitoring and commitment to academic ethics. The County should take pride, Brantley told Sokol, in the fact that it holds teachers accountable when they are caught cheating and added that it set an excellent example for students.

Top Three Takeaways:

- Cautionary tales like this illustrate the importance of embedding ethics training in every level of the teaching profession, from pre-certification courses through ongoing professional development. One of the chief benefits of the MCEE is that it can help to spark career-long conversations about what is and what is not ethical conduct.

- When I was much younger, a company called Fram ran a series of commercials to promote its oil filters. The ads all had the same basic structure: a weary mechanic in oil-stained coveralls would hold up some ruined engine part and explain how the owner could have avoided an expensive repair by purchasing a Fram oil filter. Each ad ended with the same tag line: "You can pay me now, or you can pay me later." The MCEE is the Fram oil filter of educational tools. The more time and effort we put into teaching and reinforcing its ethical precepts, the less time, energy, and money we will need to spend on the software and personnel required to detect and punish educator misconduct.

- The technology at the crux of this story—a sophisticated algorithm designed to ferret out plagiarism and cheating—is just the beginning of a fascinating technological shift in our society. Seemingly overnight, algorithms and artificial intelligence systems are going to play an increasingly signficant role in examining our behavior, rendering judgments about our choices, and in some instances, assessing penalties and job sanctions. The developers and promoters of these tools will put a lot of pressure on school boards and district administrators to buy and install them. Before doing so, however, district leaders should think carefully about their own moral and ethical obligations to protect the privacy and the safety of their employees and students.

Cautionary Tale 13-2018-US_Texas

In the fall of 2017, things were going well for Lance Hindt, the new superintendent of the Katy Independent School District in Katy, Texas. Hindt, a graduate of Katy ISD himself, previously served as superintendent in the Allen Independent School District. During his tenure there, he earned accolades for his handling of construction flaws in AISD's new $60 million football stadium and his successful passage of a major school bond issue.

Shortly after taking the position in Katy, Hindt successfully led a campaign for an even larger $609 million bond referendum that was approved by nearly 70% of the district's voters. The funds authorized by the voters allowed Superintendent Hindt to oversee the start of construction on six new educational campuses, "as well as upgrades and improvements at almost every other campus in the district."

But Hindt's professional career came to an abrupt end less than a year later. On March 19, 2018, a local businessman named Greg Barrett attended a Katy ISD school board meeting and, during public comment, accused Hindt of bullying him when they were in middle school together. (At the time, Barrett's legal name was "Greg Gay," which he said contributed to the bullying.) Hindt denied the charge in a statement issued the next day, but a video of him laughing during Barrett's comments helped draw national attention to the dispute. A week later, a watchdog website called *A Better Legacy* unearthed a 1983 lawsuit against Hindt in which he was accused of severely beating another man in a traffic dispute (the suit was eventually settled).

Things got worse for Hindt in May 2018 when Sean Dolan, the operator of the *A Better Legacy* website, published an article in early May 2018 in which he accused Hindt of plagiarism. According to Dolan, there were striking similarities between Hindt's 2012 Ph.D. thesis and one submitted in 2008 by Keith Rowland, a superintendent in Georgia:

> In 2008, Keith A. Rowland's submitted a doctoral dissertation at Liberty University titled: The Relationship of Principal Leadership and Teacher Morale. ...
>
> 4 years later, in 2012, Lawrence A. Hindt submitted a doctoral dissertation to the University of Houston titled: The Effects of Principal Leadership on Teacher Morale and Student Achievement. ...
>
> I am not an expert on plagiarism, and it's not up to me to make this call, but the similarities concern me, and I believe this is information that the public should be able to weigh in on, even if our school board won't. U of H has been notified of this, but due to FERPA laws, they can not tell me whether or not they will do anything about it.

It's not just the exact same lines used between papers that concerns me, it's the systematic similarity of the format, structure, ideas, thoughts, methods, justifications, conclusions and sources.

It's not clear how Dolan was alerted to the similarities between the two documents or what inspired him to run Hindt's thesis through Turnitin.com. However, the comparison between the two papers raised legitimate concerns about the extent to which Hindt had borrowed Rowland's content and concepts without attribution.

Just over a week later, Hindt abruptly resigned, telling the Katy ISD School Board:

My family is now my number one priority – they are innocent bystanders. In light of an organized, relentless and dishonest smear campaign against me, I cannot remain as superintendent of Katy ISD.

The controversy surrounding Hindt did not end with his resignation. The Katy ISD school board approved a severance package for Hindt of $789,000 (two years of his base pay) and also voted to appropriate $50,000 to file a defamation lawsuit against Hindt's critics. There is no evidence, however, that the board ever filed the lawsuit.

One thing that did occur, however, was that in January 2020, the University of Houston archives removed Hindt's dissertation. The University declined to disclose whether Hindt had been sanctioned in any other way (for instance, by stripping him of his Ph.D.).

Top Three Takeaways:

- Every educator, from the superintendent down to the newest student teacher, should always be mindful that "cameras are everywhere." In this case, a news station recorded Hindt's inappropriate laughter about Barrett's complaint, but it just as easily could have been captured by any of the smartphones that were undoubtedly in the room. And of course, merely remembering that cameras are everywhere is not enough these days; you also must remind yourself that thanks to the internet, photos and videos can be distributed globally with the press of a button.

- We all know that journalism is having a tough couple of decades, thanks in large part to the intensely disruptive impact of the internet. Overall, it's a terrible thing for a democracy to lose so many frontline reporters. One tiny glimmer of hope, however, lies in the fact that some people (both journalists and non-journalists) have launched websites designed to shine a bright light on specific topics or locales. *A Better Legacy for Katy ISD* is a perfect example of this trend: a group of local activists interested in promoting a better school district and keeping administrators accountable. These sites can be the digital equivalent of mayflies (**ABetterLegacy.com** does not appear to be reachable right now), but they illustrate the potential for a new mechanism of public scrutiny. Thanks to the democratizing effect of the internet, you don't have to be a reporter for CNN or the *New York Times* to break an important news story.

- Given the ease with which people can distribute information online, school boards and administrators should have a plan in place someone unfairly attacks a district employee for actions taken in the performance of his or her duties. A district, of course, has no obligation to protect an employee who is guilty of wrongdoing in his official capacity or who has said or done something controversial as a private individual. In this case, given that the alleged "smear campaign" was about the originality of Hindt's thesis, it is not clear that the Katy ISD School Board should have taken any action, particularly anything quite so dramatic as offering to fund a defamation lawsuit.

Cautionary Tale 13-2017-US_Montana

One of the standard rituals for newly-hired administrators is to send out an introductory letter or email, offering a bit of personal history and his or her plans for the future. In June 2017, John Blackman was looking forward to taking over as principal of Flathead High School in Kalispell, Montana. His cheerful introductory email praised Flathead as "a beacon of academic excellence within the great state of Montana," and acknowledged that "differentiated, rigorous, and relevant instruction which meets the needs of each student will be the vehicle to continuing the success that has already been experienced at Flathead High School."

All in all, it was a pleasant, upbeat, and forward-looking message. Unfortunately, though, it wasn't original. The bulk of Blackman's letter was copied verbatim from a letter written in 2016 by Joshua M. Wilson, the incoming principal of Strawberry Elementary School in Santa Rosa, California. A copy of Wilson's letter was available on the Strawberry Elementary website, which is where Blackman found it.

It is not clear who discovered the plagiarism and reported it to Kalispell Public Schools Superintendent Mark Flatau, but it had an immediate impact on Blackman's career trajectory. After meeting with Flatau and other school officials, Blackburn agreed to withdraw his acceptance of the principal position. Kalispell Public School officials declined to comment on the plagiarism incident. Blackburn also refused to speak to reporters.

Top Three Takeaways:

- This cautionary tale raises a couple of immediate questions. First, who is so busy that they don't have the time to compose a simple, straightforward, *original* welcoming email to parents? I certainly understand the value of looking for examples or templates online, but at the end of the day, everyone is responsible for their content. It sets a terrible example for a top administrator to use someone else's material without giving appropriate credit. Of course, even if Blackman had given credit, would it have been better? It's a little bit like copying someone else's Valentine's Day card to a spouse.

- The internet is tailor-made for gadflies and provocateurs. It is hard to imagine exactly *why* someone would bother to do an internet search to see if Blackman's welcome email was original, but it would only take a couple of minutes to find out. If the ethical considerations in the MCEE are not sufficient warning, at least consider the ease with which someone can uncover digital wrongdoing.

- The internet shines a very bright light on our activities, although it does so unevenly. When it catches us in its glare, however, there is nowhere to hide. Add Blackman to the list of educators who screw up their careers with a few ill-advised keystrokes. It really is that simple, sometimes.

Cautionary Tale 13-2013-US_North Carolina

There are a lot of little electronic mistakes that can trip up educators. For instance, you might send a text message or email to the wrong person. You might share your desktop for an online class and forget that you have some tabs open in your browser that reveal more about your web surfing habits than you might like. You might overlook an embarrassing autocorrect when typing on your phone. Most of us have experienced something along those lines.

But occasionally, small oversights can have more severe consequences. Consider, for instance, what happened to Sulura Jackson, who was hired as the principal of Chapel Hill High School in Chapel Hill, NC, in the summer of 2013. Not long after she took over, she sent a letter of condolence to one of the teachers in the school that read in part:

Everyone at Skyline is saddened to learn of the death of your mother.

Skyline is not, unfortunately, a nickname for Chapel Hill High School. Instead, it's the name of the high school in Ann Arbor, Michigan, where Jackson had previously served as principal.

That mistake inspired some Chapel Hill teachers to start a review of the other materials that Jackson had sent out at the beginning of the school year. According to a report in a local weekly, *INDY Weekly*, their research revealed that Jackson had incorporated other people's work without attribution into a variety of memos, letters, and recommendations. The teachers claimed that she copied "entire passages and letters from books, online articles and teaching resource guides." The paper's review of the contested writings backed up the teachers' research:

> In some cases, Jackson, who won a Michigan secondary school association's award for top high school principal of 2010–2011, used uncited text pulled from various sources. In others, she seems to use entire letters, such as an online welcoming letter for students posted by an Arizona principal. Sometimes she seems to have attempted to disguise the copied text by changing a single word while retaining the overall form and structure. Other times, entire passages were printed unchanged.

When contacted by the paper, Jackson was unrepentant. She offered what amounted to a "fair use" defense, telling the paper that "[t]his is not anything that I'm selling. This is not anything that I'm using for personal gain."

Unfortunately, non-commercial copying is not a defense to a claim of copyright infringement, and even more importantly, it's not a defense to an allegation of plagiarism. There was some suggestion that Tom Forcella, the Superintendent of the Chapel Hill-Carrboro City Schools, might recommend that the Board of Education take disciplinary action against Jackson. If the Board did so, however, the disciplinary action was relatively minor and went unreported. Jackson remained principal until the spring of 2018, when she took a one-year appointment as an educational liaison overseeing the construction of a new high school. A laudatory article in the *Proconian*, the Chapel Hill High School newspaper, made no mention of the plagiarism incident.

Top Three Takeaways:

- This cautionary tale starts as a relatively minor cybertrap. It's one thing to copy someone else's content, but it is not nearly such a big deal to reuse something you have written yourself. It may not be exceptionally creative, but it's not a breach of educator ethics. The unfortunate thing, of course, is that Jackson was clearly busy and did not proofread her text carefully enough. That resulted in her leaving in the name of her former school in the condolence letter. An embarrassing slip, of course, but a somewhat classic cybertrap that has undoubtedly happened to many of us.

- The problem, of course, is that these types of digital mistakes are like a loose thread in a sweater. It is far too tempting for someone to start pulling on it, and then a career can begin to unravel. It is not unreasonable to suppose, of course, that some malice contributed to the digital investigation that followed Jackson's email mistake. But regardless of the motivation, the digital research led to the discovery that Jackson had not only reused content she created but that of others as well. As a general rule, an educator who stumbles into one cybertrap is likely to find that he or she has opened a digital can of worms.

- In my experience, educators do not necessarily have a good grasp of intellectual property law and the available defenses to infringement. The concept of "fair use" does offer broad protection for educators, who are generally entitled to use excerpts of copyrighted material for "commentary or criticism." However, that does not appear to be what Jackson did here, mainly because she was not using the content in a classroom to educate students. This case does not involve anything significant in the way of monetary damage to the original copyright holders. Instead, the much more substantial issue is Jackson's intellectual integrity and the example she set for educators and students in the district.

Relevant MCEE Provisions for Chapter 13

Principle I: Responsibility to the Profession

Standards I.A.2, I.A.3, I.A.5, I.A.6, and I.A.7

Principle II: Responsibility for Professional Competence

Standard II.B.1

Principle III: Responsibility to the School Community

Standards IV.C.3, IV.D.1, IV.D.2, and IV.D.3

Principle V: Responsible and Ethical Use of Technology

Standards V.A.4 and V.C.3

Sources

The sources for the Cautionary Tales in this chapter can be viewed at the following URL:

https://link.cybertraps.com/C4E2-Sources-Chap13

Chapter 14
Lack of Productivity and Failure to Supervise

Overview

Very few of us can honestly say that we haven't lost the odd hour or two (or forty) online. Facebook, Buzzfeed, Twitter, Pinterest, DailyKos, *The Huffington Post, The New York Times, The Boston Globe* sports page, etc. (just to name a few of my favorite rabbit holes)— enticing and time-consuming distractions are scattered across the cyber universe. A random walk around the internet is not a problem on a lazy Sunday morning or even a slightly-depressing Saturday night home alone. It's a much bigger deal, of course, if you are supposed to be working.

Employers of every description are deeply concerned about the impact of the internet on productivity. They have good reason to worry. In HR circles, the phenomenon even has a new name: "cyberloafing" (or, more judgmentally, "cyberslacking"). By some estimates, cyberloafing costs the American economy billions of dollars every year in lost productivity. According to Kansas State University Associate Professor Joseph Ugrin, "the average US worker spends 60-80 percent of their time online at work doing things unrelated to their jobs."

A 2005 study by the internet research firm Websense found that 62 percent of men and 54 percent of women accessed the web during the workday for personal reasons. The available options for distraction were quite different back then: "social media" didn't even make the top five reasons for personal web use. The leading causes of cyberloafing were "news sites (81 percent), personal email (61 percent), online banking (58 percent), travel (56 percent), and shopping (52 percent)."

Less than a decade later, in 2013, *Forbes* contributor Cheryl Connor reported that while the percentage of cyberloafers had risen only slightly (to 64 percent), social media sites were now a significant part of the problem. "The winners for the time-loss warp," Connor said, "are Tumblr (57%), Facebook (52%), Twitter (17%), Instagram (11%), and Snapchat (4%)."

The concern over cyberloafing has helped fuel a multi-billion-dollar workplace surveillance industry. Employers, including school districts, have implemented a staggering array of surveillance tools, from monitoring software to closed-circuit cameras to location-based tracking (GPS, RFID, swipe cards, and the soon-to-be ubiquitous iBeacon). There are multiple reasons for such surveillance, of course, particularly in schools; cameras, swipe cards, and other tools are all integral to protecting students and staff. But there is no question that the mix of employee cyberloafing and employer efforts to prevent it has had a toxic effect on workplace morale and employee privacy.

Most teachers have less apparent opportunities to goof around on the internet than other types of employees who spend the bulk of their days on computers. It's enough of a challenge simply to ride herd on 20, 30, or even more students, while at the same time providing meaningful instruction on substantive topics. Nonetheless, a surprising number of teachers find time to surf the web when they are supposed to be working. HR specialists often list cyberloafing as an excellent way to lose a teaching job.

The temptation to cyberloaf can be intense, and it will only strengthen as more of our lives drift into the cloud, and our devices grow steadily "smarter." We all have things that we need to do online, and rarely do we have enough time to get them all done. Smart school districts, like other savvy employers, will develop acceptable use policies that have a little bit of flexibility, to give people the option to spend personal time on the web during lunch or after students have left. That can go a long way towards reducing the temptation to click on "just one more site" while students are supposedly reading or taking a test.

But a cautionary word: Regardless of the precise terms of a district's acceptable use policy, never forget that school administrators can record and review everything you do online using the school's equipment and network. The district IT department may also have deployed alerts to flag visits to inappropriate websites, which will inevitably spark further investigation. Cyberloafing is a cybertrap that is particularly easy to document, in the unfortunate event that parents complain about teacher performance, or worse, student endangerment.

Teacher discipline or termination for lack of productivity or cyberloafing does not generally result in headlines, which makes this cybertrap a little bit more difficult to research than some of the others in this book. Nonetheless, I've collected a few examples of teachers so distracted by the virtual world that they lost track of what was happening in the classroom.

Cautionary Tale 14-2014-England

Most responsible school districts have installed filters and blocklists to help limit the inappropriate use of their networks. Some percentage of students will work hard to figure out how to get around them, but one would expect that teachers would avoid doing so. One would hope even more strongly that a school's IT department would observe the very rules that it is in charge of enforcing.

In October 2014, the Information and Communication Technology (ICT) Manager at Longcroft School and Sixth Form College in Beverly, East Yorkshire, was asked to look at an issue on the computer of Dr. Thelma Geneva Fox, who was working as an IT instructor at the school. During his examination of her computer, the ICT Manager discovered that Fox had installed a Google plug-in that enabled her to bypass the school's network filtering system.

A few months later, the school's headmaster asked the ICT Manager to do a more thorough investigation. His review of the user logs for Fox's network account revealed that on several occasions, Fox had used the Google plug-in to access proxy servers. As a result, the school network could not track and record Fox's online activity.

The National College for Teaching & Leadership (NCTL) held a hearing on Fox's conduct on November 16, 2014. Fox defended herself by saying that she had not purposely installed the Google plug-in on her school computer, claiming that it automatically synced from her home computer when she logged into her personal Google account. (It's not clear if anyone asked why she would need to use a proxy server plug-in on her home computer.) She also said that she only used it to help one student (under supervision) to access a blocked site for homework and so that she could do a quick check about an expected delivery to her home.

The NCTL Board was not convinced that Fox was telling the truth. Moreover, the NCTL said, "It is satisfied that the conduct of Dr Fox in relation to the facts found proven involved breaches of the Teachers' Standards." The panel's findings regarding her efforts to circumvent the school's blocking system offer important discussion topics for all districts and are worth quoting at length:

> The use of a proxy server means that it is not possible to identify what use she did make of the internet via the School on those days, and therein lies the seriousness of the teacher's conduct. A proxy server allows access to any website, including those that have the potential to cause serious harm to the School and its students. It prevents the School from monitoring what use is being made of its IT systems, thereby preventing the School from identifying and addressing any risk of harm to itself or its students. Although there is no evidence of any actual harm resulting in this instance, the panel is satisfied that the deliberate use of a proxy server is capable of causing serious harm. The School's IT systems were set up with restrictions on internet access to safeguard students, and the use of a proxy server has the potential seriously to undermine that objective.

The panel is satisfied that Dr Fox deliberately used the proxy server, and although she says she was not aware that it was wrong to do so, in the panel's view, she should have been aware. She signed the School's IT policy which says that access to offensive or inappropriate sites should always be avoided. The purpose of a proxy server is to enable access to sites that have otherwise been deemed to be offensive or inappropriate, and to prevent that access from being detected. As an IT teacher, Dr Fox would have been fully aware of that, and yet she wilfully and repeatedly used a proxy server.

The NCTL could have struck Fox off from teaching, but because the panel did not find any evidence of actual harm to students or the school, it concluded that an order of prohibition was not necessary.

Top Three Takeaways:

- This cautionary tale can be filed under the heading of "Hoist by One's Own Petard." Every educator should be aware by now that school districts maintain computer logs of network activity, but that fact should be particularly well-known to IT instructors. The reality is that each year, it gets easier for districts to monitor and store records regarding online activity. Most school districts do not monitor the online activity of educators in real-time (apart from flagging inappropriate content). As Fox's case illustrates, however, those records can be retrieved and analyzed if there is an allegation of misconduct, even months later.

- This cautionary tale offers an important reminder: Educators should be aware of the syncing cybertrap. If you log into a browser like Google Chrome or Firefox with your personal account information on a school computer, all of your personal information—web browsing history, bookmarks, passwords, plug-ins and extensions, *etc.*—will automatically sync to the school computer. At the very least, that might be a little embarrassing, depending on your browsing activities. More significantly, it also can be a serious cybersecurity issue if you leave the browser open, and someone copies your banking passwords.

- The fact that Fox used her proxy plug-in several times on the school computer undercut the credibility of her claim that it was an unintentional syncing issue. The same is true of the evidence that she used it to give a student access to a blocked site. As the NCTL Board made manifest, that was the misconduct that raised the gravest concern. A student may have a legitimate academic reason for accessing a particular site; blocking and filtering software typically restrict access to more websites than is necessary. It sets a bad example, however, to simply bypass school filters without discussing the issue with colleagues or supervisors.

Cautionary Tale 14-2009-FL

From one perspective, teachers who surf the web during class time are committing the same offense as any other bored employee; they're not doing the job that they are being paid to do. That alone is sufficient grounds for school districts and school boards to be concerned and to take disciplinary action. But a lack of focus and attention is more dangerous in the classroom than it is in the average office since teachers are responsible for the supervision and well-being of their students.

The 2009 case of Thomas McCoy illustrates the potential dangers. McCoy worked at the Royal Palm Exceptional Center, an alternative school for special needs students in Fort Myers, Florida. While he was supposedly supervising four students, another of the school's employees walked by the classroom and saw a female student performing a sex act on a male student behind a bookcase.

The employee also told district officials that she saw McCoy using a computer with his back to the bookcase. Computer forensic analysis of the computer's browser history showed that at the time the incident between the students took place, McCoy was surfing the ESPN.com website. Six months later, the School Board of Lee County fired him.

Top Three Takeaways:

- Given the steady blurring of work and personal time, this general type of cybertrap probably arises more often than educators would like to admit. Several of the cautionary tales in this book involve educators caught using their devices for non-work-related web surfing. Time-specific events like March Madness or the holiday shopping season intensify the temptation. But educators have an ethical obligation not only to concentrate on work during the school day but in particular, to make sure that they are effectively supervising the students in the classroom. Fortunately, it is probably still quite rare that students will take advantage of a lack of supervision to engage in sexual activity.

- There are at least a couple of ways that the school could have figured out what McCoy was looking at when he was supposed to be supervising students. The first would be to review any network logs maintained by the school that show online activity. Each device connected to a school network is assigned a unique ID so that the system knows where to send data received from the internet; that same ID, however, allows the network to log activity. The second option, which is the one used here, is to examine the information a browser stores on the hard drive while someone is surfing the web. Schools have broad discretion to conduct those types of reviews when the safety of students is at issue.

- Some educators may realize that if they bring a cellular mobile device to school and use that to entertain themselves while students are busy, that eliminates the risk of network logs. That is true; however, it does not eliminate the possibility that the school will still search the device you were using. Schools do need a strong reason to examine your personal device and the search needs to be strictly limited to the reason given. In a case like this, the school could almost certainly justify exploring an educator's browser history, regardless of the ownership of the device.

Cautionary Tale 14-2008-Wales

The case of Sian Mediana, an elementary school teacher at the Fairwater primary school in Cardiff, Wales, offers an excellent example of the lengths some educators will go to mask their cyberloafing. A four-day investigation at the school revealed that Mediana had used her computer to visit a variety of non-work-related websites, including Lloyds.com (banking), eBay, and Friends Reunited (a British social networking site). One of Mediana's teaching assistants, Karen Lawrence, testified at a hearing of the General Teaching Council of Wales and said that her colleague would surf the web 2-3 hours per day.

"If she sold something on eBay," Lawrence said, "we would turn it into activity for the children and take them with us to the Post Office. [Mediana] would also look at financial sites and talk to us about it during work."

Although she resigned from the Fairwater school following the in-house investigation, Mediana strenuously contested the charges at the GTCW hearing, saying that while she did check her bank accounts and purchase school books on eBay, she never did so during school hours. She also suggested that her teaching assistants were simply lying about the amount of time she spent online and that other teachers (including her assistants) might have been responsible for the non-school activity. However, IT specialists found that all of the web activity was specific to Mediana's computer and her password.

Teaching Council solicitor Damian Phillips summed up the evidence by stating that "It is wholly unreasonable to believe other teachers were coming in during teaching hours, logging on to the internet using her computer and her identity."

The General Teaching Council ultimately found Mediana guilty of unprofessional conduct. The Council said, however, that she could return to teaching so long as she only used school computers for professional purposes, and alerted any prospective headmasters of the disciplinary order. In the months following the hearing, however, Mediana was unable to find a new position and told a reporter that she regretted submitting her resignation.

"I should never have resigned," Mediana said, "because I don't think I would have lost my job over this. I was told if I resigned it would all be over with."

Top Three Takeaways:

- It's one thing to spend a good chunk of the workday conducting personal business online; it's another thing altogether to build a field trip for students around your personal errands. It might be possible to imagine some pedagogical benefits to teaching kids about online commerce, but this seems pretty self-serving. At the very least, it suggests that Mediana failed to adhere to the ethical obligation to keep her personal life separate from her professional.

- The media reports don't discuss how this case came to the attention of administrators but there are a couple of different possibilities. First, even a dozen years ago, the network administrator for the school's computer network should have had some type of warning system that would have alerted him or her to Mediana's extensive personal web surfing. Educators who are thinking of conducting personal business during school hours should be cognizant of just how much more sophisticated such systems are these days.

- The second possibility, of course, is that one of Mediana's classroom assistants reported her conduct to administrators (which might, in turn, help explain Mediana's apparent effort to shift blame to them). One of the goals of the MCEE is to prevent these types of classroom cybertraps by first encouraging educators to reflect on their conduct and second, by encouraging an educator's friends and colleagues to raise concerns about potential issues before they become a career-ending problem.

Relevant MCEE Provisions for Chapter 14

Principle I: Responsibility to the Profession

Standards I.A.2, I.A.3, and I.A.5

Principle IV: Responsibility to the School Community

Standard IV.D.3

Principle V: Responsible and Ethical Use of Technology

Standard V.A.5

Sources

The sources for the Cautionary Tales in this chapter can be viewed at the following URL:

https://link.cybertraps.com/C4E2-Sources-Chap14

Chapter 15
Distracted Walking and Driving

Overview

During the summer of 2016, I researched and wrote the third book in my Cybertraps series: *Cybertraps for Expecting Moms & Dads*. One of the topics that I covered in that book— "Death from Digital Distraction and Other Missed Conceptions"—is unfortunately relevant to educators regardless of whether they are expecting a child or someday plan to be.

The nature of this cybertrap is straightforward and entirely predictable: Mobile devices have made us significantly less safe drivers and walkers. In a study published in 2010, University of North Texas Health Science Center researchers Fernando Wilson and Jim Stimpson estimated that between 2001 and 2007, "[d]rivers distracted by talking or texting on cell phones killed an estimated 16,000 people[.]" More recently, the U.S. Department of Transportation for the National Highway Traffic Safety Administration estimated that in 2015, distracted driving caused 3,477 deaths and 391,000 injuries.

Addressing this problem is not that complicated. It should be common sense for all of us to *put our devices away* when we are driving, crossing the street, or even walking down a crowded sidewalk. But as these statistics make clear, far too many of us either think that we are invincible or are simply too addicted to our devices to pay attention to the world around us.

According to the National Conference of State Legislatures, twenty states so far have passed laws making it a crime to use a handheld device while driving. Other states have adopted laws that expressly prohibit school bus drivers or younger drivers from doing so. A smaller but growing number of cities and towns have passed ordinances or regulations that prohibit people from using their mobile devices while in a crosswalk. Others have made physical changes to sidewalks to minimize the risk of injury; in Manchester, UK, for instance, the city marked off special lanes in the city center for people who are using devices while walking.

The first cybertrap that threatens educators, then, is the risk to themselves of physical injury. As is true for any other mobile device user, you significantly increase the risk of harm to yourself or the people around you if you are distracted while driving or walking.

But as the cautionary tales below illustrate, the second cybertrap is even more consequential. Educators and other school employees (like school bus drivers) have a duty of care to students, particularly when transporting or guiding those students on trips outside of the school. It's bad enough if you knock over students because you are staring at your phone as you walk down the hallway; it's immeasurably worse to risk their lives by using a phone when you drive. If you can't put aside your mobile device long enough to make sure your students get from Point A to Point B safely, then you have an ethical duty to defer to someone who can.

Closely related to the duty of care is the obligation to serve as a good role model. Part of the objective of primary and secondary education is to provide students with the tools to function effectively in the adult world. If they see you using your phone in a distracted or dangerous fashion, that increases the possibility that they will do so themselves. Research has shown that using a mobile device behind the wheel is even more dangerous than driving drunk. Still, at any given moment in the United States, several hundred thousand people are using a mobile device while driving. We need to reduce those numbers as much as possible, and school is a great place to start.

Cautionary Tales

Cautionary Tale 15-2019-US_New York

February mornings in New York City tend to be cold, calm, and dark. But the city is never still; the pre-dawn hours are prime time for truck deliveries of every description.

At 5:45 am on February 14, 2019, a 27-year-old teacher named Sarah Foster was crossing 37th Street near Third Avenue when she was struck and killed by an Approved Oil delivery truck turning left onto 37th. Foster was just a block or so away from her apartment on 36th Street. At the time she was struck, Foster was using headphones connected to her phone and was wearing a hoodie that cut down her peripheral vision.

Harrison, who had been teaching middle school in the Harrison Central School District for two and a half years, was declared dead at the scene. The driver, 51-year-old Steven McDermott, "was charged with failure to yield to a pedestrian and failure to exercise due care."

Top Three Takeaways:

- Although Foster's death was not connected in any way with her teaching responsibilities, it is still a valuable cautionary tale for educators. It serves as a reminder that the same physical cybertraps that threaten the general population can affect teachers as well. Not being able to hear (or see) what is happening around you is a real danger. Admittedly, the level of risk varies from location to location, but it never entirely goes away.

- On my daily runs, I frequently see teachers out with students of varying ages, and I am happy to say that I have never seen a teacher wearing headphones while chaperoning students. That would not be quite as dangerous as using a device while driving, but it would still be unsafe and set a terrible example.

- The fact that Foster was a middle school teacher makes this a particularly powerful teachable moment for her students and the others in her school. More and more middle school children are carrying sophisticated and distracting devices. Educators need to be part of their safety ecosystem, helping them to understand both the virtual and physical risks that accompany the use of these devices.

Cautionary Tale 15-2018-US_Virginia

A little after 3 p.m. on March 6, 2018, police responded to an accident on Robious Road near Polo Parkway in Midlothian, Virginia. When they arrived, they discovered that a woman named Kristen Grace Rawls had rear-ended the car in front of her. Rawls, it turned out, was an elementary school teacher at the nearby Bettie Weaver Elementary School, where she had been teaching for seven years.

It did not take police long to figure out what happened. Rawls admitted to the police that she was checking email on her phone when she rear-ended the car in front of her. That is precisely the type of distracted driving that is the subject of this chapter. The AT&T safety slogan says it best: "It Can Wait."

If Rawls's only misconduct had been a moment of distracted driving, she probably would have gotten off with a misdemeanor. But as one officer approached her car, he saw a smashed vodka bottle beside her car. After questioning Rawls about her activity during the day, officers decided to administer a field sobriety test to her, which she failed. Two hours later, the police conducted a breathalyzer test, which registered Rawls's BAC at .23, well above the Virginia limit of .08.

Drinking and drug use are not cybertraps *per se* (both have been issues for centuries before digital technology), but increasingly, we can see instances where these various activities overlap. When people are in an impaired state, they often do not make the best decisions, both online and off. One of the best aspects of the MCEE, I think, is its encouragement to educators to take care of and monitor themselves, and to have the confidence to ask colleagues and supervisors for help before problems arise. A closely-related objective of the MCEE is to give educators the confidence to reach out to a colleague who may be showing signs of emotional strain or substance abuse.

Top Three Takeaways:

- It simply can't be said often enough: "It Can Wait." Studies have repeatedly shown that digital devices are intensely distracting; in fact, the cognitive impairment of digital distractions is more severe than most levels of alcohol consumption. Let's say you take your eyes off the road for five seconds while you pick up your device, unlock it, open your message app, and read the message that just caused your phone to ding. If you are driving at 20 miles per hour, you will travel 150 feet in those five seconds. On the highway, at 60mph, you will travel roughly 440 feet before you look back up from your phone. That's a football field and a half. A lot can happen over that distance.

- Both Apple iOS and the Android operating system are now configured by default to turn off notifications and updates when they detect that you are driving. That's helpful, but since you can override that setting with the push of a button, some driver discipline is still required. Not only do we need more campaigns like "It Can Wait," but we also need both kids *and* adults to absorb the message.

- Rawls initially did the right thing by admitting that she had been distracted when she rear-ended the car in front of her. It would have been a relatively simple matter for the police to make that determination. However, one point that educators should keep in mind is that police do not have the right to examine your phone during a traffic stop or arrest unless they first obtain a warrant from a judge. Before a judge issues a search warrant, the police must list the specific information for which they are looking and where on your phone they expect to find it. They are not allowed to do a general fishing expedition to see what else might be on your phone. Of course, you can consent to a search of your phone, but it is always advisable to speak to an attorney first.

Cautionary Tale 15-2017-US_Oklahoma

Alicia Zodrow, a teacher and athletic coach at the Braggs Public School in Braggs, OK, learned first-hand that cellphones are everywhere these days. In early May 2017, someone posted a video to Facebook that appeared to show Zodrow looking down at something in her lap while driving a school bus. The video caught the attention of a local Tulsa news station, Newson6, which interviewed several concerned parents.

As Superintendent Michael Broyles made clear in a statement released to the press, Zodrow would not be allowed to drive students until the video was verified or disproved:

We were recently made aware of a video circulating online that showed one of our coaches allegedly texting while transporting students on a district school bus.

The safety of our students is of the utmost importance, therefore I am deeply disappointed by the allegations of the driver's disregard for exercising proper precautions while students were in her care.

As a result, we have suspended the coach from bus driving duties without pay pending a full investigation into the matter.

Although there was no formal report regarding the outcome of the investigation, the current web page for the Braggs Wildcats District Staff lists Zodrow as a teacher of K-8 physical education and as a coach for the elementary, junior, and high schools. Presumably, then, the investigation was resolved in her favor.

Top Three Takeaways:

- This cautionary tale is a good reminder that not every allegation is necessarily true, and not every video is dispositive. We are generally predisposed to believe something if we think we've seen it with our own eyes. But the reality is that videos can be just as misleading or downright deceptive as photos. Fraudulent videos are a problem that will steadily get worse, as computer technology makes it increasingly easy to create fake content. The concept of truth is being eroded, quite literally bit by bit.

- We have not, however, quite reached the dystopian endpoint in which nothing is believable, so educators should understand that videos can be and typically are compelling evidence. Every educator needs to continually reflect on the fact that he or she is working in an environment filled with dozens of audio and video recording devices.

- The exact mechanism by which this particular video came to light is a little unclear, and that should always compel caution. According to the local news report, the video was "circulating on Facebook," which prompted the superintendent to take action. As the reporter pointed out, however, the video is not particularly well shot, so it is not possible to see what Zodrow was looking at in her lap. It also is not clear who shot the video or whether there were even any kids on the bus. But as noted, it appears that the superintendent felt that no further action was necessary.

Cautionary Tale 15-2016-US_Florida

There is a lot of compelling television these days—or more accurately, there is a lot of fantastic streaming video, since fewer and fewer people are watching video on televisions any more. The fact that we can watch streaming video now on a wide variety of screens, many of them mobile, creates new risks and cybertraps that can snare unwary individuals.

One of the top shows in this new "Golden Age of Television" was the HBO series "Game of Thrones." Based on George R.R. Martin's sprawling and bloody fantasy, "A Song of Ice and Fire," the show attracted millions of viewers each week. In the summer of 2016, during the middle of Season 6 of the series, 12-year-old Zoe Holden saw her Lee County, Florida school bus driver watching an episode of the series while she was driving. Holden used her smartphone to shoot a video to show her parents.

Her father, Christian Holden, told local news outlets that his daughter had frequently seen the driver watching video while driving and said that on at least one occasion, she ran a red light as a result. Holden said that his daughter had told him about the driver's behavior and that he had tried to talk to someone in the Lee Country transportation department but had no success reaching anyone. His daughter decided to shoot the video so that her dad would have proof of what was going on. Holden added that his daughter is now afraid to take the bus.

News reports did not identify the bus driver by name, but a spokesperson for the Lee County School District said that she had been relieved of her bus driving duties pending an investigation. The spokesperson also said that the district has a firm rule prohibiting the use of any mobile device while driving a school vehicle.

Top Three Takeaways:

- First, we all need to be mindful of the compelling and distracting quality of the content available on our devices. From a safety perspective, one of the worst things that have happened to us is that we can now carry a movie screen, a television, a phone, and an entertainment console in our pocket. Content producers and software companies go to extraordinary lengths to make their material irresistible and addictive. They have succeeded far too well.

- Future investigative journalists are lurking in nearly every classroom and school bus, just waiting for their big break. When you pair that reporting impulse with an instinctual concern for physical safety, it is understandable that a student will have a powerful motivation to make a record of what is happening. Every administrator (and educator) should think about just how easy this all is for kids today.

- Districts should recognize the potential for student action and make sure that they have robust reporting systems that can provide alerts for this type of conduct. As this case illustrates, it is straightforward for the work of a citizen-journalist like Zoe Holden to wind up on the evening news. If the district had made it easier for parents to reach them, however, it might have avoided the notoriety that resulted from Holden's video.

Cautionary Tale 15-2015-US_Minnesota

On October 28, 2015, 79-year-old Joseph Tikalsky was between routes for his part-time retirement job as a bus driver for the New Prague School District in Minnesota. After making a cup of coffee, he went down his driveway and across the street to pick up his morning newspaper. As Tikalsky turned to cross the road back to his home, he was struck and killed by a vehicle driven by Minnesota teacher Susan Ann Russo, then 48. According to the complaint:

> At the time of the collision, 7:35 a.m., conditions were dark and rainy but the "primary" factor in the crash was that "Russo was distracted and not paying attention to the roadway ahead of her due to cellphone use," the Le Sueur County criminal complaint said.
>
> There was no indication she tried to brake before striking Tikalsky.
>
> Le Sueur County Deputy Daniel Tousley said Russo told him she had just read a text from her daughter and was typing a response. "Russo stated that when she looked back up she observed a yellow color blur and that she recognized an impact with the automobile," the complaint said. Reached on her cellphone Monday, Russo declined to comment.

During the summer of 2016, she accepted a plea offer from the local prosecutor and entered a plea of guilty. Interestingly, a forensics examination of her phone failed to reveal any messaging activity before or during the accident. However, trial judge Judge Mark Vandelist denied her motion to set aside her plea, ruling that she should have seen and avoided Tikalsky even if she was not using her phone.

The case attracted headlines in Minnesota during sentencing, thanks to the light punishment Russo received. Judge Vandelist ordered her to serve just four days in prison—two each on the anniversary of Tikalsky's death in 2016 and 2017. Other conditions imposed include two years on probation, a prohibition against active electronic devices in her car, and a prohibition against the use of drugs or alcohol. The judge also ordered Russo to pay a $3,000 fine and perform 40 hours of community service with Minnesotans for Safe Driving.

Judge Vandelist may have been influenced in part by the gracious reaction of Tikalsky's wife of 54 years, Emma Jean Tikalsky, who said that she and her family forgave Russo for the accident. "Four days or 400 days, it really doesn't matter," she said. "I know she didn't mean to kill anyone."

Top Three Takeaways:

- Educators have an ethical obligation to serve as role models for their students. There are few more essential lifestyle lessons right now than teaching new and soon-to-be drivers that they should ignore their phones while driving. As the AT&T campaign so aptly says, "It Can Wait." But teaching kids this simple concept really can't wait, and teachers should be at the forefront of doing so.

- It is interesting that the forensic examination of Russo's phone did not turn up any signs of messaging activity. It may be that Russo had not pressed send before striking Tikalsky, and the draft message was not stored in memory. It would be intriguing, of course, to find out if law enforcement examined her daughter's phone as well. It may be that they didn't feel a need to do so in light of Russo's confession.

- This cautionary tale underscores the need for districts and administrators to include educators in any anti-distraction campaigns that they implement in their schools. Everyone should be crystal clear on the fact that cellphone distraction is a more severe impairment of driving ability than alcohol.

Cautionary Tale 15-2014-US_Texas

Ashley Kelley (née Boehme), a kindergarten teacher in Beaumont, Texas, nearly died in a distracted driving accident in March 2014. As she was driving one afternoon, she tried to text a friend a photo. Kelley lost control of her car, sideswiped a chainlink fence, and slammed into a metal pole. The pole crashed through the windshield onto her head and face, causing extensive injuries.

As Kelley later told the Texas "Just Drive!" campaign, she was lucky to be alive. Her doctors said that if the pole had struck her head just a millimeter to the right or the left, she would have died instantly. As it was, Kelley suffered numerous severe injuries, "including a spinal fluid leak, a blow out to her left eye socket, bone fragments in the optic nerve, and broken nose, cheek and jaw bones."

Despite the severity of her injuries, Kelley has mostly made a full recovery (although she has some lingering vision and memory issues). She married her fiancé Brandon Kelley in November 2014 and has continued her work as a kindergarten teacher in Beaumont. She has also become an outspoken activist on the issue of texting and driving:

I'm lucky to be alive, but my life has dramatically changed. I was in a lot of pain and it's been really difficult. Before, messages of "no texting" never fazed me. I always thought, "it's never going to happen to me." Now I tell people, if you don't do it for yourself, think about how your family and friends are affected by your decision to text and drive.

Top Three Takeaways:

- Kelley is extraordinarily lucky to have survived her crash. In 2014, the year of Kelley's accident, the National Highway Traffic Safety Administration reported that 3,179 people died in accidents involving distracted drivers. By 2018, the number of victims had increased almost 50%, to 4,637 deaths. That is a tragic and unnecessary loss of life that we should all be working to prevent.

- Kelley's crash didn't have anything to do with her teaching duties *per se*. Nonetheless, as an educator, she should serve as a role model for the students in her community. To her credit, she has tried to use her unfortunate experience as a teaching tool for children across the state of Texas. It's a harrowing way to become a positive example.

- You don't need to go through a life-threatening accident to be aware of the risks of using digital devices while driving. Promoting awareness of this issue and helping students to make better decisions is squarely within the ethical precept of protecting the health and safety of all students.

Cautionary Tale 15-2013-US_Florida

At the beginning of the school year in 2013, a concerned parent tipped off an NBC affiliate in Lee County, Florida, that a school bus driver was using her cellphone to text while transporting children. NBC2 investigator Dave Elias and his camera crew followed the unnamed driver for two days, shooting video of her from a variety of angles. He observed her using an earphone cord to talk on her iPhone but also periodically looking down to read and send texts. Elias also reported that the driver often made abrupt lane changes and sometimes left her turn signal on for miles at a time.

The video shot by the news crew upset both parents and school administrators. Assistant Superintendent Dr. Greg Adkins told NBC2 that the school district had equipped all of the district's buses with surveillance cameras that let administrators review potentially dangerous situations. After a review of the recorded video verified the news report, the school district promptly fired the bus driver.

Additional research by NBC2 determined that at the time, Florida was one of 21 states around the country without a law prohibiting the use of cellphones by on-duty bus drivers. However, Lee County was able to take action against the driver because it had previously adopted a local policy prohibiting such conduct.

The bus driver's dangerous behavior put the students in a tight spot. Several told Elias that they had observed the driver's conduct from the moment they got on the bus, but weren't sure that they should say anything. Thanks to their own driver's ed classes, though, they knew it was something that she shouldn't be doing. The school district obviously agreed.

Top Three Takeaways:

- Here's a cautionary tale in which the school district received video evidence from not one, not two, but three different sources. It seems like everyone has a camera today, and that is generally true. But educators should be aware that as comprehensive as video surveillance may feel today, it is merely the tip of the surveillance iceberg that is rushing towards us all.

- This cautionary tale is a perfect example of the role that school district surveillance video typically plays in employment cases. No one in the Lee County school district was reviewing school bus footage in real-time. But the instant that a potential problem occurred, the school had footage that it could review to assess the situation. Districts will be under increasing pressure, chiefly from litigation, to do more and more real-time evaluation of surveillance video.

- This cautionary tale illustrates the importance of state and local leadership on cybertraps issues. It's quite remarkable that nearly half the states in the country do not have laws that prohibit bus drivers from using cellphones while they drive. That seems like a basic level of student protection that every state should adopt. It is arguable that under the MCEE, both administrators and individual educators have an ethical duty to advocate for these types of necessary safety measures.

Relevant MCEE Provisions for Chapter 15

Principle I: Responsibility to the Profession

Standards I.A.4 and I.A.5

Principle II: Responsibility for Professional Competence

Standard II.C.3

Principle III: Responsibility to Students

Standard III.B.3

Principle V: Responsible and Ethical Use of Technology

Standard V.A.5

Sources

The sources for the Cautionary Tales in this chapter can be viewed at the following URL:

https://link.cybertraps.com/C4E2-Sources-Chap15

Chapter 16

Creation of a Hostile Work Environment

Overview

No one can seriously argue that hostile work environments are merely an unfortunate byproduct of the internet era. Workplaces have been casually oppressive or actively hostile for women and minorities for decades, long before the rise of social media memes and emailed "jokes."

Fortunately, there has been some progress. The adoption of the Civil Rights Act of 1964 was a significant moment, as was the passage of the Age Discrimination Act of 1967 and the Americans with Disabilities Act of 1990. To varying degrees, these federal statutes have helped establish basic standards of workplace conduct, both vertically—between supervisors and employees—and horizontally—among workplace colleagues.

But the discriminatory attitudes and practices of the three-martini lunch era have not wholly disappeared. In the age of increasingly powerful digital devices and ubiquitous social media, a hostile work environment can be created and perpetuated far faster than ever before. In fact, some of the contemporary forms of harassment (particularly voyeuristic photos) would not be practical but for the remarkable development of camera-equipped smartphones.

What Is a Hostile Work Environment?

A typical "hostile work environment" claim by an employee is based on allegations of targeted harassment by a co-worker or supervisor. The U.S. Equal Employment Opportunity Commission (EEOC) defines "harassment" as follows:

> Harassment is a form of employment discrimination that violates Title VII of the Civil Rights Act of 1964, the Age Discrimination in Employment Act of 1967, (ADEA), and the Americans with Disabilities Act of 1990, (ADA).

Harassment is unwelcome conduct that is based on race, color, religion, sex (including pregnancy), national origin, age (40 or older), disability or genetic information. Harassment becomes unlawful when 1) enduring the offensive conduct becomes a condition of continued employment, or 2) the conduct is severe or pervasive enough to create a work environment that a reasonable person would consider intimidating, hostile, or abusive. Anti-discrimination laws also prohibit harassment against individuals in retaliation for filing a discrimination charge, testifying, or participating in any way in an investigation, proceeding, or lawsuit under these laws; or opposing employment practices that they reasonably believe discriminate against individuals, in violation of these laws.

Petty slights, annoyances, and isolated incidents (unless extremely serious) will not rise to the level of illegality. To be unlawful, the conduct must create a work environment that would be intimidating, hostile, or offensive to reasonable people.

Offensive conduct may include, but is not limited to, offensive jokes, slurs, epithets or name calling, physical assaults or threats, intimidation, ridicule or mockery, insults or put-downs, offensive objects or pictures, and interference with work performance.

The National Education Association, the largest teacher's union in the United States, has drafted model contract language that contains the following definition of "harassment":

Harassment/intimidation exists if an individual or group: directs personal insults (whether transmitted in writing, orally, or by electronic means) that are likely to incite an immediate adverse response from the person(s) being addressed; threatens the employee with physical harm or actually harms a person; damages, defaces or destroys private property of any person; commits an act of harassment or intimidation (as defined by statute); [or] places a person in position of feeling at risk of emotional or psychological harm.

The most common basis for a "hostile work environment" claim is sexual harassment, followed closely by harassment based on race, sexual preference, and gender orientation/expression. Although the underlying behaviors have existed for millennia, the legal concept of "sexual harassment" began to emerge in the early to mid-1970s, as an outgrowth of the civil rights and feminist movements.

The term exploded into the public consciousness in 1991, when the U.S. Senate Judiciary Committee called Anita Hill as a witness during the Supreme Court confirmation hearing of Clarence Thomas. During televised testimony on October 11, 1991, she alleged that Thomas had engaged in long-running and persistent sexual harassment of her while she served as his deputy at the U.S. Department of Education's Office of Civil Rights in 1981 and 1982. Her claims were undercut in part by the fact that when Thomas became chairman of (ironically) the EEOC, she went with him and served as his assistant for another year.

A recent survey by the National Association of Superintendents Union of Women Teachers in the United Kingdom underscores the extent to which bullying and sexual harassment remain rampant problems for educators. Among the study's findings:

- 81% of teachers report experiencing bullying or sexual harassment at work;

- 20% of teachers reported sexual harassment by "a colleague, manager, parent or pupil since becoming a teacher"

Among those who reported having been sexually harassed:

- 30% reported unwanted touching;

- 67% reported "inappropriate comments about their appearance or body";

- 51% reported undesirable or inappropriate comments about sex;

- 21% reported being propositioned for sex; and

- 3% reported being the victim of voyeuristic photos (upskirt or downblouse).

Things may be changing. In February 2020, the powerful movie mogul Harvey Weinstein was convicted on two charges of rape in a New York courtroom. His prosecution was spurred in part by the intense anger and activism of the #MeToo movement. (The phrase "Me Too" was first promoted by sexual harassment survivor Tarana Burke on MySpace in 2006 and went viral in October 2017 when it was used on Twitter by the actress Alyssa Milano.) The #MeToo movement has undoubtedly raised awareness of the ongoing problem of sexual harassment in the workplace (and to a lesser degree, other types of targeted harassment). At the same time, of course, it has also sparked various forms of backlash. It will be some time before we know how long-lasting and deep-seated any #MeToo-related reforms will be.

What Should Teachers Do If They Are Experiencing a Hostile Work Environment?

Coping with workplace harassment or a hostile work environment can be very challenging. Depending on the culture of your school or workplace, it may be challenging to have your concerns taken seriously. It may be that the harasser is your immediate supervisor or a person of importance within the organization. You may feel economically vulnerable and concerned about possible retaliation. These are all legitimate concerns.

However, you should know that there are a variety of different resources available to assist you.

For starters, your school district should have a policy in place that addresses workplace harassment (if it doesn't, then that is an important issue to raise with your HR department, your superintendent, or your school board). The specifics of that policy will vary from district to district, of course, but the basic parameters are relatively common:

- Is it possible to resolve the conflict by raising concerns directly with the other person? (*see* Standards IV.B.2 and IV.B.8 below);

- If not, then the policy usually defines a process for filing a complaint within the district with human resources or some other designated individual;

- The policy will also spell out the process for investigating a complaint of workplace harassment; and

- Retaliation against someone for filing a complaint is usually prohibited.

If you find that the resolution of your complaint by your district is inadequate or unsatisfactory, there may be additional remedies available to you under state and federal law. Most (but not all) states have an agency dedicated to the enforcement of human rights and anti-discrimination statutes or regulations. Typically, you are required to seek relief from the administrative agency before you can file a lawsuit under state law.

The requirements exist at the federal level. If you are thinking about filing a lawsuit that seeks damages for harassment or discrimination under federal law, you are required first to file a claim with the U.S. Equal Employment Opportunity Commission (www.eeoc.gov). If you fail to exhaust your administrative remedies first, the court will dismiss your lawsuit.

Filing a claim with the EEOC triggers an automatic notice to your employer and an administrative review of the circumstances of the alleged harassment or discrimination. There are a variety of possible outcomes: dismissal of your claim, a formal investigation by the EEOC, a recommendation for mediation or dispute resolution, or the initiation of a lawsuit by the EEOC against your employer. (The last action is very uncommon.)

Once the EEOC has taken all of the intermediate steps it feels are appropriate (and assuming it does not dismiss your claim), the agency will issue what is known as a "right to sue" letter. That gives you legal authority to file a lawsuit against your employer and any other individuals who may be liable for the harassment or discrimination.

Given the importance of EEOC review of your claims and the multiple deadlines involved, it is highly advisable to consult with an attorney as soon as possible when seeking relief for workplace harassment or discrimination.

Cautionary Tales

Cautionary Tale 16-2019-US_New Jersey

As I pointed out in the overview, the EEOC makes it clear (based on various U.S. Supreme Court cases) that federal law does not provide relief for "[p]etty slights, annoyances, and isolated instances" of harassment or discrimination. In many harassment or discrimination cases, the main challenge is determining whether the defendant's behavior is a relatively minor transgression of workplace or social norms, or is conduct that represents a more severe pattern of behavior.

Here's a cautionary tale that is at the more trivial end of the scale. In late 2019, Sham Bacchus, the principal of School 8 in Paterson, NJ, sent out an email with a "meme" attached that read: "As a teacher, you need to leave your family problems at HOME. Don't bring your attitude to your students, it'll only make your day worse."

There is no indication that Bacchus attached his warning to an inappropriate image or video (as is often the case with memes). Nonetheless, the Paterson teachers took grave exception to the email and accused Bacchus of creating a "hostile work environment" with his comment. Union President John McEntee Jr. said that he was "shocked and appalled" by Bacchus's suggestion that Paterson teachers were not entirely focused on the needs of their students.

The union began planning a protest but canceled the event after Superintendent Eileen Schafer quickly intervened. At her request, Bacchus issued an apology for distributing his comment and agreed that he would participate in "sensitivity training."

If the email sent out by Bacchus consisted of nothing more than the quoted sentences, there is a legitimate case to be made that the union overreacted here. The Model Code of Ethics for Educators contains a standard that urges educators to think about the state of their personal physical and emotional health and how it can affect their obligations to their students. Standard I.A.4 reads:

[The professional educator demonstrates responsibility to oneself as an ethical professional by:] Monitoring and maintaining sound mental, physical, and emotional health necessary to perform duties and services of any professional assignment; and taking appropriate measures when personal or health-related issues may interfere with work-related duties

It is not inherently unreasonable for a school principal to remind educators of this basic ethical obligation.

Top Three Takeaways:

- It is reasonable to consider whether this situation could have been handled better from the outset. For instance, if Bacchus had specific concerns about how teachers were behaving in the classroom, perhaps he could have sat down with his superintendent and the union president to craft a more empathetic message. Similarly, if he thought a particular teacher had emotional issues that were interfering with his or her job, he could have taken that educator aside and discussed the circumstances with him or her.

- The next issue is whether Bacchus needs some remedial work on what constitutes a professional communication style. The fact is that memes are dangerous. Memes are intellectual shortcuts. They lull you into thinking that you are funnier than you are. In the right circumstances, they can be very amusing to read and share, but they are rarely if ever appropriate for professional communication. There are simply too many ways the careless use of memes can cause offense and hurt feelings.

- In any situation involving digital communication, there will be issues of nuance and context that don't translate correctly to the written word (which is one of the reasons that emojis are so popular). Thanks to the remarkable speed of our devices and the internet, it is now possible to insult or upset people faster than ever before. Effective leadership, whether in the front office or the classroom, requires us to slow down and think not only about what we are saying but how we are saying it.

Cautionary Tale 16-2019-Japan

In the fall of 2019, a significant bullying scandal erupted at the Higashi-suma Elementary School in central Kobe, Japan. For a year, four teachers systematically bullied a younger colleague (the perpetrators were in their 30s and 40s, while the victim was in his 20s). According to a report in Japan's national daily, *The Mainichi*, the emotional toll of the bullying was so enormous that the victim was unable to keep working. When the news broke, the school suspended the four teachers named in the complaint without pay.

The bullies allegedly committed a variety of physical, verbal, and electronic assaults on their victim, including:

- Calling him derogatory names;

- Damaging his car;

- Locking his smartphone;

- Forcing him to send obscene text messages to female colleagues;

- Striking him with the core of a printer paper roll with enough force to leave marks; and

- Restraining his arms and forcing him to eat extremely spicy curry.

The bullied teacher filed a victim's report with the Hyogo Prefectural Police, which listed roughly 50 different types of abusive behavior. His lawyer told members of the press that the principal of the elementary school had urged the teacher to deny the harassment. The principle denied making any such request.

The city's education board launched an investigation. The Board determined that the school's principal and vice-principal not only knew about the harassment but had also verified the events with the victim.

"However," *The Mainichi* reported, "they covered up the violence in a report submitted to the education board in July, summarizing the case as 'some excessive teasing among the teaching staff.'"

The investigation also revealed an extensive history of educator misconduct at the school, leading Kobe Mayor Kizo Hisamoto to criticize by the school and the education board. "I'm infuriated," Hisamoto said. "The education board's governance is lacking." Responding to angry complaints by school parents, Hisamoto promised to hire outside experts to conduct a more thorough investigation and make recommendations.

The outside experts completed their report in February 2020 and determined that the four older teachers had been responsible for "a total of 123 forms of harassment against four colleagues." The two worst offenders—Shun Shitomi, 34, and Yusuke Shibata, 34—were both fired. A three-month suspension was handed out to the female teacher and one former administrator, while the third male teacher and the school's current principal both had their salaries docked by 10% for three months.

Top Three Takeaways:

- While some of the circumstances of this cautionary tale may flow from specific aspects of Japanese culture, there are lessons here for teachers around the world. The first and foremost of these is the extent to which electronic devices are part of our lives and the myriad ways in which someone can use them to engage in workplace harassment. The malicious locking of a colleague's smartphone, for instance, or forcing someone to send inappropriate text messages are acts that could take place anywhere (but obviously shouldn't). As we rely on these devices more and more, the potential vectors for cyberharassment steadily increase.

- That puts a premium on school administrators and building leaders to monitor staff behavior and take steps to prevent or stop any harassment that is occurring. In this case, it is quite remarkable that so many instances of harassment were allowed to happen. It is particularly disturbing that school administrators did not do more to prevent the sending of inappropriate or obscene text messages to female teachers.

- As we have learned in the recent history of U.S. politics, a cover-up only makes things worse. Administrators cannot expect ethical behavior from educators if they are not demonstrating it themselves. Mayor Hisamoto deserves some credit for stepping in to try to control the situation but left unanswered (so far) is what action, if any, has been taken against the school board or the school administrators.

Cautionary Tale 16-2019-US_Florida

A lawsuit filed in June 2019 contained explosive charges of sexual harassment by Manatee School of Arts and Sciences (MSAS) principal Richard Ramsay. Also named as defendants were Linda Brand, the registrar of MSAS; her husband Jim Brand, who served as president of the MSAS governing board; and MSAS itself (a public charter school located in Palmetto, Florida).

The plaintiffs, three MSAS teachers named Geena Gregory, Morgan Lane, and Dao Tran, allege in their 38-page complaint that Ramsay subjected them to a variety of targeted sexual and racial harassment. As the local newspaper, the *Brandenton Herald*, put it, "[t]he lawsuit included dozens of text messages and in-person statements allegedly made by Ramsay—most too vulgar to report in the *Bradenton Herald*." Many of the text messages the newspaper was unwilling to reproduce also contained images with crude sexual innuendo.

Here are some examples of some of the milder comments reproduced in the complaint:

- "Ramsay would frequently ask Ms. Gregory to 'hook him up' with her friends, specifically referring to sexual encounter requests";

- "Upon Ms. Gregory's acceptance of the gifted and talented teacher position during the winter/spring semester of 2016, Ramsay made comments to Ms. Gregory that now that she would be teaching upper level grades, the older boys would not be able to get out of their chairs; inferring students' sexual thoughts about Ms. Gregory."

- "MSAS would have popsicle days during the warmer weather months and Ramsay would repeatedly make comments to Ms. Gregory about how Ms. Lane would eat her popsicle, referring to an inappropriate sexual act."

- [to Morgan Lane] "Since you're wearing a short dress again, John and I want to know what time the show is starting" [winking face with tongue emoji]

- [to Morgan Lane] "I'm going to keep the dirty comments about you and your sister to myself. Lol. FYI. .. it's a real struggle."

- [to Morgan Lane] "Nice boobs."

The complaint further alleges that after the three teachers reported Ramsay's conduct to the MSAS board, "Ramsay issued notices of non-compliance to four teachers, three of whom were the Plaintiffs in the instant action, concerning their alleged failure to submit report cards on time." Ramsay fired all three of the plaintiffs with no warning in the spring of 2018.

Ramsay and the other defendants have denied the allegations in the complaint. The court scheduled an initial hearing on motions to dismiss for the spring of 2020.

Top Three Takeaways:

- The most obvious takeaway from this cautionary tale is the fact that these types of comments were wildly inappropriate for a professional workplace. An individual making such comments, particularly with supervisory authority, either needs substantial training on issues of misogyny and sexism or should be fired.

- Since there are numerous screenshots of the texts and images in question, there is little dispute that Ramsay made the challenged comments. That is an important reminder for every educator and administrator: If you engage in cyberharassment, it is a straightforward matter for the victim to capture and retain your messages as potential evidence. It is sometimes possible to challenge the introduction of electronic evidence at trial. In general, however, the widespread use of digital devices has made it significantly easier for victims to document this type of misconduct. It is amazing that so many people so easily forget that if you digitize something, it can be copied and preserved in an endless number of ways.

- The liability of the school and its board members will turn on whether the board was aware of Ramsay's harassing behavior and allowed it to continue. Given the fact that much of the relevant evidence is marked with timestamps, that should not be a particularly tricky question to resolve. Whether Ramsey fired the plaintiffs in retaliation for making complaints about the harassment is a slightly more challenging issue.

Cautionary Tale 16-2010-US_New York

A particularly good example of the influential role of electronics in modern-day hostile workplace cases occurred about a decade ago in the Chippewa Falls School District in upstate New York. In January 2010, a fellow teacher filed a workplace harassment complaint against fifth-grade teacher Elizabeth McElhenny, alleging that McElhenny had "target[ed] students, staff, and administration in an ongoing aggressive and belligerent effort to control and undermine the operations of Hillcrest Elementary School that spans back several years[.]"

The school district promptly launched an investigation into McElhenny's conduct during the preceding year and issued a report of its findings at the end of August 2010. Among other things, the report concluded that the amount of time that McElhenny spent using the District email system was "excessive and inappropriate."

Investigators concluded that over 169 class days from January 2009 to January 2010, McElhenny sent 3,811 emails or an average of 23 per day. Based on the timestamp associated with each email, the District was able to determine that McElhenny spent a total of 38 hours of class time and 19 hours of prep time using email (based on a highly conservative estimate of 1 minute per email).

But while the amount of time McElhenny spent emailing was a productivity concern, the real issue was what she was writing to fellow teachers. In a summary article for *The Chippewa Herald*, reporter Liz Hochstedler cited numerous examples of McElhenny's inappropriate messages:

- She alluded to alcohol as "water," and often said that she "had too much 'water' last night."

- She used the abbreviations "praz" and "vico" to refer to the prescription drugs Alprazolam and

- Vicodin, and wrote about her usage frequently. In one typical example, McElhenny wrote: "i could tell my 4:30t this morning that it was going to be THAT KIND OF DAY 1/2 praz every 3 hours started at 7:10 this morning and will continue taking a nibble of my magic relaxing potion every 3 hours."

- She used a long list of epithets for co-workers, including: "cult members," "nutjob," "crabbypants," "cuckoo woman" and "Nazi aides."

- She regaled her co-workers with descriptions of various sexual encounters.

- She frequently referred to students and parents in demeaning ways. For example, she wrote in one email: "could that student possibly be [student initials removed]? I am very familiar with that THING and also with his mother THING 2 He is the first person that comes to mind... ... Do not allow him to SUCK THE LIFE OUT OF YOU!"

McElhenny had some basic understanding that her email correspondence might be a problem; she was worried about the risk of using school email for inappropriate conversations and frequently asked colleagues to destroy the emails that she sent. However, she didn't have a useful grasp of computer forensics or the durability of digital information. Given the fact that school districts are required to maintain staff communications in most states under public records laws, it's not surprising that district investigators had little trouble recreating McElhenny's exhaustive and somewhat scandalous email correspondence.

Shortly before the investigatory report was released, McElhenny resigned from the Chippewa Falls School District. At the same time, she filed a lawsuit seeking an injunction against the release of the report but withdrew her claim the following day. A few months later, McElhenny announced her candidacy for a position on the Chippewa Falls School Board but dropped out of the race shortly before the April 2011 election. Fittingly, she announced her withdrawal in an email to supporters and the media.

"This past year or so has been very difficult for me and hard on my family," McElhenny said in her statement. "Personal aspects of my private and professional life have been made public in some media condemning me for being human." She said that her goal was to get her life "back to normal."

"I will not be able to do that," she said, "if I run for the school board and am elected, especially if I will have to butt philosophical heads with people who have little understanding of the complexity of issues that are truly important to running a school district effectively."

Top Three Takeaways:

- From an investigative and computer forensics perspective, this is quite a remarkable cautionary tale. Few cases I've researched have produced so much evidence. First and foremost, of course, is the time management analysis conducted by the district investigators. It must have taken hours to determine when McElhenny sent each of her emails; when investigators completed their report, however, it painted a devastating picture of what she was doing in the classroom.

- This cautionary tale is an excellent example of what I refer to as selfie-incrimination. The contents of the emails that McElhenny herself wrote and sent made it clear that she was acting in myriad unprofessional ways. Had she not resigned, there is little doubt that the school board would have felt compelled to fire her.

- This cautionary tale also illustrates why there is a growing concern in education circles about the phenomenon of teacher-on-teacher bullying and cyberbullying. Just as with kids, the increase in the number of mobile devices used by educators parallels this rise in not-so-collegial behavior. The perception of anonymity (however flawed) and the ability to harass someone without physical confrontation help lure adults into many of the same cybertraps that snare children. That McElhenny thought she could berate her colleagues without even the pretense of anonymity makes this cautionary tale particularly inexplicable.

Relevant MCEE Provisions for Chapter 16

Principle I: Responsibility to the Profession

Standards I.A.2, I.A.3, I.A.5, I.B.3, and I.B.4

Principle III: Responsibility to Students

Standard III.B.3

Principle IV: Responsibility to the School Community

Standards IV.B.1, IV.B.2, IV.B.4, IV.B.8, and IV.D.3

Principle V: Responsible and Ethical Use of Technology

Standards V.A.1 and V.A.5

Sources

The sources for the Cautionary Tales in this chapter can be viewed at the following URL:

https://link.cybertraps.com/C4E2-Sources-Chap16

Chapter 17

Never a Good Idea: Pornography in the Classroom

Accessing Inappropriate Content on School Property

My first book, *Obscene Profits: The Entrepreneurs of Pornography in the Cyber Age* (Routledge 2000), was published twenty years ago and was the first comprehensive look at the rise of the online adult entertainment industry. There were two trends that I identified in that book that continue to challenge schools and school districts today: employees accessing adult sites during the workday and the broader cultural changes driven in part by the online adult industry's commercial success.

By the late 1990s and the early 2000s, many employers were beginning to appreciate the economic potential of the internet. But as I did my research for *Obscene Profits* and then for *The Naked Employee* (2003), it quickly became apparent that employee access of online adult materials in the workplace had become a significant productivity concern. Online adult websites were proving to be a powerful temptation for some employees, mainly since businesses back then typically had much faster internet connections than workers could get at home. I interviewed several adult webmasters who said that they could watch the opening of businesses across the country based on the usage statistics of their sites. They also laughed about the fact that it was easy to see that some employees spent hours on their websites during the workday.

In response, employers began installing increasingly powerful software to monitor employee web surfing habits (which was part of the inspiration for *The Naked Employee*). Two decades later, it's not clear how successful computer surveillance has been in preventing on-the-job porn surfing. In September 2013, for instance, a survey done in the United Kingdom of nearly 4,000 businesses by the employment law firm Peninsula Business Services found that two-thirds of the companies had caught someone looking at porn on the job during the previous year. That was double the rate in 2008. Studies that rely on self-reporting suggest that somewhere between three and twenty-eight percent of American workers access pornography at work.

In theory, your district's filtering and monitoring software (as well as acceptable use policies) should discourage efforts to access adult content on school computer equipment, either on campus or off. The reality, however, is that some people will still try to do so, and no one yet has written software that can do a perfect job of blocking all objectionable websites.

Any educator who tries to access adult materials during school hours, especially when students are around, is behaving unethically and is risking his or her teaching career. At the very least, the educator is almost certainly violating school and district policy; if not, then there is something seriously wrong with the district's policy-making process. Also, he or she may be violating state law, particularly if he or she exposes a child to something defined under state law as "harmful to minors."

These risks are not limited to a school district's licensed educators. If a school employee's preferred form of cyberloafing involves visiting adult websites, then his or her school district may face a hostile work environment claim from other employees if they see the inappropriate content.

In the most common scenario, an employee creates a hostile work environment by purposely sharing sexually explicit material with another, typically as a form of bullying or harassment. The perpetrator may show the victim content that has been opened in a browser or by sending inappropriate materials via email or other types of messaging.

Another significant risk of accessing adult websites is the possibility of viral infection. An efficient IT department will take steps to protect the school district's network and individual devices from malware of various types. It can be difficult, however, to successfully defend electronic resources from all of the threats posed by accessing dodgy sites. If a district network does become infected, the potential consequences are wide-ranging: financial losses, identity theft, digital vandalism, ransomware, data scraping, and so on. It can't be stressed enough that using school equipment to visit adult websites is not merely an ethical lapse; it's also a profound cybersecurity breach.

You Showed That to My Child⁇!

The impact of the second trend—the broader cultural shift that's taken place over the last few decades (some portion of which stems from the online adult industry)—may be harder to quantify but is no less significant. It is unquestionably true that children of virtually all ages have much more extensive access to sexually-oriented and sexually explicit materials than at any previous time in American history. Much of that is obviously due to the enormous amount of adult materials that are available online. Equally significant, however, is the fact that so many children have access to computers and smart devices at younger and younger ages. Far too often, they are allowed to use those devices with little or no parental or guardian supervision.

We are only beginning to study and understand the developmental impact of this dramatic shift in the sexual education of our children. The studies done so far have not reached a consistent conclusion about whether this shift is good, bad, or neutral; you can find one to support whatever your assumption may be. It will be interesting to see how that research evolves.

One thing that does remain clear, however, is that the proliferation of adult content online and child access to it has changed much faster than school or parental attitudes. There is still strong resistance to formal discussions of pornography or sexuality in K-12 education (except in tightly limited instances), despite overwhelming evidence that children have extensive informal access to it. Parents and schools should play a central role in contextualizing what children see online, from disinformation to hate speech to pornography. It may take some time, however, before we are socially, culturally, and politically prepared to do so.

What this means in practical terms, as a couple of the cautionary tales below illustrate, is that teachers who show sexually explicit or provocative content to students run the risk of significant pushback and complaint from parents and possible disciplinary action by administrators.

Cautionary Tales

Cautionary Tale 17-2019-Scotland

In 2008, Israeli director Ari Folman released an animated war documentary film called *Waltzing with Bashir.* It was a stark and unflinching retelling of Forman's efforts to recover memories of his service as an Israeli soldier in the 1982 Lebanon war. The film was both an economic and critical success, winning numerous awards around the world, including a Golden Globe for Best Foreign Language Film. Twelve years after its release, it has a 96% positive rating among critics on *RottenTomatoes.com* and an audience rating nearly as high (91%). By any reasonable measure, it is a significant and influential piece of work.

It is also a work, as you might infer, that deals with difficult and painful topics through creative filmmaking and provocative imagery. The visuals are sufficiently disturbing that the film was given an '18' rating by the British Board of Film Classification, which the BBFC defines as "only suitable for adults." *Newsweek* movie reviewer David Ansen's summary of the movie's dramatic content helps explain its rating:

> The images of war that Folman and his chief illustrator, David Polonsky, conjure up have a feverish, infernal beauty. Dreams and reality jumble together. One surviving soldier fantasizes being carried across the sea riding the breast of a giant naked woman while, in reality, his fellow Israelis die in flames as their boat is bombed. Another soldier, under a hail of sniper fire, waltzes into the middle of the street, surrounded by posters of the assassinated Lebanese President-elect Bashir Gemayel, his machine gun spewing nonstop bullets in a defiant denial of death. These depictions of the dementia of war have a hallucinatory power that can stand alongside those of "Apocalypse Now."

Given those descriptions, this is a challenging piece of art that requires maturity on the part of the viewer and ample context if used as part of a school program. It's understandable, then, that when a Scottish teacher showed a portion of *Waltzing with Bashir* to an after-school group of students (some as young as 12) in December 2017, several parents were upset.

The teacher in question was Jonathan Guetta, a teacher of Hebrew at the Mearns Castle High School in Newton Mearns, East Renfrewshire (an affluent suburban community about seven miles SSW of Glasgow center). He was fired by the East Renfrewshire Council in May 2018 because he "exposed[ed] pupils to inappropriate, upsetting material, allow[ed] them access to pornographic material, and fail[ed] to seek parental consent." In support of its decision, the Council noted that even following parental complaints, Guetta shared a link to the movie with a 16-year-old student.

Following his termination, Guetta filed a complaint with the Glasgow Employment Tribunal, arguing that the Council had been anti-Semitic in its handling of his case. He told the Tribunal that he only showed the first 20 minutes of the 90-minute film and that he stood in front of the screen to block students from seeing any inappropriate content.

The Tribunal ruled, however, that the Council had not acted with prejudice towards Guetta. In ruling that his dismissal was "not wholly disproportionate in the circumstances given," the Tribunal noted that Guetta failed to provide the students with any of the information necessary to understand and process what they were viewing:

> The claimant did not provide any historical or political context to the film and the relationship between the Arab-Israeli people in the area in September 1982.

> "Furthermore no evidence was presented that the claimant provided any form of unbiased account of the moral perspectives of the protagonists of the film - the Israeli Defence Force, Lebanese Phalangists or the Muslin refugees."

Following his sacking at Mearns Castle High School, Guetta was hired at another unnamed school. Efforts to reach him were unsuccessful.

Top Three Takeaways:

- If you are reading the MCEE for guidance about whether or not you should show a movie like *Waltzing with Bashir* to young students, you will be disappointed. The goal of the MCEE is not to dictate specific outcomes but to provide a process for weighing competing ethical concerns to reach the best decision in a particular situation, taking into account a wide range of factors. This case presents several questions. Did Guetta discuss his choice of the film with any of his colleagues or his administrators? Did Guetta take into account the potential harm to his students? Did Guetta consider the impact of the film's sexuality, politics, or violence? Guetta was aware of some possible damage, insofar as he attempted to block them from seeing objectionable material, but that seems like it was an *ad hoc* decision and not the result of a deliberative process that engaged other educators in the school.

- Given the imagery in the film and the challenging psychological and political issues it addresses, it is quite remarkable that Guetta did not ask for parental consent before showing it. There are very few situations in which the need to share something controversial with students is so imperative that a teacher can't notify parents ahead of time. There is nothing that suggests that this was such a situation. Moreover, Guetta's decision to share a link to the film with an underage student even after parental complaints was reckless.

- The school's use of the phrase "pornographic material" to describe this widely acclaimed film is not accurate and not particularly helpful for this discussion. It is quite doubtful that Folman chose the film's imagery to stimulate sexual excitement. It would be more accurate for the school to have used the phrase "age-inappropriate," since that would correctly emphasize Guetta's decision-making process rather than a blanket description of the film. It is certainly possible to imagine situations in which it would be appropriate to show the film to a class of students, even though it contains some animated nudity.

Cautionary Tale 17-2019-Scotland

For several months in the fall of 2016, Claire Thompson received repeated requests from students to show YouTube videos on the smart screen at the end of her Higher Chemistry classes at Queen Anne High School, Dunfermline, Fife, Scotland. (Fife is a region of Scotland just across the Firth of Forth from Edinburgh; it runs from the famous St. Andrews in the northeast down to the town of Dunfermline in the southwest.)

In theory, that's a pleasant thing to do. If your students have put in a solid effort during class, there's no harm in spending a few minutes sharing a laugh over some amusing videos. It's undoubtedly true that YouTube has endless hours of hilarious content. At the same time, however, no teacher in his or her right mind should give students unfettered control over what gets shown on a classroom screen, particularly when the content is drawn from a loosely moderated site like YouTube.

Unfortunately, Thompson did precisely that. She allowed students to show several videos that were wildly inappropriate and offensive to other members of the class, so much so that two of her eight Higher Chemistry students complained to school officials about what had happened. Queen Anne High School officials promptly suspended Thompson and then referred her to the General Teaching Council for Scotland for disciplinary proceedings.

Each of the students who filed a report also provided witness testimony to the GTCS. One, designated Pupil A, described the events as follows:

> She confirmed that the first inappropriate video shown by the Teacher to the class was shown before Christmas 2016. The video was shown on a large Smart Board, using the Teacher's computer. The video showed a cartoon of Shrek going into a residential school and having sexual intercourse with a young orphan boy aged about 12. It lasted approximately 5 to 6 minutes. She confirmed that other inappropriate videos of a sexual nature were also shown. The Shrek video particularly stuck in her mind. … The Teacher was present in the class when the videos were played, and knew that they were on. The Teacher seemed to think that they were funny. She did not turn off the videos. Pupil A was unsure whether the Teacher or another pupil typed in the details for the videos to be played. Pupil A felt embarrassed when the videos were being played. She did not like it. She reported it to the Deputy Headmaster.

The school's headteacher told the GTCS that she had reviewed the videos after the student report and testified that, in her opinion, they were "pornographic." Given the description of the videos, there is little question that her assessment was correct.

Thompson did not appear at the disciplinary hearing, but that did not stop the GTSC from issuing an intensely critical report for allowing students to watch videos of an "inappropriate and sexual nature." After reviewing the charges against Thompson in detail, the GTSC determined that the appropriate punishment was to remove Thompson from the roll of registered teachers.

"The panel also determined," the ruling said, "that the public interest required a finding that the teacher was unfit to teach, given the need to protect children and young people, and the need to maintain the public's confidence in registrants and in the GTCS as a regulator."

Top Three Takeaways:

- Today, educators should be extremely cautious about giving students any control over the selection and display of content from the internet. At the very least, an adult should carefully vet any suggestions by students to make sure that the materials are age appropriate. By essentially ceding control to her students, Thompson violated her ethical duty to maintain a safe environment for all students.

- This cautionary tale raises some questions about whether the school had adequate software filtering in place (or any filtering at all). Ideally, the school network should have prevented the students from projecting sexually explicit content from a school computer to a school smartboard. There are also reasonably effective filters within YouTube itself that teachers can use to restrict what students view in the classroom. School administrators, in consultation with faculty and IT staff, should discuss the deployment of these tools and what exceptions, if any, should be allowed.

- This situation arose from an apparent failure of judgment, possibly augmented by lax network supervision and poor filtering. But the school does deserve some credit for creating a culture in which students felt empowered to raise concerns with administrators. Ideally, someone should have said something after the first incident, but better late than never. Part of meeting the MCEE's ethical duty of creating a safe environment for students is giving them the ability to let people in authority know when something doesn't feel safe.

Cautionary Tale 17-2019-New Zealand

As you have seen throughout this book, some educational careers quickly implode when an educator stumbles into a cybertrap, and others devolve more slowly. This is one of the latter.

In 2006, Tim Jenkinson was serving as the principal of Bayview School, a primary school in Glenfield, New South Wales, Australia (about 25 miles west-southwest of Sydney). In July, the district's IT department conducted a system upgrade for staff computers. In the course of doing so, IT personnel discovered pornography on Jenkinson's computer.

A spokesman for the local school board said that after an investigation determined that there was no threat to children, Jenkinson was given a written warning and allowed to keep his job. Shortly before the start of the school year, however, school trustees sent a letter to parents announcing the incident and the school board's action. Jenkins submitted his resignation two days after the trustees mailed the letter.

Several parents interviewed by *The New Zealand Herald* said that they felt Jenkinson had "lost community trust and the moral authority to run a school." They also sharply criticized the trustees for not notifying parents sooner. The school board spokesman defended the decision, saying that the trustees initially considered it to be an "employment relationship issue."

Ten years later, Jenkinson took a job as deputy principal at Otorohanga College, a state secondary school (Years 9-13) located about 112 miles south of Auckland in the rural community of Otorohanga, New Zealand. It is unclear what Jenkinson did in the interim, although one article alludes to an appearance on an Australian television show called "Real Crime: The Worst That Could Happen."

According to the synopsis for the broadcast, "Jenkinson found himself out on the street, jobless, in poor health, and all his available funds – including the equity in his house – rapidly dwindling."

The premise of the show was to use Jenkinson's misfortunes to illustrate the potentially catastrophic consequences of computer viruses, which Jenkinson then blamed for the presence of pornography on his Bayview School computer.

It wouldn't be the last time Jenkinson used that excuse. In February 2017, Jenkinson loaned his phone to some Otorohanga students to use as a calculator during a class exercise. A short time later, the school principal wrote to Jenkinson and said that the students had reported seeing pornography on his phone. He asked Jenkinson for an explanation, and Jenkinson replied that a virus had his phone and had downloaded adult content without his knowledge.

The principal asked the New Zealand Teaching Council's Complaints Assessment Committee to do an investigation. While the Committee found insufficient evidence to take any action, the school decided to conduct a separate inquiry.

If Jenkinson had done nothing further and allowed the school's investigation to take its course, then the whole matter would probably have blown over. However, he went one significant step too far: he forged a letter on Vodafone stationary from "Lester (Skip) Parker, Technician" that affirmed that the "innocent explanation" for the pornography on Jenkinson's phone was a virus.

The principal, logically enough, called Vodafone. The cellular phone company checked its employee lists and (surprise!) told that the principal that no one by that name worked for Vodafone.

"Our internal assessment," Vodafone wrote in an email, "indicates there is sufficient information available at this stage to conclude that the document is false and has been created to mislead or deceive."

When the principal confronted Jenkinson with Vodafone's reply, he confessed to creating the fake letter and told the principal that he made up the letter "not to cover up that I had been accessing porn because I hadn't but because I was frightened and panicked. It was a stupid and irrational thing to do and for that I am truly very sorry and ashamed."

Jenkinson resigned from Otorohanga College on June 2, 2017, and his case was referred to the New Zealand Teachers Disciplinary Tribunal. In a decision issued in January 2019, the Tribunal suspended Jenkinson from teaching for six months and censured him for "serious misconduct."

The core of the Tribunal's ruling was a finding that Jenkinson's drafting of the fake letter "strikes at the heart of the expectation for honesty and integrity that the profession and public have of practitioners." The Tribunal said that it seriously considered pulling Jenkinson's license altogether; it allowed him to retain it, however, in light of his belated admission of responsibility, his apology to the school, his cooperation with the Tribunal's investigation, and his ongoing counseling.

Top Three Takeaways:

- Educators should bear in mind that they have minimal privacy rights when it comes to material stored on school computers. When IT departments run software or operating system upgrades, they are obligated to check for any content stored on the computer that would indicate inappropriate use. Doing so is integral to maintaining a safe environment for students.

- During my years of research in this area and my work as a computer forensics expert, I've run across the "virus put porn on my computer" defense several times. It is rarely a credible argument; usually, there is amply corroborating evidence that the user was responsible for the alleged conduct. The fact that Jenkinson relied on the same excuse twice would instantly raise the eyebrows of any investigator.

- The possibility that Jenkins was using his mobile device to look at adult content is not the issue here; he certainly has a right to do so. The ethical concern is the possibility of exposing students to his browsing habits by giving them access to his phone. In general, educators should avoid allowing students to use their devices unless there is a compelling reason to do so. Even if there is nothing salacious on your device, it is inadvisable to run the risk of giving them access to whatever else may be on it.

Cautionary Tale 17-2018-Texas

"That should never have happened."

It would be challenging to come up with a better one-line summation for this book. But those words instead were uttered by 45-year-old Belton High School teacher James Edward Alleman III on September 28, 2018, when he realized that he had accidentally projected pornographic images from his school laptop onto a screen during a computer science class. When one of the students in the class reported the incident to principal Jill Ross, she called the Belton Police Department to investigate. The school district immediately placed Alleman on administrative lead, and he resigned from his teaching position on October 1.

Officers immediately seized Alleman's school-issued laptop and iPad, as well as an external hard drive and micro SD card that they found in his desk. According to an affidavit filed in support of an arrest warrant, investigators discovered that Alleman had used his school laptop to search for "pornography in Chinese and Japanese that translated in English to 'teen scandal,' 'webcam underwear teen,' 'teen video chat,' 'school girl masturbation,' and other terms[.]"

That discovery gave officers grounds to obtain a search warrant to examine Alleman's electronic devices, all of which contained pornographic images. When they did a forensic examination of the micro SD card, things got much graver: examiners located four videos that revealed a young girl changing in a residential bathroom. Investigators showed the videos to Alleman's wife, who identified both the bathroom (located in a former home of the couple) and the young girl. Police found the girl and interviewed her; she said (as had Alleman's wife) that she was unaware that someone had placed a camera in the bathroom or that videos had been recorded of her.

Two weeks after Alleman's resignation, Ross sent out a letter to the school community announcing Alleman's departure and the school's search for a new computer science teacher. Her message made no mention of the fact that Alleman had accidentally shown pornography to his students or had used his work laptop to search for illicit materials. In response to reporter questions, the school district initially said that it does not disclose "confidential personnel and student information."

In a further statement, however, the BISD defended itself by saying, "[u]pon learning of inappropriate use of technology by former Belton High School teacher James Alleman, he was immediately removed from the classroom, and Belton Police Department was notified." Parents could legitimately question why the school did not provide this necessary information to them as well.

Alleman was arrested on November 18 and charged with possession of child pornography. He posted a $75,000 bond and was released. A Texas grand jury handed down an indictment on the same charge on March 27, 2019. Five months later, Alleman pleaded guilty to a separate charge of "unintentionally showing child pornography to students," a third-degree felony under Texas law. Because he entered what is known as an "open plea," *i.e.*, without entering into a plea deal with the prosecutor, Alleman agreed to accept whatever sentence the judge decided to hand down.

At his sentencing hearing on December 5, 2019 (after the preparation of a pre-sentencing report), Alleman received a remarkably light sentence: six years deferred adjudication probation. There is no dispute that Alleman accidentally displayed child pornography to students, that he used school equipment to search for pornographic materials (including child pornography), and that he possessed voyeuristic recordings of a minor. Given all that, it is a little dumbfounding that the judge did not order Alleman to serve some portion of the 2-10 years he was facing. He is, however, required to register as a sex offender for the remainder of his life, and his teaching career is over, both of which are significant penalties. Still, one wonders what the judge was thinking.

Top Three Takeaways:

- The first cybertrap in this tale is accidentally projecting pornography from your school computer. I think that I can safely assume that no one reading this book believes that is acceptable, so we can skip right past that. The next and more pressing question is how Alleman was able to view such content on his computer. He was likely able to bypass whatever filters were in place by using non-English search terms. It is a fairly common trick but one that more sophisticated filtering programs are steadily learning to block. Administrators should ask their IT departments if their network filtering software has this capability; if not, they should implement it.

- Any cybertrap involving a digital device has the potential to become a real thread-pull. The sequence here is very typical: Educator makes a mistake in the use of his or her equipment; investigation of school device creates reasonable suspicion of other criminal activity; a court issues a search warrant for his or her personal devices; a forensic examination reveals significant illegal activity. In short, be aware that if your school district discovers that you are engaging in any conduct suggesting harm to children, law enforcement will put your electronic devices (and the rest of your life) under a very fine microscope.

- The school's response, in this case, can justly be criticized. The school should have provided more timely information to parents, given the material for which Alleman was searching and the age of his students. There are competing concerns that administrators and school boards will need to balance (preferably with the active help of school counsel), but issuing an anodyne notice issued two weeks after a disturbing event like this is inadequate.

Cautionary Tale 17-2016-California

Principle V of the Model Code of Ethics for Educators addresses the "Responsible and Ethical Use of Technology." It reads as follows:

> The professional educator considers the impact of consuming, creating, distributing and communicating information through all technologies. The ethical educator is vigilant to ensure appropriate boundaries of time, place and role are maintained when using electronic communication.

Implicit in this ethical principle is the educator's obligation to know how to safely and adequately operate technology when it is used in the classroom and to be mindful when doing so. This cautionary tale helps illustrate how easily educators can overlook that ethical obligation.

In March 2016, a high school student posted a video to the social media site Reddit.com. The video, shot by a student sitting in the middle of the classroom during a math test, showed his teacher seated at the front of the room, hunched over his laptop. The video then panned to the screen at the front of the classroom, which showed page after page of images of women in lingerie.

User D3Gamma titled his Reddit post, "Uh oh! Forget to turn off the projector?" Not surprisingly, his post attracted more than 1,200 comments. One person asked: "What happened after this OP? Did anyone say anything to him?" D3Gamma replied: "He never found out. After this class ended he switched to the next class' assignments. So he doesn't know that it wasn't turned off or 'Frozen on a screen.'"

Other users pointed out that the teacher wasn't looking at porn *per se* but was surfing the online shopping site, eBay. As numerous other commenters noted, however, that was not much of an excuse.

The teacher was initially unnamed, but his anonymity did not last long. Within four days, the video caught the attention of local San Diego television stations, who successfully identified and contacted "D3Gamma." He gave them the identity of the teacher—Paul Swanson, a math teacher and coach at Mira Mesa High School—and permitted them to broadcast the video he shot.

Officials at Mira Mesa placed Swanson on administrative leave while they conducted an investigation. Parents and kids interviewed by local reporters largely shrugged, saying that while he shouldn't have been surfing eBay during class, the embarrassment of the situation was probably punishment enough.

Although the school declined to discuss internal employee investigations and discipline, it appears that it reached the same conclusion. According to LinkedIn, Swanson is still teaching and coaching at Mira Mesa.

One person who commented on Reddit in response to the original video said it best: "I'm a teacher. I live by the assumption that the students can always see my screen."

Top Three Takeaways:

- Many of these cautionary tales work in more than one chapter, and this could just as effectively serve as a warning about educator productivity, or about how cameras are simply everywhere these days. Moreover, Swanson's choice of browsing material qualifies as "pornography" in only the broadest sense of the word. There are far worse things he could have projected onto the screen than some eBay lingerie ads. Nonetheless, this is a good reminder for educators to slow themselves down and think about how they are using the devices in their classrooms.

- The distribution of this video out into the broader world is itself a warning for educators. The young man who shot the video was able to upload it to Reddit directly from the classroom, basically providing his followers (and theirs, and then theirs) with a real-time illustration of what was happening in his class. It's not merely that cameras are everywhere; it's that they are perpetually connected to the broader world. Moreover, the rising generations of students are incredibly knowledgeable about not only how to capture content but how to distribute it effectively.

- "With great power comes great responsibility." The enormous and sometimes life-altering capability that students have to capture and distribute video puts the onus on school districts, administrators, and educators to ramp up the teaching of digital citizenship. The main focus of this book, of course, is educator ethics; we cannot overlook, however, the importance of helping students become ethical people as well. It is particularly important to do so when students are making so many decisions so quickly.

Cautionary Tale 17-2006-WI

Although this case took place nearly 15 years ago, it still illustrates some valuable ethical lessons for educators. The basic facts are straightforward: In 2006, Robert Zellner, a biology teacher and union leader in Cedarburg, WI, made the dubious decision to disable the Google Safe Search setting on his school computer and to then type the word "blonde" into the search box. Not surprisingly, many of the search results were pornographic, but as his browser history demonstrated, Zellner did not visit any of the links provided by Google. It was equally clear that he did not spend much time on the search results page: just 67 seconds.

Zellner had signed the school's acceptable use policy, which prohibited such activity, but he may not have been aware that the school's IT department had installed monitoring software on his computer (and his alone, it later turned out).

The IT department gave Cedarburg Superintendent Daryl Herrick a report of Zellner's Google Search activity, along with allegations that Zellner had surfed pornography on prior occasions, and had kept photos of bikini-clad students taken during a school trip to Hawaii. Herrick told Zellner to resign or face public disclosure and dismissal.

Zellner refused, arguing that he was concerned about students accessing adult materials on school computers and wanted to test the district's filtering software. Zellner's defense did not convince Herrick, and he ordered Zellner to appear at an unusual public hearing regarding his conduct before the Cedarburg School Board (such matters are usually handled in executive session). When the meeting concluded, the Board fired him.

After various court proceedings at the state level, all of which were resolved in the school district's favor, Zellner filed a $9 million federal lawsuit in 2008. He alleged that the school district fired him not because of inappropriate internet activity, but instead in retaliation for his union activities. If true, that would be a violation of Zellner's First Amendment rights. The U.S. District Court granted summary judgment in favor of the School District, and that decision was affirmed by the U.S. Court of Appeals for the 7th Circuit on April 29, 2011, in unequivocal terms:

> [Zellner] directly and knowingly violated a School Board Policy. He admitted as much in front of the Board at his hearing and apologized for his actions. Zellner thus failed to establish proof that the Google Image search was a pretext for firing him. Without evidence that some other teacher violated the Policy in a similar way and received a milder sanction, Zellner's "but for" case rests on conjecture. Accordingly, he cannot rebut the District's legitimate, non-discriminatory reason for his termination. The judge correctly granted the District's motion for summary judgment with respect to Zellner's First Amendment claim."

Top Three Takeaways:

- The first takeaway from this cautionary tale is the fact that even the briefest stroll on the dark side of the web can be a problem. In this case, Zellner's misconduct lasted just a fraction over one minute, but it was still enough to derail his career. Even fifteen years ago, the monitoring software available to districts was powerful; today, it is many software generations faster and more invasive. I believe districts and schools should be transparent about the tools used to monitor computer use. Still, educators would not be amiss in assuming that school districts are doing more monitoring and collecting more data than they admit.

- Zellner's decision to disable the Safe Search setting was an ethical breach, if well short of the most serious discussed in this book. It is not clear to what extent the Board took into account the claims that he had photographed students on a beach trip, but it undoubtedly contributed to a sense of disquiet and concern about why he disabled the search filter.

- The last key lesson here is that powerful software, faster processors, and virtually unlimited cloud storage combine to give school districts the ability to reach far into the past to harvest evidence of possible misconduct. The real risk for employees, as I wrote some years ago in *The Naked Employee*, is not that employers are conducting real-time surveillance. Instead, it's that districts are storing large quantities of digital data that the district can review at its leisure if it is looking for justification to terminate someone.

Relevant MCEE Provisions for Chapter 17

Principle I: Responsibility to the Profession

Standard I.A.5

Principle II: Responsibility for Professional Competence

Standard II.C.3

Principle III: Responsibility to Students

Standards III.B.1, III.B.2, III.B.3

Principle IV: Responsibility to the School Community

Standards IV.B.8 and IV.D.3

Principle V: Responsible and Ethical Use of Technology

Standards V.A.5, V.A.7, and V.B.1

Sources

The sources for the Cautionary Tales in this chapter can be viewed at the following URL:

https://link.cybertraps.com/C4E2-Sources-Chap17

Chapter 18
Intimate Photos or Videos on School Property

Overview

This cybertraps covered in this chapter arise from two separate but not-unrelated trends. First, there has been a dramatic expansion in the availability of explicit adult content over the past thirty years. Second, a remarkably high percentage of people use their camera-equipped smartphones to take nude photos or videos of themselves in utterly inappropriate settings. It would be great to be able to say that schools and educators have not been affected by these trends, but in fact, they have been.

The Sexting Revolution

As I discussed in *Obscene Profits*, someone likely took the first nude self-portrait within months (or even weeks) of the announcement of Louis Daguerre's photographic process in 1839. The same phenomenon occurred when the process of making movies developed a half-century later, although it took a little longer for movie equipment to become available to the average hobbyist. Each significant jump in consumer imaging technology—home movie cameras, Polaroids, camcorders, digital cameras, *etc.*—has contributed to an incremental but steady increase in the creation of personal pornography.

When computers and the web emerged in the 1980s and early 1990s, it led to what I described as the "democratization of porn production." While not everyone takes nude photos of themselves or makes homemade adult films, enough people have done so (and shared the material online) to alter the economics of the adult industry. The vast amounts of freely-available amateur content have led to the shuttering of major magazines like *Playboy* and most commercial adult film companies.

Given all that, it was perhaps inevitable that the combination of cameras and phones in the early 2000s would accelerate this trend. It took only three years after Sanyo released the first widely-available camera phone in 2001 for the word "sexting" to make its way into the dictionary. Just three years after that, when Apple released the first iPhone, it became much simpler to send images and videos via text message and to upload that content to websites.

In the years since those innovations, study after study has shown that growing numbers of teens and young adults share nude photos and videos with their romantic partners and significant others. Both a long-term trend—the rise in online dating—and a hopefully short-term exigency—enforced social distancing and lockdown during the worst of the coronavirus pandemic—have encouraged more people to get playful with their smartphones.

To paraphrase the British actress Beatrice Campbell, does it really matter what adults do with their smartphones, so long as they don't do it in the streets and frighten the horses? It shouldn't, but the problem, of course, is that all too often, what people do with their smartphones doesn't remain private. Photos and videos can wind up in the hands of the public in a variety of ways, ranging from purposeful sharing to careless handling to unauthorized and abusive dissemination.

Public disclosure of intimate photos can be embarrassing for anyone but particularly so if the person photographed is prominent (*i.e.*, celebrity victims of phone hacks) or holds a position of responsibility or authority in the community. Educators need to be particularly careful about taking and sharing photos that could lessen their credibility in the classroom or cause a disruption in the school.

Creating Inappropriate Content on School Property

It should go without saying, of course, that if an educator does decide to use his or her smartphone to take intimate photos or videos, he or she should not do so on school grounds. But unfortunately, a surprising number of educators take wildly inappropriate photos in equally unacceptable locations. For smartphone users (teachers included), all the world's a stage, with clothes or without.

Few things are more likely to undermine a teacher's moral authority, however, than the news that he or she has taken nude photos in a classroom or school bathroom. It sets a terrible example for children and makes the school and the school district look bad. The cold reality is that if your school district catches you taking such photos on school property, you probably will lose your job.

It's good to remember the old internet adage that "Information wants to be free." You can't be embarrassed by a photo you don't take.

Cautionary Tales

Cautionary Tale 18-2019-US_New York

One of the things that I learned during my research for *Obscene Profits* is that adult webmasters can be impressively creative in their efforts to lure people to their websites. One of the most notorious examples occurred in the early days of the web. Not long after President Clinton oversaw the creation of the first White House website (whitehouse.gov) in the mid-1990s, an enterprising adult webmaster registered the domain name "whitehouse.com."

At the time, people did not necessarily understand the distinctions among the three main top-level domains (.com, .gov, and .edu), so it was a common mistake for someone to type in "whitehouse.com" when they were trying to get to the White House home page. But what they reached instead was a political humor site with a substantial amount of adult material. The White House sent a cease and desist letter, but thanks to the First Amendment, website creator Ransom Scott simply ignored it.

In addition to trying to fool people into visiting similarly-named websites, adult webmasters also keep an eagle eye out for "legitimate" domain names that have expired. If they can swoop in and register otherwise unobjectionable domain names, then they can redirect visitors looking for the original content to a website they've filled with spurious offers, various types of adult content, or even malware.

Here's how that can be a problem for educators. In December 2019, an unnamed teacher at Ray Middle School in Baldwinsville, NY, shared a Google Doc with students that contained links to various websites for use in a homework assignment. Unfortunately, the teacher did not test all of the hyperlinks before sharing his document; one of the resources the teacher listed had shut down sometime earlier, and an adult website operator had purchased the domain name. The content viewed by students when they clicked on the link may have been "educational," but certainly not in the way the teacher intended.

Not surprisingly, complaints flooded into school and district offices, and the teacher was put on paid administrative leave while the district launched an investigation. The school sent out a letter to parents explaining the situation that same day and reported the incident to both the NY Department of Education and the local police. The school also set up counseling for all of the students in the teacher's class.

It didn't take long for the Onondaga County Sheriff's office to announce that the teacher would not face any criminal charges, since it concluded that the teacher did not act with criminal intent. However, the Baldwinsville School District said that the teacher would remain on administrative leave while the district continued its review of relevant policies and procedures. Citing personnel privacy concerns, the school district refused to say what actions it might take against the teacher.

Top Three Takeaways:

- The first and most apparent takeaway for this cautionary tale is to always, always test the links that you send out to students. Another related pro tip: If you send students links to videos on Youtube, you should carefully watch the videos through to the very end or, at the very least, do a good sampling of different spots in the video. There have been instances of people discovering that someone has inserted inappropriate content into otherwise inoffensive videos.

- Second, educators should be aware that virtually every state has a statute that makes it a crime to distribute explicit content to minors. In some states, the material must be "obscene," while others use the lower standard of "harmful to minors." As this cautionary tale illustrates, the police may investigate a cybertrap that is mere carelessness as a criminal matter.

- The swiftness and thoroughness of a district's response are critical. This particular district deserves high marks for the thoroughness of its communication and its support for both students and parents. It is clear that the administration was well-prepared for this type of situation and properly executed its response plan. Most of this book understandably focuses on individual educator ethics, but many, if not most of its precepts apply to the organization as well.

Cautionary Tale 18-2019-US_Florida

If you are of a certain age and have sufficiently dubious taste in movies, you may have seen one or more of *The Naked Gun* films in the late 1980s and early 1990s. It's been quite a while since I saw any of them, so when I looked them up on Wikipedia, I was reminded that the first one—*The Naked Gun: From the Files of Police Squad!*—had quite a cast. In addition to the lead, Leslie Nielson, there were roles for Ricardo Montalbán (of *Fantasy Island* fame), Priscilla Presley (best known for her first marriage), and O.J. Simpson (who needs no introduction).

The connection between those silly films and the facts of this cautionary tale will be quickly apparent. I have included this object lesson not so much because I think any reader will fall into this cybertrap (hopefully not!) but because it serves as an example of how private photos can become public in the most unexpected ways. It is a perfect illustration of the central point that your best protection from an embarrassing photo is not to take it in the first place.

In April 2019, the Osceola County Sheriff's Office began investigating a personal incident involving a female member of the department and her husband. The unnamed female officer served as a school resource officer at the Imagine Kissimmee Charter Academy in Kissimmee, Florida.

During its investigation, the Sheriff's Office examined the contents of the female officer's phone. They were shocked to discover that just before Christmas 2018, the officer had recorded a 45-second nude video of herself in a bathroom at the Charter Academy and had sent it to her husband, along with three nude photographs. Among other things, the video showed the officer's uniform, gun, and pepper spray all lying on the floor of a bathroom stall.

When confronted with the material from her phone, the officer reportedly defended herself by saying that she was on a break at the time. She also said that she had carefully locked the bathroom door so that there was no chance anyone would see her.

The Sheriff's Office was not impressed with her defenses. As the department's investigative report dryly put it, "Even though she was on a lunch break, she was subject to recall at any time, and due to her disrobed state, it would delay any immediate response."

The report also noted that the officer eventually admitted that she had made a mistake but that she did not think the department should fire her. The department disagreed and fired her, saying that she could no longer be fully trusted to perform her duties properly.

Top Three Takeaways:

- This particular cautionary tale is, in many ways, a perfect distillation of our current era. It is almost impossible to imagine a school resource officer recording a nude video of himself or herself before the introduction of smartphone cameras. But it's not just that we have the technical capability to record ourselves, it's also that our cultural mores have shifted so dramatically. A lot of that has to do with the online adult industry but not exclusively; we also have an aggressive celebrity culture that has normalized the taking of nude or nearly-nude selfies. Reviewing and discussing the MCEE principles laid out below is an excellent opportunity to consider whether your selfie habits are inspired more by celebrities or professional ethics.

- Even members of law enforcement sometimes overlook the fact that "information wants to be free." If you create a digital image or file, it can be challenging to keep it private. It is simply too easy for someone to copy information, misappropriate it, hack into your devices, or uncover it in some unexpected legal or investigative proceeding. (A video like this, for instance, could easily be offered as evidence of parental unfitness during a divorce proceeding.)

- It is worth noting how much trouble can flow from a remarkably brief decision-making process. Most cybertraps, like this one, are not the result of long planning or reflection but instead, are triggered by an impulsive decision. In many ways, the most critical skill for educators in the digital era is impulse control. One of the central objectives of the Model Code of Ethics for Educators is to help educators with that precise problem, by encouraging personal reflection and regular consultation with colleagues and supervisors before making what can be life-altering decisions.

Cautionary Tale 18-2018-Pennsylvania

This particular cautionary tale doesn't have a lot of specific details, but there's enough information for it to be instructive. The basic facts are straightforward: a Brashear High School student found some nude selfies of a substitute teacher on a school computer, and the Pittsburg school district promptly fired her.

According to reports, the substitute teacher used a student computer to log into a "personal account" but forgot to log out of her account when she stopped using the computer. A short time later, a 10th-grade student sat down to use the equipment and saw photos that showed the substitute teacher fully nude. The girl sent the pictures to her mother and then notified another teacher about what she had seen.

Unfortunately, the coverage of the incident does not contain specific information about the type of account the teacher left open or how the photos were viewable by the student. However, there is a range of different possibilities: the teacher might not have realized that she had synced pictures from a personal account, or she might have left open her Dropbox, or Google Drive, or iCloud—there are a large number of possibilities. Of course, it doesn't matter exactly how the student was able to see the photos (assuming no inappropriate conduct on her part). The salient point is that the substitute teacher should have taken much more care to make sure that she did not leave intimate photos where a student could see them.

Although this particular cautionary tale offers a good reminder for educators to slow down and think about what they are doing when they log into digital devices on school property, it is perhaps an even more useful warning for school administrators. This was not a significant incident; the level of student exposure was minimal, and the school acted promptly in dismissing the teacher. But there was some controversy over whether the administration's communication regarding the incident was as effective as it should have been.

At some point shortly after the district fired the teacher, the school principal sent a letter home with students explaining what had happened. The letter said that "[p]arents and guardians of the students directly involved in the issue have been contacted." That statement upset the father of the girl who saw the teacher's photos. He claimed that the letter was the first that he had heard of the incident. He called a local news station to complain about how the school was handling the situation.

"I'm still waiting," he told a reporter. "I'm being patient. Will we ever get that call? Will they accept responsibility? Bathtub pictures. Top and bottom. Full body shots. I'm ticked off, I'm angry, I'm hurt. When my child came on and went to go log on, her and one of her friends, she seen the nude pictures. She could've did other things – sent it throughout the school to other students. Humiliated the young lady. But she sent it to her mother and then she went and alerted a teacher."

The local news station contacted the school district about the father's comments, but administrators insisted that they had spoken to the parents of the students involved. Regardless of who is correct in this, "he said, school said" situation, it's a good reminder for administrators to be thorough in their outreach to the parents of affected students. It is always better for parents to hear a clear and consistent account before hearing about it from children or other parents.

Top Three Takeaways:

- One of the most challenging aspects of digital technology is that it has virtually wiped out the distinction between our personal and professional lives. Far too many companies and organizations expect their employees to check and respond to email from home or even while on vacation; far too many employees find it hard to resist doing so, even if it's not explicitly required. The overlap between our personal and professional lives is exacerbated by the fact that we use the same programs in both environments and can access our data anywhere. The MCEE propounds an ethical duty for educators to keep their private and professional lives separate, but as this case illustrates, it takes some real discipline to do so.

- "Information wants to be free." Once something is captured in digital form, it is surprisingly challenging to prevent it from spreading. Note how simple it was for the student to copy the images and send them to her mother, for instance. Before taking intimate photos of yourself or allowing a trusted partner to do so, think about how you will retain control over who sees them. At the very least, having them automatically sync to iCloud or Google Photos is probably not the best idea.

- The timeliness and openness of a school district's communication are critical to parents. For obvious reasons, parents want to know if an upsetting or disturbing situation has arisen so that they can discuss it with their children. Districts often feel that personnel privacy concerns limit what they can tell the public, but administrators should not rely on those concerns as an excuse for hiding necessary information. Districts should parents as partners in these situations, not necessarily hostile adversaries.

Cautionary Tale 18-2016-England

Here's a headline that you don't want appearing on the first page of Google when someone searches for your name: "Teacher allowed to continue work after bringing massive cache of porn to school." But that's the challenge facing Joel Gunning, a former teacher of English and Head of Drama at Bungay High School in Bungay, England.

In the spring of 2016, a student found a USB memory stick on the floor of a classroom and turned it into school officials. When they examined the drive, officials found a collection of nearly 2,500 pornographic images and videos. Many of the pictures depicted hardcore sexual activity, including scenes of bondage and sadomasochism.

It's not clear precisely how school officials traced the drive to Gunning, but when administrators interviewed him, Gunning admitted that the USB drive was his and that he had accidentally dropped it in the classroom. The school immediately suspended him and turned the USB drive over for further examination by the Suffolk Police Hi-Tech Crime Unit. The police computer experts did not find any pornographic images involving children.

School officials reported Gunning to the National College of Teaching & Leadership, which conducted a hearing on the matter on March 29, 2017. Before the start of the hearing, Gunning submitted a Statement of Agreed Facts in which he admitted to "unacceptable professional conduct and conduct that may bring the profession into disrepute."

In its opinion, the NCTL panel said that its primary objective to be "protection of public interest." Among the concerns raised by Gunning's conduct were the potential exposure of children to pornography, the damage to the profession the panel did not treat his behavior with "the utmost seriousness," and the importance of "declaring proper standards of conduct in the profession."

At the same time, the panel noted that there were several mitigating factors. Gunning was a highly regarded teacher who had taught at Bungay High School for ten years without incident. There was no evidence that any children were exposed to the contents of the drive, and the panel was confident that it was a "one-off incident." They found no evidence of intent on Gunning's part and noted that none of the pornography on the USB drive contained images of children.

In the end, the panel elected not to issue a prohibition order that would have prevented Gunning from teaching again. Instead, it issued a public finding "of unacceptable professional conduct and conduct that may bring the profession into disrepute conveys moral blameworthiness and is likely to affect his professional reputation." The panel said that the public embarrassment and damage to Gunning's career stemming from its ruling would be sufficient punishment.

Top Three Takeaways:

- This cautionary tale raises several questions. The first, surely, is why a teacher would store a significant amount of hardcore pornography on a USB drive and bring it to the school at which he teaches? At the very least, it raises the possibility that he intended to view it while he was at the school, which would be a separate and perhaps more disturbing offense.

- School districts should teach all students to do precisely what the student in this case did: bring any found electronic devices into the central office of the school. Don't take it home, don't look at what's on it, just turn it in. Gunning would have faced a much more damaging situation— and probably career-ending—if the student had looked at what was on the drive.

- The key finding was that none of the content involved children in any fashion. For obvious reasons, that would not be anything the school administration or the NCTL could overlook (let alone law enforcement). In general, educators should be entitled to their personal sexual preferences, as long as they are consensual, legal, and private.

Cautionary Tale 18-2014-Italy

There's not a lot of detail associated with this particular cautionary tale, but it illustrates a specific cybertrap that is easy to overlook: the potentially embarrassing consequences of using borrowed technology in the classroom.

In January 2014, the Italian wire service *Agenzia Nazionale Stampa Associata* carried a report that fifth-grade students at an unnamed Catholic school in Vincenza had accidentally been exposed to pornography during one of their classes.

According to the report, the teacher had borrowed a USB drive from a parent so that she could use it to store some 1980s music videos and project them onto a digital blackboard. When the teacher started playing the videos, however, the first one contained sexually explicit content. The report implicitly suggests that the parent was responsible for putting the adult video on the USB drive, but that's not the only possible method by which it got there.

Another possibility is that the teacher herself accidentally downloaded it when she was downloading videos; not all web sites do a great job of curating their videos or labeling them correctly. Or, for that matter, it the music video itself might have contained sexually explicit content; as someone who was a teenager when MTV debuted, I recall that some of the videos were pretty raunchy. Some of you may remember, for instance, that Tipper Gore led a spirited campaign against the music industry in the mid-1980s, in part because of her concerns about kids watching music videos.

Top Three Takeaways:

- The primary lesson to take away from this cautionary tale is to make sure that you look to see what might be lurking on any external drives or devices that you borrow from parents to use in the classroom. It doesn't matter how well you think you know the person involved; it's irresponsible and unethical not to take reasonable precautions to protect your students from exposure to inappropriate material.

- Despite some diligent searching, I found only one article about this particular incident. Part of that might be because I don't read Italian, but a more likely answer is that the school's response was exemplary. The principal issued a prompt apology and explained to parents exactly how the incident occurred. The school also called in counselors to provide psychological support to the students, including "explanations about human behavior to help them understand the images they saw."

- The news report, not surprisingly, offers no detail as to precisely what it was that the students saw. Given that these are elementary students and that they attend a Catholic school, exposing them to any sexually explicit conduct in the classroom is pretty shocking. However, as adults and as educators, we do need to come to grips with the fact that thanks to the combination of the internet and digital devices, children are gaining access to adult materials at very non-adult ages. The average age of exposure to online adult materials right now is about ten years old, or fifth grade. We should confront that reality and incorporate it into the education of our children. More than anything else, we have a responsibility to provide them with the context for understanding what they already see online.

Cautionary Tale 18-2009-US_California

"Dad, is that Ms. Defanti?"

That's a fairly innocuous question to get from your 10-year-old son when you are standing in line at the movies or shopping in the grocery store. It can sometimes be hard to recognize a teacher when they're out of the context of the classroom or dressed more casually then they are at work.

It's a much more difficult question to answer, however, when you're frantically trying to turn off the DVD player to limit your child's exposure to his teacher's homemade sex video. One unfortunate father in this cautionary tale told a local reporter that "[w]e were up until midnight doing the 'birds and the bees.'"

The sharp-eyed boy was correct. The solo star of the video was, in fact, Crystal Defanti, a fifth-grade teacher at the Isabelle Jackson Elementary School in Sacramento, California. In the spring of 2009, she prepared a year-end DVD with video clips of class projects, field trips, *etc.*, and sent a copy home with each student. Later that evening, Defanti learned that when she copied videos from her computer onto the DVDs, she accidentally spliced in a six-second clip of a home sex tape that she had made of herself on her living room couch.

The young man's father said that Defanti "called his home the day after his child got the DVD, crying hysterically, profusely apologizing, and asking the man and his wife to call every parent they knew to stop their kids from seeing the DVD too."

The school's reaction was surprisingly understanding. It began an investigation to determine how the explicit material wound up on the DVD, but there was no outcry among parents for the dismissal of the highly-popular teacher. A spokeswoman for the school advised parents to destroy the DVD distributed by Defanti and said that the school would send out a new version "once it had been reviewed."

It's not clear whether the school district took any disciplinary action; the only sure thing is that the Isabelle Jackson Elementary School web site does not list Defanti as a member of the staff. A search did not turn up her name in any other educational institution.

Accidents can happen to anyone. The school took a reasonable and rational approach to the incident, balancing the misconduct against the actual harm. But obviously, school districts would prefer that this type of thing not happen in the first place. So what can be done to minimize the risk of this type of incident? I have some suggestions.

Top Three Takeaways:

- Teachers should take whatever steps are necessary to create digital barriers between their personal and professional lives. There is an ethical obligation for teachers to do so concerning social media, but often overlooked is the necessary separation of digital content on devices. Ideally, educators should have separate accounts *and* digital devices for each aspect of their lives. If that is not possible, however, then particular care should be taken to create and maintain digital separation in hard drives and folders.

- Schools should adopt and enforce policies that require educators to either get the approval of digital content that will be shared publicly or, at the very least, mandate that a colleague vets it before distribution. In the rapid, fast-paced world of social media, that can seem like an unnecessary drag, but as this cautionary tale illustrates, it only takes one mistake to damage if not trash a career.

- At the end of the day, though, the final responsibility lies with the educator sharing the content. It's far too easy to imagine that Defanti was rushing to finish this project before the end of the school year and didn't take the time to review each of the video chapters that she added to the DVD. When an educator uses digital technology of any kind, he or she should know how it works and be sufficiently familiar with it to avoid significant screw-ups. As my fourth-grade math teacher drilled into me, "Slow down and always check your work!"

Relevant MCEE Provisions for Chapter 18

Principle I: Responsibility to the Profession

Standards I.A.2, I.A.3, and I.A.5

Principle II: Responsibility for Professional Competence

Standard II.C.3

Principle III: Responsibility to Students

Standard III.B.3

Principle IV: Responsibility to the School Community

Standards IV.B.8, IV.D.1, and IV.D.3

Principle V: Responsible and Ethical Use of Technology

Standard V.A.5, V.A.7, and V.B.1

Sources

The sources for the Cautionary Tales in this chapter can be viewed at the following URL:

https://link.cybertraps.com/C4E2-Sources-Chap18

Chapter 19
Cameras and Microphones Are Everywhere

Overview

In the 18th century, British philosopher Jeremy Bentham conceived of a novel new prison design that he called the "Panopticon": a circular building with an observation tower in the middle and the cells arranged in a circle around the core of the building. In theory, a single prison guard could watch every prisoner. Bentham's key concept was that the prisoners would regulate their behavior because they could never know if the guard was looking at them at any given moment. George Orwell incorporated precisely the same concept into his dystopian novel, *1984*, in his chilling and prescient description of the telescreens installed in each apartment:

> There was of course no way of knowing whether you were being watched at any given moment. How often, or on what system, the Thought Police plugged in on any individual wire was guesswork. It was even conceivable that they watched everybody all the time. But at any rate they could plug in your wire whenever they wanted to. You had to live—did live, from habit that became instinct—in the assumption that every sound you made was overheard, and, except in darkness, every movement scrutinised.

Orwell (and to a lesser extent, Bentham) has gotten a lot of attention lately, as surveillance cameras and facial recognition have become increasingly common features in our world. I've spent the last year living in the United Kingdom, which is the most surveilled nation in the Western hemisphere. 2020 opened with the news that the Metropolitan Police in London are combining public surveillance cameras with a facial recognition system in an attempt to identify known criminals and suspected terrorists, even though the system routinely generates false positives.

Given the unrelenting gun violence that afflicts American schools, it should come as no surprise that technology companies have been remarkably successful in selling surveillance technology to schools. By 2016, 81% of public schools reported the use of surveillance cameras to monitor activity on school grounds and in public areas within school buildings.

For obvious reasons, schools are reluctant to put surveillance videos in classrooms, let alone more intrinsically private areas like locker rooms and bathrooms. But they don't need to put surveillance cameras in classrooms. At any given moment, the average class has 20-25 cameras in it, each capable of taking photographs or recording video and broadcasting it to the world (or, more importantly, to the parents, the principal, the superintendent, or directly to law enforcement).

When Bentham conceived of his panopticon, he imagined the government would apply the structure of his prison to other institutions, including hospitals, factories, and schools. The construction of most school buildings bears no resemblance to Bentham's circular panopticon, but in functional terms, we are pretty close to what he imagined. At any given moment, educators should assume that someone in the classroom may be making a video or audio recording of what is taking place in the school.

Cautionary Tales

Cautionary Tale 19-2019-US_Arizona

School districts have been installing cameras in school buses for about thirty years now. The primary motivation has been to prevent bullying and fights between students, but on occasion, the cameras also record misconduct by the bus driver or another adult on the bus.

That's always struck me as rather remarkable, given the fact that there is no secrecy about the fact that a bus is camera-equipped. Still, people have bad days, and it is easy to forget a piece of technology that hangs silently above your head. That's the most charitable explanation for the actions of Arizona school bus driver Jamie Danielle Tellez, whose abusive meltdown was recorded in excruciating detail by the multiple cameras installed on her bus. On October 4, 2019, Tellez was driving a route for the Mesa Public Schools when a young male student leaned over the railing of the front seat and tried to throw some paper at the wastebasket under the dashboard.

Unfortunately, his aim was off, and things went south very quickly, as Tellez began yelling at the kid who had thrown the paper. "You better get your shit down there and pick that up right now," she barked. "I'm gonna knock the shit out of you."

By itself, that would have been enough to merit disciplinary action, but Tellez then made matters much worse by slamming on the brakes. Two kids were standing in the aisle while the bus was moving, and the one in front was thrown head-first into the windshield with enough force to crack it. Tellez grabbed him and threw him back up the aisle.

"What did I tell you? See what happens when you're standing in the fucking aisle?!" When the child said it wasn't his fault, Tellez got more abusive. "It IS your fault!" she said, "because if you were behind a seat, then you wouldn't be flying around the bus, would you?!"

Tellez finished her broadside with a disturbing threat: "'The truth of the matter is I can't touch you, but every day I would like to beat the shit out of your little ass! You understand that?"

The student who hit the windshield was taken to the hospital by his parents with head and hip injuries. Tellez was later arrested and charged with child abuse, threatening or intimidating, endangerment, and reckless driving. Upon being notified of the charges, Mesa Public Schools fired Tellez.

Top Three Takeaways:

- For entirely understandable reasons, the rise in the use of surveillance cameras in school settings (including transportation) has been dramatic. Eighteen months ago, school surveillance was estimated to be a $2.7 billion industry, and it is not likely to decline significantly in the foreseeable future. Factor in the smartphones carried by students and American schools may be the most photographed and recorded workplaces in the world.

- "What you say can and will be used against you." In the early days of video surveillance, the video recordings would be stored for some time in case something happened that required investigation, but most of the videos went unwatched. This case is an excellent example of how a specific stored video might be reviewed because of the injury to the students. The days of unwatched videos, however, are rapidly coming to an end. More and more security firms are offering school districts AI-based analysis of recordings, looking for specific behaviors of concern or statements that might merit closer evaluation.

- For the MCEE to have its most significant impact on our educational system, we need to employ an expansive definition of the word "educator," one that includes everyone responsible in one way or another for the health, safety, and education of children. All of the MCEE provisions regarding respect for students, protection of their health and safety, and need for self-care are just as applicable to someone like Tellez as they are to any classroom teacher.

Cautionary Tale 19-2019-US_Louisiana

"This is happening at East Ouachita Middle School."

That was the caption of a Snapchat video that was shot and distributed by a middle school student in East Ouachita Middle School in Monroe, Louisiana (the video can is still available online but fair warning: it is disturbing). The footage showed substitute teacher Andre Fuller in an aggressive confrontation with another student. The video opens with Fuller standing over the student at a desk. The student says, "Get out of my ear. Go sit down, please." Fuller tells the student, "Do not say that no more," as the student leaves his desk and moves away from Fuller.

Fuller follows the student as he moves around the room, at one point using his arm to press the student against a window. As the two move around the room, Fuller bumps into the student several times and gives him a shove. Throughout the video, Fuller continues to shout at the boy, saying, "What are you going to do? Why are you doing that? Who are you yelling at?"

The Snapchat video spread rapidly through the school community and quickly came to the attention of administrators, who contacted the Ouachita Parish Sheriff's office. Deputies went to the school, interviewed the individuals involved, and escorted Fuller off school property. Officers gave Fuller a court summons but did not charge him. Nonetheless, the district quickly terminated his contract as a substitute paraprofessional.

Fuller told both school administrators and media outlets that he had been in "full self-defense mode." He said that the student had threatened him with a chair before the Snapchat video started and added that he got close to the student to prevent him from swinging anything at him. Even if Fuller's statement was correct, it is no justification for Fuller's lengthy verbal and physical harassment of the student (particularly given the fact that Fuller was at least twice the size of the student).

Top Three Takeaways:

- We already know how easy it is to manipulate photos. It is almost as easy to alter videos. Thanks to automated tools like artificial intelligence, it will soon be possible for any tech-savvy kid to create a "deep fake," i.e., a morphed video that purports to show someone doing and saying things that have no basis in reality. Very soon, the only thing that will be certain is the need for us to view digital content with thorough skepticism and much better critical thinking skills.

- The facts of this particular cautionary tale offer an excellent opportunity to reflect on the value of video evidence in particular. The minute or so of recorded video is disturbing, and there is not much ambiguity about what is taking place in the classroom: a large man is intimidating a much smaller teen and verbally harassing him. But school administrators and other investigators should always be prepared to ask some hard questions before taking action based on a video recording. For instance: 1) Is there any ambiguity in what the video depicts? 2) Can everyone be heard and seen clearly? 3) Is there any possibility that someone might have edited or otherwise altered the video? 4) Why does the video start or stop at a particular moment? Is there anything relevant that occurred before or after the start of the video? 5) Does the creator of the video have an ax to grind? Did that influence his or her recording in some way?

- When people hear the word "Snapchat," they reflexively assume that we are talking about content that automatically disappears. As this cautionary tale should illustrate, that is not necessarily true. There are numerous ways to capture and preserve Snapchat content; as this case demonstrates, once someone transfers an image outside of the app, it can be like redistributed like any other piece of digital content.

Cautionary Tale 19-2017-US_Indiana

Late in the fall of 2017, one Indiana teacher overlooked two significant facts: first, that for various policy and safety reasons, the vast majority of school classroom doors have some type of glass panel, and second, that at least three-quarters of high school students carry a smartphone capable of shooting high-quality photos and videos.

At 11:30 a.m. on November 22, 2017, area police came to Lake Central High School in St. John, Indiana, and arrested 24-year-old Samantha Cox on suspicion of possessing an illegal narcotic. School officials called the police after students shared a video on YouTube that appeared to show Cox drawing lines of cocaine on a textbook and then snorting the powder.

The police brought a K-9 to the school with them to examine Cox's classroom. The dog pointed to a drawer in the teacher's desk, where officers found "a clear tightly twisted bag with multiple small rolled up pieces of tin foil." A search of Cox's car turned up a variety of other drug paraphernalia. Cox told police that she typically bought drugs after school but "was feeling sick and needed some" earlier in the day. Her first opportunity was a mid-morning free period.

The videographer was a junior named Will Rogers, who saw his English teacher acting strangely in the locked classroom and decided to record a video. He later told Chicago television station WGN9 that he didn't know what he had recorded.

"When I actually watched the footage again and again," Rogers said, "I just realized that my english teacher just did cocaine."

In a press statement, district officials praised Rogers and other students for their actions:

School Officials and Police want to recognize and praise the student witnesses that brought this information to the attention of the Principal very quickly. Their actions showed a tremendous amount of grit and integrity and enabled staff to address this situation promptly.

Top Three Takeaways:

- Kids these days... They know stuff. They see stuff. They record stuff. And they report stuff.

- Here's another reason that digital citizenship training for students is essential. All of those budding private detectives need to learn that it is not fair and can be quite harmful to put photos or videos of the alleged crime on social media without discussing the contents with a trusted authority figure. It appears in this case that the administration found out about Cox's recreational activity when they saw the video on YouTube. It would have been much better for Rogers to take the video to the principal directly. That's something that parents and schools should teach kids because their natural impulse is to put content online.

- Cameras are everywhere. That's it. That's the takeaway.

Cautionary Tale 19-2016-US_Maryland

Like many states and municipalities, the City of Baltimore operates a program designed to bring people from other fields into the teaching profession. The Baltimore City Teaching Residency (BTCR) was founded in 2002 and, according to the program's website, "is designed to transform talented professionals into great teachers through practical, classroom-centered coursework, with a sharp focus on the core skills and mindsets teachers, need to be successful."

Prospective teachers in the program attend training sessions for 10-12 hours per day, five days a week, for six weeks. Candidates work with "[o]utstanding local teachers [who] will prepare you to manage a classroom, to deliver the content your students must learn, and to support students in meeting high expectations by building bridges between challenging academic content and students' unique values and experiences."

Assuming that all goes well, BTCR graduates are eligible to start teaching in the following school year. For the first half of the year, BTCR educators work with a mentor in the classroom and are required to do additional training, including courses that focus on diversity. According to city statistics, just under 82% of Baltimore's 83,000 K-12 students are Black.

In the fall of 2016, someone posted a video to Facebook showing a confrontation between an unnamed white 8th-grade science teacher and some of her students (all Black). At the start of the recording, the teacher is seen grabbing the hoodie of a Black male student and repeatedly yelling, "Get out of my class!" As the other students erupt in laughter, she escorts the student to the door of the classroom, repeatedly telling him loudly to leave.

When she turned her attention back to the rest of the class, she shouted, "Who else needs to leave?" That was all bad enough, but things quickly went further south. As she looked at the unruly class, she yelled:

> You are getting zeros for doing nothing! I gave you the work! You're idiots! You have the chance to get an education. But you want to be a punk ass n****r who is going to get shot. You're stupid!

If you have any illusions about the power of social media, here's an opportunity to put them aside. Erica Gales Deminds, the mother of the student initially thrown out of class by the teacher, posted a copy of the video to Facebook. In just 12 hours, over *1 million* people viewed it. Deminds went to her son's school to complain about the teacher's behavior. When she got there, however, the school informed her that the district had already fired the teacher.

In an interview with local news station WMAR, Deminds said that she disagreed with the district's decision to fire the teacher and expressed empathy for the challenges she faced in the classroom:

> I don't want people to see the video and think that she's such a monster or she's such a racist or she doesn't like black kids. Absolutely not. She loves the children. It was a messed-up situation and you gotta think about—I got two teenagers myself. I can't deal with two! I can imagine dealing with 34!

In a separate interview with CNN, Deminds said that she was "floored" and "disgusted" by what she saw on the video. However, she reiterated her praise of the teacher: "The teacher was a really good teacher, she was one of my son's favorite teachers. I had met her a few times and she was always very pleasant. She just must have reached breaking point."

The Baltimore City Public Schools issued a terse two-paragraph statement detailing its responses:

> On Tuesday, November 15, a middle school science teacher at Harlem Park Elementary/Middle School engaged in verbally abusive behavior and made racially charged comments directed at students. The teacher involved in the incident is no longer employed by City Schools.

At Baltimore City Public Schools, we are committed to creating positive and equitable learning environments in school communities where all members are welcome, supported, and valued. No form of discriminatory behavior of any kind is or will be tolerated.

Top Three Takeaways:

- This particular cautionary tale raises legitimate policy questions about alternative certification programs like BTCR, the most significant of which is whether six weeks of admittedly intensive training is adequate to prepare people for the rigors of K-12 teaching. It also underscores the importance of ethics training and the role that the MCEE can play in preparing all educators to face the challenges that arise while teaching.

- One fundamental ethical breach by the teacher is crystal-clear: the teacher's lack of respect towards her students and her use of a profoundly offensive epithet. Less obvious but equally important, however, was her failure to practice self-care. Did she, as Ms. Deminds graciously suggested, simply reach a breaking point? Did she have the self-awareness to anticipate that something like this might happen and seek help? Did any of her colleagues (especially her mentor) see any warning signs? The ethical standards in the MCEE can help educators answer all of these questions. Reviewing and discussing those standards have the potential to lessen the chances of this type of situation occurring.

- All of us have days that are more difficult or upsetting than others. Educators must confront the reality that they spend difficult days in the company of smartphone-equipped students who are more than happy to record any awkward moments they experience. Ideally, that awareness should inspire educators to heed the ethical obligation of self-care. If you feel yourself reaching a point where your emotional control is slipping, that's a good time to ask a colleague or a supervisor for some help.

Cautionary Tale 19-2016-US_West Virginia

Had this particular cautionary tale ended differently, it might have been a good fit for Chapter 17, which discusses educators accessing inappropriate materials on school property. But in this case, the teacher in question couldn't control his temper, which created the opportunity for him to serve as a reminder to all educators that cameras are everywhere.

In August 2015, East Bank Middle School in East Bank, West Virginia, hired Thomas Yohn to teach math. In mid-April, a sixth-grade student named Jeffrey Province walked into Yohn's classroom and allegedly saw him looking at adult materials on his school computer.

As Province later said to a local news station, "I saw something no 13-year-old should ever see in a school." He said that he turned around and went to tell the school principal what he had seen.

Later that same day, Yohn interrupted Province's English class and began yelling at him. One of Province's classmates filmed Yohn's tirade. The surreptitiously-recorded video does an excellent job of capturing Yohn's tirade:

> Yohn [shouting]: Next time you open your big stinking mouth, pal, I will write you up and send you to the office for coming into my room without permission. Is that clear?
>
> Province: [unintelligible]
>
> Yohn [shouting]: What I watch as an adult is my choice. You as a child wait in the hall until you're invited into my room. Is that clear? How many times have I made this clear to you now?
>
> Province: [unintelligible]
>
> Yohn: Keep going.
>
> Province: [unintelligible]
>
> Yohn: The fifth time, you get written up!
>
> Other adult: [unintelligible]
>
> Yohn: I'm not putting up with this. And he tried to blackmail me! So go ahead, tell! Isn't that what I told you to do? Now I'm telling you, you keep your big flap shut.
>
> Province: [unintelligible]
>
> Yohn: Because I'm a grown up and can watch whatever I want. And if you ever step in my room again without permission, it'll be the last time you step in my room. Is that clear?

To be fair, the facts of this confrontation are somewhat ambiguous. During the initial local news station report on the controversy, Province's mother, Carmeline Short, conceded that her son is "no saint" and had not gotten along well with Yohn all year. But Province insisted that he was not attempting to blackmail Yohn for a better grade.

As is standard procedure in most districts or schools, Yohn was placed on paid administrative leave while the school district conducted an investigation. According to school officials, an examination of Yohn's computer revealed "nothing questionable," but they told local media that the inquiry was continuing.

Yohn's LinkedIn page is similarly ambiguous. He has two entries for teaching in the Kanawha County School District: one that shows his service ending in May 2016 and another that says he is still working there. However, he also says that he has been working as an Airgas Help Desk employee since May 2016, so it is certainly possible the school district terminated his employment shortly after the video was released.

Top Three Takeaways:

- The circumstances of this cautionary tale are ambiguous. The case involves two people who don't get along and a serious allegation that the school can't quickly and effectively verify. The only thing not particularly ambiguous is the video recording of a teacher's tirade. In the end, regardless of whether the allegation of viewing pornography was proven, it was probably the recording of Yohn yelling at the student that cost him his job.

- The ambiguity of this case is itself an important takeaway. When a student makes a serious allegation against a teacher, school administrators should not instantly assume that the student is telling the truth. In the course of my research, I've run across numerous instances in which students made things up, tried to frame educators with false profiles, and so on. This type of situation helps make a case for good internet filters and network logs so that there is some objective evidence regarding how employees or students are using district equipment.

- It is not difficult to imagine that Province misinterpreted what he saw on Yohn's computer or even that he made up the charge altogether. Had Yohn not stormed into Province's English class, there is a decent chance that he would have kept his job. But, when an educator loses his or her temper like that and publicly berates and humiliates a student, it's neither surprising nor inappropriate that the district would take action.

Cautionary Tale 19-2015-US_Washington

Towards the end of the school year in 2015, a 14-year-old female student at the Evergreen High School in Vancouver, Washington, reported a disturbing incident to the school resource officer. The student alleged that her teacher (later identified as Matthew Morasch) used the camera in his phone to either photograph or record a video of her under a classroom table.

The student learned about Morasch's behavior when one of her classmates showed her a photo the classmate took of Morasch holding his camera under the table while talking to the alleged victim and two other students. Other of the victim's classmates told police that they also observed Morasch holding his phone under the table, and one said that he could see that the phone was in recording mode. (This cautionary tale is also relevant to the issue of voyeurism by educators discussed in Chapter 25.)

School administrators and the student resource officer met with Morasch during the next class period and immediately placed him on administrative leave. School officials reported the incident to the Vancouver Police Department, who interviewed Morasch and asked him to surrender his phone, which he did.

In the meantime, students posted several photos to social media that showed Morasch holding his smartphone under a lab table and pointing it towards the legs of his female students. In one image shared on Facebook, you can see Morasch sitting in an awkward position; you can also see the faces of the students that he is trying to photograph or record under the table.

A forensics exam of Morasch's phone failed to recover the video he allegedly shot in his classroom. However, investigators did find another photo of a female student taken surreptitiously by Morasch, as well as an "upskirt" video of an adult woman that he recorded at a nearby Goodwill store. Morasch was arrested on two counts of voyeurism on June 23, 2015, and briefly held pending bail of $5,000.

The mother of the girl allegedly recorded by Morasch in the classroom told a local TV station that she thought Morasch's behavior that day was part of a larger pattern:

> [The video] was clearly shown - my daughter's legs. She had a dress on that day.
>
> He was grooming my daughter. He asked her on several occasions to stay in at lunch. [He] was just always complimenting her and just kind of weird stuff. I mean, she kind of, of course, thought something of it but not like that until this happened.

Two years later, Morasch was convicted on one count of voyeurism and two counts of attempted voyeurism. At trial, the young woman testified that she was the target of both the attempted video recording and the still photograph found on his phone.

At sentencing a few weeks later, she asked Judge Derek Vanderwood to give Morasch the maximum sentence—364 days in jail. Despite characterizing Morasch's conduct as "a significant violation of trust," Judge Vanderwood decided to sentence Morasch to six months in prison, along with a suspended sentence of 184 days to expire after two years. Once Morasch served his sentence, the judge ordered him to register as a sex offender, undergo a psycho-sexual evaluation, and complete any proscribed treatment plan.

Morasch posted $25,000 bail and was allowed out on supervised release pending an appeal of his conviction. The court prohibited him from having any contact with minors or the underage victim in the case. He was also forbidden to use a cellphone equipped with a camera.

In April 2019, the Washington Court of Appeals ruled that the warrant permitting law enforcement officers to search Morasch's phone was too broad and voted to suppress the evidence found on it. As a result, the Court overturned Morasch's felony conviction for the upskirt video and one of the two gross misdemeanor charges of attempted voyeurism.

Six months later, he was re-sentenced by Judge Vanderwood to the same 364 days in jail for the remaining count of attempted voyeurism. This time, however, Judge Vanderwood suspended 229 days of the sentence and gave Morasch credit for 18 days already served, which left him with about four months of incarceration. Following his release in the spring of 2020, Morasch is serving 12 months of probation and must register as a sex offender for eight years.

Top Three Takeaways:

- Many of the criminal cybertraps discussed in this book flow from the fact that the commission of the crime just looks so natural. Voyeurism is a good example: every smartphone contains a miniaturized camera/video recorder, and some people think that they can discreetly dangle it underneath a table or hold it over the top of a bathroom stall without being caught. The very simplicity of the criminal act overwhelms the judgment of some people, leading them to end or severely damage their careers with the click of a button. Online content typically fuels these impulses; over the years, people have uploaded millions of voyeuristic photos and videos to various websites, which has the effect of implicitly normalizing the behavior.

- It's a little bewildering that Morasch somehow thought no one would observe his attempt to record up the skirt of one of his students. Morasch was sitting at a lab table at the front of the classroom, with his back to the bulk of the class, and his students could see him holding his phone below the table. That would be suspicious enough for a bunch of teenagers but add in the fact that they all know what it looks like when a phone is recording, and you can understand why several of them used their phones to record the scene.

- Even though the phone evidence got thrown out in this particular case, it still serves as a good reminder that if the police come across other evidence of wrongdoing when investigating a separate crime, that evidence can and will be used against you. As this case illustrates, computer forensics tools and techniques are not perfect, but more often than not, they are capable of retrieving all kinds of content that you may have thought was forever deleted.

Cautionary Tale 19-2010-Canada

It was a lot harder to go viral in 2010, but two Canadian teachers at Winnipeg's Churchill High School managed to do it. At a school pep rally in February 2010, Chrystie Fitchner was paired with a new colleague Adeil Ahmed to compete in a teacher dance-off. Ahmed suggested to Fitchner that she sit in a chair while he danced in front of her. When the music started, Ahmed straddled Fitchner, began grinding against her, and at one point, simulated oral sex with her.

In an interview published eight years after the pep rally, Fitchner admitted that as students started cheering, she began to get into the routine and actively encouraged Ahmed's salacious lap dance. Even without the possibility of viral notoriety, Fitchner and Ahmed should have realized that what they were doing was wildly inappropriate in a gymnasium full of children. But even in 2010, the fact that a significant percentage of the audience was carrying a smartphone turned a brief, poor decision into a life-changing moment.

As copies of the video spread rapidly around the internet, parents began calling the Winnipeg school offices to demand that the district take disciplinary action. School officials suspended Fitchner and Ahmed (initially with pay and then without) pending an investigation. In April, the Winnipeg School Division declined to renew Ahmed's short-term contract and accepted Fitchner's resignation. She later said that she was forced to resign but did not elaborate on how that was done.

Fitchner left Manitoba and eventually married an American firefighter. She's the mother of two daughters and occasionally teaches part-time using her husband's last name. But the incident, she said, "blackballed her" and made it impossible for her to find a permanent position.

Top Three Takeaways:

- Fitchner's description of the aftermath of her moment of viral fame highlights a couple of essential issues that run through this book. First, her resignation, combined with her notoriety, had a devastating impact on her life. After losing her job, she lost her apartment in Manitoba and, for some time, lived in her car or on friends' couches. It is difficult for any of us to pause and contemplate possible long-term consequences during an exciting situation. One of the goals of the MCEE is to help educators develop a level of ethical "muscle memory" that will help guide decision making even when things get lively.

- Second, there was a distinct difference between how the media and the public treated the two teachers. Fitchner received the bulk of the blame for the incident, and critics raided her Facebook feed for potentially provocative photos. Media outlets made extensive use of a vacation photo that showed Fitchner in a bikini, which had nothing to do with the situation at hand. Since the video was seemingly everywhere (it even wound up on the Howard Stern Show and TMZ), Fitchner found herself being harassed and slut-shamed by total strangers. Rooting out sexism and misogyny is not going to happen overnight, but hopefully, we will make some headway as a society. In the meantime, however, female educators do need to be aware of how these double standards can manifest themselves when cybertraps occur.

- The ultimate lesson here: The internet does not forget easily. Type the search terms "teacher gym lapdance" into YouTube, and two different videos of the pep rally dance are still in the top ten results, a decade later.

Relevant MCEE Provisions for Chapter 19

Principle I: Responsibility to the Profession

Standards I.A.3, I.A.5, and I.B.3

Principle III: Responsibility to Students

Standards III.A.3, III.A.5, III.B.2, and III.B.3

Principle IV: Responsibility to the School Community

Standards IV.B.2 and IV.D.3

Sources

The sources for the Cautionary Tales in this chapter can be viewed at the following URL:

https://link.cybertraps.com/C4E2-Sources-Chap19

Chapter 20
Assignments or Teacher Comments That Go Viral

Overview

If you lose your temper or act outrageously in the classroom, it probably won't come as a shock that one or more of your students has channeled their inner Spielberg by using their smartphone to capture the moment. You may not like the fact that smartphones have turned your students into small hordes of *paparazzi* with global distribution networks at their fingertips, but there's no easy way to put that particular genie back in the bottle. As we'll see in the final section of this book, some schools have adopted policies designed to take devices out of student's hands during class, but there is often significant pushback from students and parents.

The cybertrap of classroom smartphones is not merely limited to the documentation of physical misconduct. As more and more teachers are discovering, the combination of mobile devices and social media has created a situation in which *any* action by an educator — homework assignments, quizzes and tests, and student feedback—can be offered up for global scrutiny and feedback. To be fair, it has always been necessary for teachers to be sensitive to the mores and values of the school community in which they teach. But a variety of forces have combined to make the teaching environment far more challenging than it used to be.

The first and foremost of these forces is the decades-long attack on public education in general and the teaching profession in particular. For most people my age, the parental presumption when issues arose was that the teacher was correct until shown otherwise (which was rare). That presumption, however, has faded. Too many parents reflexively side with their child or even encourage him or her to be confrontational with teachers. Such disrespect is not universal, of course, but the change in social attitudes is disturbing.

Closely related to that trend is another: the profound polarization that has gripped our country, especially over the last four years. One consequence of the political shift is that parents on both ends of the political spectrum are hypervigilant about the concepts and information taught to their children in school.

Twenty or more years ago, if a parent were upset about a homework assignment, a quiz question, or an assigned book, they would complain about it to the teacher, the principal, the superintendent, or perhaps even the school board. Doing so required an investment of time, so parents had to weigh whether the issue was important enough to merit the effort involved. That approach also enabled people to have actual conversations aimed at resolving any disagreements.

All too often today, of course, parents vent their spleen by quickly snapping a photo of the offending material and sharing it with a worldwide audience. If the grievance is provocative enough, a virtual firestorm can erupt that can quickly spill over into the real world, including everything up to and including death threats (seriously, what is wrong with some people these days?). Sadly, school districts often do not give an educator a chance to explain his or her actions before being attacked. The ferocity of public reaction often blindsides school officials, and local school boards must deal with a public relations nightmare that is often vastly disproportionate to the actual scale of the problem.

No individual educator, school, or school district is going to be able to single-handedly solve the social ills that have led to this sorry state of affairs. Still, certain things can be done at each level of a school community to minimize the chances of viral blowback for ill-worded or ill-conceived assignments.

First, every educator should remember that he or she has an ethical duty to reflect on the students in front of them and the community in which they teach. Education can and should be challenging, but in a polarized environment, assignments require thoughtfulness and tact. Second, you should always take the time to discuss potentially controversial assignments, quizzes, *etc.*, with a colleague or supervisor. (If you don't recognize that your current events assignment might be controversial, that's a more profound concern.) It's always easier to cope with social media outrage if your supervisors have been given a heads-up and are prepared to support you.

The main lesson of this chapter is that the world has changed dramatically in a brief time, and a very bright spotlight can shine on the decisions you make in the classroom. The way to handle this brave new world is to be thoughtful and reflective about what you do and to build a team of supporters within the school to help manage whatever controversy might arise. A central theme of the Model Code of Ethics for Educators is the importance of communication among educators and school officials. The more that occurs, the easier it will be to address potential controversies.

Cautionary Tales

Cautionary Tale 20-2019-US_Missouri

When I was younger, one of my favorite computer games was "Oregon Trail." The basic concept was straightforward: You are about to embark on a trip from Independence, Missouri to the Pacific Northwest. You have $1,600 to purchase oxen, a Conestoga wagon, and enough supplies to keep yourself and your "family" safe and fed on the long and treacherous journey to Oregon. If you never had a chance to play the game or now realize just how much you miss it, there's an online emulator of the 1985 software that you can play. Be warned: the odds are good that you will drown, starve, or be eaten by wolves long before you make it to the Willamette Valley. And not surprisingly, the stereotypes of Native Americans in the game are deeply offensive (especially as the game presumes that you are racing to settle on land from which they have been dispossessed—or worse).

I was reminded of "Oregon Trail" by a homework controversy that arose in St. Louis, Missouri, at the end of 2019. It's a great illustration of how just how easily an insensitive and poorly-conceived class project can generate vast amounts of negative publicity for an educator and a school district.

As is so often the case, all it took was a smartphone camera, and a social media account to cause an uproar. On December 8, 2019, a woman named Lee Hart posted a photo to Facebook of a class assignment, which she captioned as follows:

> A friend of mine's child brought this home from Blades Elementary School, 5th grade. It is so wrong on so many levels ⓜ ⓝ ⓞ   What do you think the plan of action should be?

> This was supposedly a westward expansion lesson. Some were given food, wood, water, and...slaves!!!!!!!!!!!

The apparent goal of the assignment was to introduce students to the concept of trade and a market economy. Unfortunately, the teacher did not spend enough time considering the emotional and social impact of the question:

> You own a plantation or farm and therefore need more workers. You begin to get involved in the slave trade industry and have slaves work on your farm. Your product to trade is slaves.

> Set your price for a slave. _____ These could be worth a lot.

> You may trade for any items you like.

The comments responding to Hart's Facebook post shine a grim light on the polarization of the country, with some decrying the insensitivity of the assignment, others defending it as a legitimate reflection of U.S. history, and still others suggesting that Hart made the whole thing up.

Hart did not fabricate the story; the school district quickly placed the teacher on administrative leave and began an investigation. Blades Elementary principal Jeremy Booker said that the exercise was a misguided effort to teach market forces. He agreed that the assignment was "culturally insensitive" and told parents in a letter that the teacher had expressed "considerable remorse."

Mehlville School District Superintendent Chris Gaines went further in his statement:

> Asking a student to participate in a simulated activity that puts a price on a person is not acceptable. Racism of any kind, even inadvertently stemming from cultural bias, is wrong and is not who we aspire to be as a school district. I am sorry and disappointed that this happened in our school.

Both Booker and Gaines said that the district would be providing teachers with professional development specifically focused on concepts of "cultural bias."

Top Three Takeaways:

- Social media increasingly serves as the great and general court of our age, and the unfortunate reality for educators is that there are thousands, if not millions of people ready to sit in judgment on the pedagogical choices that you make. It's a sobering situation for teachers since the possibility always exists that someone, somewhere will be offended by a class assignment or test question. Whether and to what extent the threat of social media criticism changes how you teach and the homework you hand out is something you will have to decide.

- Sometimes, of course, social media criticism is well-earned. It is difficult to defend the educator in this case. At a minimum, she demonstrated a lack of sensitivity for issues and concerns that are at the forefront of the national conversation right now. More broadly, her assignment displayed an obliviousness to how those conversations might be affecting students. As the MCEE makes clear, educators are obligated to try "to understand students' educational, academic, personal and social needs as well as students' values, beliefs, and cultural background." All of those factors can be influenced not only by our national history but also by the events taking place right outside classroom windows.

- The prevalence of social media and its ready availability to parents as a tool for broadcasting, protest, and organization presents both challenges and opportunities to educators and school districts. The problems are grave—increased scrutiny, the potential for widespread criticism, harsh language, trolling, *etc.*—but the opportunities for robust—deeper engagement with the school community, quick and timely assignments, dynamic conversations with parents and students, and so on. It may be tempting in instances like this to view social media merely as a threat, but we should not ignore its positive potential as well.

Cautionary Tale 20-2019-US_California

Teacher feedback is a critical part of the educational process. Students may not always like it, but the goal is to give them guidance on how they can improve their work and their understanding of the material they are studying. Of course, it helps if that feedback is at least moderately constructive. As much as we might like to think otherwise, however, that's not always going to be the case. Everyone has bad days, and most of us have said or written things we later regret. The challenge for educators lies in the fact that they are always under scrutiny by parents, all of whom have access to social media to air any complaints or objections.

Alyssa Rupp Bohenek, a second-grade teacher at Valley View Elementary School in York, Pennsylvania, discovered the frightening power of social media in the spring of 2019. She handed out a 50-question math quiz to her second-grade students and gave them three minutes to complete it. Bohenek was unimpressed with the efforts of one of her students, a young boy named Kamdyn Piland; she scrawled across the top of his quiz in red ink, "Absolutely pathetic he answered 13 in 3 min! sad ☹"

Piland later told a local news station that "[s]he made me really sad and upset. I was really mad. And [it was] really mean to do. It broke my heart."

Kamdyn Piland was not the only one upset. His father, Christopher Piland was irate about Bohenek's comments. "You don't write that on anybody's paper, let alone a little 7-year-old, second grader's paper," he said.

Piland messaged Bohenek to tell her that he thought her conduct was "was extremely unprofessional and just very rude[.]" He said that Bohenek texted back and said that she was sorry he felt that way.

Upset with Bohenk's dismissive attitude, Piland wrote a post on Facebook to ask his family and friends what he should do. He also included a photograph of his son's quiz with Bohenek's comments visible at the top. Not surprisingly, Piland's post went viral, with people weighing in from around the world. A petition was started on Change.org that called for Bohenek's dismissal; it garnered over 17,000 signatures in the first week (it currently has just over 20,000). She even starred as a short-lived hashtag on Twitter: #AlyssaRuppBohenek.

Valley View School District Superintendent Rose Minniti said that the district was aware of the controversy and was investigating the incident. However, she said, "It's a personnel issue and the results of that are not going to be dictated by social media. It's going to be dictated by the facts and evidence. As always with everything, we're going to try to do what's best for the students and what we need to do for the employee under investigation."

The staff director for Valley View Elementary School still lists Bohenek as a second-grade teacher. However, emails sent to the addresses listed for Bohenek both bounced so that that information may be out of date.

Top Three Takeaways:

- This cautionary tale is a straightforward example of the ethical obligation to treat students with respect. (*See* the provisions of the MCEE at the end of this chapter.) It is an ethical duty that exists wholly apart from the threat of internet shaming. It doesn't hurt to reflect on the fact, however, that abusing or ridiculing a student can far too easily make you an online villain.

- For better or worse, the internet has upended long-standing power structures in myriad institutions, and education is one of them. Educators and administrators are much more vulnerable to parental criticism these days, given the potential of parents to harness the power of public opinion on social media with a single photograph or angry post. The shift in the power dynamic is irreversible (unless social media somehow vanishes overnight), but it need not be a catastrophe for teachers or administrators. Parents will be far less likely to invoke the awesome power of social media if educators adhere to the ethical principles in the MCEE, communicate clearly and reasonably with students and parents, and promptly address any concerns that arise. These are all things that schools should be endeavoring to do regardless of social media and its lurking hordes of trolls.

- It is also a good reminder that these types of social media controversies put a strain on district and building administrators. It is essential, even in the glare of what appears to be worldwide condemnation, for district leaders to keep a cool head, follow established procedures, and base their actions on facts and not emotion.

Cautionary Tale 20-2019-US_Texas

The great Texas writer Molly Ivins spent much of her illustrious career chronicling the oddities and quirks of the Texas Legislature, or as she affectionately called it, "The Lege." Ivins was a native Californian with excellent journalistic credentials (Smith College, Columbia School of Journalism, *The New York Times*, etc.) and a wonderful sense of humor. She took great delight in affectionately poking fun at some of the more foolish legislative actions (or inactions) that occurred in Lone Star state capitol.

In her 1991 book, *Molly Ivins Can't Say That, Can She?*, she revealed that during each two-year legislative session, the Austin press corps would vote on "the ten stupidest members of the Legislature."

"For the last three sessions," she wrote, "the title of Number One Dumb has been captured by a Republican, leading to no small degree of ill feeling among loyal Democrats." To overcome the fact that some legislators hid their eligibility for this award by simply not saying anything during the legislative session, Ivins said, the press corps developed a sub-category called "The Top Ten Pieces of Furniture."

All of which brings us to Briscoe Cain, a member of the Texas House who represents District 128, a somewhat-convoluted district a little bit east of Houston. First elected in 2016, the young lawyer got off to an ignominious start when he headlined a list of "The Worst" legislators compiled by *Texas Monthly*:

> We typically exempt freshmen from the Worst list. We usually forgive their transgressions, because they don't know how the Legislature works. So just know that we tried. We tried really hard to give Briscoe Cain a pass. But he left us little choice.
>
> When we asked Capitol insiders for Worst list suggestions, his name, almost universally, was the first one mentioned.

One of the main reasons for Cain's selection, *Texas Monthly* said, was a moment on the Texas House floor that would have been classic fodder for an Ivins column (who sadly died of breast cancer in 2007). During a 2017 budget debate, Cain used the term "death panel" to describe "a state council that promotes palliative care[.]" Incensed, the deeply-conservative Cain proposed an amendment to reduce the council's budget to zero.

As the debate over his amendment progressed, his incredulous colleagues slowly realized that Cain didn't know the meaning of the phrase "palliative care," *i.e.,* "the treatment of terminally ill people for pain and anxiety to ease their passing." As *Texas Monthly* neatly summed up:

[Cain] eventually withdrew his amendment, but not before he'd very nearly zeroed out funding for a good program without actually knowing what it does. Thankfully his colleagues saved him from himself in that instance. Unfortunately, there was no one to save the rest of us from Briscoe Cain.

The *Texas Monthly* article serves as a useful background for understanding Cain's involvement in a controversy that erupted in the Goose Creek Consolidated Independent School District (GCCISD) in March 2019. Chris Felder, a parent of a GCCISD student, sent Cain a copy of an assignment on "Inference" given to his child by an unnamed 7th-grade teacher. The teacher told students to read a short essay entitled "Trump Against American Values." The students were then asked to identify two conclusory statements with which the author would agree and provide a brief answer to the question, "What is the author implying about Donald Trump?"

Upon receiving Felder's message, Cain decided to post his thoughts on Facebook. He made his disapproval extremely clear:

> This individual has violated the sacred trust that every parent has with the State of Texas when they send their child into a public school. They have lost the privilege of being in a classroom with Texas children, and forfeit the title of teacher. No teacher should attempt to indoctrinate a child to their ideology, no matter who is in the White House.

Cain did not mention the fact that the district had already resolved the matter at the campus level.

Having read the short essay, I think it is fair to say that reasonable people can disagree about the extent to which it attempts to indoctrinate children. At most, it suggests that the President of the United States should exhibit basic standards of decency and set an example for the very children for whom Cain expressed such concern.

Activist politicians of any stripe have a duty to consider the potential consequences of their words, particularly given our wildly polarized political landscape. In the wake of Cain's Facebook post, the district received several disturbing phone calls, including some death threats, from people upset about the perceived slight to President Trump. The school district issued a statement expressing its concern:

> We received many calls at the district following the issue of a media release and social media post that told part of the story and did not reflect the fact that the matter had been resolved within the district. Many of those calls were deeply disturbing and threatening in nature. While we all agree that the particular passage should not have been used, the teacher made a simple error in judgment. Like all of us, teachers are human and make mistakes from time to time.

When asked about the threatening calls, Cain ignored the district's concerns and instead touted his role in bringing the matter to light (again, ignoring the district's resolution of the case).

> Some view this incident as a simple mistake, others see it as a betrayal of parents and students. Sunlight is the best remedy to inappropriate behavior in the classroom. The importance of Texans being made aware of such actions is to ensure public accountability to indoctrination in the classroom.

It is disingenuous for Cain or any legislator in this day and age to blatantly disregard the potential impact of inflammatory social media posts. Legislators do have the right, if not the duty, to publicize misconduct in public institutions. But in doing so, it is incumbent upon them to provide complete information about what has occurred.

Top Three Takeaways:

- The cybertrap into which this teacher stumbled is one about which every educator should be aware. In our highly politicized and polarized society, it is essential to think carefully about the materials that you use for classroom assignments. I am a staunch free speech advocate, and I genuinely believe that educators should take a full part in our vibrant political debate. That is the right and duty of every citizen. At the same time, it is also vital for every educator to reflect on the potential social, political, and emotional impact of the material they use for class assignments.

- There is no foolproof way to prevent assignments from being distributed on social media, where they can be misinterpreted or manipulated for partisan purposes. The only recourse is always to be aware of that possibility and to make sure that you have the backing of your building and district supervisors in case things go sideways. There isn't the time or need to discuss every potentially controversial homework assignment with your building supervisor(s). Your political radar, however, should be sufficiently fine-tuned to anticipate which homework assignments might be particularly provoking.

- One of the challenges of our current era is not merely the possibility that things can go sideways but that they can go sideways so incredibly quickly. Sadly, we can now measure the time required to go from parental outrage to death threats against a school in mere hours. That it happens at all is, of course, a terribly sad commentary on the state of society. Both educators and school administrators should prepare for what can often be very fast-moving social media storms. Have a response plan in place, one that lists (at a minimum): a) the people who should be called and in what order; b) the types of statements that should be issued and who should issue them; c) the law enforcement agencies that should be contacted; and d) the physical safety measures that should be put in place.

Cautionary Tale 20-2019-US_California

Social media is a fascinating phenomenon and offers endless pedagogical opportunities for teachers. Every couple of weeks or so, for instance, I'll see another tweet from a teacher asking people for retweets to help demonstrate just how far and fast information can spread. It's the digital equivalent of using messages in a bottle or balloons with postcards to illustrate ocean and air currents.

Not all assignments involving social media, however, are created equal. There is a fine line between those that teach a useful lesson about how this relatively new mode of communication works and those that are vaguely unethical and borderline creepy. This cautionary tale involves a social media assignment that manages to straddle that line.

Brian Kwan, a junior high school government teacher at Anaheim Discovery Christian School in California, is well-known for his practice of starting the school year by giving his students an unusual extra credit assignment. For 2019, Kwan decided to issue what he called the "Katy Perry Challenge":

> Any student that can bring Katy Perry to this school and have her talk to me, you get an automatic A+ for my class; a video of her talking and saying my name (shout-out) get [sic] you an automatic B+.

As Kwan told *Buzzfeed News*, his goal in giving the assignment—which he described as a "complete joke"—was to demonstrate to his students that he could "relate" to them (always a dangerous motivation). As he explained in more detail:

> I thought, 'What kind of an assignment that can get them to laugh but at the same time have a shot at it – be it a long shot?' I am a fan of her music and totally enjoyed her *Teenage Dream* album, along with her *Prism* album. It was then that I was inspired to create this assignment and have the students at least know I have heard of her.

The educational content of the assignment shot up considerably when Jonathan Delos Angeles, one of Kwan's students, had a bright idea. He sent out a tweet on January 21, 2019, asking the Twitterverse to "please do its thing," either by getting Perry to come to Kwan's class or do a video shoutout.

Angeles's Twitter experiment was wildly successful. Thanks to Perry's enthusiastic fans, it quickly spread into timelines all across Twitter (by most recent count, it has been liked by almost 73,000 people and retweeted by just over 42,000). Like all experienced Twitter users who suddenly discover that they've gone viral, Angeles took the opportunity to do a little self-promotion: "i also make music so check me out katy perry if you find this [emojis]"

But more significantly, his attempt at Twitter networking *almost* paid off. Somehow, *American Idol* co-host Ryan Seacrest learned about the class assignment and shot a video for Angeles (and Kwan) with the three Idol judges: Lionel Ritchie, Luke Bryan, and Katy Perry. Ironically, the only member of the group who didn't say Kwan's name in the video was Perry.

Top Three Takeaways:

- The responses to the tweet by Angeles are a gold mine of teachable moments and ethical concepts. Some people questioned whether Kwan was wasting his students' time or effectively bribing them so that he could satisfy some life-long dream of meeting Perry. Others suggested that he should spend more time teaching. A few took the opportunity to argue that the government teacher had shown who really controls society (*i.e.*, celebrities). Still others touted whacky conspiracy theories (My favorite: "Makes sense that your government teacher would like her. She is a product of @CIA cultural department, wittingly or unwittingly. Same for Elvis Presley, Frank Sinatra, Justin Bieber, etc., etc..".)

- This particular cautionary tale did not end badly, but there are still some potential ethical pitfalls that Kwan should have considered. Actively incorporating social media into a class assignment, even one that is just for extra credit, is like starting a campfire during a drought. You may be able to keep things under control and successfully cook dinner, but you might also ignite a raging inferno. You might also inadvertently expose your students to some of the less-balanced people that lurk online.

- Educators should always be clear about their motivations when they craft assignments. It's one thing to name-check a singer in a homework assignment because you like his or her music. It's another thing altogether if you are effectively drafting your unwitting students into helping you to cyberstalk your celebrity crush.

Cautionary Tale 20-2019-US_Kansas

A perfect example of how a social media campfire can rage out of control occurred in February 2019 at Klein Oak High School in Spring, Texas (just north of Houston). A teacher at the school asked students to create a fake news story as part of the Klein Independent School District (KISD) Digital Citizenship Program. Among other things, the goal of the program is to teach KISD students "about being safe, ethical, and productive citizens while online."

The facts of this cautionary tale perfectly illustrate a central theme of this book: if something is digitized, it is extraordinarily difficult to keep it from spreading. What appears to have happened is that one student wrote a fake news story with a headline that read in part "Principal of Klein High School Arrested for Cocaine Drug Trafficking and Firearms Charges." A subheading added the additional detail that the principal was facing charges for possession of cocaine with intent to distribute to a student.

From a production perspective, the student deserved top marks; the story looked like a legitimate news outlet produced and distributed it. Had the story remained on the student's computer, everything would have been fine. But predictably, someone took a photo of the fake news story and shared it on Snapchat. From there, the phony story spread like wildfire to other social media channels and eventually to traditional media.

Interest in the story got so intense that KISD issued a statement explaining the situation and denying the allegations against the school administrator. The statement read in part:

> One student created a fake post outside of the scope of the assignment about a Klein Oak employee which has been shared repeatedly online. This post is NOT TRUE.

> Creating and spreading false and defamatory information about someone is illegal and could result in legal action.

> Social media has the ability to connect us in ways we've never had before. It is a powerful tool when used for the right reasons. It is just as powerful when used— knowingly or not— irresponsibly. This is the unfortunate power of social media.

> This is a teachable moment. Families can use this to start the conversation about the power of social media -- and the damage fake news can create.

Despite the rapid spread of the fake story, the controversy appears to have died down fairly quickly. Nonetheless, it provided KISD with a powerful lesson for its students and the broader school community about how easily false information can travel the globe.

Top Three Takeaways:

- At first blush, this seems like it was a brilliant assignment. A significant part of practical digital citizenship training is helping students develop critical thinking so that they can better evaluate the accuracy of the news they read. What better way to demonstrate how easy it is to create fake news than to ask the students to do so purposely? It probably would have been prudent to make it off-limits to write a story accusing someone of a crime (also an important part of digital citizenship), but perhaps the teacher assumed that none of the students would do so. Oops.

- This teacher overlooked two other essential points. First, he or she neglected to take into account the remarkable design and technical skills that some kids have these days. In what should serve as a warning to every cybersecurity expert worried about phishing attacks, the task of creating a highly realistic fake news article was quite literally child's play.

- Second, the teacher overlooked the remarkable distribution capabilities of every single smartphone in the room. A couple of clicks of a button and what was intended as a purely in-class exercise soon began rocketing around the world. Teachable moments abound. The very speed with which the story spread is instructive, as is the number of news outlets that were fooled by the quality of the work. And hopefully, the students learned how difficult it is to put the horse back in the barn. Fortunately, the article does not appear to have caused real harm. Still, teachers should frequently remind every student that when you break some things by misusing the internet, you can't necessarily put them back together.

Cautionary Tale 20-2018-England

Many if not most of the cases that I use as cautionary tales in this book can be neatly summed up by asking "What was he or she thinking?!?"—but some are in a category by themselves. This is such a case.

For nearly 16 years, Karen Hutchinson served as the Head of Art at the Priory City of Lincoln Academy, a co-educational secondary school in Lincoln, UK. The school is a little over fifty years old and has about 1,000 students.

During the 2018 fall semester, Hutchinson assigned her students a final project on the female form. An 18-year-old female student asked Hutchinson if she could take topless photos of a female classmate as a visual aid for her work, a planned abstract painting. Hutchinson agreed and lent the student her camera to take the pictures. She also had the students take the photos in a classroom closet and locked the door to make sure that they were not disturbed.

The images taken by the student were neither explicit nor readily-identifiable, as they just depicted the torso of the model. Still, the fact that Hutchinson facilitated such a photoshoot, especially on school grounds, was problematic. Her next step, however, severely exacerbated the situation. Hutchinson downloaded the photos from the camera and then sent them to the student photographer using her personal email account. By doing so, she bypassed the school's monitoring software.

There is some ambiguity regarding who may have seen the photos after Hutchinson sent them to her student. *The Sun*, one of England's notorious tabloid newspapers, breathlessly reported that the art student had shared the images with the examiners of her final project. The paper also claimed that the photos were then pinned to a portfolio board where they could be viewed by, among others, male students at the school. Headteacher Richard Trow told a local Lincoln news outlet, however, that only the student's original artwork was shared and subsequently displayed.

Upon learning about the photo session, the school immediately suspended Hutchinson and started an investigation. Less than three days later, the school fired Hutchinson and referred the matter to the Teaching Regulation Agency, the United Kingdom's educator licensing authority. Since the young woman who did the modeling for her classmate was just 17, the school asked the Agency to consider whether Hutchinson should be struck off (*i.e.*, lose her license) on the grounds of distribution of child pornography.

During the two-day Agency hearing, Hutchinson conceded that she had failed to maintain appropriate professional boundaries but said that she was unaware that the photography model was underage. Agency officials sharply criticized Hutchinson for her poor judgment in facilitating the photoshoot and her apparent effort to hide her actions from the school's IT department. They also underscored her violation of the "Priory Contract," which, among other things, requires staff members to "[e]nsure that students wear their uniform appropriately at all times." (Although to be fair, in the context of this case, that's like giving someone a ticket for failure to keep right after they've caused a serious car crash.)

In the end, however, the Professional Conduct Panel issued a statement on December 11, 2018, that it "did not find the case proved." Although Hutchinson avoided being formally struck off, her LinkedIn profile indicates that she has moved on from teaching and is now the Duty Manager at the Thames Ambulance Service, Ltd. in Lincoln.

Top Three Takeaways:

- Educators should always be ready to encourage the creative and artistic impulses of their students. At the same time, however, they should not abandon all common sense when they do so. And perhaps most importantly of all, they should not give students the means to break the law and thus digitally document the educator's lack of common sense.

- Hutchinson's use of her personal email account to share the photos with the student artist strongly suggests that she recognized that administrators at the school would have a problem with what she did. What Hutchinson did not fully understand is that even if she used her personal email account, there is an excellent possibility that investigators could still find copies of the photos themselves on the school computer, even if deleted. And the school, of course, would have complete authority to search its equipment as needed.

- There is no substantial evidence that anyone other than the photographer and her subject saw the photos in question. (Whether the student's abstract drawing of her classmate's torso might constitute child pornography is a question for another day and not directly relevant to Hutchinson's case.) But what Hutchinson should have taken time to consider is the fact that she arguably facilitated the commission of a crime. As noted above, it was not proven that Hutchinson knew the model was just 17. However, it is a possibility she should have considered before agreeing to her student's request.

Relevant MCEE Provisions for Chapter 20

Principle I: Responsibility to the Profession

Standards I.A.2, I.A.3, and I.A.5

Principle II: Responsibility for Professional Competence

Standards II.B.2 and II.C.3

Principle III: Responsibility to Students

Standards III.A.1, III.A.3, III.B.1, III.B.2, and III.B.3

Principle IV: Responsibility to the School Community

Standard IV.A.2 and IV.D.3

Principle V: Responsible and Ethical Use of Technology

Standards V.A.1 and V.A.5

Sources

The sources for the Cautionary Tales in this chapter can be viewed at the following URL:

https://link.cybertraps.com/C4E2-Sources-Chap20

Chapter 21

Accidental or Intentional Violations of Student Privacy

Overview

The main legal background for this chapter is the **Family Educational Rights and Privacy Act**, which was passed by Congress and signed into law by President Gerald Ford on August 21, 1974. There are entire books devoted to exploring the intricacies of FERPA, the accompanying regulations, the subsequent amendments, and regulatory tweaks, and the policies and procedures schools should adopt to comply with the law. This is not one of those books.

The goal here is to provide a brief overview of the law as it might apply to two specific types of online activity: social media use by teachers and students, and distance learning. If you would like to delve more deeply into FERPA and how it might apply to your classroom or your school, one excellent place to start is the section of the U.S. Department of Education's website that is devoted explicitly to student privacy: https://studentprivacy.ed.gov/.

Key Definitions

FERPA has two main objectives, which are neatly summarized by the Electronic Privacy Information Center (epic.org/privacy/student/ferpa/):

> First, it gives students the right to inspect and review their own education records, request corrections, halt the release of personally identifiable information, and obtain a copy of their institution's policy concerning access to educational records. (20 U.S.C.S. § 1232g(a)). Second, it prohibits educational institutions from disclosing "personally identifiable information in education records" without the written consent of the student, or if the student is a minor, the student's parents. (20 U.S.C.S. § 1232g(b)).

Schools or school districts that violate FERPA risk triggering one of Congress's preferred penalties: the loss of federal funding. Districts also face the possibility of a lawsuit by an affected student or his or her parents under state law for various privacy-related torts.

To avoid those undesirable consequences, it essential to understand: 1) what constitutes an "education record" (particularly in the fast-moving world of digital communications and social media) and 2) what types of information are encompassed by the phrase "personally identifiable information."

The Code of Federal Regulations (specifically, 34 CFR § 99.3) contains some specific definitions for the terms used in FERPA. The term "record," for instance, covers a wide range of familiar materials, including handwritten notes, printed documents, computer files, photos, videos, audio recordings, *etc.* The phrase **"education record"** is defined as a record that is:

1. Directly related to a student; and

2. Maintained by an educational agency or institution or by a party acting for the agency or institution.

As you might expect, the list of "personally identifiable information" (PII) contained in FERPA is somewhat lengthy and detailed. It includes:

a. The student's name;

b. The name of the student's parent or other family members;

c. The address of the student or student's family;

d. A personal identifier, such as the student's social security number, student number, or biometric record;

e. Other indirect identifiers, such as the student's date of birth, place of birth, and mother's maiden name;

f. Other information that, alone or in combination, is linked or linkable to a specific student that would allow a reasonable person in the school community, who does not have personal knowledge of the relevant circumstances, to identify the student with reasonable certainty; or

g. Information requested by a person who the educational agency or institution reasonably believes knows the identity of the student to whom the education record relates.

This definition of PII provides a baseline for understanding the types of student information that you *should not share* on social media. However, the law contains at least one glaring internal contradiction: the ability of a school to distribute so-called "directory information" routinely, provided that parents have not explicitly opted out. This contradiction is one of the reasons that there is such a booming supply of FERPA-related materials (and litigation).

Under the FERPA regulations, a school may classify some or all of the following PII as "directory information":

the student's name; address; telephone listing; electronic mail address; photograph; date and place of birth; major field of study; grade level; enrollment status (e.g., undergraduate or graduate, full-time or part-time); dates of attendance; participation in officially recognized activities and sports; weight and height of members of athletic teams; degrees, honors, and awards received; and the most recent educational agency or institution attended.

It is worth noting that the last time the United States Department of Education considered any changes to the definition of "directory information" was nearly a decade ago, back in 2011. Some commentators urged the DOE to narrow the definition of "directory information" to better protect students from possible identity theft, but the DOE declined to make any changes:

> The definition of "directory information" in FERPA is generally a guideline for schools to use in designating types of information as directory information. A school is not required to designate all of the types of information given as examples in FERPA as directory information. The decision to designate certain types of information as directory information, such as the student's address, is left to the discretion of the individual educational agency or institution. We share the concerns raised by commenters that certain directory information items may make identity theft easier in our modern information age. We encourage school officials to be cognizant of this fact and, if feasible, to work hand-in-hand with parents and eligible students in their community to develop a directory information policy that specifically meets their needs and addresses legitimate concerns.

A lot of software and hardware changes have occurred since 2011. It is essential to ask whether your school or school district has done a thorough analysis of the potential misuses of directory information and updated its parental consent form accordingly. Keep in mind that this is not a one-time exercise; as existing technologies evolve and new ones emerge, there is an ongoing need to think carefully about how best to protect student privacy and safety.

Here is the fundamental question: What is the minimum amount of information that can be routinely shared while still accomplishing the education and social goals of the organization? It's not particularly useful pedagogy to educate students about digital citizenship and online privacy at the very same time that their school and school district is casually handing out "directory information."

In general, my recommendation is that neither schools nor individual educators should casually rely on the "directory information" exemption contained in FERPA. While it may be *legal* to ask parents for permission to distribute all of that information once they consent, it may not necessarily be *ethical* to do so. Each educator has an overarching ethical duty of care that is owed to students and their parents, as does the organization as a whole.

Besides, it's necessary to keep in mind that many parents will sign the consent form without giving it much thought since they have neither the time nor inclination to research and ponder these issues. As I discussed earlier, educators have specific ethical obligations not only to students and parents but to the school community as a whole. In this context, that means educating parents about the potential consequences of sharing directory information and then limiting the amount of such data that is publicly shared.

Social Media and Student Privacy

The widespread use of social media has created numerous potential cybertraps for educators, as you can see in the chapters below. The use of social media by educators presents two main concerns when it comes to student privacy: 1) are educators violating student privacy if they look at what students share online? And 2) do educators violate student privacy (and possibly FERPA as well) if they post photos or comments about students on social media?

The first question is relatively easy to answer. Students, like adults, have no reasonable expectation of privacy concerning anything they post on social media. But the mere fact you can view the public social media posts of students without infringing their privacy rights does not mean that it is ethical for you to do so. As you can see from the various standards listed in the section below, the intersection of student privacy and social media implicates the highest number of MCEE standards in this book. That reflects both the critical importance of student privacy and the extent to which technology and social media have woven themselves into our lives.

Of the various standards listed in the section below, the most important in this context is **Standard V.B.2.**, which states that educators should respect student privacy on social media *unless* given consent to view their content *or* if the educator thinks there might be evidence of harm to the student. And I would go one step further: even if a student invites you to view his or her social media feed, you should refrain from doing so unless you discuss the invitation and your reasons for accepting it with a colleague. Even more important: don't use that permission as an excuse to communicate directly with the student in a private or non-transparent fashion.

More broadly, educators should avoid searching for their students online, encouraging them to share their user IDs (let alone their passwords!), or asking students to follow their personal social media accounts. The MCEE encourages educators to develop separate online accounts for their professional posts and their personal activities and opinions. Violating these guidelines raises the potential for confusing and perhaps dangerous multiple relationships with students.

Educator posts *about* students on social media are somewhat more complicated. Here's the first question: if a teacher takes a photo of a student in his or her classroom, is that an "education record" as defined by FERPA? There is no clear answer, unfortunately. A close-up photo of a student, for instance, does contain personal identifying information (his or her face, at the very least), but it is probably not a record "maintained by an educational agency or institution." Instead, a photo taken by a teacher is perhaps more akin to a personal note that a teacher writes during the day.

The next question that arises is whether the photo itself depicts anything that might be considered an educational record. Here a few possibilities to keep in mind:

- Are student homework assignments or tests visible?
- Is it possible to read names, grades, or other personal identifying information in the photo?
- How easily can individual students be recognized?
- Was the photo taken in the classroom or at an event that is open to the public?
- Does the photo show documents on your desk that might reveal personal information? Keep in mind that with each new generation of smartphones, camera resolutions get steadily better, so a piece of paper that was unreadable in an iPhone 4 photo might be surprisingly legible in a photo taken with an iPhone 11.

It bears repeating that none of this is a problem if you take a photo and keep it for yourself. But in the current era of social media, the chances that the public will see your classroom photos are quite high. It is increasingly common for educators to feel pressured by school administrators and parents to share photos. In an era of rising education costs and tight budgets, school districts have a strong incentive to show how they are serving students and the public and to demonstrate their cutting-edge use of technology. All too often, there is also a subtle competition among educators to be the most tech-savvy teacher in the school, since that often can lead to professional accolades, promotions, and raises. And of course, parents are always interested in seeing what their children are doing in school, so teachers commonly view the enthusiastic use of social media as part of their service to the school community.

The chief peril, as always, is the technology-fueled acceleration of our decision-making. Baked into social media is the fierce (but ultimately false) urgency of NOW, that relentless sense that we must not delay a single instant in tweeting, posting, uploading photos and videos, *etc.* The faster we do things, however, the more likely it is that we will make a mistake, overlook something we should have noticed, or unintentionally cause harm that we could have avoided. Ideally, school policies and procedures can help regulate the content that is shared online. It is ultimately the responsibility of individual educators to slow themselves down and be thoughtful about the content they share from their classrooms.

Even if it is entirely *legal* to share a classroom photo on social media, thanks to FERPA's vast "directory information" safe harbor, every educator should stop and think about the potential consequences of photo sharing. Is there a possibility that someone will use the photo to bully or harass the students pictured? Will it cause friction with parents whose kids are not portrayed? Will it create an impression of favoritism? If the photo is particularly cute or funny, is there a possibility that someone will misappropriate it for use in advertising or a mocking meme?

There are many good reasons to post photos online. Doing so ethically, however, requires a solid understanding of how the technology works, a thoughtful set of school and school district policies and procedures to guide educators, and as limited distribution as is possible. At the very least, educators should rarely, if ever, post classroom photos on globally-accessible social media accounts. Instead, save them for school-run websites or community-restricted social media pages.

Online Learning and Student Privacy

Interest in online or distance learning has been growing steadily over the last twenty-five years, thanks to the powerful pedagogical tools made possible by the World Wide Web. That use of distance learning has dramatically accelerated (out of necessity) thanks to the coronavirus pandemic that first hit in late 2019 and early 2020 (which is ongoing as I write this). It is unlikely that there will be a wholesale abandonment of face-to-face instruction in K-12 schools, in no small part because schools provide so many vital secondary services, ranging from meals to childcare. At the same time, however, I don't think there is any question that online learning will get a significant boost from this crisis, now that we've been reminded what "going viral" really means.

Unfortunately, the growing use of distance or remote learning raises myriad student privacy issues, most of which will not get the attention they deserve in a rush to preserve some level of learning in the spring of 2020 (and possibly longer). At some point, districts need to spend some time reviewing what student data online learning platforms are collecting from students and how they are handling that data. In theory, both FERPA and the Child Online Privacy Protection Act (COPPA) offer some protection of student data. As many people have observed, however, data is the new oil, and it is central to the economy of the internet and the success of internet-related businesses.

Earlier this spring, *The Washington Post* noted that that the Federal Bureau of Investigation had issued a warning in 2018 about the data threats to K-12 students stemming from the growing use of educational technology (including online learning). The *Post* summarized the FBI's findings as follows:

> The FBI said the types of data that can be collected on students include personally identifiable information; biometric data; academic progress; behavioral, disciplinary and medical information; web browsing history; students' geolocation; IP addresses used by students; and classroom activities.

The primary long-term concern here is the use of this information for fraud or identity theft, if student data should ever be lost or stolen (the odds of which unfortunately are quite high). Even if the data is adequately protected, it undoubtedly will be used to tailor advertisements and commercial offers for students as they grow older. That may not sound like much imposition, but it is not possible to foresee all future uses of collected data. At the very least, it is a considerable invasion of privacy for a student to lose control over his or her educational information.

In the short term, as teachers and students are discovering, the sudden use of videoconferencing is raising several challenging issues. At a structural level, it is revealing suspected but inadequately quantified (or addressed) disparities in access to necessary equipment and broadband internet connections. The Model Code of Ethics for Educators makes it clear that educators should take the following steps:

- advocate for "adequate resources" for their students (Standard I.C.5.);

- advocate for "equitable educational opportunities" (Standard II.A.3.);

- provide access to resources that will ensure an "equitable educational experience" (Standard II.C.1.);

- demonstrate "a commitment to equality, equity, and inclusion (Standard IV.A.2.); and

- advocate for "equal access to technology for all students." (Standard V.D.1.)

To be fair, these standards focus primarily on the equity of access to resources and technology in the classroom or the school environment, where educators can have a much more direct impact. Five years ago, nobody was contemplating the equity issues arising out of a sudden and massive adoption of online learning in response to a global pandemic. Addressing those systemic-level disparities needs to occur at pay grades well above that of the average teacher.

But equity is not the only ethical issue highlighted by distance learning. With so many teachers and students broadcasting from home, a host of other concerns about privacy, multiple relationships, the duty to report, *etc.*, are now being raised.

When it comes to potential invasions of privacy, not all distance learning systems are created equal. The rule of thumb, logically, is that the more widespread the sharing, the higher the privacy risk. It is much more challenging to separate your professional and personal lives when you are teaching your students while broadcasting from your home. It's equally hard to respect the privacy of your students on social media (Standard V.B.2.) when they are sharing a portion of their home with you on a distance learning platform (which is, after all, just a specialized form of social media).

You should take some basic steps to minimize privacy risks. On your end, the most obvious thing to do is to create a professional backdrop (a whiteboard, for instance, or a wall decorated with maps, posters, etc.) and consistently use that for your video broadcasts. Your students may or may not be able to do the same thing, but at the very least, each should be encouraged to think about what might be showing onscreen when they broadcast from their home.

Distance learning platforms typically use video in one of the following ways: a gallery view, where each participant can see all of the other participants at the same time (think, for instance, Google Hangout or Zoom), or a broadcast view, in which each student just watches the teacher's video feed. Some platforms are more flexible, allowing the teacher to see all students at once, focus on a single student, engage in group or one-on-one chat, and so on.

Let's put aside for the moment the various risks that arise out of direct communication, either video or chat, between a teacher and a specific student. I'll discuss those particular risks in the context of multiple relationships, grooming, *etc.* The more immediate focus here is on your ethical obligation if you observe certain types of behavior during an online class.

Some behaviors do not present much of an ethical dilemma. If you see a student cyberbullying another student during a virtual class, you have the same obligation to take action that you would if the behavior was occurring in front of you in the classroom. You probably can't send the student to a virtual principal's office (as much as you might like to do so). However, you should be sufficiently familiar with the distance learning platform to be able to shut off a student's chat or video if need be.

If you are recording your virtual classes, that may be useful for documenting student misconduct, but it does raise additional issues for you to consider. The most significant is that recordings of virtual classes are almost certainly "educational records" as defined by FERPA, and you should treat them with the same care and confidentiality that you would manage other FERPA-designated documents.

The most tempting social media/privacy risk of recordings lies in the fact that undoubtedly, one or more of your students will do something amusing or mildly embarrassing while they're on camera in your virtual classroom. Regardless of how humorous it is (and we can all use more humor these days), that doesn't give you license to make them an involuntary social media star. It is evident that this is a significant temptation: Within days of the corona pandemic shut down, people started posting clips from videoconferences and college classes that showed various *faux pas.*

An unfortunate woman named Jennifer, for instance, gained considerable internet notoriety when she forgot that her webcam was on during a video class. A recording of the class discussion (in gallery view) showed Jennifer broadcasting herself to her classmates as she walks down a hallway, clearly carrying her computer. She turned into her bathroom, put her laptop on the floor, and then dropped trow before sitting down to use the toilet. A clip from the online video class—and the hysterical reactions of the other students—can be seen on YouTube under the title "Video Conference Gone Wrong - EPIC FAIL," where it was viewed more than 3.2 million times as of March 30, 2020. (And here's another lesson: as of August 15, 2020, the original video has been deleted from Youtube, undoubtedly at Jennifer's impassioned request—but at least a half-dozen copies can still be viewed.)

The most significant ethical issue for educators in this area arises from the fact that distance learning platforms offer a video window into the home lives of your students. The potential privacy infringements or boundary blurrings are bad enough, but what if you see or hear something that makes you think that a student is in physical or emotional danger? In most states, educators are mandatory reporters if they suspect child abuse, so this is something that you should discuss with your colleagues and supervisors as part of the set-up process for online teaching.

The language of the mandatory reporting requirement in the state of New York is reasonably representative of similar statutes around the country:

> Mandated reporters are required to report instances of suspected child abuse or maltreatment only when they are presented with reasonable cause to suspect child abuse or maltreatment in their professional roles.

In the context of online learning, what does "presented" mean? Do you need to witness child abuse on camera, or should you take action if you hear something happening off-camera while the class is going on? What constitutes "maltreatment" for mandatory reporting in the context of online learning? The simple fact of the matter is that the more online teaching you do with your students, the more you will learn about their personal lives and that knowledge may not always make you comfortable. The core ethical issue is figuring out when discomfort crosses over the line to a duty to report. The more discussion you can have beforehand with your colleagues about the appropriate parameters, the better.

Cautionary Tales

Cautionary Tale 21-2019-US_Tennessee

During my research for this book, I have frequently felt sympathy for building administrators and school officials. I know that they spend a lot of time and money providing training to educators on a variety of critical topics. FERPA, thanks to the potentially draconian penalties and expensive consequences for violations, is a popular topic for professional development sessions. At the very least, school districts frequently remind educators to review district policies regarding the handling of confidential student information. Nonetheless, there are still far too many examples of educators who simply ignore the warnings or don't hear them in the first place.

Take, for example, the case of Aaron Miller, a former theater arts teacher at the Tullahoma High School in Tullahoma, Tennessee. In mid-November 2019, the school announced it had suspended Miller from teaching for more than two weeks, pending an investigation into various allegations of misconduct.

The news reports are a little sketchy, but according to the investigative reports released by the school, Miller was charged with "possible violations of the Federal Educational Rights and Privacy Act (FERPA), violations of school policy, inadequate safety concerns on school field trips and 'multiple violations of the Tennessee Teacher Code of Ethics.'"

School officials alleged that among other things, Miller posted copies of student theater audition forms on social media, even though those forms clearly showed "student names, phone numbers and email addresses." He also apparently provided parents with information regarding other students (although it is not clear that social media was involved in those disclosures).

Following the school's investigation, Miller agreed to resign his teaching position effective October 28, 2019. He released a statement that read in part:

I'd like to say that it was my honor to serve students as an educator in Tullahoma City Schools. My family and I love this community. Professionally, it is time I move forward in another direction. It was a difficult decision, but one that I felt was in the best interest of students, the school and myself.

According to LinkedIn, Miller is currently working as a voice over artist and podcast producer, as well as assisting his wife in the operation of her clothing design company.

Top Three Takeaways:

- In this day and age, it is a little bewildering that anyone would need to be told not to post private student information online, notwithstanding the provisions of FERPA. There have been so many stories about the misuse of personal data that simple common decency would compel the careful handling and protection of student records.

- This cautionary tale does not even offer the excuse of accidental disclosure. Teachers should always carefully examine the photos they take in the classroom or on field trips before posting them online. Educators should always be aware of the potential for some confidential student information to be lurking in the background.

- Many of the consent forms that I've seen during my research are incredibly cursory. Schools and school districts should give both parents and students a solid understanding of their privacy rights concerning the posting of photos, videos, and other information online. I understand that blanket permission is simplest from a school or district perspective, but a more nuanced approach is not only more respectful but increasingly expected.

Cautionary Tale 21-2019-US_North Carolina

Here's a pro tip: the use of a social media digital sticker is not enough to save your job if you make fun of a student online. In August 2019, a teacher at Mooresville High School was looking forward to accompanying her students on a field trip. She ended up not going on the field trip and decided to create an Instagram video to let her friends and family know what had happened.

The video opens with a picture of the unnamed teacher and a caption that reads: "One student created an unsafe bus environment for my class, so guess who had to stay back with an unruly child while the rest of the class goes on a field trip?" The next thing you see is the teacher recording herself in a classroom; over her left shoulder is a student in a wheelchair, with a sticker over the child's face that reads "Ugh." She then offers her version of what happened:

This girl has not made a peep since we got into the classroom from the bus. Her unruly behavior was literally just to get out of the field trip and now we both get to sit here and stare at each other for the next three hours while the class is gone. Happy freakin' Wednesday.

The video closes with the teacher's captioned lament that she did not pack lunch because she thought she would be having pizza on the field trip. She ends with a plea: "Send food, send patience."

If the teacher was hoping for a sympathetic response, she badly misread the room. A community resident posted a copy of the teacher's video on Facebook, and it quickly attracted a lot of negative attention.

As the public outcry grew, the superintendent of the Mooresville Graded Schools quickly began an investigation. Within 48 hours, the teacher resigned from the school system. The district spokesperson issued a brief statement:

> The teacher who posted the video to social media voluntarily resigned her position with the Mooresville Graded Schools this morning, August 30, 2019. By law, the school board cannot comment on any specific employee matters. However, it is important for parents and the community to understand that anytime a question arises regarding the conduct of a school employee specific to their job, the Superintendent and school administrators work diligently to ensure the best possible outcome for our students.

Top Three Takeaways:

- This cautionary tale easily could have been included in Chapter 7, which discusses the cybertrap of mocking or criticizing students. I added it here because it goes beyond "mere" mocking or criticism. Notwithstanding the use of the cruel "ugh" sticker over the student's face, it is clear that the unnamed educator is talking about a female student who uses a wheelchair. It is likely that this teacher only has a few female students who use a wheelchair, or perhaps just one. In either case, it would not be difficult for someone in the school community to figure out the identity of the disciplined student.

- Although you can argue that the teacher's Instagram video is not an "education record" under FERPA, there is no question that the student's identity is, as is the fact that her teacher disciplined her for misbehavior. And even if it was not a FERPA violation *per se*, it unquestionably was a violation of the student's reasonable expectation of privacy.

- Instagram allows users to create and share video in two different formats: 1) as a traditional post, which is part of your permanent Instagram feed, and 2) as part of an Instagram Story, which is a collection of photos and videos shared by a user on a particular day. After 24 hours, Instagram Stories disappear. The goal, Instagram says, is to allow you to "share all the moments of your day, not just the ones you want to keep on your profile." It is a little unclear in this case, but it appears this educator posted this video as part of an Instagram story. It illustrates the overarching theme that some people do not always realize that there are some moments they just shouldn't share.

Cautionary Tale 21-2012-US_Florida

It's no great secret that students often use social media to talk about their teachers, nor is it particularly surprising that they often say things that are rude or unpleasant. Understandably, teachers are often curious about what students are saying about them, and that makes sense. No one wants to be the victim of cyberbullying by students or have their reputations trashed (for examples, *see* Chapter 20). But educators need to think carefully about just how far they should go to monitor student conversations on social media. It's one thing if the students are making comments on a publicly-accessible social media feed; it's another thing altogether if an educator uses underhanded methods to view the content.

In January 2012, Angela Cruikshank, a Spanish teacher at Land O'Lakes High School in Pasco, Florida, caught wind of a private Facebook page that allegedly contained unflattering comments about her. When she was unable to locate and access the page herself, she ordered one of her students to come to the front of the classroom and log into the page using Cruickshank's personal cellphone.

After perusing the comments on the page, Cruikshank allegedly compiled a list of the students that she suspected had made derogatory remarks. She then gave the roster of names to a small group of students and asked them to write "ok" next to the name of any student who did not write something negative. One parent alleged that Cruikshank also projected her daughter's private Facebook group onto a screen in one of her classes. More significantly, Cruikshank refused to give permission slips for a field trip to the nearby Salvador Dali Museum to those students she suspected had made negative comments online.

Parents of the disciplined children, not surprisingly, were furious at Cruickshank's *ad hoc* investigation. Several wrote emails or called district superintendent Heather Fiorentino to complain. After a short inquiry, Fiorentino sent a termination letter to Cruickshank that read in part: "This situation is very troubling to me. You seem unaware of student privacy concerns and used extremely poor judgment in taking the steps you took to address these concerns."

A hearing on Cruickshank's termination was held in July 2012, and her appeal was denied. At its September board meeting, the Pasco County School Board voted unanimously to uphold her dismissal. Board Vice Chairwoman Cynthia Armstrong aptly summed up the problem with Cruickshank's conduct:

> In reviewing the documentation and testimonies of the students and the teachers, the one thing that really stood out in my mind is that the teacher is a professional, and needs to act like a professional and needs to act like the professional in the room. I don't think that happened.

In an interview with a local news outlet following her firing, Cruickshank claimed that she was protecting students from cyberbullying and investigating whether the private group was being used by students to share tests. She was, she said, trying "to channel that into a teachable moment." The Pasco County School Board declined to comment further.

Top Three Takeaways:

- If you are an educator, don't involve any of your students in your attempts at digital investigations. If you have concerns about content online, talk to your IT department, your building supervisor, or law enforcement (if the content is criminal or threatening a criminal act).

- Do not attempt to bypass school filters by using your device to access prohibited or blocked content. Again, if you feel you have good reason to view the content, discuss the situation with someone who has the authority to help you do so.

- Above all, do not project the private information of students onto a classroom screen and do not coerce students into becoming digital informants on each other. Do not unilaterally punish students for statements they allegedly made on social media, particularly if you do not have proof that they did anything wrong. If you suspect that students have violated your school's acceptable use policy, you should follow your school district's policy and report the offense so that administrators can investigate it. Social media can make us all feel a little paranoid sometimes, but even students are entitled to information privacy and digital due process.

Cautionary Tale 21-2011-US_Illinois

School Photo Day can be a wonderful occasion for kids—particularly in the lower grades—to dress up a bit and show a little flair. In the fall of 2011, 7-year-old Ukailya Lofton persuaded her mother, Lucinda Williams, to recreate a hairstyle that she saw in a magazine—tight braids with Jolly Rancher candies dangling from the ends.

It ought not to have been a big deal. But when Ukailya went home that evening, she told her mom that her computer teacher, Dana Fitzpatrick, had taken her photo during the day and said to the young girl, "My husband is not going to believe this." Williams also heard from friends that Fitzpatrick had posted photos of Ukailya to her Facebook page and that people were mocking her hairdo.

When she took a look at Fitzpatrick's personal Facebook page, Williams discovered that Fitzpatrick had captioned the photos of her daughter: "Right! This is for picture day." One photo showed Ukailya from behind, and the other showed her face in profile. Some of Fitzpatrick's friends added their own critical opinions, ranging from "if you are going to make your child look ridiculous, the least you can do is have them matching," to "yeah, this is foolishness," to "I laughed so hard that my contact popped out."

Ukailya's reaction was completely understandable: "My mama told me she put it on Facebook and then I felt sad."

Williams told a local television station that the teacher had deleted the photos and comments from Facebook and apologized to her but not to her daughter. On April 6, 2011, Williams filed a lawsuit against the Chicago Board of Education and Dana Fitzpatrick, seeking $29,000 in damages for intentional infliction of emotional distress to her daughter. A court eventually dismissed the lawsuit in 2012, but Fitzpatrick did receive a Warning Resolution from the Chicago Board of Education for "unsatisfactory conduct."

Top Three Takeaways:

- One of the perpetual problems with social media is that it trains us to think that we each have an "audience," a group eagerly awaiting our next humorous photo or witty comment. It pushes us into continually looking for an image or incident about which we can be sarcastic or mocking or just plain mean. I think that is what happened here.

- The brazenness with which Fitzpatrick acted is a little breathtaking. From the moment the photo was taken, Ukailya clearly understood that her teacher intended to make fun of her. Ten years ago, a 7-year-old might not have guessed that a picture would wind up on Facebook, but she was certainly old enough to understand what it meant when her teacher did so.

- This cautionary tale drives home the point that most cybertraps are not about the technology; they are about the behavior that people engage in when they use technology. That is one of the reasons that the MCEE is so essential; it provides tools for helping educators think carefully about their values and those of the profession. Over time, the use of and reflection upon the principles and standards of the MCEE can help educators avoid cybertraps by modifying the behavior that can lead to them astray.

Relevant MCEE Provisions for Chapter 21

Principle I: Responsibility to the Profession

Standards I.A.2, I.A.3, and I.A.5

Principle II: Responsibility for Professional Competence

Standards II.B.5 and II.C.3

Principle III: Responsibility to Students

Standards III.C.1, III.C.2, and III.C.3

Principle IV: Responsibility to the School Community

Standards IV.A.4, IV.B.3, and IV.C.3

Principle V: Responsible and Ethical Use of Technology

Standards V.A.1, V.A.5, V.A.6, V.A.7, V.B.2, V.B.3, V.C.1, V.C.2, and V.C.3

Sources

The sources for the Cautionary Tales in this chapter can be viewed at the following URL:

https://link.cybertraps.com/C4E2-Sources-Chap21

Chapter 22

Cyberbullying and Cyberharassment of Educators by Students and Parents

Overview

The issue of cyberbullying among students has gotten a lot of attention over the past decade, particularly as the percentage of children using mobile devices has more than quadrupled since 2004. Increasingly, cyberbullying has been identified as a severely disruptive threat to the school environment, one that poses a significant risk to the mental and physical health of the children involved. Only recently, however, have people begun to focus on the fact that some students and their parents bully educators.

As with so many of the other issues discussed in this book, the underlying behavior is not a new phenomenon. Students have been playing pranks on teachers for a long, long time: crickets in the ceiling, frogs in desk drawers, tacks on the seat, and so on. However, those were localized events, and quickly dealt with; none of them, in today's vernacular, "went viral." Today's technology has not only changed the nature of the pranks that kids can play, but it also has dramatically expanded the potential audience. Kids no longer harass teachers for the sake of a few moments of laughter from their classmates; they are now competing to see how many hits or likes they can get on YouTube, Facebook, Instagram, and the like.

There is little disputing the fact that digital abuse of teachers is a growing problem. A 2006 survey by the National School Boards Association found that 26% of teachers in the U.S. had been targeted by cyberbullying. In 2011, a study of United Kingdom teachers by Plymouth University found that 35 percent of respondents had experienced some kind of cyberbullying. Teachers reported that 72 percent of the bullying was done by students and 26 percent by parents. A more recent UK study by the National Association of Schoolmasters Union of Women Teachers (NASUWT) found a lower rate of cyberbullying overall (roughly 21%). However, the NASUWT also found that the bullying was arguably more derogatory and involved a greater age range of children (including some as young as 4–7 years of age).

The tools used to cyberbully teachers will be familiar to anyone who has studied the issue of cyberbullying among students. That makes sense, of course; students are generally adept at using technology and can turn it to whatever ends best serve their purpose at the moment. Teachers report that they have been bullied via text messages, on social media posts (mainly Facebook, Twitter, and Instagram), in chat rooms and other online fora, on websites like RateMyTeachers.com or even on student-created websites targeted at embarrassing or libeling a specific teacher. The surveyed UK teachers reported that 47 percent of the online comments consisted of assorted insults, and 50 percent were critical assessments of their performance; over one-quarter of the remarks included photos or videos that students took without the consent of the targeted teacher.

Many of these online attacks come within the scope of general anti-cyberbullying statutes, so some relief is available. The problem of educator bullying has grown sufficiently severe, however, that the North Carolina legislature recently adopted a law (arguably unconstitutional) that imposes up to a month-long jail sentence and/or a $1,000 fine on any 15–17-year-old who "intimidate[s] or threaten[s]" a teacher. Of course, given the fact that UK researchers found that the "vast majority" of the online bullying of teachers was committed by students 11–16, it's not clear that the North Carolina law will have the preventative effect that the legislators hope.

One of the interesting questions is whether a specific law against bullying teachers will encourage more teachers to report abuse. It is discouraging but not surprising to note that nearly 60 percent of the teachers who admitted to being bullied did not bother to report the harassment to their administrators or, presumably, to the online services involved. Much of the reluctance educators feel arises from the sheer difficulty of identifying the perpetrators; it is far too easy for online bullies to hide their identity, at least on a superficial level. As someone who has worked in the field of computer forensics for more than twenty years, I can attest that it is more complicated than people realize to achieve true anonymity online. But in the case of most online bullying, the time and effort required to ferret out the people responsible are much higher than the actual harm caused by the bullying.

Disturbingly, some teachers also report a reluctance to report online bullying due to fear that the allegations will result in discipline by skittish administrators more concerned about potential liability than conducting a fair investigation. To be honest, we've made progress since the early days of the World Wide Web, when administrators and school boards had a much harder time believing that students were capable of using internet tools to malign their teachers. Few have any remaining illusions on that score.

Cautionary Tales

Cautionary Tale 22-2019-US_California

The Elk Grove Unified School District (EGUSD) is a relatively large school system a few miles south of Sacramento, California. In an interview for a video about the district's Positive Behavioral Intervention and Supports (PBIS) program, Associate Superintendent Mark Cerutti noted that the school district is essentially a small city, with over 62,000 students and approximately 6,000 employees. It is the 5th largest school district in California, with a total of 67 schools spread over an area that is 320 square miles in size. If EGUSD were a city, it would be the 20th largest in the United States.

It is, Cerutti said, also "an incredibly culturally and ethnically diverse community," with students speaking more than 110 different languages. According to a fact sheet produced by EGUSD for the 2019-2020 school year, the four largest populations among the students are Hispanic (26%), Asian (23%), White (21%), and African American (13%). The ethnic composition of the district's 3,251 certificated employees is somewhat different: White (67%), Hispanic (10%), Asian (7%), and African American (5%).

The district's website describes EGUSD as a "top performing district ... recognized throughout California and the nation as a leader in progressive education." The PBIS is an excellent example of the type of program in which the district prides itself.

"PBIS," Cerutti said, "is a comprehensive approach to understanding and supporting students from both a behavioral and an academic perspective. ... PBIS is about getting students to understand and having every student on campus have common behavioral standards and values and feel valued and value others."

It is fair to ask, however, just how effective a program like PBIS can be in a nation that is so profoundly politically polarized and riven by its unresolved legacy of racism. That's one of the questions that was raised by an incident that occurred in the spring of 2019. An unnamed elementary school teacher at Zehnder Ranch Elementary School in Elk Grove walked into her classroom one May morning and discovered that someone had "etched the 'N-word' into a whiteboard in the classroom." At about the same time, someone set up an Instagram account and used it to harass the teacher with similar racial epithets. It is not clear whether the same student was responsible for both instances of harassment.

The incidents were upsetting to members of the community in general, but the fact that an elementary-age student was responsible for at least one of them was particularly disturbing. The EGUSD immediately contacted Instagram to have the account taken down and issued a detailed statement that read in part:

We take all matters of hate speech very seriously and in solidarity with our entire school community, bullying, hate speech, expressions of hate and hateful acts of any kind are not and shall not be tolerated here or at any school within the Elk Grove Unified School District. School officials are working to support the teacher, address the educational needs of the student by working with the student and their family with regard to the classroom situation and with those involved on the Instagram situation and look toward healing for all involved.

Zehnder Ranch parent Katherine Spero told a local news station that her son told her what had happened in the school. "Even, unfortunately at age 11, they start saying things that are inappropriate," she said. "We just discussed it and said, 'Yeah, it's not appropriate for him to say that.'"

In the end, Spero said, "[i]t's definitely up to the parents to look at the stuff and check what your kid is doing and say, 'OK, what you're doing and what you're little friends are doing is not appropriate[.]'"

Hopefully, Elk Grove's PBIS will make significant strides in promoting respect and civility in EGUSD and beyond.

Top Three Takeaways:

- If anyone has any doubts about the need to start digital citizenship training as early as possible, this cautionary tale should resolve them. The social issues that we are grappling with both online and off affect our children as much as ourselves. That is true in part because children have access not only to the internet's wonders online but also to its far less savory aspects as well.

- It is not clear that the student who defaced the smartboard was the same as the one who set up the harassing Instagram account, but it easily could have been. Few 10- or 11-year-olds would find it particularly challenging to manipulate Instagram like that.

- Both parents and tech companies need to do more to monitor online activity by young children. Elementary-aged children are not old enough to set up Instagram accounts and should not be allowed to do so, either by their parents or Instagram. I understand the challenges but until we do a better job of age-gating children and/or supervising their online activity, these types of incidents will continue to pop up.

Cautionary Tale 22-2019-Australia

In addition to the Cybertraps series, I've been working for a year or so on a book entitled *The Rise of the Digital Mob*. It is a mainstream nonfiction book that explores the impact of digital communication technology on society and politics, with a particular focus on the United States from 2015-2020.

One of the main topics on which I have focused is on the rise of "trolling," which is the act of using various internet tools to upset, harass, or enrage another person or group of people. It's a practice that dates back to the earliest days of the internet, when experienced users would "troll" for new users, or "newbies," by posting outrageous statements in various newsgroups. Then they'd sit back and watch with glee as the uninitiated victims reacted with outrage, writing long screeds to refute whatever nonsense the greybeards dangled in front of them.

Over the years, unfortunately, the practice of trolling has taken a far more sinister and malicious turn. Increasingly, the aim of trolling is not to pull someone's leg and help initiate them into the brotherhood of internet users; instead, the objective is to hurt or wound someone, further a political or social agenda, or just sow chaos and havoc online. Trolls can accomplish these objectives because the internet facilitates maximal impact minimal effort. Also, numerous tools on the internet can make it very difficult (although not impossible) to establish the identity of a particular troll. It is hard enough for someone to cope with a single troll, but when the trolls conducting an online attack number in the dozens, hundreds, or thousands, it can be utterly terrifying.

One of the problems that educators face is that there is no age requirement for trolling; far from it. As we know all too well, many, if not most, children are enthusiastic users of digital technology in general and social media in particular. They are, as a group, well-versed in the creation and use of "memes," the evocative blend of images and text that can be used for good (humor) or ill (vicious trolling). (If you want a quick and safe-for-work primer on the first category of memes, search Google for "Ryan Gosling hey girl.").

An unnamed teacher at Mandurah Catholic College (MCC) in Western Australia learned this the hard way. MCC is a K-12 school located in Mandurah, Australia, on the western coast about 45 miles south of Perth. According to its website, it is "a Christian community and seeks to provide an environment supportive of the development of Christian values, attitudes, beliefs and practices. It is a place where the young should encounter people of faith who show that they care deeply for the individual and are willing to share their own experience of faith."

The principles espoused by the school were called into question by four students, who set up an Instagram account in the spring of 2019 and propagated it with a series of memes intended to suggest that the teacher in question was a pedophile. The Instagram account was registered in the name of "mccmemesboi," with a subtitle "if yk, yk" (which Urban Dictionary defines—tautologically—as "if you know, you know"). The memes posted to the Instagram account implied or stated that the teacher was a rapist and liked girls between 12 and 17 years old.

Despite the efforts of the students to remain anonymous, the school quickly identified three boys and a girl as the creators of the Instagram account. Reports of the incident do not explain how the school identified the perpetrators. However, there are a variety of possibilities, ranging from a confession by an informant, an IP trace leading to a laptop or phone, or even logs from the school's network servers. Regardless of the precise methodology, when the school identified the perpetrators, it immediately suspended the students, removed them from all school activities, and told them that it would be necessary for them to interview for re-admission to the school.

The school offered limited information about the investigation but did issue the following statement:

> All members of the College community have responsibility to ensure that all online communications keep within the Catholic ethos of the College of supporting and caring for all students and teachers.
>
> Whether cyber bullying of our students occurs during school time or after school hours, it constitutes a breach of College policy and the student or students involved face disciplinary action.
>
> All reports of cyber bullying and other misuses of technology are thoroughly investigated by the College and the protection of students, staff and members of the community remain our number one priority.
>
> Mandurah Catholic College is committed to ensuring a safe physical, emotional and spiritual environment for staff, students and our wider College community.

Top Three Takeaways:

- Get in the habit of doing online searches of your name, not just in the major search engines but in specific social media services like Facebook, Twitter, Instagram, and so on. Ideally, someone will alert you if they see something derogatory, but it is good to be proactive in protecting your personal and professional reputation.

- In situations like this, school district and building leaders need to act promptly and make it clear that the district will not tolerate such conduct. In this case, it appears that the administration did exactly that.

- Any time someone has used a third-party service to harass or bully a student or teacher, it is imperative to get law enforcement involved as soon as possible. The sooner an investigation of online misconduct begins, the more successful it is likely to be. Also, school administrators should keep in mind that they are likely to get little or no cooperation from social media services without the assistance of law enforcement.

Cautionary Tale 22-2019-US_Florida

Between the start of the 2018-2019 school year and early February 2019, Miami-Dade County Public Schools logged nearly 60 threats of violence or harm directed at the schools on social media or in verbal/written form. Few were as disturbing as the one directed at an unnamed female teacher and her children, including a newborn baby.

The incident occurred at Southwood Middle School in Palmetto Bay, about 15 miles south on Route 1 from Miami. The teacher told investigators that she received a friend request and a direct message on Instagram. The message read:

> You and your children are next on Valentine's Day for making my life. I'm finna [*sic*] kill all yo family and shoot up to (expletive) ass school.

The person who sent the message also tagged a recent photo of the teacher's newborn daughter with an exclamation point.

Understandably shaken by the message, the teacher immediately contacted the police. No one missed the significance of the date referenced in the direct message: February 14, 2019, was the 1st anniversary of the shooting at Stoneman Douglas High School in Parkland, Florida, about 60 miles to the north, where Nikolas Cruz shot and killed 17 students and teachers and wounded 17 others.

Law enforcement officers were able to identify the IP address used to post the threat and traced it back to the home of a 13-year-old boy named Payton Rolle. When they went to his house and interviewed him, Rolle admitted sending the message and said that his 12-year-old friend Claudio Torreslara had helped him post the threat. Both juveniles were arrested and "charged with aggravated stalking and written threats with intent to kill with bodily injury."

A statement issued by Schools Superintendent Albert M. Cavalho made it clear that the district would not take such threats lightly:

Recent arrests of students for hoax social media threats demonstrate clearly and unequivocally that Miami-Dade County Public Schools has a zero-tolerance policy related to this type of activity. Parents and students must understand that any threat — real or fabricated — to schools and students is a serious matter. It is unacceptable and those involved in such activity will be prosecuted. Prank and hoax threats made against a school are counterproductive to the life-saving work of law enforcement and compromise the safety of everyone.

Contacted by local reporters, Torreslara's mother said that the message was "a joke in bad taste." It is not clear whether the young men have tried or sentenced yet.

Top Three Takeaways:

- In this day and age, never assume that something like this is a joke. It is far better to be reassured by the appropriate authorities that something was a hoax than to discover in tragically painful ways that it was not.

- The belief that you can be anonymous on the internet is deep-seated and powerful, but it is almost entirely a myth. (True anonymity online requires advanced technical skill, time-consuming and meticulous attention to detail, and more than a little luck.) Nonetheless, that belief lures individuals into doing and saying things that will get them into considerable trouble, as was the case here. Kids should be taught, of course, not to make threats like this in the first place, but parents should regularly remind them that as a practical matter, they almost certainly will get caught if they do so.

- Cavalho's statement can serve as a template for districts around the country. Both parents and children should have no illusions about the seriousness of making this type of "joke" online.

Cautionary Tale 22-2018-India

Uday Nare is a teacher at the Hansraj Morarji Public School in Andheri, a suburb in the northern part of Mumbai, India. He is one of those educators that you run across occasionally who has a vibrant network of media contacts. When I Googled his name, he popped up in numerous articles about education and technology issues in India. For instance, in a 2013 story about so-called "confession pages" on Facebook and other social media sites, Nare warned about the potential consequences of the anonymous comments that get posted:

[S]tudents are overriding us with such non-sense. The kids of class 5-6 are innocent but at the same time they are vocal and tech-savvy. They need to be sensitised about repercussion of their fun[.]

He has also criticized a government regulation that "made it mandatory for teachers to take selfies with students with irregular attendance and upload them … to a government database," and defended a teacher caught grading exam papers in a restaurant while watching a cricket match.

Nare must have felt some chagrin, then, when the media spotlight got turned on him. Over the summer of 2018, some students alerted Nare to the fact that he (and numerous other teachers) had become the target of memes posted to Instagram. One, for instance, showed Nare's face photoshopped onto a person lying in bed with the caption "Nare going through parents' phone numbers that he got... Collection is growing." (Nare, called "mobile man" by some of his students, would routinely ask misbehaving students for the mobile numbers of their parents.) Another showed him looking downcast with a caption that read, "That reaction when in canteen there is special food for students, but not for staff."

In an interview with the *Mumbai Mirror*, Nare complained that "Former students have taken to social media to mock their teachers, their dressing styles and their idiosyncrasies. Some posts romantically link teachers, while some others are downright vulgar." He also warned that students may be violating the law: "Some photos used in the memes have been lifted from teachers' personal Facebook accounts. This is a crime. Students should understand this."

Under Indian law, Nare could have asked the cybercrime unit of the Mumbai police to investigate and take action. Instead, he drafted a letter to then-Maharashtra Minister of Education Vinod Tawde, asking him to step up efforts to educate students about online misconduct. He wrote in part:

> The posts on Instagram have caused grave anxiety among teachers. If we complain to the cybercrime cell, students will have to face an inquiry. Teachers are wondering exactly what they are supposed to do. It is important to educate students about the benefits, drawbacks and ill-effects of social networking sites. The current generation is savvier with social networking sites than teachers, but due to lack of proper guidance, they could commit an offence.

There are no reports that Nare received any response from the Minister of Education regarding his concerns. But he's not the only educator to be worried about the impact of the internet and social networking on India's enormous child population (at 470 million or so, the largest in the world). Digital communications have played a role in some truly horrific incidents of bullying and sexual assault, and there is a growing concern (as there is in the United States) about their role in the radicalization of susceptible youth. In partial response to those concerns, the Maharashtra cyber department has developed a standardized "Cyber Safe Women" presentation that it is rolling out to dozens of schools, colleges, and universities around the country.

Top Three Takeaways:

- These cybersafety initiatives are essential and vitally necessary, not just for children, but for adults as well. Teachers need training on social media so that they better understand the potential for how it can be misused. It is also crucial for teachers and administrators to learn how to check the various leading social media channels to make sure that students or parents are not unfairly targeting them.

- This cautionary tale does an excellent job of illustrating the shift in the power dynamic that has occurred over the last 25 years or so. Student access to powerful devices and the endless resources of the internet has given them unprecedented ability to embarrass, shame, or harm their teachers. In many instances (if not the majority), they don't understand the potential consequences of what they are doing. Creating and sharing a meme just seems like an amusing thing to do.

- That is just one of the reasons, as Nare suggests, that every department of education and school district should aggressively instruct students on how to be good digital citizens and how to avoid the risks of online misconduct. A significant issue is that more and more children are carrying incredibly powerful devices, and with great power comes great responsibility. Unfortunately, we have not been as quick to provide responsibility training as we have been in handing out the devices. Uncle Ben would agree; we need to do a better job.

Cautionary Tale 22-2018-Northern Ireland

If someone says something about you that is not merely unkind or untrue but actively damages your reputation or livelihood, can you do anything about it? As with most areas of the law, the answer depends on several factors.

In general terms, untrue statements are known as defamation, and they fall into one of two categories: 1) **Slander**, which involves oral comments, and 2) **Libel**, which encompasses written or printed statements. Without getting too deeply into the weeds on this, a plaintiff suing in the United States must show that the defendant's statement was an assertion of fact and not mere opinion, that he or she transmitted the statement to a third party, and that the false statement caused harm. It is more difficult for a "public figure" to successfully sue for defamation, since he or she must show that the person who made the statement did so with actual malice (*i.e.,* with actual knowledge that the statement was false, or with a reckless disregard as to its veracity).

Although the basic parameters are pretty much the same from country to country (and state to state), there are occasionally local variations regarding standards of proof, availability of damages, and so forth. In fact, even in the United Kingdom, defamation law varies among the four constituent jurisdictions (England, Scotland, Wales, and Northern Ireland). This particular cautionary tale arose in part because Northern Ireland is considered to be a more plaintiff-friendly place to file a defamation lawsuit. Among other things for instance, no showing of "serious harm" is required to recover damages.

That helps explain the outcome of this cautionary tale, as well as why a lawsuit was filed in the first place. In May 2017, a woman named Caroline Coulter wrote a post on the Facebook page of St. Joseph's Convent Grammar School in Donaghmere, a small town near Dungannon in Northern Ireland. Her comments (which were cross-posted to her personal Facebook feed) criticized Roisin Corr, who was and still is head of music for the school.

For obvious reasons, the articles covering the case did not reprint Coulter's comments. However, we can reasonably infer that the remarks were unpleasant and deeply upsetting to Corr, given that she sued Coulter for libel. In her lawsuit, Corr described the comments as "unfair and derogatory," and said that they had caused such extreme emotional distress that she had been on medical leave for stress since the incident occurred.

A little over a year later, the parties announced in court that they had reached a settlement, in which Coulter agreed to apologize for her public comments about Corr. Her barrister read the brief apology in open court:

> I made unfair and derogatory comments on Facebook about Roisin Corr. I take this opportunity to formally withdraw my comments and apologise to Mrs Corr for making those comments. In particular, I apologise for any hurt and upset I may have caused and shall desist from any such conduct in the future.

Corr told reporters that she was looking forward to returning to work and urged the Northern Ireland Department of Education to use her case as grounds for establishing a firm policy to protect teachers from online abuse.

> It is essential that the Department of Education and all schools develop a robust social media policy to safeguard teachers, their good name and professionalism from defamatory comments made by others. In the current age of social media a recurrence of similar events for other teachers is inevitable. The impact that this ordeal has had on myself as a professional, but also on my family should prompt an urgent implementation of such a policy.

In response, the Department of Education basically shrugged its shoulders and said that it is not the Department's responsibility to police school social media sites or those of parents. It also noted that the various social media platforms all offer tools to report misconduct.

Mark McTaggart, the assistant northern secretary of teachers' union the Irish National Teachers' Organisation (INTO), offered a stirring summary of the problem faced by Corr and other educators:

> It's becoming a major issue for teachers. We regularly receive calls to this office in relation to it – the school gates have moved onto social media. For teachers or even children in schools, there's a policy in place for these people if they use or misuse social media. The problem we have is that parents don't have that. They haven't signed up to any code of conduct which prevents them from putting things onto social media. It's something this union has been calling for – something to be put in place to protect teachers from things said on social media by parents.

In the United States, a robust First Amendment makes the idea of a Parents Code of Conduct highly unlikely, if not impossible. Perhaps the successful defamation claim in this case will give some parents pause for thought (although the matter does not appear to have led to a flood of lawsuits by teachers, as some worried). Arguably, the most effective solution, in the long run, is persistent outreach by schools to parents about acceptable behavior and the training of good digital citizens in the classroom.

Top Three Takeaways:

- It does seem clear, based on both anecdotal reports and initial research assessments, that teachers are experiencing more online abuse. There are a lot of reasons for that: competitive parenting, the rise of hostility online (and in real life), the availability of numerous channels on which to complain, and so on. Educators should prepare themselves for this more challenging environment by studying the scope of the problem, discussing possible techniques for de-escalation, and how to practice self-care.

- We need to be more pro-active in assisting and protecting educators from online abuse, particularly by parents. We can do more at every level— legislature, departments of educations, school districts, and schools—to educate parents about proper interaction with educators. The critical point is that digital citizenship begins in the home, and parents should be setting a positive example for their children.

- As an initial step, schools should ask parents to read and sign an acceptable use policy regarding their interactions with the school and with educators. Such an approach is more likely to be effective if the policy lays out a mechanism for dispute resolution that is readily accessible to all interested parties.

Relevant MCEE Provisions for Chapter 22

Principle I: Responsibility to the Profession

Standards I.A.4 and I.C.2

Principle III: Responsibility to Students

Standards III.A.2 and III.A.3

Principle V: Responsible and Ethical Use of Technology

Standards V.A.2, V.A.7, V.B.1, and V.B.3

Sources

The sources for the Cautionary Tales in this chapter can be viewed at the following URL:

https://link.cybertraps.com/C4E2-Sources-Chap22

Chapter 23
Hacks and Unauthorized Intrusions by Students

Overview

In the classic 1983 movie *War Games*, Matthew Broderick plays a bored high school computer geek. One afternoon, his classmate (played by Ally Sheedy) gives him a ride home on her Vespa and accepts his invitation to check out his computer set-up. Eager to impress her, he demonstrates how he can log into the school computer system and offers to change one of her recent less-than-stellar test grades. Broderick explains to Sheely that each week, the school secretary writes down a new system password on a piece of paper taped to the metal writing shelf in her desk. One glance when the secretary steps away from her desk, and he's got access to every student's grades and attendance record. To her credit, Sheely declines his offer to boost her grade (although Broderick secretly does it anyway after she leaves).

War Games was a prescient and compelling film that remains fresh and entertaining to this day. The central premise was so novel and disturbing that after President Ronald Reagan watched it at Camp David one weekend, he demanded a security audit of Department of Defense computers, which in turn led to a significant revamp of U.S. military computer security. But the real insight of *War Games* was that on a day-to-day basis, the biggest cybersecurity threats for schools are inquisitive students, insecure computers, and sloppy password practices by educators and staff. Thirty-seven years later, that fundamental dynamic has not changed. Students continue to search for ways to gain access to protected systems, and educators are not necessarily as careful as they should be about securing the passwords necessary to do so.

Institutional Cybersecurity

As part of their routine operation, school districts collect and store a great deal of information about students and staff. Cybercriminals are continually looking for weaknesses to exploit large caches of sensitive data. They either try to steal it to commit identity theft or, more commonly, hold school districts hostage in a ransomware attack. (Make backups! Always make backups!) But that information is also of great interest to the segment of the school community that generates the most data daily: the students themselves.

As any IT professional can tell you, there are a seemingly endless number of ways to attack the cybersecurity of a school district (or any other organization, for that matter). However, two cybersecurity weaknesses are responsible for the bulk of school data breaches: the failure to update or patch software, and poor password management.

In general, educators aren't responsible for software updates (particularly of network operating systems and other similar district-wide programs). However, you should keep in mind that if you download and install software on a networked computer without the knowledge or approval of your district IT staff, then you've introduced a new vulnerability for the network as a whole. If you install poorly-written software or you ignore a critical security update, there is a chance that someone will find the flaw, exploit it, and hack the district network.

For individual educators, the most common cybersecurity lapse is poor password control. The three most common mistakes are 1) inherently insecure passwords, 2) careless handling of passwords, and 3) succumbing to a phishing attack.

In this day and age, there is simply no excuse for using easily-guessable passwords or ones that might be vulnerable to a so-called dictionary attack. The safest and most reliable solution is to use a password manager like Dashlane (my personal favorite), Keeper, LastPass, or Password Boss. All of those programs make it easy to create complex passwords using letters, numbers, and symbols, and then store them for instant use in your browser. The only thing you have to remember, then, is the master password that lets you unlock your password manager. All of my passwords, for instance, are thirteen characters long and look like a drunk cat walked across my keyboard. But you won't find any of them in a dictionary.

Of course, you will dramatically decrease the usefulness of any password manager if you write your master password on a slip of paper or a post-it where someone can easily see it. You are primarily responsible for making sure that you have not left your network login on or around your computer. However, your district or building IT staff should also periodically do a visual inspection as well (perhaps as part of their routine sweep to make sure that no one has installed a keylogger). Making sure that you keep all of your passwords in a well-locked password manager will significantly reduce the chances that you will be responsible for a destructive network break-in.

Avoiding the cybertrap of phishing emails is admittedly more challenging. These attacks have grown steadily more sophisticated, and it often tough to distinguish the look-and-feel of a fake email from its genuine counterpart. Many online resources are available that can teach you how to identify the clues that an email is bogus; the security firm KnowBe4, for instance, runs a resource site called Phishing.org that contains a lot of useful information. The Federal Trade Commission also has compiled a helpful tip sheet entitled "How to Recognize and Avoid Phishing Scams." Your school district or your building may also have purchased or subscribed to an online anti-phishing training program for its employees. If it hasn't, then I recommend that it consider doing so.

Personal Cybersecurity

Every admonition regarding the protection of your workplace passwords applies to your personal ones as well. In theory, you shouldn't have to worry about personal passwords at all when you are at work, but of course, most of us carry one or more personal devices with us and any of the online services we use can be accessed just as easily at work as they can at home.

The first and most basic way to protect your personal data is to remember always to lock your devices and use strong passwords for your data and your services (particularly social media). Even now, it is still startling how often teachers have problems in school because they left a phone or tablet unlocked where kids could find it. Students, of course, should not be touching or accessing someone else's equipment or online accounts, and schools (and parents) should discipline when they do so. At the same time, adults should anticipate that some children may succumb to temptation and should take responsibility for locking down their devices and accounts. In these kinds of situations, a few seconds of prevention outweighs hours or days of cure.

One handy feature of the password managers listed above is that they can all store multiple passwords for a single service. So, for instance, if you have a separate log-in for your classroom Facebook page and for your personal Facebook account (and you should), it's easy to keep them separate. One of the main benefits of a password manager, both at work and at home, is that they make it easy to create and use a unique and difficult-to-guess password for all of your online services. Far too many of us tend to repeat passwords from one service to another, which means that if one service gets hacked, cybercriminals can try to use your stolen user ID and password on any other service you might use. It would be a real shame if the user ID/password combination that you use to log in to Netflix also allows someone access to your bank records or your Gmail account.

Given how busy most educators are and the large number of students with whom they interact every day, the best advice for lowering the risk of personal data loss and many educator cybertraps is to reduce the overlap between home and work. Bring as few personal devices to school as possible, make sure that each is locked or auto-locks as quickly as possible, and avoid accessing personal social media accounts or other online services during the workday (particularly on school computers). There may be times and situations when the overlap is unavoidable, but the less it occurs, the safer your personal data (and your career) will be.

Cautionary Tales

Cautionary Tale 23-2019-US_New Jersey

Here are a couple of recent examples in New Jersey schools that illustrate the risk that schools face from students. In February 2019, four students at Dickinson High School in Jersey City, NJ, found a way to install keylogger software on computers used by various teachers. When the teachers logged into their accounts on the system network, the software recorded each of their keystrokes. The students then used teacher logins to change their grades and possibly those of their friends as well. Once the intrusion was detected and IT staff identified the perpetrators, the district called in Jersey City police to arrest them.

About a month later, the Elizabeth Public Schools (EPS) also discovered that several students had broken into the district network and tried to change some grades and attendance records. The initial perpetrator allegedly stole a teacher's password (the method of the theft was not disclosed) and then shared it with several of his classmates, who made alterations to their own data.

Superintendent Olga Hugelmeyer sent a letter home to parents announcing the hack, criticizing the students' "poor choices," and calling it a "sad day for Elizabeth Public Schools." She added that "[t]he consequences for the individual(s) who lead [*sic*] the data compromise are likely to be severe. Due to student privacy laws, we're restricted from disclosing more information but we can assure you that we are working within the full extent of the law and our Student Code of Conduct Board policy[.]"

Pat Politano, a spokesperson for the district, said that "[t]he district has and is continuing to increase technological security by changing and increasing the complexity of passwords to its system and other security measures."

Both of these intrusions were severe breaches of student ethics, of course, but there were other failings as well. Obviously, without more information, we don't know exactly how the student in the EPS incident managed to steal his teacher's password. The obvious question, though, is whether the teacher took adequate steps to prevent it. Was the password written down on a post-it or some other piece of paper on the desk? Did the teacher type it in while the student was watching? Did the student use a smartphone to record a video of his or her keystrokes? There are myriad ways that the data leakage might have occurred, and a capable IT department will run periodic training to educate or remind administrators, teachers, and staff about the basics of password security.

And speaking of IT departments, it is an organizational failure if a student can install keylogger software on *any* computer attached to the school network. IT departments should configure all networked computers to block the installation of software by anyone other than authorized staff. I know that such restrictions can be frustrating to educators, particularly those who try to be innovative and creative in their use of digital technology. But the reality is that the risks to data privacy and network integrity are simply too significant.

The other thing that IT departments should keep in mind is that software is not the only way for kids to capture keystrokes. Using a physical keystroke logger is even more straightforward, and it avoids any restrictions on software installation. Hardware loggers are small electronic components that can be attached to the USB cord connecting a keyboard to the computer. Such devices are easily overlooked, can store megabytes of keystrokes, and can be quickly and quietly retrieved.

Top Three Takeaways:

- IT departments should routinely and regularly examine all computer cable connections to make sure that no one has installed a keylogger or some other nefarious device.

- IT departments should regularly provide professional development to educators and administrators on proper password handling and implementation.

- School districts should regularly remind students of the academic and legal consequences of unauthorized access into district or building computer systems.

- [Bonus takeaway] Parents should be reminded every year (if not more frequently) of the importance of monitoring the computer activities of their children and teaching them ethical values.

Cautionary Tale 23-2019-US_Ohio

In a majority of cases, the motivation for limiting student access to a district's computer network is to prevent potential harm to the system itself. Any rational educator or district IT department should want to minimize the possibility that confidential information has been stolen or altered by a student, or that the student has inadvertently created a vector for the insertion of malware.

In some rare instances, however, a cybersecurity breach can have much more sinister implications. In the spring of 2019, a 13-year-old boy at Columbus City Preparatory School for Boys "hacked" into a teacher's district computer account (the precise method was undisclosed) and copied confidential information of about five dozen classmates. He then set up a website with the title "User Names and Passes for Columbus Schools" and posted all of that personally-identifying information to the site.

That alone is disturbing enough, but what set people on edge was the fact that the student told some of his classmates that he had created a "hit list" and that he threatened to "shoot up their houses." The ensuing investigation revealed that this was not his first "hit list." Law enforcement had told school officials about a similar list created by the student in December 2018 following a bullying incident. Administrators let the matter drop, however, when they couldn't find a copy of the alleged list.

It is difficult to provide precise advice to educators or administrators on how to avoid this type of situation, given the limited amount of information available. The central question here is whether the boy's teacher was careless in protecting his or her password, or whether the student was able to record or otherwise crack it. It does appear that the school identified the potential threat reasonably quickly and took appropriate action. Still, it is certainly worth discussing how the student was able to break into the network in the first place.

School officials contacted the parents of all of the students named on the "hit list," but some parents suggested that the district should have informed the entire school community. As parent Bridgett Class—whose son was listed on the website—put it, "Even if your son's not on the list, my son hangs out with your son so in my opinion all the parents need to know. Not just the ones on the list." Other parents were upset that the district did not inform them about the December threat or investigate it more thoroughly.

To be fair, it can be challenging to trace online activity, and sometimes things do just disappear. Nonetheless, given the prevalence of school shootings in the United States and the level of parental concern, it probably would have been advisable to give members of the school community some type of alert. Of course, while transparency is generally a virtue, it needs to be tempered by respect for student and family privacy and the importance of avoiding unnecessary alarm.

Top Three Takeaways:

- School district administrators and IT staff should never underestimate the technical skills of their students. It is necessary, of course, to guard a school district network against outside attacks, but sometimes the most serious threats come from someone physically in the school.

- A school district's cybersecurity is only as strong as the weakest password. Cybersecurity best practices should be a regular part of professional development, with a particular emphasis on selecting a strong password and keeping it secure. This cautionary tale should illustrate to educators that protecting passwords is part of maintaining a safe environment for students.

- Administrators should err on the side of providing more information to the school community, not less. It is, of course, inadvisable to advertise your vulnerabilities by revealing the method used to break into your computer network. At the same time, but parents do have a right to know when someone steals information about their children and makes threats against student safety in the school.

Cautionary Tale 23-2018-US_California

In the spring of 2018, David Rotaro, a sophomore at Ygnacio Valley High School in Concord, California, sent a phishing email to staff at the school. In an interview with a local news outlet, Concord Police Sgt. Carl Cruz said that Rotaro "made an e-mail [with a link to what] looked like a Mount Diablo School District site asking to log in to refresh your password or reset something and, when one of the teachers did it, he captured their log-in information." In a separate interview with another local station, Rotaro smugly said that "it was like stealing candy from a baby."

Armed with the teacher's login and password, Rotaro logged into the MDSD network and changed grades for several students (the marks of those he liked (including his) went up, while those of people he disliked went down). Rotaro was not quite as smart as he thought, however. The MDSD IT department detected the intrusion and contacted the Contra Costa County Sheriff's Office and the U.S. Secret Service to help investigate the break-in. While officials did not reveal the specific details of the investigation to the media, investigators likely were able to glean enough data from Rotaro's phishing email and from MDSD network logs to identify his internet protocol address. Once investigators had that information, they were able to obtain a search warrant for his physical address.

In a clear demonstration of how the Costa County Sheriff's office is on the cutting edge of digital investigations, a K-9 "officer" named Dug accompanied officers during the search of Rotaro's home. Law enforcement agencies around the country have been training canines to use their phenomenal sense of smell to identify and locate hidden electronic devices, and Dug did not disappoint. He pointed investigators to a Kleenex box with an SD memory card hidden inside; the card contained incriminating evidence that officials used to charge Rotaro.

Following the search, Rotaro was arrested and charged with 14 felony counts of unauthorized computer system access. The school district also suspended him for the remainder of the school year. With his father's consent, Rotaro gave an interviewed to a local news station and offered an apology for his actions. "I'm very sorry for all the people that I put grades up and grades down," he said. "And I'm sorry for the teacher that I hacked."

Rotaro also reportedly told police that he had hacked the school network in part to highlight what he described as poor cybersecurity practices and added that he hoped to work in IT someday "at a high level."

Top Three Takeaways:

- These types of phishing attacks are one of the biggest cybersecurity threats facing organizations right now. Every employee needs ongoing training on how to recognize fake emails and to avoid disclosing security information without being entirely confident that the request is legitimate.

- There are a large number of companies that offer online training for employees in this area, but most phishing attempts can be defeated by following one simple rule: "Trust but verify." Anytime you are asked for confidential or personally identifying information, double-check the alleged source with a phone call. If your district's IT department needs you to refresh your password, someone in the office will be able to confirm it. A few seconds on the phone can spare hours and hours of hassle, let alone the potential loss of confidential information and harm to the district's network and data.

- As this cautionary tale illustrates, district and building administrators must have a clear response plan in place before cybersecurity breaches occur. At the very top of the list should be the names and numbers of the law enforcement agencies that can assist you in responding to an incident as quickly and as effectively as possible.

Cautionary Tale 23-2016-US_New York

On January 13, 2015, Angela Costa, a Brooklyn social studies teacher, sent a very private Facebook message to her then-boyfriend, in which she thanked him for the physical pleasures of the previous night. Nearly 18 months later, she was horrified to walk into her workplace, the Urban Action Academy in Canarsie, and discover that students had made color photocopies of a screenshot of that conversation and were distributing them throughout the entire school building.

In an interview with the *New York Post*, Costa said that the first mystery was how the students had even obtained the screenshot. She said that she had no recollection of ever accessing social media on a school computer. The only possibility Costa could think of was that in the fall of 2015, three students had stolen her smartphone. Costa told reporters that she feels that they might have been able to access her Facebook account while they had her phone, although she didn't know why they would wait so long to use the screenshot.

The second mystery, Costa said, was why the administration at the school was so slow to respond to the invasion of her privacy and file the required incident report with the New York State Department of Education. In a letter to her union rep and a subsequent report she filed with the local police, Costa said that Urban Action Academy Principal Steve Dorcely and assistant principal Jordan Barnett engaged in a coverup by failing to interview staff or students promptly. Dorcely also lied, Costa claimed, when he told her that it was not possible to identify any students in a school surveillance video showing a hallway where students distributed some of the photocopies. When Costa reviewed the video herself with the help of the school's assistant principal for security, however, they quickly identified several students distributing the flyers and snapping photos of them with their smartphones.

In light of the incident (which the police designated as "aggravated harassment") and the administration's seemingly indifferent response, Costa said that she no longer felt safe at the school and wanted a transfer to a different location.

Following the publication of the *Post*'s initial article on the matter, the Department of Education announced that its Office of Special Investigations would be looking into Costa's claim and the school's handling of its internal investigation.

Top Three Takeaways:

- Any device that you bring on to school grounds should be securely locked at all times unless it is under your direct control and supervision.

- Every school district should have clear policies and procedures for investigating alleged bullying or harassment of educators or students, and administrators and staff should follow those policies and procedures promptly and consistently each time an incident occurs.

- Never underestimate the ubiquity and spread of digital evidence. This case highlights the potential evidentiary value of security videos (which should be self-evident, since that is their purpose).

- [Bonus takeaway] Students should routinely be reminded that if school officials see them photographing or video recording an incident in school, the school may be entitled to review all relevant photos or videos on their phone as part of an investigation.

Cautionary Tale 23-2016-US_Texas

"What's on YOUR phone?" and "How quickly does your phone lock when you put it down?" are two questions that educators should routinely ask themselves. It is a safe guess that virtually all of our phones contain various levels of personal information, from private text messages and emails to financial information to photos and videos we might not want to become public. Depending on your level of irritation with your phone's lock screen, your phone may auto-lock anywhere from 1 to 5 minutes after you stop using it. If you work in an environment filled with tech-curious children, you should be clear on this critical point: it is risky and careless to turn off the lock-down feature altogether.

That was a lesson learned by an unnamed female percussion teacher working on a contract basis at Katy High School in the Katy Independent School District in Texas. At the beginning of the school year, she dropped her unlocked cell phone somewhere in the school, and a student found it. Before turning the phone into the central office, he looked through her photo album and discovered that she had taken nude photos of herself. He used his phone to take pictures of the images and then sent his photocopies to several other students.

One of the students who received the images informed a family member, who then reported the incident to district officials. KISD immediately fired the music teacher, asked her to leave the school, and told her that the district would not renew her contract. District officials also contacted the Katy ISD Police Department, which interviewed the students involved and confiscated several of their phones as well. An official press release summarized the events:

> On September 15, 2016, Katy High School administration became aware of inappropriate photos belonging to a contracted instructor, not employed by Katy ISD, circulating among students. Katy ISD's Human Resources and Police Department immediately investigated and determined that the photos were located on the instructor's personal cell phone, which she lost shortly before the start of the school year and was recovered by students. The students who distributed the contracted instructor's inappropriate photos are being disciplined according to the Student Code of Conduct, and the contracted instructor, who was removed from the classroom on September 15, will not be returning to the District.

In a subsequent interview with *The Dallas Morning News*, Katy ISD spokesperson Maria Corrales said that the district terminated the Booster Club-funded instructor for two reasons: first, because of "the sensitive nature of the incident," and second, because "the nude photos were readily available to students[.]" Corrales added that because the photos were "believed to be distributed to quite a few people," "[i]t was not in her interest to stay there."

Shortly after the story first broke, the instructor contacted *Covering Katy News* and disputed the district's account of what happened. She said that her phone was locked when she lost it and that she took the photos found on her phone for "medical reasons." She also said that she would not be embarrassed to return to work at Katy High and thought that the students would be supportive. She did not explain, however, of how a student would have been able to access her photo album if the phone was locked.

Top Three Takeaways:

- Any device that you bring on to school grounds should be securely locked at all times unless it is under your direct control and supervision. You should also set it to lock in two minutes or less. That is particularly true if you have photos or videos that you do not want your students or your colleagues to see. Never underestimate the curiosity of the people around you.

- Every school district should have policies and procedures that address the use of personal devices on campus by educators and staff, including under what circumstances those devices can or should be loaned by educators to students. Those policies and procedures should be a routine part of professional development.

- Every school district should have policies and procedures that address the unauthorized access of another person's digital devices or online accounts. The district should integrate those policies and procedures into the district's Student Code of Conduct, Acceptable Use Policy, and parental information packet.

- [Bonus takeaway] Students should routinely be reminded of the civil and criminal implications of accessing another person's digital device without permission, as well as the consequences for copying or redistributing any content thereon.

Cautionary Tale 23-2016-US_South Carolina

It is reasonable to assume that someone who works in a school district technology office would be reasonably careful about his or her personal cybersecurity. But mistakes, of course, do happen. In an ideal world, we could all leave our device unsupervised and unlocked without having to worry that someone might start pawing through it.

In mid-February 2016, Leigh Anne Arthur, a teacher in the Union County (SC) Career and Technology Center, brought her cellphone to school. An incident occurred involving her phone and not surprisingly, there are at least two different versions of what happened.

Arthur, who taught mechatronics for 12 years in the Union County School District, said that she left her unlocked phone on her desk and stepped out into the hallway briefly to greet incoming students to her class. While she away from her desk, one of the early-arriving students picked up her phone, opened her photo album, and saw some nude selfies that Arthur had taken to send to her husband on Valentine's Day. The student pulled out his phone, took photographs of Arthur's selfies, and then shared them with some of his classmates via text and social media.

Interim Superintendent David Eubanks, who demanded that Arthur immediately resign or face disciplinary proceedings, issued an initial statement that was the administrative equivalent of "slut-shaming."

"I think we have a right to privacy," he told one reporter, "but when we take inappropriate information or pictures, we had best make sure it remains private." About a week later, Eubanks issued another statement that presented a starkly different version of the events described by Arthur:

> It is truly unfortunate that a teacher charged with proper supervision and care of students failed to fulfill that responsibility in her classroom. Evidence indicates that Leigh Anne Arthur was not in her assigned position at the time of the incident. Evidence also indicates that she allowed students to use her personal cell phone on a regular and routine basis.
>
> Evidence also indicates that the phone was routinely left on her desk for student use and was never locked.

Initially, Eubanks had expressed uncertainty as to whether the district would punish the student involved in the incident, but that quickly changed. The student was charged with one count of aggravated voyeurism and one count of second-degree violation of South Carolina's computer crime statute (for posting Arthur's photo to an online service). Eubanks later said that the district might expel the student for his actions.

In mid-April, the student pleaded guilty to the computer crime charge (the voyeurism charge was dropped) and left the school district. At about the same time, Arthur filed a lawsuit against Eubanks and Union County School District in which she alleged "Breach of Contract, Breach of Implied Covenant of Good Faith and Fair Dealing, and Defamation." She sought damages for "injury to reputation, mental suffering, and emotional distress[.]" Among other things, Arthur's suit claimed that her actions did not violate any district policies.

In early December 2016, however, Arthur dropped her lawsuit without public explanation.

Top Three Takeaways:

- Any device that you bring on to school grounds should be securely locked at all times unless it is under your direct control and supervision. You should also set it to automatically lock in two minutes or less. That is particularly true if you have photos or videos that you do not want your students or your colleagues to see. Never underestimate the curiosity of the people around you.

- Every school district should have policies and procedures that address the use of personal devices on campus by educators and staff, including under what circumstances those devices can or should be loaned by educators to students. Those policies and procedures should be a routine part of professional development.

- Every school district should have policies and procedures that address the unauthorized access of another person's digital devices or online accounts. The district should integrate those policies and procedures into the district's Student Code of Conduct, Acceptable Use Policy, and parental information packet.

- [Bonus takeaway] Students should routinely be reminded of the civil and criminal implications of accessing another person's digital device without permission, as well as the consequences for copying or redistributing any content thereon.

Relevant MCEE Provisions for Chapter 23

Principle I: Responsibility to the Profession

Standards I.A.4 and I.A.5

Principle II: Responsibility for Professional Competence

Standard II.C.3

Principle IV: Responsibility to the School Community

Standard IV.D.3

Principle V: Responsible and Ethical Use of Technology

Standards V.A.5 and V.A.7

Sources

The sources for the Cautionary Tales in this chapter can be viewed at the following URL:

https://link.cybertraps.com/C4E2-Sources-Chap23

Section Four
Criminal Cybertraps

With a few short keystrokes, the network we now know as the internet sprang into being on October 29, 1969. Originally called "ARPANET" (Advanced Research Projects Agency Network), the infant network was a research initiative of interest only to scientists and academics. What we think of as the internet today did not begin to emerge until the late 1980s. It exploded into public consciousness in 1993 and 1994, when the release of the first graphical web browser, Mosaic, made it possible to easily view text, images, and even videos on the same screen.

In the early days of the internet, very few people gave much thought to the possibility that criminals might use the emerging network for illicit purposes. To be fair, it didn't take long for annoyances to arise: the first spam, for instance, was sent over the ARPANET on May 3, 1978, by Gary Thuerk, a marketer for the now-defunct Digital Equipment Corporation. And just four years later, when Apple still held its lead as the dominant personal computer brand, a fourteen-year-old named Rich Skrenta created the first virus, a boot-sector infection called "Elk Cloner." Despite its significant place in computing history, however, Skrenta's virus was relatively harmless; every fiftieth time that an infected disk was used to start an Apple II personal computer, the virus would first display a poem written by Skrenta.

In the thirty-five-plus years since Skrenta's little joke, however, cybercrime has become a multi-billion dollar business and a massive global problem. A 2019 report by Cybersecurity Ventures estimated that the worldwide cost of cybercrime and cyber espionage could be as high as **$6 trillion**. Admittedly, that's just a tiny slice of the planet's $142 trillion of gross domestic product (GDP) in 2019, but any way you slice it, $6 trillion is real money.

The range of criminal activities that occur online is discouragingly impressive. A small but representative list of electronic crimes includes virus and malware distribution, hacking, cybertheft, software piracy, copyright infringement, fraud, cyberharassment and cyberstalking, phishing and Trojan attacks, identity theft, voyeurism, sexting, and so on. And of course, new and disturbingly creative criminal activities pop up with remarkable frequency.

Crime statistics, cyber or otherwise, are unfortunately not broken down by the profession of the person who committed the crime, so there is no easy way to tell if educators are more or less likely to commit some types of cybercrimes than those who work in other professions.

Based on more than a decade of researching online activity, however, I can state with some confidence that educators do not commit most cybercrimes with any more frequency than other types of professionals. If anything, the overall percentage of electronic misbehavior by educators is probably below average.

The unavoidable reality, however, is that some small percentage of educators unquestionably do commit online crimes, which run the gamut of possible offenses. As the following cautionary tales illustrate, teachers can all too easily find themselves entangled in a variety of different criminal cybertraps. The motivations for these crimes by teachers are no different from the impulses that spur criminal behavior in any other segment of the population: lust, greed, desperation, jealousy, anger, bitterness, sociopathy, terrible judgment, even mere boredom.

While not technically a "cybertrap," it's worth noting in passing that for some teachers, computers are not so much the instruments of a crime as the object of the crime itself. In the fall of 2013, for instance, the Rhinelander (WI) Board of Education unanimously terminated the contract of high school English teacher Joshua Juergens after police charged him with stealing over $9,000 of school computer equipment.

Of all the possible cybercrimes that educators can commit, those involving sexual activity with students are the ones that draw the most attention and public dismay. Many of you will read the cautionary tales in the following chapters and confidently say to yourself that you would *never* engage in any of the behavior described in those stories. I certainly hope that is true, and for the vast majority of readers, it undoubtedly is. Nonetheless, every educator has a duty of care to his or her students that extends beyond his or her own behavior. If you see another educator doing something that might be criminal or could lead to criminal behavior, then you have an ethical duty to speak up, either to the individual involved or to someone with authority to investigate further or both.

If human history tells us anything, it's that crime will happen and that no profession is immune from criminal misconduct. I have no illusions that this book will somehow prevent all illegal activity by educators and administrators. Inevitably, some percentage of teachers will use electronic devices and online services to commit criminal acts.

However, I also believe that the education profession can reduce the incidence of illegal activity through an emphasis on ethical guidelines and conduct (with the MCEE as a guide), professional development, and appropriate district supervision.

Chapter 24

Cyberbullying, Cyberharassment, and Cyberstalking

Overview

Over the last twenty-five years, cyberbullying has become such a widespread disciplinary problem that districts and schools devote enormous time, effort, and resources to mitigating the problem. As most educators are well aware, when it comes to cyberbullying in schools, the vast majority of cases occur among students. However, students sometimes use their impressive technical skills to bully teachers, and even parents occasionally get in on the act. Stemming the rising tide of educator abuse will take ongoing education of both students and the broader school community.

Although statistically, it is a much smaller problem, we should not overlook the genuine harm that educators can cause when they cyberbully, cyberharrass, or cyberstalk students. In some cases, the educator does not want to do anything more than criticize or emotionally harm his or her victim, which is bad enough. In other more severe cases, however, these behaviors can be a prelude to egregious physical assaults.

Regardless of the motivation or perceived provocation, educators obviously should not be engaging in these types of behaviors. The provisions of the Model Code of Ethics for Educators selected for this chapter focus on the overall ethical duty of educators, their obligation to monitor their emotional state, their duty to provide a safe learning environment for all students, and their responsibility to use technology appropriately. The bottom line, ultimately, is that educators are supposed to be the adult in the room (quite literally) and should take seriously their obligation to model not only proper use of technology but also decent behavior in general.

One final note: Some of the most disturbing cases of student harassment (or even assault) involve teachers who get into trouble in one school district are told to leave, and then commit similar offenses in a new district. Some school districts are all too willing to engage in the process of "passing the trash" to minimize the harm to their students and avoid possible litigation with the disgraced teacher. Other institutions—notably the Catholic Church—have engaged in similar practices. But no child down the road should suffer preventable harm; every school district should promptly and honestly disclose when any educator is released or disciplined for harassing or assaulting a student.

Cyberbullying and Cyberharassment

Although it is common to use the terms interchangeably, "cyberbullying" is generally used to refer to behavior among students. "Cyberharassment," by contrast, is typically used to describe a situation in which an adult is the one doing the bullying. From a legal perspective, cyberbullying and cyberharassment are often lumped together in a single state statute, or a state will have a prohibition against one type of electronic misbehavior and not the other.

According to the website **stopbullying.gov**, "cyberbullying" is defined as follows:

> Cyberbullying is bullying that takes place over digital devices like cell phones, computers, and tablets. Cyberbullying can occur through SMS, Text, and apps, or online in social media, forums, or gaming where people can view, participate in, or share content. Cyberbullying includes sending, posting, or sharing negative, harmful, false, or mean content about someone else. It can include sharing personal or private information about someone else causing embarrassment or humiliation. Some cyberbullying crosses the line into unlawful or criminal behavior.

Not surprisingly, the definition of "cyberharassment" is quite similar: "threatening or harassing email messages, instant messages, or blog entries or websites dedicated solely to tormenting an individual."

In those states that do not have a separate cyberharassment statute, it is common for prosecutors to rely on the more general harassment statute to cover acts involving social media and other types of electronic communication.

Cyberstalking

Cyberharassment and cyberstalking are two variants on the concept of cyberbullying, but with an added component of obsession that typically goes beyond the more ephemeral and often temporary nature of cyberbullying.

"Cyberstalking" is defined by the National Conference of State Legislatures as "the use of the Internet, email or other electronic communications to stalk someone, and generally refers to a pattern of threatening or malicious behaviors ... posing a credible threat of physical harm." The credible threat may consist of an explicit statement, or may simply stem from the pattern of behavior. Whether particular conduct should be classified as "cyberstalking" or mere "cyberharassment" depends on the facts and the specific language of the state statute in question.

In some jurisdictions, the line between cyberharassment and cyberstalking is a little blurry. For instance, North Carolina defines cyberstalking in part as:

electronically mail or electronically communicate to another and to knowingly make any false statement concerning death, injury, illness, disfigurement, indecent conduct, or criminal conduct of the person electronically mailed or of any member of the person's family or household with the intent to abuse, annoy, threaten, terrify, harass, or embarrass.

Cautionary Tales

Cautionary Tale 24-2019-US_Colorado

Most of the cautionary tales in this section involve educators who harass or stalk a student they know. But thanks to the incredible speed and reach of social media, educators now have the opportunity to harass a student they've never even met.

As many of you no doubt remember, an incident occurred on the National Mall on January 19, 2019, involving some male high school students from Covington Catholic High School in Covington, KY, and a Native American activist named Nathan Phillips. The students, many of them wearing the red "Make America Great Again" baseball caps promoted by President Trump, were in Washington to attend a "March for Life" anti-abortion rally. Phillips had traveled to D.C. to participate in the simultaneously-scheduled Indigenous Peoples March.

A controversy arose thanks to a short video clip that appeared to show the students from CCHS—and in particular, a MAGA-capped student named Nick Sandmann—crowding into Phillips's personal space. Sandmann and his classmates seemed to be jeering and smirking at him while he chanted and played his drum. The video was viewed millions of times and spread rapidly around the internet on social media. Reaction to the video, predictably, split along political lines. Subsequent videos, however, showed a much more complicated situation than was initially reported—but by then, of course, public opinion had largely ossified.

In the Douglas County School District in Colorado, a seventh-grade social studies teacher named Michelle Grissom saw a tweet containing the original video of the incident. She did a little internet research and wrote a reply in which she purported to identify the young man standing directly in front of Phillips [Sandmann]:

> His name is Jay Jackson. His twitter account is closed to non followers so we won't interfere with his training in the #HitlerYouth.

But—predictable plot twist—Grissom was wrong. Her comment was arguably slanderous enough even if she had correctly identified the student, but it was incredibly reckless and hurtful when applied to someone utterly uninvolved in the situation. Jackson's father, Dr. John Jackson, wrote a reply to Grissom's tweet that read:

> I assure you this is not Jay Jackson…he played in a varsity basketball game last night in Park Hills Kentucky and another game today in Middletown Ohio…the person has been identified please remove this post and apologize for accusing someone without evidence

Grissom initially refused to back down, saying that "if it's not him, he must have a twin bc he's a dead ringer for the guy above." Eventually, however, after numerous other people chimed in on Twitter to defend the Jacksons, Grissom issued an apology:

> I officially retract using Jay Jackson from Covington Catholic High School as the racist and disrespectful student who mocked Native American, Nathan Phillips. I apologize to Jay Jackson and his family.

But by then, as you might expect, the damage had already been done, both to the Jackson family and Grissom's 20-year teaching career. On January 24, 2019, the Mountain Ridge Middle School sent a letter to parents announcing that Grissom had been removed from the classroom and placed on administrative leave. At the same time, Grissom resigned from her position as a member of the executive board of the Douglas County Federation of Teachers.

Grissom's tweets (and similar online comments by DCSD Board of Education member Kenneth Leung) led to a tense confrontation between parents and the BOE regarding board policy. As is the case in many communities, school boards ask members of the public in advance to speak at board meetings. However, this particular board also asks people to state the subject on which they plan to talk. Before the BOE meeting on January 24, the board secretary called several prospective speakers to tell them that they would not be allowed to comment on the Twitter remarks by Grissom, since the incident was a personnel matter and therefore confidential.

That decision angered several parents. One speaker addressed the board and said that "[h]ere we are a community incensed by a teacher's social media posts, nobody wants to be here discussing this but no matter how uncomfortable, we must confront this." As soon as he mentioned Grissom's name, however, he was told to stop speaking and was escorted from the meeting by officers.

Five months later, the DCSD and Grissom reached a separation agreement in which the district agreed to pay her for fourteen weeks accrued vacation and an additional $25,000 in exchange for her covenant not to sue the school district. Under the agreement, she also cannot be employed in the DCSD again.

This resolution did not sit well with everyone. A local news blog called "Colorado Peak Politics," which describes itself as "Colorado's Conservative Bully Pulpit," summarized it this way:

Abuse students and collect $25,000. Only in government does a person who should have been fired on the spot receive a lump sum payout after months of paid leave after committing extreme behavior on the job.

Yesterday marked the conclusion of another shameful episode from the union-owned Douglas County School Board (and it's hand-picked superintendent). ...

Not only was this a breach of decorum, a marginalization of Nazi atrocities, and a demonstration of a complete ignorance of history, but it was also a glaring violation of the district's social media policy on cyber bullying, which, by the way, was written to punish students, not teachers who should be above this sort of thing.

Top Three Takeaways:

- One of the more disturbing recent trends on the internet is the rise of digital vigilantes. This phenomenon took off following the Boston Marathon bombing in 2013, when armchair detectives scoured the internet for photos of the crime scene, tried to ID possible suspects, and devoured catalog listings of pressure cookers and backpacks. Over time, people got into the habit of circulating videos of people misbehaving and asking social media users to help identify them, with the express goal of publicly shaming them or even getting them fired. There are a lot of problems with this, but one of the most significant is that sometimes people are misidentified. The resulting emotional and even economic harm can be substantial.

- No one should engage in these types of mob takedowns, but most assuredly, educators should not. Teachers do not have the training to be investigators, no matter how savvy they may think they are at sniffing out student misconduct. More importantly, no educator should take it upon himself or herself to call out or "identify" a minor as an alleged perpetrator outside of a formal investigation. As this case amply illustrates, there is a profound risk of misidentification, with all the potential harm that entails.

- As an attorney and former school board chair, I understand the reluctance of the DCSD Board of Education to entertain public discussion of the incident. But that rule may need to be adjusted when an educator has engaged in public misconduct. It would, of course, be inappropriate for the board to publicly discuss its internal investigation or its disciplinary options (all of which do have significant legal implications). None of that, however, should prevent the board from listening to the concerns of the citizens about publicly-known information. Clamping down on speech in this fashion is an unfortunate misstep that undermines public confidence in the actions of the district.

Cautionary Tale 24-2018-US_Michigan

On December 4, 2018, 18-year-old Maison Hullibarger—a top-notch football player and straight-A student studying criminal justice at the University of Toledo—committed suicide.

Three days later, a funeral for Hullibarger was held at Our Lady of Mount Carmel Catholic Church in Temperance, MI, a small town just north of the Ohio border near Toledo. The purpose of such gatherings is two-fold: to honor the life of the deceased and to provide comfort to the bereaved. Unfortunately, Hulliberger's funeral fell short on both counts. In his homily, Rev. Don LaCuesta repeatedly referenced the fact that Hullibarger had committed suicide and speculated about whether his actions might prevent him from entering Heaven due to his mortal sin. He also tried to stop Hullibarger's parents from speaking to the mourners, but the parents' funeral director told the organist to stop playing and offered the parents a chance to talk about their son. As pallbearers carried Hullibarger's casket from the church, the parents told Father LaCuesta that they did not want him to attend the burial.

The priest's comments undoubtedly were upsetting enough, but that was not the only disruption. Hullibarger's former high school football coach, Jeffrey Wood, showed up at the church after explicitly being told that the family did not want him to attend. Hullibarger had been a star linebacker at Bedford High School under coach Wood, but according to his parents, the experience was not positive. As Jeff Hullibarger, Maison's dad, put it, "We've had four boys who played for him. He's been bullying kids for many years[.]"

When Wood entered the church, one of Maison's brothers went and asked him to leave. Wood did so but later posted a snide comment on Facebook:

> I was just asked to leave a funeral by a family member of a deceased football player. If you need someone to blame, I'm your man, I'm your fall guy. This is how society is when things go not as planned. We blame others for our own shortcomings. This tragedy is not about me or you. It's about looking in the mirror as a human being and being real and honest with yourself.

The Hullibarger family did not appreciate the post by Woods. They reported his remarks to the Bedford Community Schools, and on December 10, Woods was relieved of his coaching duties. BCS Superintendent Carl Schultz issued a statement that read in part:

> The district holds all of its staff to the highest standards of professionalism (but) recently received allegations that those standards may not have been met by the coach. Therefore, we are in the process of thoroughly investigating those allegations.

Top Three Takeaways:

- It's not clear why Wood showed up at the church after being asked by the family not to do so. Even before we get to the ethical issues, this is a failure of courtesy and common decency. Educators can avoid many of the cybertraps discussed in this book by showing a willingness to abide by community and social norms.

- Wood's initial unkindness had nothing to do with the internet, but social media is always there to help make matters worse. It appears from the text of his post that Wood was either responding to statements made offline or, in some way, continuing an earlier disagreement. In either case, Wood should not have added to the family's pain by sharing his thoughts on Facebook.

- Educators should keep in mind that one of the unintended byproducts of social media is that it can dramatically speed up disciplinary proceedings. It's much more difficult to contest an allegation of misconduct when your superintendent or school board is staring at a printout of your own words. There are cases where words or even videos can be ambiguous, but more often than not, impulsive educators will discover that they have made life very easy for investigators and supervisors.

Cautionary Tale 24-2018-US_Pennsylvania

On February 20, 2018, 18-year-old Kixx Alderette Jr. attended a meeting of the New Castle Area School District (NCASD) School Board. He was at the meeting to talk about his senior project on bullying, which he told the board was based in part on his own experience with bullying in the district.

In particular, Alderette said, he was assaulted by two NCASD students as he was returning from classes at the Lawrence County Career and Technical Center. Despite the injuries caused by the students and the significant risk to his health (he lives with a metal bar in his chest), Alderette told the board that his assailants were never disciplined by the school district nor charged by police (who described the incident as a "mutual fight"). He specifically criticized the lack of action by NCASD Superintendent John J. Sarandrea.

It's not clear that the NCASD board took any action in response to Alderette's report, but Superintendent Sarandrea unfortunately did. Following the board meeting, Sarandrea found Alderette's Facebook page and sent him an instant message at 12:36 a.m. The tone, to put it mildly, was unkind:

> Good Evening Kicks....I can't begin to tell you what a pleasure it was having you grace us with your presence at tonight's board meeting.

> It is nice to see you becoming a chip off the old block and following the example of blaming others for your shortcomings.

In reference to your request for my assistance in helping you toward finishing your cyber school graduation project, let me point out the following:

The NCASD posts its entire policy manual on its website.

Do the research, you will learn much.

Most of the data you requested is either not available until year's end or not accumulated.3) While I am honored that you chose me to assist you in this very important endeavor, unfortunately my position and its time demands will not permit me to assist. Perhaps Superintendent Rich at Laurel could be of better assistance since I know you hold him in equally high esteem.

Best wishes for a successful project and may you go on to become wildly successful like your parents.

Warmly,

Mr. Salandrea [*sic* -- Alderette had accidentally misspoken Sarandrea's name at the hearing]

In mid-June 2018, Alderette attended another NCASD school board meeting and provided copies of Sarandrea's Facebook message to the board. He also said that when his parents met with Superintendent Sarandrea to discuss the incident, Sarandrea threatened to have Alderett's locker searched by police and falsely accused him of carrying a razor blade on the school bus. Following that meeting, Sarandrea had Alderette's father (Kixx Alderette Sr.) cited for disorderly conduct by the New Castle police and also sent him a certified letter banning him from entering the Croton Administration Building (NCASD district headquarters). Sarandrea later withdrew the disorderly conduct citation Alderette Sr. appeared before a magistrate and pleaded not guilty.

At the same school board meeting, Silk Alderette (Kixx's mother) said that her family was considering the possibility of filing a federal civil rights lawsuit against the district, Sarandrea, and other district personnel. She accused them of failing to take action to prevent the physical bullying of her son, the abusive message from the superintendent, and the false charges filed against her husband. Sarandrea responded by saying that "I see this for what it is. Have at it, people."

Six weeks later, the NCASD board voted 8-1 to approve a severance package that paid Sarandrea $210,000 over four years, along with annual health care coverage valued at $2,000 per month. Sarandrea, who had served as NCASD superintendent since 2013, had another two years left on his contract and would have earned an additional $600,000 had he stayed. Before the vote, Silk Alderette spoke at public comment and accused the board of engaging in a "'zero tolerance for bullying' cover-up."

On July 21, 2018 (ten days before Sarandrea's departure from NCASD), the Alderettes did file a federal lawsuit that alleged various civil rights violations against Sarandrea, NCASD, the Lawrence County Career and Technical School, and the school's director, Leonard Rich. The Alderettes alleged that Sarandrea violated their son's First Amendment rights by sending him a message intended to silence his criticism of Sarandrea's handling of bullying in the schools. They also sought damages for Sarandrea's attempt to use the criminal process against the father without reasonable cause.

In January 2019, a federal judge dismissed the charges against the NCASD and Rich, but the suit against the Technical School and Sarandrea is still ongoing.

Top Three Takeaways:

- Here is one bright-line rule that should emerge from this book: If you ever find yourself thinking about messaging a student after midnight, just don't. Very little good can come of it. And yes, of course, it is possible to imagine some dire emergency in which doing so would be justified. In the vast majority of instances, however, there is no good reason that the message can't wait until the following day. And if you do postpone writing, the odds of making a better ethical decision rise considerably.

- Similarly, it is not appropriate to seek out and use a student's personal social media account to communicate with that student. Most social media channels allow for both public and private messaging, and the use of either method is problematic. The potential ethical pitfalls of using private social media messaging are well-illustrated throughout this book. As this case demonstrates, however, potential ethical problems can arise even when communicating publicly. Sure, there's transparency, but if your message is scornful and sarcastic, you are still acting unprofessionally.

- The ethical problems associated with making false accusations against a student and threatening him with an unlawful search should be self-evident.

Cautionary Tale 24-2016-US_Alabama

Sometimes, a cautionary tale appears to be useful for illustrating one type of cybertrap and then offers lessons on a different digital risk. Few instances, however, offer quite the buffet of digital misconduct and ethical lapses as this one does.

Jeremiah Hunter, an 8th-grade science teacher and cheerleading coach at Hankins Middle School in Theodore, Alabama, was arrested in mid-February 2016 and charged with the second-degree stalking of a student. The Mobile County Sheriff's Office (MCSO) said that Hunter had become obsessed with a student when he was in Hawkins's class. Over the next three years, Hawkins and the student exchanged over 18,000 text messages. During that time, Hunter twice was warned by law enforcement to stop contacting the child but continued to do so, even going so far as to change his phone and use various social media apps to hide his stalking. Police also later learned that Hunter occasionally showed up at the teen's workplace unannounced and tried to talk with him.

The duration of the stalking led to some predictable finger-pointing, with MCSO Lt. Paul Burch suggesting that the school district had not responded quickly or forcefully enough to the initial reports of Hunter's behavior. Mobile County School System Superintendent Martha Peek, however, strongly disagreed with Burch's comment. She said that the district had been working with both the boy's family and law enforcement all along but that the school district did not have sufficient grounds to take any disciplinary action until the MCSO arrested Hunter.

Peek also implied that the district was hampered by the fact that it could only monitor public social media activity. School districts are not able to monitor text messages or one-to-one social media messages exchanged between two individuals like Hunter and his victim.

Following Hunter's arrest, the MCSO executed a search warrant of his home. Burch told reporters that the MCSO seized a variety of items from Hunter's house. The collected evidence included assorted electronic equipment, a photo of the victim that was on his nightstand next to his bed, and a cellphone that used a picture of the boy as its screensaver. Both the cellphone and Hunter's iPad used the victim's birth date as a passcode. Burch also said that it was clear that Hunter was aware of the investigation and was proactively soliciting support from students and parents in the event police arrested him.

The 39-year-old Hunter—a former "Teacher of the Year" at Hankins Middle School—was re-arrested 11 days later on a single charge of "tampering with physical evidence." The charge stemmed from a request Hunter made to a friend to remove a backpack from his classroom before the police could find it.

Ultimately, the evidence tampering charge was dropped by the state of Alabama because Hunter's case was taken over by the U.S. Attorney's office in March 2016. The switch to federal court stemmed from the fact that an FBI computer forensics analyst found extensive evidence that Hunter had solicited and had received sexting photos depicting as many as nine different male students at the Hankins Middle School. Many of the pictures were taken by one of the children involved and sent via text message to Hunter.

The computer forensics exam also revealed that Hunter had conducted Google searches for terms indicating a sexual interest in young men, and had also searched for techniques and apps that would enable him to text anonymously.

Although Hunter admitted texting with the middle school boy and receiving photos of him and other middle school boys, he testified during his trial that he was investigating whether middle school students were sharing nude photos. He said that he didn't report the photos or child sexting to administrators because "it was so common." If he started reporting all the sexting, Hunter added, he would have spent most of his time in his office filling out paperwork.

Despite Hunter's best efforts to explain and excuse his conduct, it took the jury less than 10 minutes to reach a unanimous guilty verdict when given the case on July 22, 2016. Four months later, the U.S. District Court judge sentenced Hunter to ten years in federal prison. Hunter appealed his conviction because, he said, the photos that he received from the student did not meet the statutory definition of child pornography under federal law. Specifically, Hunter argued that the images could not be "pornography," child or otherwise, because he did not find them arousing. His only was only interested in the contents, Hunter said, so that he could report what was happening to the school principal (which he admitted that he did not do).

The Court of Appeals for the 11th Circuit affirmed his conviction, noting that there was ample evidence for the jury to conclude that Hunter found the photos sexually arousing. Among other things, the Court pointed to his conversations with the student who provided the images, Hunter's request for a picture of another specific student, and the contents of his Google search history.

"[T]he jury," the Court dryly wrote, "was free to disbelieve Defendant" when he testified that the images were not arousing.

Top Three Takeaways:

- Despite the somewhat defensive tone of Superintendent Peek, she is correct that neither school districts nor law enforcement can monitor direct messages exchanged via text messages or apps. At the same time, however, it is fair to conclude that whatever steps the district took to address Hunter's behavior were not nearly sufficient. The fact that Hunter was able to exchange 18,000(!) messages with the primary victim is a strong indication that the district's supervision and intervention were ineffective.

- The fact that Hunter was able to engage in his grooming of these victims over such a long time also suggests that the school district should have done more to create a better climate of cybersafety for the students. What guidance were students given, for instance, on how to recognize inappropriate contacts from a teacher and how to report them safely? What information did the district provide to parents on monitoring their children's use of mobile devices or on how to recognize warning signs? Lastly, were district educators

- trained on recognizing potential grooming situations and encouraged to raise concerns?

- Many people have tried to defend their possession of child pornography as part of an amateur "investigation." All of those people are in jail. There is no vigilante exception to federal and state child pornography laws. And, if someone *ever* sends you an intimate image of a minor, you should contact law enforcement immediately. (For more on the proper handling of student sexts, *see* Chapter 29.)

Cautionary Tale 24-2013-US_Pennsylvania

In the late winter of 2014, Michael David Garet, a Spanish teacher at Penn-Trafford High School in Harrison City, PA, was suspended after being charged with stalking, harassment, and disorderly conduct. Police allege that Garet started messaging a 17-year-old male student on Google+ Hangouts, and then on other social media channels, including Facebook and Twitter. He repeatedly invited the student to spend time alone with him or go on trips, and then began trying to set up meetings with the boy at his workplace.

The young man grew concerned about the tone of Garet's messages, mainly since his younger sister was about to enter high school in the fall. He was worried that Garet might approach her in the same way. He printed out the messages and showed them to his mother, who reported the situation to another teacher in the school on January 31, 2014. The teacher, in turn, promptly told school officials what was going on. Garet was suspended without pay and escorted off the campus by police on the morning of February 4.

Law enforcement officials noted that none of the messages Garet sent to his victim were "overtly sexual." Taken together, however, they indicated an effort to groom the young man for sexual contact. As Penn Township Police Chief John Otto put it:

> There was definite, inappropriate and – in our opinion – criminal conduct on behalf of Garet. We were able to capture and view a significant number of text messages from Mr. Garet's phone to the victim in this case's phone and evaluate those for content. In our opinion, those text messages were very inappropriate and in fact criminal. These texts, while they may not have been directly sexual in nature, were certainly disturbing, certainly put this young man in fear for his own personal safety and certainly crossed the line from inappropriate into criminal conduct.

The response of Superintendent Matt Harris should be a guide for every school district administrator. As he told reporters, "You don't take chances, and you turn over everything." The school district was praised by law enforcement for its swift and effective response to the situation.

Top Three Takeaways:

- This case is a particularly good illustration of how multiple unsupervised communication channels can abet educator misconduct. Whether the conversations are welcome or unwelcome, mobile devices and apps make it possible for teachers and students to have conversations at any time of the day or night, and frequently without anyone else knowing that they are occurring. Educators have the primary ethical obligation to monitor their behavior and to refrain from any interaction that is inappropriate or creates the appearance of impropriety.

- As you read through these cautionary tales, you will realize that it is not uncommon for a child or student involved to demonstrate more ethical behavior than the adult. That's what happened here; thanks to the combination of his upbringing, school lessons, and his sense of moral conduct, the young man recognized that there was a problem and took steps to prevent potential harm to himself and his sister. Parents and schools should partner to create an environment in which every child feels comfortable enough to report something that concerns them.

- It's not enough for a school district to draft handouts on cybersafety and provide the occasional lecture to faculty and students. The school must also demonstrate its commitment to student safety in practical ways when the occasion arises. The key attributes of a good district response are promptness, transparency, cooperation, and due process. Invariably, the districts and administrators that experience the most difficulty in educator misconduct cases are those that fail to demonstrate one or more of those qualities.

Relevant MCEE Provisions for Chapter 24

Principle I: Responsibility to the Profession

Standards I.A.2, I.A.3, I.A.4, and I.A.5

Principle II: Responsibility for Professional Competence

Standard II.C.3

Principle III: Responsibility to Students

Standards III.A.2, III.A.3, III.A.7, and III.B.3

Principle IV: Responsibility to the School Community

Standards IV.D.1, IV.D.3, and IV.E.1

Principle V: Responsible and Ethical Use Technology

Standards V.A.1, V.A.5, V.A.7, and V.B.2

Sources

The sources for the Cautionary Tales in this chapter can be viewed at the following URL:

https://link.cybertraps.com/C4E2-Sources-Chap24

Chapter 25
Electronic Sexual Assault: Voyeurism and Child Pornography

Overview

This chapter covers two separate but not unrelated cybertraps: voyeurism and child pornography. As with so many other cybertraps in this book, digital technology has made two serious social ills far more problematic.

A brief word about terminology: when I was at a tech conference a few years ago, there was a conversation about the phrase "revenge porn" and whether it is an accurate description of how such images are captured and used. I proposed the phrase "electronic sexual assault" to describe any intimate image that is taken or distributed without the consent of the person depicted. I later wrote a blog post entitled "Reclaiming the Conversation: It's Not 'Revenge Porn,' It's 'Electronic Sexual Assault.'" I came to realize that this terminology encompasses several of the cybertraps discussed in this book, including both voyeuristic photos and child pornography (which, as we'll see, frequently overlap).

The reason that the incidence of both voyeurism and child pornography has increased recently is simple. As I've frequently stated in my professional development presentations, the *de facto* "Olympic motto" of the technology industry is "Smaller, Faster, Cheaper." If you look at advertisements for digital equipment over the years, you will see that the size of electronic components has steadily shrunk, the processing speeds have accelerated dramatically, and that even with these improvements, the overall cost of electronics has steadily dropped.

There is probably a no better illustration of these trends than digital photography. Back in 1995, just as the World Wide Web was starting to take off, Fuji and Nikon joined forces to produce what became known as the "B-2 Stealth Bomber" of digital cameras. It had a 1.3-megapixel digital sensor and used 131 MB cards capable of storing up to 70 photos. All of this technical wizardry could be yours for just $20,000. You may want to read that again: $20,000.

Just twelve years later, Apple released the first iPhone. It came with a 2-megapixel rear-facing camera, and in its largest storage configuration (8 GB), could store more than 1,000 photos. The cost of this technical wizardry? $599. Every week, it seems, we continue to see remarkable advances in the digital technology available to consumers.

Earlier in this book, I discussed one of the major implications for educators resulting from the ever-shrinking camera: the fact that more and more students every year are carrying camera-equipped smartphones. Thanks to their myriad apps and global connectivity, if anything amusing, interesting, outrageous, or even criminal happens in front of a student, he or she can record and broadcast the event to a worldwide audience in seconds. #CamerasAreEverywhere.

But an equally important implication, unfortunately, is that shrinking camera sizes pose a powerful temptation for a small percentage of educators.

Voyeurism

The practice or fetish of voyeurism has been around a lot longer than computers or digital cameras. According to Merriam-Webster, "voyeurism" is defined as "a: the practice of obtaining sexual gratification from observing others," or "b: the practice of taking pleasure in observing something private, sordid, or scandalous." The English language borrowed the term "voyeur" from French around 1900, but the nearly-synonymous English phrase "Peeping Tom" has been around since the middle of the 18th century. And undoubtedly, whoever Tom was, he wasn't the first.

Even the practice of taking surreptitious photos predates our modern era. Back when the Kodak Brownie camera was the must-have consumer product, people would drill holes in the side of a lunch box, hide a camera inside, and rig a string to trigger the shutter from a safe distance. These days, of course, it is much, much easier to take secretive and voyeuristic photos. As I detailed in my earlier books, *The Naked Employee* and *American Privacy*, there is an entire industry devoted to hiding cameras in household items. For example, one home security company, PalmVID, hides its cameras in smoke detectors, air purifiers, clock radios, television soundbars, DVD/Blu-Ray players, routers, computer speakers, desk fans, clocks, carbon monoxide detectors, bathroom clothes hooks, planters, and so on. Another company, BrickHouse Security, offers cameras hidden in tissue boxes, lamps, a teddy bear, light bulbs, and even wall plugs. BrickHouse's promotional video on how to select the most useful hidden camera for your personal "security" needs is, quite frankly, Orwellian.

The widespread availability of hidden cameras helped spark a new social movement in South Korea, where the practice of voyeuristic photos appears to be particularly prevalent. One woman, Chung Soo-young, is selling a wildly popular anti-spy cam kit to women across the country. The kit contains a tube of silicone sealant to fill holes, an ice pick to break tiny camera lenses, and stickers reading "Don't look at me!" to put over possible camera hiding places." In part because of the response to Soo-young's product, the South Korean capital of Seoul announced that it would deploy 8,000 municipal workers to regularly inspect the city's more than 20,000 public bathrooms for hidden recording devices.

Unfortunately, far too many educators have fallen victim to this particular temptation. Teachers have committed a range of hidden camera-related voyeurism offenses: including taking upskirt photos during music lessons or science class; hiding a camera in a packet of hotel coffee to videotape a student showering; hiding a camera in a theater dressing room; and putting a digital camera in a bottle of shampoo to record both faculty and students in a locker room shower. That is, unfortunately, just a small sampling of the disturbing misuses of tiny cameras over the past decade.

To be clear, not every voyeuristic photo is *ipso facto* illegal. It is not a crime, for instance, to take a surreptitious photo of a clothed individual in a public place (for example, on the street or public transportation). The possibility of being observed or even photographed is one of the trade-offs we make when we use public spaces. There are limits, however. Some jurisdictions have made it a crime to take or attempt to take so-called "upskirt" or "downblouse" photos in public spaces, for the obvious reason that no one consents to such invasive photographs merely by going outside. The laws, however, are not consistent from state to state.

Child Pornography

Not surprisingly, the category of electronic sexual assault that attracts the most attention and concern is child pornography (the only crime that surpasses it for public outrage and concern is sexual assault on a student). Wholly apart from a teacher's duty to serve as a role model in society, the fact that a teacher who works with children for hours each day has any involvement with child pornography is alarming. There is considerable debate among academics, researchers, and law enforcement about whether the collection and/or production of child pornography inevitably leads to the sexual assault of children. This book is not the place to either summarize or try to resolve that debate. There is an innate logic, however, to the argument that someone who works with children all day is at higher risk of transitioning from passive consumption of child pornography to active assault.

"Child pornography" is defined under federal law as "an image or picture, whether made or produced by electronic, mechanical, or other means, of sexually explicit conduct, where the production of such visual depiction involves the use of a minor engaging in sexually explicit conduct…" (Most state laws use a similar statutory definition.) The law defines a "minor" as someone under the age of 18, which covers most students in a K-12 school system.

Child pornography images presumed to be "obscene" under federal and state law and therefore are not entitled to First Amendment protection. A judge or jury can disagree with the prosecutor about the designation, of course, but the presumption of illegality is an onerous burden for a defendant to overcome.

The possession, production, and distribution of child pornography is a crime under federal law and the law of all fifty states, and each offense carries its own mandatory minimum prison sentence. An individual convicted of child pornography almost certainly will be required to register as a sex offender and also may have to pay substantial restitution to the victim. His or her license to teach, of course, will evaporate upon conviction.

Educators who engage in the practice of digital voyeurism may not necessarily intend to create child pornography images *per se*. When someone points a camera lens at children in spaces where they change clothes or go to the bathroom, it is virtually inevitable that they will create contraband images. If a photograph or video constitutes a "lascivious exhibition" of the intimate areas of a minor's body, then it can be considered child pornography even if the child is fully clothed. Determining whether a particular image or video falls within the category of child pornography depends in part on the intent of the photographer. As a result, the covert nature of a voyeuristic photo would factor into the analysis of a potentially illegal image.

Of course, some percentage of educators who engage in digital voyeurism specifically intend to create child pornography. In most digital voyeurism cases, the perpetrator is taking the images and videos for his or her sole gratification. However, it is far too easy to share digital content with the entire world, and there is unquestionably a thriving market for illicit images of schoolchildren. School districts and individual educators have a compelling ethical obligation to immediately report any concerns that a colleague might be abusing his or her position as an educator in this fashion.

I have focused much of this section on the interplay between digital voyeurism and child pornography for one simple reason: When an educator is the one taking voyeuristic images, he or she is almost certainly doing so in a school building. As a result, students are the most likely victims. That is a direct and personal breach of trust with the school community and a particularly visceral ethical breach.

At the same time, however, it is vital to keep in mind that the potential cybertrap of child pornography extends well beyond the temptations of hidden cameras or hallway creepshots. Over the past thirty-five years, the combination of three technologies—scanners, digital cameras, and the World Wide Web—has fueled a tragic explosion in the global production and distribution of child pornography.

Once a tiny, niche phenomenon, child pornography has become a problem of global significance and a significant priority for law enforcement agencies worldwide. Scanners can give new life to old print images, thus perpetuating acts of abuse that took place decades ago. Digital cameras and now camera-equipped smartphones make it far too easy to produce new images without running the risk of film developers reporting suspicious photos to the police. The World Wide Web has facilitated both nearly-instantaneous global distribution of contraband images and the development of far-flung underground communities devoted to the sharing and sale of these images.

Complicating matters immensely, and adding significantly to the scope of the problem, is the fact that significant percentages of children use their smartphones to take and share sexting photos of themselves and their classmates. Often, neither they nor their parents are aware that they are producing and distributing child pornography when they do so.

Like people from every other walk of life, teachers have found it all too easy to fall into the particularly heinous cybertrap of possessing or distributing digital contraband. Not a single week goes by without multiple reports of teachers being arrested, indicted, or convicted of this crime. The stories are a living journal of the constantly-evolving cat-and-mouse game between perpetrators and police. Law enforcement agents have caught teachers in a host of innovative ways: using peer-to-peer software, offering to trade child pornography in chat rooms, setting up meetings in classrooms to exchange child pornography on USB sticks, taking surreptitious photos of students on field trips, soliciting and receiving sexting photos from underage students, and so on.

It is essential to reiterate that these types of cases, while horrifying, are fortunately exceedingly rare. The actual number of educators involved in child pornography in any manner is a minuscule percentage of the roughly 3 million K-12 teachers employed in the United States. Nonetheless, even a single perpetrator (or victim) is one too many. We should deploy every available tool—pre-certification training, ongoing training in the Model Code of Ethics for Educators, adequate background checks, professional development, and effective supervision—to protect children from the life-altering harm caused by this crime.

Cautionary Tales

Cautionary Tale 25-2019-US_Texas

Given that the title of this book is *Cybertraps for Educators 2.0*, it makes sense that the bulk of the cautionary tales are about classroom teachers. But administrators and educators should not lose sight of the fact that these cybertraps can ensnare anyone who is working in the schools. Fulfilling the ethical obligation to protect students means being aware of that fact and taking appropriate steps if there is reason to believe that anyone in the school is doing something that might harm students.

Into this broader category of potential misconduct falls the case of 42-year-old Scott Gelardi. In the fall of 2019, Gelardi was working as an employee for Aramark at the Northside Elementary School in El Campo, TX. Aramark is a well-known national food services corporation that the El Campo ISD hired to provide meals for schools in the district.

In mid-November, school maintenance workers discovered a hidden camera in the boys' bathroom. The camera contained both pictures and videos of boys using the restroom. Police reviewed surveillance footage recorded by the school in the hallway outside the bathroom and identified Gelardi as the most likely suspect.

None of the victims were readily identifiable in the images and videos, since their faces were not visible. In a statement, the El Campo Police Department said that there was no evidence that Gelardi had any physical contact with any of the victims.

Based on the contents of the hidden camera, the Department said, "Gelardi was charged with invasive visual recording in a bathroom, possession of child pornography and possession of child pornography with intent to promote[.]" Investigators obtained a search warrant for Gelardi's vehicle, his school office, and his apartment. During the search, police seized additional equipment and said that additional charges might be brought depending on the results of a forensic examination of the evidence. Gelardi was held overnight in jail before posting bail of $70,000.

The school district released a limited comment:

> El Campo Independent School District is saddened, disturbed, and angered by the alleged actions of this individual. We thank and applaud the El Campo Police Department for its work related to this incident.

For its part, Aramark insisted that it had taken all the necessary precautions before hiring Gelardi:

> Yesterday we were made aware of very disturbing allegations involving one of our employees. We immediately launched an investigation and terminated his employment. The employee passed a background check, including a sex offender registry check, prior to starting work in the El Campo ISD. We are fully cooperating with the authorities on their investigation into this matter.

In the meantime, the school district instructed maintenance workers to examine all bathrooms in the district; they did not find any other hidden recording devices.

Top Three Takeaways:

- It should be a goal of every school and every school district to create a culture of cybersafety that suffuses the entire organization. Every person who works in the organization, whether directly or through a subcontractor, should be given clear information about his or her responsibilities in promoting cybersafety for students (which includes refraining from certain types of behavior). School districts should require any subcontractor working on campus to help promote a culture of cybersafety.

- Courts have made it clear that businesses and organizations cannot install surveillance cameras in places where individuals have a reasonable expectation of privacy (bathrooms, locker rooms, etc.). In this case, the district made the smart decision to install a surveillance camera near the entrance to the bathroom, which provided valuable evidence during the investigation of this crime. Since bathrooms and locker rooms are often the sites of voyeurism crimes, other school districts should consider taking similar steps. There are some practical considerations. For instance, school districts will need to think about how long they are willing to store surveillance footage. Depending on the size of the school district, data storage can quickly become a logistical and financial burden. The economic cost places a premium on regular sweeps of private spaces for hidden devices. The sooner a camera or recording device is discovered, the more likely it is that you will have a record of who might have planted it, and the more quickly the district can discard or overwrite old camera footage.

- Any educator who engages in this type of conduct should not be surprised when law enforcement subsequently scrutinizes every nook and cranny of his or her digital life, up to and including material that he or she tried to delete. Over the last twenty years, the software and hardware resources of law enforcement computer forensic experts have grown incredibly powerful. If you do anything that triggers that level of official scrutiny, don't expect any unpleasant secrets to remain hidden.

Cautionary Tale 25-2019-US_Kentucky

Thanks to digital devices and social media, criminal investigators have a powerful new tool at their disposal: "selfie-incrimination." I apply that term to situations in which the perpetrator either records himself committing a crime or boasts about it afterward on social media. Just in the last few months, for instance, people have been arrested for some incredibly thoughtless oversharing:

- Committing domestic abuse on a video game live-stream;

- Committing assault and robbery while recording a Snapchat video;

- Racing and crashing two Corvettes in New York's Lincoln Tunnel and then sharing a dashcam video on Instagram;

- Vandalizing an expensive Bentley and sharing selfies with the damage on Instagram; and

- Urinating into a Kellogg's Raisin Bran production line and posting a video of the act online.

The concept of selfie-incrimination comes to mind thanks to the facts of this cautionary tale. In late April 2019, the staff at Murray High School in Murray, Kentucky, noticed that someone had installed a recording device in the bathroom of the school nurse's station. It perpetrator carefully positioned it to record people as they were disrobing or changing clothes.

When law enforcement examined the device, they discovered that the person installing it had accidentally recorded himself. Police were able to identify the person as Mark Boggess, 53, a health and physical education teacher at the high school.

Boggess was charged "with three counts of possession or viewing of matter portraying a sexual performance by a minor and four counts of voyeurism." Under Kentucky law [Ky. Rev. Stat. § 531.300(4)(c)], "sexual conduct by a minor" includes "[E]xcretion for the purpose of sexual stimulation or gratification," i.e., for that of the viewer or recorder.

Murray Independent School District Superintendent Coy Samons promptly suspended Boggess without pay, and he resigned his position with the district later that same day. Samons also issued a statement to the school community that read in part:

> I want to assure our MISD families that when unfortunate events such as this occur, I will take action to protect our students and staff. The situation in no ways defines Murray Independent Schools.

In August 2019, Boggess was back in court on five new charges of "possessing or viewing matter that depicts a sexual performance by a minor," charges which presumably stemmed from the forensic examination of his digital devices. Five months later, in early January, he accepted a deal with the prosecution in which he pleaded guilty to "eight counts of possessing/viewing matter portraying a sexual performance by a minor and eight counts of voyeurism." Under the terms of the deal, Boggess could be sentenced to as many as ten years in prison. He also will be required to register in Kentucky as a sex offender for the remainder of his life.

Top Three Takeaways:

- Detectives and prosecutors order an extra round when they discover that a suspect has recorded himself or herself committing the crime. It is quite remarkable how many people video record themselves committing a crime or boasting about it afterward. You would think that people might want to make the whole investigation thing harder, but apparently, the need for self-aggrandizement outweighs prudence.

- This cybertrap was inspired in large part by Boggess's evident belief that he could successfully hide a tiny recording device. That belief was no doubt inspired by two main factors: 1) the remarkably small size of recording devices these days and 2) the fact that there is so much voyeuristic content available online. The reality is that if someone has a predilection for such material, there are far too many websites that not only normalize the behavior but host communities of people who offer tips and advice on how best to hide cameras and recorders. Educators have an ethical obligation to avoid criminal behavior like this and should seek professional help if they feel any temptation to become a digital voyeur.

- Schools can and should try to prevent digital voyeurism by routinely conducting professional development that discusses unacceptable conduct (including digital voyeurism) and highlights for educators the serious harm such privacy invasions can cause. Unfortunately, however, mere warnings are not sufficient. As remarkable as it may sound, schools now have an affirmative duty to routinely scan ostensibly private spaces (bathrooms, changing areas, locker rooms, *etc.*) for possible hidden cameras. Staff can conduct such inspections visually or by using a device specifically designed to detect tiny camera lenses. There are a growing number of products and apps available to assist with this, in part because of a recent spate of hidden cameras discovered in Airbnb rentals.

Cautionary Tale 25-2019-US_California

Anderson W. Clark Magnet High School is located in Glendale, California, and is managed as part of the Glendale Unified School District. For twenty years, 60-year-old Christian Axelgard worked at the school as a physical education teacher. In January 2019, however, his teaching career came to an ignominious end when police arrested him for "allegedly taking voyeuristic photos of female students."

A couple of months earlier, students noticed that Axelgard was openly taking photos of young women while they were doing push-ups during gym class. Sgt. Dan Suttles, a spokesperson for the Glendale Police Department, said that Axelgard was taking the photos for his sexual gratification and that the pictures were not limited to gym class.

> It was during class, while [students] were participating in sports activities or just a girl walking in the hallway. It was whenever he felt there was an opportunity to take a picture of a girl.

A student cell phone video showing Axelgard photographing students helped buttress the November report of Axelgard's misconduct.

Following the complaints by the students, the district conducted an investigation that included, among other things, an examination of Axelgard's personal cellphone, his school-issued computer, and interviews with students. Based on that data, the district concluded that Axelgard had been taking covert photos of students for at least three years. In a letter sent to Axelgard on March 22, 2019, Assistant Superintendent Cynthia M. Foley summarized his misconduct:

> These pictures/videos were all taken while on school campus as evidenced by the photos of students found on your personal cell phone (pictures of female students' chests and buttocks, picture of two female students against a school wall backdrop). A review of surveillance cameras confirms you held your cell phone close to your chest with your camera application open, facing female students, while they waited in the cafeteria line. You further shared this behavior goes back to 2016. These images were captured unbeknownst to students and without their permission. During student interviews, students shared your behavior was known among students commented this made them feel extremely uncomfortable.

On March 1, 2019, Axelgard was charged with "two misdemeanor counts of 'unlawfully annoying or molesting a child under the age of 18[.]'" He pleaded not guilty to both charges. GUSD placed him on administrative leave, but Axelgard accelerated his retirement, which he previously planned to take at the end of the 2018-2019 school year.

If convicted of the two misdemeanor charges, Axelgard will be required to register as a sex offender for the remainder of his life and will no longer be able to teach. He also could face a year in jail and a $5,000 fine on each count.

Top Three Takeaways:

- Cameras are everywhere. That may be the most critical message of this book. We live in a constantly photographed and recorded world, and we should act accordingly. Unfortunately, some small percentage of people believe that the ubiquity of cameras means that they can photograph and record others with impunity. That's not actually how it works; everyone should continue to observe standards of decency and propriety. (For instance, all but the most unethical employers refrain from putting surveillance cameras in bathrooms or locker rooms.) People who use cameras disconcertingly or creepily (particularly educators!) will inevitably be photographed or recorded themselves, either by school surveillance cameras or by one of the digital natives roaming the halls.

- This cautionary tale does raise the question of how Axelgard went unreported for so long. In the school environment, with hyper-digitized teens and surveillance video, it is remarkable that no one sounded an alert sooner. The progression is predictable: the longer Axelgard seemed to get away with his voyeurism, the more emboldened he became. Eventually, as always happens, he was so openly inappropriate that students could no longer disregard his behavior. Arguably, the school district should have done more to foster a climate in which Axelgard's behavior was detected and reported sooner. The school district could have educated the students on how to be were more aware, or it could have evaluated its surveillance videos more regularly (assuming they exist).

- A reminder: If law enforcement officers obtain a warrant to search your devices, all bets are off. Whatever secrets might be lurking on your hard drive or smartphone will show up in the digital colonoscopy that they will give your devices. Time and again, a relatively minor infraction can lead to much more draconian charges once the forensic examiners start delving into your electronic data. Axelgard's eagerness to photograph female students doing push-ups led, inevitably, to the discovery of multiple years of covert photography.

Cautionary Tale 25-2018-US_Massachusetts

On the afternoon of November 21, 2018, Bellingham (MA) Superintendent of Schools Peter D. Marano sent home a disturbing notice to parents. He told them that one of the district's teachers, Scott McDonald, had been arrested "on two felony charges concerning possession of illicit images of a minor." The charges arose, Marano said, from the discovery of a hidden camera in a Bellingham Memorial Middle School faculty bathroom that McDonald had been using to record young boys. The camera was spotted by a 12-year-old boy who was instructed by McDonald to use that specific bathroom. Marano added:

> As an educator and a parent, I am absolutely appalled anytime a teacher violates the awesome trust and responsibility given to teachers by the parents of the children placed in our care on a daily basis. We will not tolerate any behavior by any member of the staff or faculty of our school district that violates that trust.

Marano instantly pulled McDonald from the classroom and put him on administrative leave. At some point in early 2019, the school district fired McDonald from his teaching position.

Over the next few months, law enforcement technicians did a computer forensics analysis of various devices seized from McDonald's home. That analysis ultimately led prosecutors to file a total of 61 charges against McDonald: "20 [were] for photographing an unsuspecting nude person; 20 [were] for enticing a child under 16; and 21 [were] for posing a child in a nude, lascivious pose/exhibition." At a hearing on March 28, 2019, prosecutors told the court that they had identified twenty different victims, now ranging in age from 12 to adult. Several said that McDonald had recorded in various states of undress both at school and in his home. The videos dated back as far as 2012.

At his arraignment in July 2019, McDonald entered pleaded not guilty to each of the charges. Worcester Superior Court Judge Janet Kenton-Walker declined to increase the amount of McDonald's bail but ordered him to serve house arrest with a GPS monitoring cuff. She instructed him to stay off social media and to have no contact with any of the victims or any unsupervised interaction with any child under 16, apart from his own. McDonald was also required to sign a waiver allowing the Massachusetts Probational Department to get notes and reports from his therapist.

Five months later, McDonald accepted a deal with the state in which he agreed to plead guilty to 14 counts of enticing a child under the age of 16, 14 counts of photographing an unsuspecting nude person, and 15 counts of posing a child in a state of nudity. The judge sentenced him to two and a half years in prison for the 14 enticing charges and then two and half years for the 14 voyeurism charges. After his five years in jail, McDonald must serve three years probation for the charges based on posing. He is also required to register as a sex offender and continue to observe the no-contact guidelines.

The mother of the boy who first discovered McDonald's hidden camera told the court that her son "no longer uses a bathroom without being anxious." His father added that the young man had been "a model, A-B student before the incident and then his grades plummeted, he didn't want to go school and feared for his life." He concluded his remarks with this powerful statement:

> So please, Scott, do not insult my son, his mother, myself, the entire community of Bellingham by stating you're now low-risk. You got caught. Otherwise, you would continue to use your manipulative, arrogant ways and your powers to victimize children. You were preying on children that legitimately believed in Santa Claus. If it was my decision, you would spend the rest of your life behind bars.

Top Three Takeaways:

- I often tell school audiences that "it's the behavior, not the technology" that is responsible for the various cybertraps I discuss. But sometimes, to be fair, it's a little bit about the technology. While people have been taking surreptitious photos for at least 100 years, it is vastly simpler these days than it used to be. Camera lenses have shrunk to the size of a pinhead and can now wirelessly transmit the photos they take to a remote storage device. Those capabilities give some people ideas that they shouldn't have. If you are thinking about doing something you would not want your colleagues or supervisors to discover, that is your best answer as to whether you should stop yourself before causing harm to others—and yourself.

- Of course, an educator's behavior is the most important indicator that something is amiss. None of us has the time or inclination to continually check every nook and cranny of the bathrooms or locker rooms we use each day. But we can and should pay attention to how our colleagues and our students behave since those types of changes often are much more easily identified. If you see a teacher acting oddly or there is something that appears to be upsetting one or more students, you have an ethical duty of inquiry. Likewise, you and your colleagues should be actively promoting the development of a school culture in which students feel comfortable reporting anything that makes them uncomfortable. In this case, the sharp-eyed 12-year-old realized that he should report what he had found and fortunately felt empowered to do so.

- It is not easy to shame people who engage in this type of self-gratifying activity, but I hope that everyone will pause and contemplate the genuine, long-lasting harm that this type of behavior can cause to children. In case after case, children and parents document in excruciating detail the pain and suffering that is inflicted by invasions of privacy and physical assault. Every educator has both an ethical and moral duty to refrain from such behavior and to take action if a colleague might be at risk of causing injury.

Cautionary Tale 25-2018-US_New York

Up until the early 1980s, the United States Postal Service did a pretty effective job of tracking and interrupting the efforts of U.S. citizens to order child pornography from overseas producers. While I was clerking in the U.S. District Court in western Massachusetts, we had several cases stemming from searches coordinated by U.S. postal inspectors. After identifying an order for suspected contraband, the inspectors and the local postal carrier would agree on a delivery time for the package. Then the inspectors (and local police officers) would knock on the suspect's door fifteen minutes after the package was delivered. By that time, they could be reasonably confident that the suspect had opened the shipment and could no longer deny knowledge of what it contained. In those rare cases that went to trial, it never took the jury long to reach a verdict.

The internet, of course, has made the battle against child pornography vastly more complicated. The number of sources and the sheer volume of material has exploded beyond the capacity of any law enforcement agency to suppress effectively. Still, both national and international law enforcement agencies around the globe do their best to identify and prosecute the producers and distributors of contraband materials.

Here in the United States, one of the lead agencies now in the battle against child pornography is the Department of Homeland Security and, in particular, a subdivision called Homeland Security Investigations (HSI). In June 2019, HSI received a tip that someone using the ID "EJD" was spending time on a Thai website, which was allegedly an open site containing child pornography.

Working with Thai officials, investigators were able to trace the email address associated with the ID "EJD" to 60-year-old Scott Aikens, a middle and high school agriculture teacher in the Clymer Central School District, in the very southwestern corner of New York. Law enforcement officials said that they found evidence that Aikens had purchased credits for use on the website, had posted comments about some of the material, and had downloaded videos and images. However, investigators reassured school district officials that there was no evidence that any of the activity had occurred on district devices or involved children with whom Aikens interacted.

On September 14, 2018, Homeland Security and the New York State Police executed a search warrant on Aikens's home, seizing his computer and various other electronic devices. Aikens was arrested and charged with possession of child pornography. He was immediately placed on administrative leave by the district. He later submitted his resignation effective the day of his arrest.

While law enforcement agents executed the search warrant, others interviewed Aikens about his activities. He admitted viewing child pornography and said that investigators would find contraband on his computer. Ultimately, a forensics examination uncovered 683 videos and 22 images of child pornography. Prosecutors told the court at sentencing that some of the contraband involved children under 12, and some also contained "sadistic or masochistic conduct or other depictions of violence."

Aikens was sentenced on December 11, 2019, "to serve 54 months in prison and five years supervised release." The judge could have been sentenced him to as many as twenty years in prison.

Top Three Takeaways:

- Every educator should understand that sexually explicit or intimate images of minors are illegal in virtually every national, state, and provincial jurisdiction around the world. There is tremendous cooperation among international law enforcement agencies in the fight against the production and distribution of child pornography. When law enforcement agents raid an illicit website, any usable information will be distributed rapidly to the appropriate jurisdictions for investigation. Unfortunately, the internet does make it easier to obtain contraband material, but at the same time, it provides investigators with remarkable amounts of potential evidence.

- This cautionary tale should underscore the need for an alert and competent IT staff that can install filtering and monitoring software on network activity. Most commercial programs can look for the tell-tale signs of this type of internet activity and flag data for further inspection. If a school employee uses the district network to access contraband material, there is a strong likelihood that law enforcement will shut down and seize some portion of it to conduct forensic examinations. Having regular backups is the only thing that will minimize the disruptions that will cause.

- There is, unfortunately, relatively little that districts can do to prevent these types of incidents from occurring in the first place. If someone is intent on viewing or downloading contraband, a professional development presentation is unlikely to stop him or her from doing so. And understandably, when the person who commits this type of crime is someone who works with children, that fact will feature prominently in any news coverage. The best thing a district can do, as it did here, is to promptly remove the educator from the classroom and place him or her on leave pending further investigation.

Cautionary Tale 25-2018-US_Massachusetts

In the summer of 2018, law enforcement officials were investigating the possible use of Dropbox and the Kik messenger app to share child pornography. As part of that investigation, they interviewed a math teacher at Narragansett Regional High School in Baldwinville, MA, named Warren Anderson. When asked if he knew why investigators wanted to talk with him, the 26-year-old reportedly replied, "because of my Internet activity." He allegedly admitted to the investigators that he had accessed the so-called "dark web" to obtain and trade child pornography. He also told law enforcement that he had between 20 and 30 gigabytes of pornographic videos depicting boys under the age of 8.

For those not familiar with it, the "dark web" refers to internet resources that are hidden from most search engines and can only be accessed using a specialized browser called **Tor**. The chief feature of the Tor browser is that it anonymizes the online activity of people who use it. The main reason that operators of dark websites are so eager to hide from search engines and anyone with a shred of human decency is that much of what is available on those websites is highly illegal. Dark websurfers can not only find sites offering child pornography, but also: those that offer a wide range of stolen financial information, weapons of various description, a cornucopia of drugs, credentials for various subscription sites (want a lifetime Netflix account for just $6??), and software tools for hacking into computer systems or merely wreaking digital havoc.

Following his interview with law enforcement, Anderson was arrested and charged with "one count each of receipt and possession of child pornography." Narragansett Regional Schools Superintendent Dr. Christopher Casavant expressed his disbelief to reporters: "It's shocking. It's not what we do. We're educators, we take care of kids." He reassured parents that "[a]t this time there is no evidence of localized victimization of any student, past or present during Mr. Anderson's two-year tenure with the district."

Anderson pleaded guilty in July 2019 to one count of receipt and one count of possession of child pornography. Three months later, U.S. District Court Judge Allison D. Burroughs sentenced Anderson to 45 months in prison, followed by five years of supervised release. She noted that the forensic analysis of his computer uncovered thousands of contraband images and videos (depicting both boys and girls), as well as evidence that he had used a dark web messaging tool to locate and trade child pornography images.

Top Three Takeaways:

- Don't use the dark web. Seriously. There is no good reason to do so. First, it's complicated and almost entirely criminal; if you want to shop at the online criminal bazaar, you'll have to learn how to use bitcoins or other digital currency to do so). Second, you'll expose your computer and whatever network you are on to a fascinating array of viruses and other malware. So really, just don't.

- No one needs course work, professional development, or a code of ethics to know that an interest in videos of young children engaging in sexual activity is just wrong and that downloading such images is both legally and professionally disastrous. If that's the kind of thing that revs your engine, get help. Get help fast.

- If you are caught with contraband materials and you know that there is no credible defense, the single best thing you can do for yourself is to admit what you did and cooperate fully with law enforcement. Obviously, consult with an attorney first, but if you minimize the workload of the court system and potentially provide useful information to law enforcement, your sentence may be significantly shortened. In this case, Anderson could have been sentenced to as many as 20 years in prison but instead received a sentence of less than 4 years. It is likely that his quick admission played a role in the sentencing, even if he wasn't able to provide other useful information.

Relevant MCEE Provisions for Chapter 25

Principle I: Responsibility to the Profession

Standards I.A.2, I.A.3, I.A.4, and I.A.5

Principle II: Responsibility for Professional Competence

Standard II.C.3

Principle III: Responsibility to Students

Standards III.A.2 and III.A.B

Principle V: Responsible and Ethical Use of Technology

Standards V.A.5 and V.C.3

Sources

The sources for the Cautionary Tales in this chapter can be viewed at the following URL:

https://link.cybertraps.com/C4E2-Sources-Chap25

Chapter 26

Sexual Solicitation and Distribution of Sexual Content to a Minor

Overview

The previous chapter covered two cybertraps that are significant ethical violations—voyeurism and child pornography—but don't necessarily involve interaction with a particular student in the educator's district or school. By contrast, the cybertraps discussed in this chapter and the next are the most consequential of the ethical violations presented in this book. These are situations in which an educator is targeting a specific student (or students) for highly inappropriate interaction and potentially abusive conduct.

Sexual Solicitation

The specifics of this cybertrap will vary from state to state, as each jurisdiction has separate definitions for what constitutes "solicitation." In its broadest sense, "solicitation" means to entice or encourage someone to engage in illegal activity. When the victim is a minor (as is typically the case when the perpetrator is an educator), it takes on a more specific meaning: an effort to persuade the victim to engage in some type of sexual activity.

This chapter focuses on non-contact examples of solicitation, *i.e.*, instances in which an educator asks a minor to send nude or partially nude photos of himself or herself to the educator. Such a request can constitute solicitation because it is a crime (production of child pornography) for a person to take a nude photo of a minor, even if the person taking the picture is himself or herself under the age of 18. It is a separate crime for that same minor to send child pornography (his or her nude photo) to someone else.

Distribution of Sexual Content to a Minor

There are a variety of ways in which an educator can solicit inappropriate photos or videos from a student. The most obvious way, of course, is simply to for them. But another common approach is for an educator to send nude or semi-nude photos of himself or herself to a student, with the expectation that the child will reciprocate.

This adds a separate criminal act to the solicitation since virtually all states make it a crime to share material with minors that are either "harmful" or "obscene." The standard for what is "harmful to minors" is lower than the standard for what is "obscene," but the general concept is similar. The presumption is that there are materials to which minors should not be exposed, and it is a crime for someone to do so, especially when that person is in a position of trust.

It is a discussion for another day whether "harmful to minors" laws are realistic in light of the reality of how minors are using digital devices and the material they regularly see on the internet without the assistance of adults (and typically, without the supervision of adults). In truth, we are still figuring out what is harmful to minors. It may be both more and less than we anticipate. The unfortunate reality is that we are running a lengthy and ill-conceived study on our children, the results of which may not be known for a generation.

In any case, the fundamental concept of this cybertrap is straightforward: an educator who sends inappropriate photos or videos to a student is violating the law, district policy, and numerous standards of the Model Code of Ethics for Educators. These cautionary tales offer some insight into the circumstances in which these transgressions can occur.

Cautionary Tales

Cautionary Tale 26-2019-US_West Virginia

"The Girl with the Green Fiddle." That was the nickname given to Kentucky bluegrass musician Ramsey

Carpenter started playing her much-beloved instrument at the age of 8. In her early teens, she and some other musicians formed a group called County Line Bluegrass and began to play at events and gatherings throughout Kentucky and the nearby states.

In the summer of 2014, Carpenter's skill as a fiddler helped her win the crown of Miss Kentucky, which in turn earned her a slot in the 2015 Miss America pageant that fall in New York. Carpenter won the talent portion of the national competition and finished as one of the twelve semi-finalists.

At both the state and national level, Carpenter talked about her experience living with multiple sclerosis. She first experienced tingling in her fingers and physical weakness in 2010 and was diagnosed with MS later that year. She underwent extensive physical therapy to regain muscle strength and finger dexterity so that she could keep playing the fiddle. Following her participation in the Miss America competition, Carpenter served as a spokesperson for the National Multiple Sclerosis Society.

As she prepared to hand over her crown in 2015, Carpenter told Kentucky Educational Television that she was looking forward to her new career "as a teacher of children with learning and behavior disorders." Her plans changed slightly; she ultimately took a job as an 8th-grade science teacher at the Andrew Jackson Middle School in Cross Lanes, West Virginia. (Cross Lanes is a small town of about 10,000 people, located in Kanawha County just northwest of Charleston.) Following her marriage in 2016, Carpenter changed her last name to Bearse.

Unfortunately, all of her early achievements have been overshadowed by events that took place in the fall of 2018. In early December, the parents of a 15-year-old boy in the Kanawha County Schools discovered that he had inappropriate photos on his phone and learned that they had been sent to him by Bearse. The boy had been a student at Andrew Jackson Middle School when Bearse began teaching.

A year after her arrest, Bearse entered a guilty plea on "one count of possessing material depicting minors in sexually explicit conduct." During the hearing, Bearse told the court that she used Snapchat to keep in touch with her former middle school students to find out how they were doing. Bearse acknowledged, however, that her interaction with one male student (the same one who received the photos) went further than it should have gone:

> [He] asked a lot of questions and I crossed the line and shared too much information of what I was going through at the time. Basically, that my husband was working all the time and was too distracted and overwhelmed with work to pay attention to me. In addition, since I moved to West Virginia, I felt like I was completely alone. None of my family lives here, and I didn't have any friends.

Exchanging personal and even intimate information with a student is problematic enough. The real transgression, however, occurred when Bearse stumbled into a well-worn cybertrap: sending a message to the wrong person. She told the judge that she had taken a topless photo to share with her husband but accidentally clicked on the student's name, which was listed right below her husband's. The student then asked if she could send more photos, and Bearse said, "she panicked."

"I was afraid to not appease him," Bearse said, "and when he asked for more, I sent him more photos of me." Ultimately, she sent at least four photos to the student over several weeks.

Bearse took full responsibility for what occurred. "Since I am the adult, and he was just a teenager, it is my fault, and I accept full blame for the situation," she said. "So that's how I'm guilty of this crime. I messed up big-time."

Before entering a sentence, the court ordered Bearse to undergo a psychiatric evaluation. Just as this book was going to print, Bearse was sentenced on July 17, 2020, to two years in a West Virginia prison, followed by ten years of probation and lifetime registration as a sex offender.

Top Three Takeaways:

- This cautionary tale is a toxic blend of digital carelessness, poor judgment, and inadequate self-care. Together, those elements combined to derail a potentially promising teaching career. To be clear, we only have Bearse's word that she sent the student the topless photo by mistake. It is entirely possible to read her statement and imagine that she purposely sent the topless picture to the student as part of their growing emotional intimacy. In either case, this underscores the peril of using non-transparent channels to communicate with students, whether active or former. As a general rule, educators should not engage in non-professional communication of any kind until students have left the district and have reached adulthood. Similarly, Bearse should not have used Snapchat to communicate with current or former underage students under any circumstances. The school district should have made it clear that doing so was inappropriate.

- Bearse's major ethical lapse was sending nude photos to her former student, but her predicate ethical lapse was her failure to recognize her need for self-care. Schools and districts should do a much better job of making emotional health resources available to employees. However, educators have the primary responsibility to recognize when their emotional vulnerability may be leading them into ethically fraught situations. Electronic communication can be much more emotionally intimate than we realize, and as this case illustrates, it often flattens differences of age, status, and power. It is far too easy for an older person to delude themselves into thinking that a minor is much more mature than he or she is, especially when the older person is experiencing emotional vulnerability.

- Bearse's case is one of several that is remarkable for just how quickly her teaching career ended. The precise timing is a little vague, but it appears that she was only in her second year of teaching when she was arrested. Bearse's case underscores the systemic need for better training on the risks of cybertraps for new teachers, as well as better institutional support and greater awareness of the emotional and psychological stresses that young teachers experience. School districts certainly should not ignore the mental and emotional health of older teachers. I'm merely suggesting that the evidence is clear that teachers in their first 2-3 years need special attention, mainly because the smaller age gap between them and their students can be more problematic.

~ 356 ~

Cautionary Tale 26-2019-US_Massachusetts

This cautionary tale begins with the ethical breach of solicitation but then segues into an example of a job-ending incompetent investigation. The underlying offense should never have occurred in the first place, but once it did, school officials had an affirmative duty to conduct a prompt and thorough inquiry. Spoiler alert: that didn't happen.

Public awareness of this case first arose in late October 2019, when 42-year-old Dorothy Bancroft Veracka, a math teacher at Nashoba Regional High School, was arraigned in Massachusetts District Court. The state prosecutor alleged that between September 2018 and March 2019, Veracka had sent nude photos to a 15-year-old student and had actively solicited nude pictures from him in return. She was charged with "possessing child pornography, distributing obscene matter to a minor, and posing or exhibiting a child in the state of nudity."

Nashoba Regional School District (NRSD) Superintendent Brooke Clenchy told reporters that Veracka had been placed on administrative leave on September 30 but declined to comment further on the specifics of the case.

Court documents, however, revealed that Veracka and the student had exchanged photos and messages on Snapchat, and that the student had saved the communications. When confronted by law enforcement with the snaps, Veracka admitted sending and receiving the messages. The judge ordered Veracka to stay away from the victim and to have no unsupervised contact with minors, apart from her own three children.

Over the next several months, it became clear that there were some significant issues with how the school district had handled the Veracka matter. In March 2020, the NRSD school committee announced that immediately following Veracka's arraignment, it hired a local attorney named Tim Norris to investigate whether the district correctly followed its policies and procedures. The committee also placed high school principal Paul DiDimenico on administrative leave following Veracka's arraignment.

In a lengthy and detailed report, Norris identified numerous lapses in the handling of the Veracka matter.

He determined that Veracka and the student had exchanged nude photos between September 2018 and January 2019. At a party in mid-June 2019, the victim showed a group of classmates a series of snaps depicting a woman's naked body. Although the photos did not show the woman's face, the student identified her as Veracka. The student also said that he had sent pictures of himself to Veracka.

One of the students who saw the photos on the victim's phone reported the incident to his parents, who then contacted DiDimenico. The principal spoke with their son, who gave them the name of the victim and other students with potentially relevant information. DiDimenico tried to arrange a meeting with the victim and another student; the victim, however, did not keep his appointment, and the other student never returned the principal's call. DiDimenico did not follow up on either interview and did not conduct any additional investigation into the matter. Norris concluded that DiDimenico did not have any specific knowledge about the nature of the photos exchanged by Veracka and the student, but only because he allowed the investigation to lapse.

In September, one of the parents of the student who first reported the nude photos found out that Veracka was still teaching at the high school. The parent called DiDimenico for an explanation, and he said that the matter had been resolved. On September 20, 2019, the parent filed a report with the Bolton Police Department, which set in train the series of events leading to Veracka's arrest and arraignment. Superintendent Clenchy placed DiDimenico on administrative leave on November 7, 2019.

On March 9, 2020, Veracka pleaded guilty to one count of distributing obscene matter to a minor. Prosecutors dismissed the charges of posing a child in an obscene manner (*i.e.*, by requesting nude photos) and of distributing pornography. The court gave her a suspended sentence of two and a half years in prison and two years of probation. She also was ordered to register as a sex offender, to undergo mental health treatment, to refrain from any unsupervised contact with children under the age of 16 (except for her own children), and to avoid having any contact with the victim.

About a month after Veracka was sentenced, the Norris report was made public. Two days later, the school committee accepted DiDimenico's letter of resignation.

Top Three Takeaways:

- Veracka committed a serious and justifiably career-ending ethical breach by sending nude photos to a 15-year-old student. But it is worth highlighting that she had two other related lapses in judgment: first, trusting in the discretion of a 15-year-old and second, relying on the purported security of Snapchat. Neither was a good idea. I'll leave the analysis of the discretion of 15-year-old boys to others, but I can comment on the limitations of the automatic deletion by Snapchat. There are numerous guides online on how to preserve snaps past their scheduled expiration, with the simplest method being the most common: just use another device to photograph the Snap before it disappears. Here too, the psychology and skill set of many 15-year olds are relevant; if someone is sufficiently motivated, there is a way around almost any technical limitation.

- The real heroes of this story are the young man who reported what he saw and the parents who not only reported the incident but followed up when it appeared that the school district took no action. That is precisely the culture of cybersafety that should be cultivated by every school district.

- DiDimenico's handling of this incident was objectively terrible, and his resignation was wholly appropriate. It appears, fortunately, that Veracka was more infatuated than predatory. However, it is not difficult to imagine a scenario in which DiDimenico's dithering might have allowed an educator to victimize other students. The best mechanism for districts to prevent this type of situation is to follow meticulously well-established policies and procedures each time a student or parent reports this type of situation. The failure to do so could expose a district to significant legal liability if an administrator's failure to take effective action permits further victimization of students.

Cautionary Tale 26-2019-England

One of the things that educators and administrators need to keep in mind is that some of the most treacherous cybertraps are those that pop up in unexpected places. A particularly good example is apps that are written for one purpose (for instance, distributing audio and sharing music) but also have social media components, like user-to-user messaging. Multifunctionality is an increasingly popular practice among software developers. They have learned that such social features increase the amount of time people spend using their app and make it more likely that people will get their friends to download or purchase it.

Educators should be leery of using a non-monitored app or online service for any number of reasons, but especially if they plan to engage in back-channel communications. As I hope the various cautionary tales in this book have made clear, it is far too easy for such unmonitored conversations to create an inappropriate sense of intimacy that can lead to even more serious ethical violations.

In September 2017, Nottingham Girls' High School hired 27-year-old Alexander Day to teach psychology and English. The school is located just outside of downtown Nottingham in central England and has students ranging from 4-18 years of age.

Day's teaching career did not last long. In May 2018, the school headmaster learned that Day and a female student had been seen together, "both in School and outside the School setting." School officials immediately began an investigation and discovered, among other things, Day and the student (called "Pupil X") exchanged a massive number of emails, many of which were sent and received in the middle of the night.

School officials concluded that the emails were evidence of an inappropriate relationship because they made "reference to topics outside of the academic and school setting, such as personal interests, films, books, music, hobbies, moving house and holiday destinations." Also, it was evident that Day and Pupil X were using "coded talk" to plan get-togethers without actually appearing to make plans to meet.

School officials concluded that Day had furthered his inappropriate relationship with Pupil X by communicating with her through messaging tools on Soundcloud (a service used to distribute music, audio files, *etc.*). In a written statement to the disciplinary panel, Day admitted utilizing the music site to upload songs he wrote and performed but denied communicating with Pupil X.

Neither Day nor Pupil X testified at his disciplinary hearing, but two other students (Witnesses A & B) did provide evidence. They told the panel that that Pupil X had talked about music produced by Day and had seen that she was following a SoundCloud account that listed those titles. One of the students also testified that she could see that Pupil X had exchanged instant messages with the SoundCloud account in question. The panel noted that one of the emails between Day and Pupil X contained a link to that same SoundCloud account and discussed one of the listed songs. The panel concluded, after weighing all of the evidence, that Day had a SoundCloud account, that Pupil X had followed that account, and that Day had used the account to communicate with Pupil X.

After reviewing the large quantity of email correspondence between Day and Pupil X, the review panel concluded that:

> [T]he emails showed the progression of a relationship between Mr Day and Pupil X, with the content of the emails initially covering work and pastoral matters, and gradually becoming more detailed, discussing matters of an increasingly personal nature and expressing views on matters relating to love and relationships.

Given the contents, the panel said, "the emails contained an intellectual intimacy, created through the use of 'coded talk.'

> The panel considered that the emails were designed to move the relationship between Pupil X and Mr Day forward and that there was an underlying sexual current to the emails. The panel did not consider that there was any other reasonable explanation for the exchange of such emails and did not accept Mr Day's explanation for the purpose of the emails.

> The panel did not have sight of direct messages sent between Pupil X and Mr Day on SoundCloud, but noted the title of the song "longing." Again, the panel considered that this showed the development of the inappropriate relationship between Pupil X and Mr. Day.

Although the panel concluded that Day's communications were "sexually motivated" and there was testimony from Witnesses A & B that Day and Pupil X had met outside of school (including, allegedly, at Day's nearby flat), the panel concluded that the allegation was "not proven." A significant factor in the panel's decision was the fact that Pupil X declined to participate and so the credibility of her statements could not be assessed.

At the recommendation of the panel, a prohibition order was entered, barring Day from teaching. He is also required to wait at least five years before seeking reinstatement of his license (less severe cases typically receive a two-year review period).

Top Three Takeaways:

- I've been researching educator misconduct for nearly a decade, but I'm reasonably confident that this is the first time that SoundCloud has made an appearance in my case files. Still, this underscores an important point that I've been making for years: educators have an almost infinite number of ways to communicate privately with a student. Since we can't even catalog all the options available today, let alone what might become available in the future, we need to focus on the *behavior* of educators and students. Educators need to understand that there is a zero-tolerance policy for non-transparent or non-archivable communication with students.

- As with Snapchat (among others), the inability of investigators to access the specific contents of the SoundCloud messages was not a huge impediment. Investigators are skilled at compiling related pieces of digital information to construct motive and intent, as they did here. It was particularly useful for investigators to have access to the emails archived by the school, which underscores the importance of retrievable communication methods.

- The sheer number of emails between Day and Student X raises a practical question: Did the school have any filters or flags that would alert administrators to potential problems or, at the very least, to the need to review Day's email account? It is not enormously challenging to come up with a threshold number of emails that might raise concerns: more than ten a day? 100 per week? School districts can play around with different levels to see what works best. But yes, the sheer volume of interaction between an educator and a particular student can be cause for concern, and school districts have a duty to recognize a potential problem sooner rather than later.

Cautionary Tale 26-2019-US_Florida

In mid-August 2018, the Orlando Science Charter School hired Jaelen Alexander, 19, to work as a part-time office assistant. It was a bit of a homecoming for Alexander, who had previously attended the school and served as its student body president. At some point during the fall, after starting his new job, Alexander created a group text chat under the title "M&Ms" and offered to mentor students in the school. School officials later said they were unaware that Alexander had launched this unofficial mentoring program.

On or about March 26, 2019, a 14-year-old student told the dean of the school that Alexander had been using Snapchat to send partially nude photos to him and two other boys at the school. During the ensuing investigation, the school discovered that Alexander had requested nude pictures from one of the boys and offered him $50, a pass to get out of class, and free Viagra. After Alexander sent him a photo of his penis, however, the boy blocked him on Snapchat.

Another child said that he was dealing with depression and thought that Alexander was providing him with emotional support. As their conversations progressed, however, Alexander also asked him for nude photos. The boy said that he felt Alexander was trying to take advantage of him in his depressive state.

One of the boys involved allowed in the group chat allowed an investigator to impersonate him and conduct an undercover chat with Alexander. During the conversation, Alexander said that he was sorry for asking for nude photos and admitted that he knew the boy was just 14. However, he repeated his request for nudes and asked the "boy" if he had any romantic interest in him.

When investigators confronted Alexander with the statements by the boys and the photos he sent, he apologized for his actions and resigned from his position with the school on March 29.

Despite the nature of the incident, the school waited a month before reporting it to the resource officer assigned to the school. He alerted his colleagues at the Orlando Police Department (OPD), which launched it's a separate investigation. That led to the arrest of Alexander on May 16 on multiple charges of "attempted lewd or lascivious conduct, solicitation of a minor and lewd conduct of an authority figure." He spent a night in the Orange County Jail before being released on bail the following day.

The school notified parents nine(!) days later, issuing a statement that implicitly defended its handling of the matter but offered no explanation for the delay in contacting police or parents:

> At Orlando Science Schools, student safety is our No. 1 priority. Upon being notified of these allegations, our administration took immediate action to investigate the claims, and Mr. Alexander's employment ended on March 29.

The delay in reporting Alexander's actions to the school resource officer and the OPD angered members of the Orlando School Board. Chairwoman Teresa Jacob told local reporters that she was calling for an investigation into the delay in notifying police. In a letter to the school, Jacobs raised the possibility of canceling the school district's contract with OSCS, which would have the effect of shutting down the school. She noted that the school was in the process of applying for a new contract to open and run a K-8 school and questioned whether school officials were trying to hide the reports of Alexander's misconduct to avoid any negative impact on their application.

Like many states, Florida has a mandatory reporting law that states that **any** resident "who knows or has reasonable cause to suspect that a child is being abused ... **must** immediately report that knowledge or suspicion to the Florida Abuse Hotline of the Department of Children and Families." The state statute does not define what time frame is contemplated by the word 'immediately,' but presumably, it is something less than 30 days.

In response to a query from local station WFTV, the Florida Department of Education effectively ignored the language of the statute. The agency said that "charter schools are supposed to adopt policies and procedures related to misconduct for themselves."

Notwithstanding Chairwoman Jacob's concerns, it does not appear that the board took any action against OSCS for its dilatory reporting. It is also unclear, thanks to a lack of media follow-up, how Alexander's criminal case was resolved.

Top Three Takeaways:

- This case is as much about staff training and the cultivation of a culture of cybersafety as it is sexual misconduct. It is rather remarkable that Alexander was able to set up an *ad hoc* "mentoring" without the knowledge of other school officials. It is equally noteworthy that none of the mentees happened to mention it to anyone until Alexander started requesting nude photos from participants. It is a reasonable goal for a school district to create a culture in which students feel confident enough to ask if text message "mentoring" is officially sanctioned. At the very least, school districts should teach students to verify any proposed digital communication activity that is run by just one teacher or staff member.

- To be fair, the young men in this cautionary tale recognized that some of Alexander's behavior was highly inappropriate and correctly reported him for soliciting nude photos. All educators are well-advised to note that many law enforcement officers are highly skilled in impersonating minors, both male and female, in the course of digital criminal investigations. There's an old joke among defense attorneys that somewhere between 40 and 50 percent of the people in internet chat rooms are law enforcement agents trying to lure each other into inappropriate conversations. Whether that is true or not is debatable, but the reality is that when you are communicating electronically, you can never be 100% certain that the person on the other end is who he (or she) says they are.

- It is fair to criticize the school's handling of this incident on several points. First, it's not clear that it did adequate training or supervision of Alexander during his employment. Second, there is no apparent reason for the month-long delay in reporting his conduct to the police. And third, waiting for more than a week beyond that to notify parents is both dilatory and disrespectful. Revealing this information would not reflect well on the school, but students and parents have a right to expect prompt and transparent handling of incidents like this.

Cautionary Tale 26-2019-US_Virginia

Alison Briel, 25, launched her education career as a marketing education teacher and advisor for the Distributive Education Clubs of America (DECA) at Loudon County High School in August 2017. Within just a few weeks, however, she set in motion a series of events that quickly brought her career to a crashing halt.

On April 30, 2019, Briel was arrested and charged with "three misdemeanor counts of contributing to the delinquency of a minor." According to the charging documents filed by the police, Briel spent nearly a year—from December 2017 to November 2018—sending "salacious pictures" of herself to two 16-year-old and one 17-year-old student using the social media app Snapchat. She also propositioned the two 16 year-olds to have sex with her, although there is no evidence that any inappropriate contact occurred.

Because of the automatic deletion of messages by Snapchat, law enforcement officials were not able to recover the images that Briel sent to the students. However, it turns out that Snapchat does keep records of how often one user sends photos to another, and the social media service told investigators that Briel had sent "hundreds" of pictures to her three victims in just a few months.

After her arrest, Briel was temporarily held on $2,500 bail and immediately suspended without pay. Less than a week later, she pleaded guilty to each of the counts against her. The judge sentenced her to one year of probation and three years in jail, with the prison time suspended pending successful completion of her probation. The court also ordered her "to undergo a mental health and psychosexual evaluation, and [said that] she is not to have any contact with the victims or unsupervised contact with any juveniles."

Top Three Takeaways:

- Although law enforcement was unable to recover the images sent by Briel in this case, educators should not necessarily rely on the auto-deletion feature of Snapchat. There are far too many ways in which people can save Snapchat photos (it isn't any more complicated than pointing a second camera at the receiving device). And in some instances, law enforcement has been able to recover ineffectively deleted snaps. I can't stress often enough that the computer forensic capabilities of law enforcement are already enormously impressive and grow more so every day.

- This cautionary tale also illustrates how routine data collection can create a presumption of misconduct. As part of its regular operation, Snapchat tracks how many messages and photos each user sends. If law enforcement discovers that you have sent "hundreds" of Snaps to a minor, they will have some hard questions for you about what you sent and why you did so.

- School districts do not have any mechanism for monitoring the use of social media apps by students and teachers. However, districts can facilitate the handling of these types of cases by adopting acceptable use policies that make it crystal clear that educators shall not communicate with students using unapproved and non-transparent digital communication tools. A school district should immediately put any educator or staff member who does so on administrative leave pending a full investigation of the circumstances of the communication. At the same time, school districts should regularly remind students that they should not solicit or encourage covert digital communication with adults.

Cautionary Tale 26-2019-England

Few cautionary tales better illustrate the darkest potential of the internet than that of Alaric Bristow, a 31year-old science teacher from Coventry, England. In September 2018, Bristow was arrested by officers of the West Midlands Police Online Child Exploitation Team (OCSET) when they raided the home that he shared with his mother and his brothers. Reports of suspicious internet activity triggered the raid and arrest, but officers were not prepared for the scope of what they would find.

While analyzing Bristow's electronic equipment, technicians uncovered thousands of images and videos of young boys, ranging in age from 13-15, that Bristow had collected over the preceding years. They also uncovered evidence that showed that Bristow had set up multiple social media accounts in which he posed as various young women. He did so by collecting images of girls from around the web and using those photos to flirt with boys online. Over time, he persuaded a large number of boys to send photos of themselves or engage in on-camera sex acts. A team of 20 investigators eventually identified 213 different victims, some of whom were students of Bristow.

The scientifically minded Bristow, police said, kept detailed spreadsheets with "the names of the boys, the false profiles he used when contacting them, and the images sent and received." He insisted to investigators, however, that he never had any intention of trying to meet the young men or to harm them in any way.

Following his arrest, Bristow was released on bail. One of the conditions of his release was that he not use a computer. Nonetheless, he obtained a laptop and continued his online activity, amassing another 1,000 photos before being arrested again in December 2018 and held without bail.

Bristow eventually agreed to plead guilty "to 12 charges of causing a child to engage in sexual activity, nine of making indecent images of children and one of having prohibited images." On May 10, 2019, Judge Peter Cooke sentenced Bristow to five years in prison, six years of probation, and lifetime registration as a sex offender.

In court, Judge Cooke provided a stern summary of Bristow's misconduct:

> When [the boys] thought they were flirting with a girl their own age, they were being recorded and lusted over by one of their own teachers, a man they were supposed to be able to trust. You were leading a double life, imparting knowledge during the day, but leading a dark secret life at night.
>
> I am satisfied there is a significant risk that you will commit further specified offences in the future and cause serious harm to members of the public, most likely young people.

Top Three Takeaways:

- One of the most robust and most persistent myths of the internet is that you can hide your identity and do things that you would not normally do using your own name. As the amazingly prescient 1993 *New Yorker* cartoon put it, "On the Internet, no one knows you're a dog." But the reality, however, is that it is **not** that easy to completely hide your identity or, more typically, the IP address from which you are conducting your illicit affairs. In general, law enforcement can and will find you.

- When news like this breaks, the first thing parents want to know is how the perpetrator managed to get through the hiring process? The unfortunate reality is that there sometimes aren't any obvious red flags. It is not uncommon for the district to receive its first notice that there's a problem with a teacher when law enforcement shows up at district headquarters or the teacher's classroom. And of course, no district is eager to consider the possibility that one of its teachers is engaging in sextortion. Still, every school district or private school should offer detailed professional development about the harm that this type of behavior can cause.

- You can see in this cautionary tale the germ of an argument by Bristow that he was somehow less culpable because he did not intend to have any physical contact with the boys he sextorted. While districts and schools cannot prevent every assault on students, they can make it unequivocally clear that electronic sexual assault can be equally damaging to physical attacks. Essentially, Bristow manipulated these young men into being co-conspirators in their own abuse, which is a challenging psychological harm to overcome. It is time to recognize the fact that the societal changes wrought by the internet require us to help protect our children by speaking and educating much more openly about sexual matters. The earlier we do so, the safer our children will be. An effective culture of cybersafety depends on giving children the ability to speak openly about sexual issues. We need to catch up to the sexual education (and occasional threat) that the internet is providing our children every single day.

Relevant MCEE Provisions for Chapter 26

Principle I: Responsibility to the Profession

Standards I.A.2, I.A.3, I.A.4, and I.A.5

Principle II: Responsibility for Professional Competence

Standard II.C.3

Principle III: Responsibility to Students

Standards III.A.2, III.A.3, III.B.3, III.B.7, and III.B.8

Principle V: Responsible and Ethical Use of Technology

Standards V.A.5 and V.C.3

Sources

The sources for the Cautionary Tales in this chapter can be viewed at the following URL:

https://link.cybertraps.com/C4E2-Sources-Chap26

Chapter 27
Sexual Assault

Violation of a Sacred Trust

The Model Code of Ethics for Educators unequivocally states that "[e]stablishing and maintaining an environment that promotes the emotional, intellectual, physical, and sexual safety of all students" is a core value for educators (MCEE Standard III.B.3.) As I've discussed in this book, there is a range of educator cybertraps that can threaten student safety, but none do so as thoroughly and with so much potential for permanent harm as sexual assault.

Thanks to the combination of social media and the global distribution of news on the internet, it would be easy to conclude that the sexual assault of students by educators is now raging out of control. That is not remotely the case. The percentage of educators who violate this most critical of ethical standards is still very, very small, and we should not allow hysterical media accounts to color our perception of the profession or its members.

Still, it is undeniable that digital communication technology has increased the potential for educator misconduct, up to and including sexual assault. As I've detailed throughout this book and in my lectures, there is an almost endless number of apps specifically designed for communication and an equally large number of apps that include communication capabilities as a feature of an otherwise innocuous app. In some minuscule number of cases, predatory educators use these new capabilities to groom vulnerable students as potential assault victims. In a more significant amount of unfortunate instances, the inherent speed and intimacy of digital communications lured unwary educators into life-altering cybertraps of solicitation and assault.

Human nature being what it is, there is no silver bullet policy or procedure that can entirely prevent these types of ethical lapses. But well-designed policies and ongoing education can minimize the risks. Schools can help teach parents how best to supervise the digital devices their children use. Districts can cultivate a culture of cybersafety, one in which children know what to do if a conversation gets uncomfortable or threatening. Staff and colleagues can learn how to spot potential grooming situations and how best to intervene or report, rather than discount or overlook. And administrators can practice cooperation and transparency so that both the public and future employers are informed of ethical and criminal violations by educators.

I learned to drive in the early 1980s, just as the big push against drunk driving began. As part of my driver's ed class, we had to watch a short film showing car crashes caused by drunk drivers. Today, one of the benefits of digital technology and the internet is that it is increasingly common for news outlets to post video clips from the sentencing hearings for educator sexual assault cases. Time and again, I've listened to mothers, fathers, and guardians describe in excruciating and heart-rending detail the psychological and emotional harm caused by sexual assaults. School districts should consider playing two or three such recordings at the first faculty meeting of each school year.

Some Cruel Double Standards

When you start reviewing educator sexual assault cases, it doesn't take long to realize that there are several blatant and corrosive double standards at work. None are justified, but each reflects deep-seated social biases that will take years, if not decades, to root out.

The first is the salacious attention given to female educators who assault students. If you go by headlines alone, you might conclude that women have committed the majority of sexual assaults over the last five-plus years. There is, unfortunately, a lack of reliable data on the gender breakdown of educators who commit sexual assault. After having studied this for nearly a decade, however, I can confidently say that headlines are deceiving. While there probably has been a small percentage increase in the number of female teachers assaulting students, the number of sexual assaults committed by male educators is vastly higher than female educators both in terms of raw numbers and per capita.

We should not ignore any trends regarding the sexual assault of students by teachers, but we need a lot more hard data about what is taking place. Are the number of assaults up or down? What is the gender breakdown of perpetrators? What other factors contribute to assaults? What role does technology play? What policies and procedures are most effective in reducing the incidence of assault? These are all critical policy questions that require detailed investigation. Until we do the demanding and meticulous research to answer those questions, the editorial on assaults by female educators is little more than salaciousness masking as journalism.

A second double standard relating to women is driven, I am sure, by the prevalence of male editors and reporters. The regrettable reality is that if prosecutors charge an educator with an assault who is attractive by conventional standards, the media will cover her case with an intensity that is often vastly disproportionate to the actual severity of the offense. In the cautionary tales below, the case of Brittany Zamora is a good illustration of this phenomenon. There was wall-to-wall media coverage of her case in various Arizona media outlets, and it is hard to square the vast number of videos and column inches with the actual crime.

The final double standard affects young men who are assaulted by female teachers. If you read the comments posted to news articles or television videos, the most common response is along the lines of "Why didn't *I* have a teacher like that when I was in [x] grade??" Only rarely is there ever any awareness of the emotional damage that boys suffer in the vast majority of these assaults. The trope of a male child gleefully accelerating his sexual maturity is a myth; the vast majority of the time, the female educator is using the child for her own emotional and physical needs.

In those exceedingly rare instances in which the child is the initiator, the educator is still, at the end of the day, the adult and the participant who is morally and legally responsible for what takes place. We do need to have frank and honest conversations about the increased sexualization of our children due to exposure to online content, but that is no excuse for educators. Regardless of the developmental changes taking place in teens and pre-teens, teachers should always be the ones to draw the appropriate boundaries and model ethical behavior.

I have some experience with how this particular double standard can play out. Not long after I got off the Burlington, VT school board, the news broke that a female high school teacher had assaulted a male student. The victim happened to be in the same class as one of our sons. When we asked him what he had heard about the incident, he said that the only thing his (male) classmates were saying was that the victim had suffered just one injury: a "sprained wrist from all the high fives." Our son probably didn't get the reaction from us that he might have hoped: suffice it to say that there was no laughter, and lectures ensued.

The reality was that the assault had a terrible effect on the young man; it severely damaged many of his friendships, he was in therapy for many months, and he postponed going to college. The consequences were even more severe, of course, for the teacher, who happened to live just a couple of blocks from us: she was fired, lost her teaching license, got divorced, and has four years remaining as a registered sex offender in the state of Vermont.

Cautionary Tales

Cautionary Tale 27-2019-US_Florida

In every criminal trial, the prosecution must prove its case "beyond a reasonable doubt." This legal standard is a high bar to conviction, which is appropriate given the life-changing consequences of a criminal conviction. Over the years, courts have struggled to come up with a precise definition for the phrase "reasonable doubt." In general terms, however, if a member of the jury can come up with a credible alternative explanation for a given set of facts, then it is appropriate for him or her to conclude that there is reasonable doubt about the prosecution's case.

Every so often, of course, there are those cases in which there simply is no other alternative explanation for the evidence. Take, for instance, the case of 27-year-old Desiree Cartin Rodriguez, a teacher of English at Doral Academy Prep in Doral, Florida. In mid-December, 2019, local police received an anonymous tip that Rodriguez was assaulting a 15-year-old student.

The police brought the young man in for an interview, and he confirmed the anonymous report, saying that the relationship with Rodriguez had begun at the start of school in August. He also told the officers that he had used his smartphone to record some of his sexual encounters. For investigators and prosecutors, of course, that's like winning the lottery [cue "Law and Order" sound effect].

After the police reviewed the videos, they brought Rodriguez in on December 20, 2019, for questioning. When confronted with the videos, she confessed to the relationship. The married teacher told police that she thought she was in a consensual relationship with the student and that she was in love with him. The police promptly arrested Rodriguez and charged her with "two felony counts of lewd and lascivious assault on a child." That same day, Doral Academy fired her.

Doral Police spokesperson Rey Valdes said that there was no question that the woman in the video was Rodriguez. He also said that she obviously was aware that the student was recording her (even if the camera had been hidden, of course, her actions would still be a crime):

> The young man took the video; the video was not hidden. It wasn't like it was a hidden camera. She was aware that there was video. You can clearly tell by the proximity of her face to the camera that she was aware she was being filmed.
>
> I'm not going to go into details, but I can tell you it's graphic and explicit, and we'll leave it at that. I guess everybody can make their own summations.

Valdes added that even if the young man was a willing participant, Rodriguez still committed a crime, since the victim was too young to consent to the sexual act. Rodriguez was held briefly at the Turner Guilford Knight Correctional Center in West Miami-Dade and released after posting a bond of $7,500.

It does not appear that the court has set a trial date yet.

Top Three Takeaways:

- **#CamerasAreEverywhere.** This maxim is particularly true when you are dealing with minors, who increasingly document their lives and communicate with each other through photos and videos. One of the reasons for the popularity of Snapchat among children is that it dispenses with all that time-sucking typing; you can tell your friends where you are and what you're doing simply by taking a photo or sending a short video clip. As a result, it is completely second nature for them to capture images of what they are doing (or what someone is doing to them).

- For some young people (and many adults, I might add), the online adult industry serves has normalized the recording of intimate conduct. To be fair, adults began making home videos of sexual activity long before there was any available distribution network. Now, of course, the recordings made by the young man could be distributed around the world before the two of them put their clothes back on. The mere possibility that a student might record this type of sexual encounter should be enough to give pause to any educator thinking of an illegal relationship with a minor. It's hard to know what to make of a teacher who was seeming unfazed by the fact that she had a starring role in a gonzo video.

- From an institutional perspective, it's a little hard to figure out how Rodriguez wound up in a classroom without being very clear about the fact that she could not have a consensual relationship with a student. It's a basic concept that should have been driven home during her teacher education courses, the certification process, and her employment training and orientation at Doral. Familiarity with the MCEE would undoubtedly have helped as well: the realization that she was experiencing strong emotions towards or even falling in love with a student should have been a signal that she needed to seek professional help.

Cautionary Tale 27-2019-US_Alabama

"It was a new school year for me and him. He sent me a Facebook request in September."

Those were the words of a 15-year-old female student during a forensic interview with a criminal investigator in Alabama. Her meeting with law enforcement was part of an inquiry into allegations that David Burkhalter, a 30-year-old math teacher at Randolph County High School (RCHS), had sexually assaulted the young woman.

The investigation began in early February 2019, after another student told the school principal about the alleged sexual relationship. A court issued an arrest warrant for Burkhalter on February 13, and the police arrested him shortly after that. Prosecutors charged him with "two counts of rape in the second degree, one count of sodomy in the second degree, one count of enticing a child, two counts of electronic solicitation of a child for sex and two counts of school employee sex act with a student less than 19 years of age." Burkhalter was held in the Randolph County Jail on $1.5 million cash bail.

Superintendent John Jacobs told reporters that he placed Burkhalter on administrative leave following his arrest. He said that other students had raised concerns with the principal and that the district was investigating each report. He urged any other students with information to come forward.

Within 48 hours of Burkhalter's arrest, the district asked Tri-County Children's Advocacy Center's Executive Director Jacqueline Burgess to speak to RCHS students about the arrest. Burgess stressed the importance of using the incident as a teaching moment.

> The message in the Randolph County Schools is—this thing has happened, and what can you do now to move forward, and what can you do if you know something, or if there's something else happening that you're uncomfortable with? What can we do as a community now? What do these children need to do now with this information that they may have?

> If we don't talk about these things with our kids, if we act like they're not happening, then it's more likely that they're going to keep it a secret because they're ashamed of it and feel like mom and dad won't understand.

Prosecutors presented the forensic interview of the victim and other evidence to Randolph County District Court Judge Amy Newsome at a preliminary hearing on April 23, 2019. In addition to the Facebook request, the victim told the investigator that she and Burkhalter communicated via text, calls, and Snapchat. "We stayed in contact 24/7," she admitted.

When rumors started circulating among students in the fall of 2018, the two stopped hanging out in the school building but stayed in touch on social media and by phone. She said that after the New Year, Burkhalter took her to a Motel 6, where they first kissed and then had sex. She told the investigator that on two other occasions, she and Burkhalter had sex in his car after driving around on dirt roads in Randolph County.

Prosecutors told the court that the victim buttressed her account by identifying tattoos on portions of Burkhalter's body not ordinarily visible in public. They also said that both the victim and Burkhalter were currently undergoing medical treatment for chlamydia.

By the middle of December 2019, Burkhalter was facing a total of 15 separate charges from three different counties relating to the assault on the student. They broke down as follows:

- **Randolph County:** two counts of second-degree rape, one count of sodomy, two counts of electronic solicitation of a child, two counts of violation of the school employee sex act and one count of enticing a child to enter a vehicle;

- **Clayton County:** one count of electronic solicitation of a minor and interference with child custody surrounding the relationship; and

- **Calhoun County:** one count of second-degree rape, two counts of second-degree sodomy, one count of violation of the school employee sex act and one count of second-degree sexual abuse.

Burkhalter successfully posted bail. A trial date has not been set yet.

Top Three Takeaways:

- The Model Code of Ethics for Educators makes it clear that educators should not seek out the personal social media accounts of students, either for mere lurking or active interaction. This case illustrates why that is a necessary ethical standard. The risks inherent in "multiple relationships" should be immediately apparent if you try to add "Facebook friend" to your role as a teacher. The same is abundantly true for Twitter, Instagram, and **especially** Snapchat.

- As is often the case, the sheer volume of messaging between Burkhalter and his victim raises numerous questions about supervision, both at home and in school. It is difficult to believe that there was not a single adult who observed any change in the behavior of either person or that someone did not ask the victim name of the individual with whom she was messaging so often. The fact that once again, fellow students perceived a relationship to which adults were oblivious is further evidence of our need to do a better job empowering students to raise concerns.

- In that respect, Executive Director Burgess's remarks were right on point. Every district needs to ask itself what it has done to create an environment where any student can report an unpleasant truth or something that makes them uncomfortable. It is essential, of course, to make it clear that there are consequences for false or malicious reporting. Still, given the fact that we now routinely entrust children with powerful electronic devices, we should also give greater credence to what they see and hear.

Cautionary Tale 27-2018-US_Arizona

There are a lot of things that schools can and should do to protect students from the risk of sexual assault by educators. But there is no question that the single most effective tool for keeping kids safe is ongoing parental supervision of the use of digital devices by their children.

That is not an easy task, especially if parents first decide to exert their supervisory authority when the child is in middle or high school. Digital parenting is much, much more effective if the adults establish supervision as a house rule from the moment they first hand an electronic device to a child. (For some suggestions on digital parenting at all ages, see my recently-published book, *Raising Cyberethical Kids.*) Of course, while the best time to start supervising a child's device was when he or she started using it, the next best time is right now. That is particularly true if parents see unexplained or upsetting changes in their child's behavior.

To some degree, parents can automate the process of supervision by installing computer software or an app to track online behavior and flag potentially suspicious keywords. That's how the parents of a 13-year-old Arizona boy learned of a disturbing situation involving their son and Brittany Zamora, a 27-year-old teacher at Las Brisas Academy in Goodyear, Arizona. After they began noticing some behavioral changes in their son, they installed an app on his phone called **Sentry Parental Control**. The app recorded several different messages between Zamora and their son. When the parents reviewed them, they realized that Zamora might be sexually assaulting their son.

The parents took screenshots of the flagged text messages and showed them to the school's principal, who immediately called police. He also asked Zamora, who had only just started teaching at Las Brisas the previous fall, to come meet with him; when she arrived at the school, the police arrested her.

Digital communication technology was integral to this assault. The victim told his parents that Zamora got bored one day and asked students to message her on **Classcraft**, an educational app designed to engage students by gamifying aspects of learning. She and the victim soon began exchanging flirty messages and then transitioned to exchanging messages by text and on Instagram. At some point during these conversations, Zamora and the boy exchanged nude photos, although it is not clear which communication channels they used to do so. Eventually, Zamora and the victim engaged in various types of sexual activity in her classroom and her car. In one instance, they asked an 11-year-old boy to stand guard while they had sex in her classroom; Zamora later sent naked photos to that boy as well.

The original victim's father reported to police that before Zamora's arrest, she and her husband called and pleaded with the parents not to report the assault. Zamora's husband said that he and the father should "meet up" so that they could "settle this," but the father declined and hung up the phone.

Shortly after police arrested Zamora, a local TV station reported that the Las Brisas Academy principal had received three statements from classmates of the victim in which they complained that Zamora was showing favoritism towards him. The letters were all written in early February 2018, less than a week after Zamora's sexual assault of the victim began.

According to Liberty Elementary School District Interim Superintendent Dr. Richard Rundhaug, Las Brisas Academy principal Tim Dickey immediately interviewed the three students, Zamora, and the victim, but found no evidence of any inappropriate behavior. Zamora specifically reassured Dickey that her relationship with the victim was professional, as she did not want to "jeopardize anything in her life."

Some weeks later, *The Arizona Republic* obtained Dickey's investigation notes through a Freedom of Information Act request. The notes showed that several students alleged that Zamora and the victim were "dating" or "in a relationship." However, Dickey was not able to find any proof that an inappropriate relationship was taking place. In an interview with the paper, Interim Superintendent Rundhaugh defended the response of school officials:

> We did investigate. We determined there were some elements of favoritism, and we gave the teacher some very specific direction on not allowing that favoritism to continue, and then we monitored to make sure those directions were followed.

Zamora, was held in a Maricopa County jail for failure to post bail of $250,000. On April 6, 2018, she pleaded not guilty "two counts of molestation of a child, nine counts of sexual conduct with a minor, one count of furnishing harmful material and one count of public sexual indecency." Prosecutors laid out a trove of evidence of the interaction between Zamora and the victim, ranging from electronic messages and photos to handwritten mash notes. Some of the digital images that Zamora sent to the victim showed her in lingerie that was subsequently discovered by police when they executed a search warrant on her home.

Two months later, on June 10, Zamora accepted a deal with the prosecution in which she agreed to plead guilty to "sexual conduct with a minor, attempted molestation and public sexual indecency." Even with the reduced number of charges, Zamora faced a potential sentence of up to 44 years in prison. As is typically the case, the agreement of the parties to a plea deal eliminated the need for the victims to testify at trial.

At a highly emotional hearing on July 12, 2018, Maricopa County Superior Court Judge Sherry Stephens heard arguments from the prosecution and defense, a statement by Zamora, and victim impact statements by family members and representatives of the victims. Zamora's mother pleaded with the court to impose a lighter sentence, while the mothers of the victims both argued for the maximum penalty possible. Despite concluding that "the circumstances of the offenses [are] especially aggravating," Judge Stephens sided with the defense and gave Zamora the lightest possible sentence: 20 years in prison, with credit for the 478 days already served since her arrest. When she is released, Zamora will be required to register as a sex offender and remain on probation for the remainder of her life.

Notwithstanding Zamora's statement of contrition in the courtroom, her attorney Belen Olmeda Guerra told reporters that the prosecution offered a skewed view of the facts. "This was not between a young child and Brittany," Guerra said, "this was a teenager." She alleged that Zamora had asked school officials to move the victim to a different classroom due to boundary issues and what Guerra described as "obsession" with her client. Guerra denied, however, that she was trying to blame the victim for what happened.

In August 2018, the victim's parents filed a lawsuit against the Las Brisas Academy Elementary School for failing to properly report the allegations that Zamora and the child were "dating" or "in a relationship." The lawsuit also alleges that Dickey neglected to supervise communications on the Class Craft platform and conducted an incomplete and ineffective investigation of the claims of favoritism. The litigation is still pending.

It's worthwhile to give the final word in this cautionary tale to Laurie Roberts, a columnist for *The Arizona Republic*, who wrote:

> The message here – to teachers, to principals, to Sunday school teachers, to Boy Scout leaders, to anybody who works with children – is obvious:

> Err on the side of believing the child – or at least considering the possibility that kids could be telling the truth. (Especially if there are three of them.)

> If you aren't sure, then turn it over to someone whose job it is to figure it out.

Top Three Takeaways:

- From the moment children begin their education, schools and parents should form an active partnership to keep them safe. A school can only legally inspect a child's device if it has reasonable and articulable suspicion that the device contains some evidence of misconduct. Parents, on the other hand, have a legal right and the responsibility to check their children's electronic devices regularly. It also would be helpful if schools provided parents with some information once or twice a year on how to check devices and the software they can install to monitor digital activity for potential harm. A district might reasonably tell parents that the installation of such software is a necessary precondition for bringing devices on campus (with fiscal assistance for those who need it). And through their digital citizenship curricula, schools can educate children on their parents' legal rights as the actual owners of devices and data plans.

- Both schools and parents can sometimes get overwhelmed by the sheer number of communication channels available to misbehaving educators and vulnerable students. That's understandable; it does not seem like a week passes without teens glomming onto some new social media service or app, which can make the task of supervision seem daunting. But it is worth remembering that the most effective approach is to monitor children themselves. Many of the problems that children experience online will be reflected in their behavior, so if you are attentive to a child's conduct and emotional state (this applies to both parents and teachers), you will generally be alerted to anything that requires further investigation.

- This case is hard to view as anything less than a supervisory and investigative failure by the district in general and the interim superintendent in particular. One wonders what filters or flags were in place on the Classcraft software. Were the messages Zamora exchanged with her students saved, and if so, where? That's particularly relevant given the timing of this matter. When the victim's classmates alerted the administration to a potential problem, there may well have been relevant evidence in the Classcraft records. The stored data might have been concerning enough to lend credence to the students' complaints and perhaps encourage the involvement of law enforcement at an earlier stage of this assault. Administrators should automatically take every student statement at face value, of course. Conscientious administrators and educators, however, will reflect on the fact that in case after case, it eventually is shown that classmates were aware of a transgression long before adults.

Cautionary Tale 27-2017-US_Florida

Every case of sexual assault of a student by a teacher raises two similar categories of questions. The first category deals with the assault itself: What happened, how did it happen, and could it have been prevented? The second category focuses on the organization: What steps has it taken to avoid sexual assault in general, did it do enough to protect the victim of this particular assault, does it have adequate procedures in place for investigating allegations of assault, and were those followed in this case? This cautionary tale illustrates what can happen when almost all of the answers to those questions are bad.

For many years, Wendell Nibbs, 51, served as a physical education instructor at Brownsville Middle School in northwest Miami-Dade County. On November 30, 2017, he was arrested on "two counts of sexual battery on a child 12 years of age or older but less than 18 by an adult while in familial/custodial authority." He was booked into Miami-Dade County's Turner Guilford Knight Correctional Center and held without bond. That same day, Nibbs submitted his resignation from the district for "a personal reason."

An affidavit filed by a detective with the Miami-Dade School Board Police said that he had begun investigating allegations of sexual misconduct against Nibbs in the spring of 2015. One female student, 15, told the detective that she and Nibbs had exchanged naked photos using the KIK messaging app and that they would have sex in his classroom during the school day. She told the detective that her classmates bullied her and Nibbs provided her with positive attention and understanding. Another girl separately reported to the detective that Nibbs had asked "to see her privates."

Nibbs denied the allegations, but when the detective brought up other claims of suspected abuse, Nibbs replied, "I can see why the district is looking into this allegation. I have a few other allegations attached as well. I guess when there's smoke, there's fire."

According to an affidavit filed in support of the arrest warrant, detectives spoke to four different female students. Each reported "inappropriate sexual behavior" by Nibbs over the years ranging from 2004 to 2013. A spokesperson for Miami-Dade County Schools could not explain why Nibbs was allowed to continue teaching. The district did, however, issue a brief statement:

> Miami-Dade County Public Schools will not tolerate actions by employees that endanger or violate the safety of children. Our highest priority is to protect their physical and emotional well-being. The allegations against the employee are unconscionable and do not comport with the standard of excellence and integrity of our workforce. He is no longer an M-DCPS employee.

Prosecutors filed additional charges against Nibbs on March 21, 2019, when two more female students alleged that he had raped them on multiple occasions on school property (one suggested that he might also be the father of her child). In addition to the numerous physical assaults, Nibbs forced his victims to pose for nude photos.

Shortly after the filing of the additional charges, *Miami Herald* reporter Colleen Wright said that the paper had reviewed more than 400 pages of documents obtained from the school district under a public records request. She wrote that the paper's review raised "questions about how two powerful institutions – the United Teachers of Dade and Miami-Dade County Public Schools – dealt with 12 years of allegations against the veteran educator."

In excruciating detail, Wright's article details the myriad complaints made by female students against Nibbs, which the district left unheeded for years. Eventually, Miami-Dade Public Schools Police Detective Bernise Charley received a tip that a student had information that Nibbs and a 17-year-old student were having intercourse. When Charley began investigating the report, she learned that the reporting student had seen nude photos of Nibbs and her friend in her friend's KIK messenger app. Nibbs repeatedly reminded his victim to delete the images, but a state computer forensics expert was able to retrieve some of the deleted photos.

Wright noted that numerous district employees had reviewed the claims about Nibbs but that no one took any action. Part of the reason, she suggested, was that Nibbs was an influential member of the United Teachers of Dade and served as the building steward for the Brownsville Middle School. Wright also observed that union president Karla Hernandez-Mats shared several photos of her and Nibbs on social media; one posted on February 16, 2016, shows her and Nibbs standing in front of a sign that read in part "UTD We Are Keeping Kids Safe." Irony may not be completely dead, but it does seem like it's on life support sometimes.

On January 23, 2020, Nibbs pleaded guilty "to three counts of sexual activity with a child." The court sentenced him to eight months in prison and ten years of probation. He will also be required to register as a sexual predator for the remainder of his life.

Top Three Takeaways:

- This cautionary tale is remarkable for the number of victims, the length of time over which they were victimized, and the relative notoriety of the abuse. The fact that there were reasonably credible allegations of abuse stretching back over a dozen years reflects a near-total breakdown of institutional integrity. The district's handling of this matter raises disturbing questions about its commitment to protecting the health and safety of its students in general and its young women in particular.

- It is difficult to avoid the conclusion that raw political power played a significant role in this case. In a district the size of Miami-Dade County, the union is a powerful force working on behalf of its members. In general, I believe strongly in the role unions play in helping to redress the power imbalance that can exist between employers and employees. I will admit that a decade on the Burlington School Board dampened my enthusiasm somewhat (although not entirely), as I watched unions fight vigorously to save the jobs of teachers who behaved stupidly, unethically, or criminally. While I respect the need for employee advocacy, unions also need to have zero tolerance for child abuse. It is possible to defend due process without excusing or implicitly condoning the sexual abuse of children.

- From an ethical perspective, this cautionary tale offers a buffet of lessons. Nibbs was taking advantage of young women in difficult or vulnerable circumstances, which created a sense of dependency and made them less likely to report the abuse. The district did not successfully develop a culture of cybersafety, lessening the chance that the students would tell anyone about the abuse. And when a student finally did say something, the school district sent a clear (and discouraging) message by not taking action. And even though he was unsuccessful, Nibbs tried to obstruct justice by instructing one or more of his victims to delete photos from KIK. Just a final word of warning: you can still be charged with obstruction of justice even if you are not successful at it. As this case illustrates, computer forensics technicians are often able to frustrate efforts to delete relevant evidence.

Cautionary Tale 27-2017-US_California

Like all of the cautionary tales in this chapter, this is a depressing story of educator misconduct (facilitated by technology) that is not merely unethical but seriously criminal. However, it is the perfect final cautionary tale for this chapter because it illustrates several of the major themes in this book.

As is so often the case, the story began with a relatively short and not overly-detailed story in a local paper. On October 6, 2017, Samuel Neipp was arrested by San Jose police "on suspicion of lewd and lascivious acts with a minor under 14 years of age, oral copulation, possession of child pornography and extortion." The article noted that at the time of his arrest, the 34-year-old Neipp was a music teacher at two San Jose area schools, Dartmouth Middle School and Branham High School.

The few details provided were shocking enough: Neipp was accused of using his teaching position to sexually assault a student (Victim A) over three years. Victim A allegedly was 13 when the assaults began but did not report Neipp until he threatened to publish nude photos of her.

Just four days later, Neipp was in court facing new charges as Victim B, now 20, came forward. She told prosecutors that Neipp had molested her for two years, also beginning when she was 13. Prosecutors filed 35 felony charges against Neipp, "including 17 counts of lewd and lascivious acts with children under 14." If convicted, prosecutor Michel Amaral said, Neipp could be incarcerated for more than 100 years. She encouraged any other victims to contact the San Jose Police Department. In light of the seriousness of the charges against him, the judge set bail at $2.375 million.

As is increasingly common in these situations, litigation ensued. A little more than a year after Neipp's arreset, attorney Robert Allard announced the filing of a lawsuit against the Union School District. In addition to his claim for damages for Victim A and a third unnamed Victim C, Allard said that he was asking the courts to order significant changes in how schools handle these types of situations. As he said at his press conference:

> Time and time again, and we've all been here many times before, school districts like this one have demonstrated that they are utterly unable to regulate themselves and protect students entrusted to their care from predator coaches and teachers.

Allard's list of proposed changes included:

training of school staff to identify possible grooming situations and to take action; removing the ability to lock the door to a teacher's office from the inside; instituting policies designed to limit isolated contact between teachers and students; and prohibiting social media and smartphone communication between teachers and students and instead, require use of a school-archived email system with copies sent to an administrator and/or parent.

Allard's lawsuit contained numerous allegations that the school had failed to monitor Neipp's activity in the school building and had failed to report credible allegations of abuse to law enforcement. For instance, Victim A said that much of her abuse by Neipp took place in his office, progressing over time from kissing to sexual intercourse. Victim C was the daughter of a district employee, who shared with supervisors examples of highly inappropriate text messages sent by Neipp to her daughter. One, for instance, read, "the only girl I want anything to do with is you! The rest are dead to me."

Instead of alerting law enforcement, the Union School District hired an outside law firm to do an investigation. Attorneys warned Neipp that his texts to the girl were "inappropriate and did not show good judgment," but the district did not take any disciplinary action. In fact, Neipp was assured that the matter would be kept confidential.

The girl's mother continued to report disturbing interactions between Neipp and her daughter, including texts exchanged late at night, but school officials still did nothing to stop Neipp's conduct. Allard's complaint alleged that even after being told he was not exercising good judgment, Neipp sent hundreds of text messages to Victim C.

Two weeks later, a second lawsuit was filed against the district on behalf of Victim B by Los Angeles attorney David Ring, seeking unspecified damages and similar changes in the district's practices. The factual allegations were very similar: the new lawsuit alleged that when the plaintiff entered middle school in 2009 at the age of 12, Neipp quickly began texting and emailing her. During her second year, Neipp asked her to be his classroom assistant and, over time, transitioned from suggestive comments to physical abuse. She said she would occasionally visit the middle school after going to high school, and that Neipp used those visits as an opportunity to continue his abuse. It was not until she read of his arrest, when she was a senior in college, that she felt she could report what he had done over the years.

In September 2019, Neipp accepted a deal in which he agreed to plead no contest to 14 separate counts on charges including:

- lewd and lascivious acts with a minor under 14 by force, violence, duress, menace or fear;

- sexual penetration, oral copulation, unlawful sexual intercourse, and sending harmful matter to a minor with intent to commit a sex crime, all with a minor under 16 by an offender over 21; and

- possession of child pornography.

As part of the plea deal, Neipp agreed to accept a sentence of 56 years in prison. The civil lawsuits are proceeding.

Top Three Takeaways:

- More and more school districts are facing litigation stemming from acts of solicitation or assault by educators and staff. Thanks in no small part to the ready availability of damning digital evidence, juries are handing out increasingly large damage awards to victims and their families. These verdicts damage the reputation of schools, raise insurance rates, and threaten educational budgets at a time when districts simply cannot afford unnecessary expenses. School districts have a moral obligation to do all they can to protect the students in their care; that alone should be sufficient motivation to act swiftly to prevent or stop sexual assault. If that somehow is not enough, however, districts also have powerful economic incentives to do so as well.

- If true, the allegations in the lawsuits regarding the school's response are shocking. Of course, the failure began long before officials allegedly attempted to sweep Neipp's conduct under the rug. The district did not do enough to create a climate in which harassed or assaulted students could come forward and seek help. There are a lot of factors that contribute to these situations, but schools should work diligently to create an environment in which it is more difficult for abuse to occur and easier for students to report.

- The measures proposed by Attorney Allard are generally sensible and are similar to ones that I have been recommending over the last several years. Two of his recommendations deserve specific comment. First, it is a sad reflection on our current social situation that a suggestion designed to address one problem—minimizing the possibility of sexual assault by removing the ability to lock doors—is probably outweighed by another depressing consideration—the sometimes desperate need to lock doors in an active shooter situation. The world in which we live, however, continually presents us with these grim balancing acts. Second, I think that the most important of his recommendations is the one dealing with electronic communication. Every district should make clear to educators, staff, students, and parents that teacher-student communication must be either archivable (and effectively monitored) or transparent, i.e., with more than one adult involved in the conversation.

Relevant MCEE Provisions for Chapter 27

Principle I: Responsibility to the Profession

Standards I.A.2, I.A.3, I.A.4, and I.A.5

Principle II: Responsibility for Professional Competence

Standard II.C.3

Principle III: Responsibility to Students

Standards III.A.2, III.A.3, III.B.3, III.B.7, and III.B.8

Principle V: Responsible and Ethical Use of Technology

Standards V.A.5 and V.C.3

Sources

The sources for the Cautionary Tales in this chapter can be viewed at the following URL:

https://link.cybertraps.com/C4E2-Sources-Chap27

Chapter 28

Failure to Report

Statutory Requirements to Report

Almost fifty years ago, the United States Congress passed the Child Abuse Prevention and Treatment Act (CAPTA) (Public Law 93-247 [1974]). According to the National Low Income Housing Coalition, the goal of the original legislation "was to provide funding for the prevention, identification, and treatment of child abuse and neglect." Among other things, the law established the National Center on Child Abuse and Neglect and the National Clearing House on Child Abuse and Neglect Information.

Since its initial adoption, Congress has amended the statute numerous times to address different types of child abuse and implement new programs aimed at curbing harm to children. The law was most recently changed in 2015 when Congress passed the Justice for Victims of Trafficking Act. That legislation expanded the definitions of "child abuse and neglect" and "sexual abuse" to include children who are victims of "sex trafficking or severe forms of trafficking in persons."

While educators should be on the look-out for all kinds of abuse, they should pay particular attention in the school context to possible sexual abuse by colleagues. As I hope this book has convincingly demonstrated, the rise of digital communication technology has exacerbated the risk of inappropriate teacher-student relationships and accelerated the pace at which such interactions occur.

The states all use slightly different language to define what constitutes "sexual abuse," but Monster.com's "Teaching Community" offers a useful summary of the minimum provisions:

- Employment, use, persuasion, inducement, enticement, or coercion of any child to engage in, or assist any other person to engage in any sexually explicit conduct or any simulation of such conduct for the purpose of producing any visual depiction of such conduct; or

- Rape, and in cases of caretaker or inter-familial relationships, statutory rape, molestation, prostitution, or any other form of sexual exploitation of children, or incest of children.

Who Is Required to Report Sexual Abuse or Suspected Sexual Abuse?

The Children's Bureau of the Administration for Children & Families (a division of the U.S. Department of Health & Human Services) has created an excellent website, https://www.childwelfare.gov/. The site contains vast quantities of information, programs, and initiatives aimed at protecting children and promoting their welfare.

Included in that material is a detailed report on mandatory reporting requirements around the United States entitled Mandatory Reporters of Child Abuse and Neglect. Although the specific terminology varies—"teacher," "school employee," "school personnel," etc.—classroom educators are identified explicitly as mandatory reporters of suspected abuse in virtually every state statute addressing the issue. The website **Findlaw.com** also has an excellent collection of materials entitled "Child Abuse Information by State."

As some of the examples below make clear, the failure to report the suspected abuse of a student by another teacher or administrator can result in criminal charges. If you are a teacher or classroom educator, you have a responsibility to familiarize yourself with the applicable laws of your state. If you are a school community leader—a building administrator, a district official, or a school board member--I strongly recommend that you consult with your school or district attorney regarding mandatory reporting requirements. Make sure that your policies are in line with the applicable state law and that they do not create any possible grounds for confusion. It is also essential to make sure that all school personnel receives regular and thorough professional development on their responsibility to report suspected abuse.

Institutional Requirements to Report

In addition to the mandatory reporting requirements of the state in which you work, your school or school district may (and should!) have internal policies and procedures regarding the reporting of suspected abuse. It is essential to keep in mind that state statutes take precedence over institutional policies or procedures; put another way, a school district policy cannot contradict or even limit a teacher's legal obligation to serve as a mandatory reporter. Just to underscore the point, fifteen states currently have laws that explicitly state that "regardless of any policies within the organization, the mandatory reporter is not relieved of his or her responsibility to report."

Along the same lines, seventeen states have adopted statutes that expressly prohibit an employer "from taking any action to prevent or discourage an employee from making a report."

Cautionary Tales

Cautionary Tale 28-2018-KY

The vast bulk of the "failure to report" cases in this book (and in real life) arise because an educator or administrator is aware of a sexual assault against a student and does not alert the appropriate authorities. Increasingly, however, legislatures are imposing mandatory reporting requirements for other types of serious situations. For instance, many if not most school building administrators around the country are required to alert district officials or law enforcement when there is a possible threat of violence against the school or its students.

School districts are working diligently to draft and implement response procedures for threats of violence. As a case in Knoxville, Tennessee illustrates, however, there still are occasionally holes in the system. On February 15, 2018 (the day after the school shooting in Parkland, Florida), two female students told Holston Middle School Principal Kathryn Lutton and 8th Grade Principal Sara Greene "that they had overheard a male student saying something about 'bringing a gun to school[.]'"

Twenty minutes later, Lutton contacted the boy's mother by phone, who reportedly was shocked by the news and said that there were no guns in the family's home. Lutton told the boy's mother that she would meet the child the next morning when his bus arrived at school and interview him with the school resource officer. Contrary to Knox County School protocol, however, Lutton did not contact law enforcement regarding the alleged threat.

Technology disrupted Lutton's plan for handling the incident. That same evening, another student used Snapchat to post a picture of the boy and repeat his threat. The social media post quickly came to the attention of the Knoxville Police Department (KPD), which immediately began an investigation. Using information obtained from a Knox County Schools security dispatcher, the KPD was able to identify the boy and assess the extent of the threat. Although the KPD concluded that the threat was not serious, the department was upset to learn that Lutton had known about the boy's comment for hours without contacting the KPD.

KPD Sgt. Jason Hill wrote an email to his supervisor that sharply criticized the Knox County Schools:

> My purpose of writing this email to you is to discuss what I believe to be a flaw in the notification system by Knox County Schools. This is not the first time that we have been notified about these types of threats, only to find out that the school system knew several hours prior.... I believe that school principals are operating on an outdated threat matrix because by their actions they seem to think they have time on their side and, additionally, believe that they can handle the issues internally.

Sgt. Hill noted that in addition to Lutton's failure to relay the alleged threat, the contact information for the school security personnel was outdated (which hindered the investigation) and a school community alert system (Text-a-Tip) had been out of service for several weeks.

The Superintendent of the Knox County Schools, Bob Thomas, told reporters that the district would conduct a comprehensive review regarding the communication failure and that "there is going to be accountability for not following the protocol." There were no reports, however, of any specific disciplinary action taken against either Principal Lutton or Greene.

Area law enforcement officials described the security protocol for the Knox County Schools as "sound" but admitted that it could use some "tweaking." Knox County Schools Security Chief Gus Paidousis said that "the agencies will revisit their safety plan and make sure school staff, most notably principals, are aware of its contents and set up training for the approximately 4,000 teachers in the district's 90 schools."

Top Three Takeaways:

- Knox County Schools could have offered a model example of school responsiveness, but instead, it's a cautionary tale. Whether through parental training or school culture or some combination of both, at least two of the district's students were aware that they should let school officials know that they heard someone talk about bringing a gun to school. In this day and age, it does not matter if their classmate was joking; as the Transportation Safety Administration has made abundantly clear, there are just comments that are just not funny.

- This cautionary tale illustrates that a district's policies and procedures are only as effective and meaningful as the people charged with implementing them. To be fair, mandatory reporting requirements can seem extreme, particularly in situations where an educator or administrator knows the child and perhaps the parents, and suspects that the "threat" may have been nothing more than off-hand, immature remark. But unfortunately, it only takes one mistake in judgment for serious harm to occur. Nobody would want it on their conscience that they could have prevented a tragedy and failed to do so, especially when they have an ethical and legal obligation to take specific actions.

- One of the primary reasons to have mandatory reporting policies is to make sure that all relevant parties receive essential information as soon as possible and through appropriate channels. The fact that a random student posted his classmate's comment on Snapchat helps show how easily school officials (and law enforcement) can lose control of a situation. It is not difficult to imagine threats or assaults of the young man as a result of the social media rumor. Nobody should have any illusions about the ability of social media to take a tense situation and make it worse. Effective policies and procedures and training are the most critical components for effective incident response; however, every school district also should give some thought to providing media and crisis PR training to appropriate officials.

Cautionary Tale 28-2018-TX

Haynes Northwest Academy is part of the Wichita Falls Independent School District (WFISD) in northern Wichita Falls, about 150 miles northwest of the Dallas-Fort Worth metro region. Like many other schools, Haynes provides iPads to its students. Many schools have discovered to their dismay that students don't necessarily use the devices for their intended purposes. Last fall, it was Haynes's turn; but this time, it cost a school principal her job.

According to an arrest warrant filed on February 5, 2018, by the Wichita Falls Police Department, a teacher in the school had discovered on October 25, 2016, that three elementary students had used one of the school's iPads to take a series of "inappropriate photos" in a classroom. The teacher reported the incident to Haynes principal Cindy Underwood that same day and showed her the photos on the iPad.

Texas law states that if an individual operating in his or her official capacity learns of or suspects abuse of a child, he or she is legally required to file a report with the police or with Child Protective Services within 48 hours. In this case, the Wichita Falls Police Department alleges that Underwood disregarded her legal obligation and merely informed the parents of the boys about the incident. In doing so, the WFPD said, Underwood risked further abuse of the boys, who "should not have knowledge of sexual acts exhibited in the photos unless they have seen or experienced it."

Law enforcement began investigating Underwood's conduct after a parent of one of the boys filed a report with Child Protection Services on October 31, alleging that his son had been sexually assaulted at Haynes. Investigators then interviewed Underwood, who acknowledged seeing the photos. She was able to identify the classroom, name the children involved (all age 6), and describe the sex acts that the children had photographed. She told the investigators that since all three boys are visible in the photographs, they must have taken turns using the iPad. A computer forensics examination of the iPad confirmed the presence of the photos, which matched the description that Underwood provided. During forensic interviews, each of the young students made statements consistent with the behavior depicted in the images.

Following Underwood's arrest on February 5, she was placed on administrative leave by the WFISD. A couple of days later, WFISD Superintendent Michael S. Kuhrt offered a firm endorsement of Underwood and another WIFSD principal who was charged with failure to report in a separate incident.

"I know the character of both administrators in question," Kuhrt said, "and I am confident that neither of those administrators would deliberately hurt a child."

After a three-month investigation, police dropped the failure to report charge filed against Underwood, and the school district removed her from administrative leave. Since Underwood's position as the Academy principal had been filled, the school district assigned her to serve as the district's Early Learning Program Support coordinator.

Top Three Takeaways:

- One-to-one device initiatives like this raise a host of challenging technical issues, not least of which is the taking of inappropriate photographs. Even first graders, unfortunately, are aware of the use of mobile devices to play a game of 21st-century doctor, and schools and parents have a responsibility to intervene and help children understand the risks of what they are doing. A necessary part of that responsibility is notifying people trained to handle these types of situations (i.e., Child Protective Services).

- I suspect that one-to-one device initiatives are increasingly less common in schools these days, mainly because more and more schoolchildren show up with their own devices. However, schools still have a responsibility to supervise how students are using those devices on campus. Even if they are using electronic devices that they brought to school, students need to understand that they still are required to abide by the rules and regulations of the school. Failure to do so should result at the very least in the confiscation of the device and possibly more serious consequences depending on the behavior in question.

- It's hard not to conclude that Superintendent Kuhrt missed the point here. The question was not whether the administrators "would deliberately hurt a child," but instead, whether they would follow applicable reporting requirements. At the very least, it seems clear that Underwood did not follow the explicit provisions of state law, so her intent to hurt or not hurt children was irrelevant.

Cautionary Tale 28-2017-KS

In May 2016, Dan Nasalroad, a school resource officer at Prairie View High School (PVHS) in La Cygne, Kansas, received a report that a teacher had sexually assaulted a student. Following an investigation, the Linn County Sheriff's Department met with PVHS English teacher and basketball coach Keaton Krell in the office of Superintendent Chris Kleidosty. Sheriff Paul Filla arrested Krell on charges of violating a Kansas statute prohibiting sexual relations with students. In subsequent comments about the case, Sheriff Filla made a point of praising Kleidosty for the assistance and cooperation of the school administration in the investigation. Two weeks later, police rearrested Krell on ten additional counts of unlawful sexual intercourse.

Coincidentally, on the same day that Krell was arrested at PVHS, Kleidosty accepted a new position as superintendent of the Tonganoxie Public Schools, located about 70 miles north-northwest of La Cygne. He told the Tonganoxie school board that he would continue to assist the Linn County Sheriff's Office with its investigation into the Krell case.

That investigation took an unexpected turn, however, when police arrested both Kleidosty and PVHS Principal Tim Weis in mid-February 2017 on charges that they were aware of Krell's actions and failed to report the assaults. The news shook La Cygne, a small town of 2,000, where angry parents asked why the school officials did not do more to protect children.

There's some suggestion that members of the community had long-standing suspicions of their own. Helping to illustrate the challenges faced by school boards and administrators in this digital age, an online petition calling for an investigation into the actions of Linn County and PVHS school administrators garnered over 385 signatures (a not insignificant number in such a small town). The petition drive was started by Melody Beeker, who drafted a ringing call to action:

> As you all know the Linn county Kansas sheriff's department is doing an investigation into things involving inappropriate relationships between teacher and students at Prairie View high school. Apparently the county attorney isn't wanting to go after administration who by law are required to report any indiscretion or complaints about inappropriate behavior. They knew that this stuff was happening yet even after years of concerned parents and students reporting things, repeatedly, NOTHING WAS DONE TO STOP IT!! A pedophile/ predator was allowed years of unrestricted access to our children by things not being reported AS MANDATED BY LAW. I am asking you please sign this petition to help the sheriff's department get everyone who has been/was/is involved held accountable. If those who we trust with our children cannot be trusted to do the right thing, where does that leave us? PROTECT PRAIRIE VIEW STUDENTS!!

There is no specific suggestion that Beeker's petition had an impact on the investigation and arrest of Kleidosty and Weis. What is clear, however, is that the professional fallout for the two administrators was swift and far-reaching. Both Kleidosty and Weis were suspended with pay following their arrests. A few months later, the Tonganoxie school board voted to rescind a one-year contract extension that it had given to Kleidosty.

For Kleidosty, matters came to a relatively positive conclusion: in early August 2017, Linn County State's Attorney James Brun announced that he was dismissing the charges without prejudice. While that did leave open the possibility that Brun might recharge Kleidosty, there is no indication that he did so. In theory, Kleidosty could have returned to his position as superintendent in Tonganoxie. Instead, he submitted his resignation in October 2017 and the school board accepted it.

For PVHS Principal Weis, the outcome was less good. Almost a year after his arrest, he entered a plea of no contest to a single charge of failure as an administrator to report child abuse/neglect. At his change of plea hearing, prosecutors told the court that their investigation revealed that Weis had disciplined Krell on three separate occasions for "inappropriate contact." Instead of taking disciplinary action, Weis ordered Krell to read *Innocence Denied: A Guide to Preventing Sexual Misconduct by Teachers and Coaches*, by William L. Fibkins (2006). Investigators also found that Weis had ignored complaints from numerous people about Krell's conduct.

In his statement to the court, Weis cited his 31-year career as an educator and his desire to prevent further emotional harm to the victims by forcing them to testify. His attorney added that his professional life is "in tatters," with numerous employers withdrawing job offers after hearing about the legal proceedings.

At the conclusion of the hearing, the court sentenced Weis to serve eight days in the Linn County Jail, spread over three months; to serve one year of probation; to make payment of court fees; and to write letters of apology through the District Court Services officer to both victims of the original two misdemeanor counts.

Top Three Takeaways:

- This cautionary tale should serve as an excellent reminder to educators and administrators that the newsgathering landscape is much more unpredictable than it used to be. Some school officials may have taken grim satisfaction in the economic problems besetting the news industry, having no love lost for inquisitive local reporters (like my soon-to-be daughter-in-law). But one of the under-reported aspects of the internet and social media is the democratization of news-gathering. As this cautionary tale illustrates, a single passionate parent and a website together can provide local coverage with the same effectiveness as a team of New York Times reporters. Although it was not a factor in this case, school officials should keep in mind that Facebook especially strong influence and organizing power to parents and political gadflies. Yes, there is a significant risk of disinformation and libel, but ignore those news feeds at your peril.

- As you can tell from the recitation above, there's an information gap here. What exactly was it that led Weis and Kleidosty (to a lesser degree) to protect Krell instead of the student he assaulted? For all the research I've done on this topic, it is still bewildering to me that educators and administrators do not do everything possible to protect the health and safety of students. Anything less is a moral and ethical failing.

- The answer, of course, lies in the fact that some people put a higher value on their personal relationships rather than their professional responsibilities. One of the objectives of the Model Code of Ethics for Educators is to remind all members of the educational community that they should adhere to ethical standards that transcend personal relationships. You may be deeply pained by what you need to do, but if it is in the interests of your profession and consistent with your ethical obligations, then you should do it nonetheless. You should not sacrifice the well-being of any student on the altar of your personal friendships.

Cautionary Tale 28-2014-IL

For 18 years, Michael R. Vucic taught at the Gavin South Middle School in Ingleside, Illinois (just west of Chicago). On August 25, 2014, a former female student told relatives that she had been sexually assaulted by Vucic when she was a student at the school (she was under the age of 13 at the time). The following day, Vucic fled to Bosnia-Herzegovina to avoid arrest. He successfully hid in Sarajevo for three weeks before being arrested on an international warrant. It took another three months for U.S. authorities to extradite Vucic to the United States.

During the subsequent intense investigation, the Lake County Sheriff's office identified three Ingleside colleagues of Vucic who they believed should have suspected ongoing child abuse and reported it to the proper authorities. Two teachers, April Courtney and John Keehan were also teachers at Gavin South when Vucic fled to Europe. The third, Michael Lanners, had once worked at Gavin South with Vucic and was still friendly with him, but at the time of the alleged assault, taught at Mundelein School District 75 about 10 miles away.

Both Courtney and Keehan were placed on administrative leave at Gavin South on September 24, 2014, and fired three weeks later for their failure to report suspected child sexual abuse. The Mundelein School imposed a similar penalty on Lanners. Arrest warrants were issued for all three on November 12, charging them with a Class A Misdemeanor.

The Daily Herald, a local newspaper based in Arlington Heights, obtained personnel records for both Courtney and Keehan. According to Keehan's file, "Vucic told him that he was engaged in a sexual relationship with a former student who was a minor." The records do not indicate when Vucic told Keehan that information.

Courtney's file revealed that Vucic told her not once but twice about illegal interactions with students: first in 2013, when Vucic said to her that he was having sex with a student, and then in 2014, when he talked about sexting with a student on social media. Courtney told district officials that she did not believe Vucic, who she described as a teller of "tall tales." However, just as he was fleeing to Bosnia-Herzegovina, Vucic met Courtney outside the middle school and handed her a bag of CDs and DVDs. When Courtney eventually looked at the contents, she saw that one was labeled with the name of a sex act and took the bag to the police. The video recordings, several of which Vucic recorded in his classroom, revealed the identity of a second assault victim.

In July 2015, Courtney agreed to plead guilty and was sentenced to 30 days in prison. She earned a stern rebuke from Lake County Associate Judge Helen Rozenberg:

> The fact that he made a statement that he had sex with a child and nothing was done is abhorrent. I found Ms. Courtney's behavior outrageous and callous and led to substantial suffering by a child.

Four months later, Keehan also agreed to plead guilty and "was sentenced to [12 months of] conditional discharge, ordered to pay a $2,100 fine and donate $500 to two child abuse agencies."

The third teacher, Lanners, opted for a bench trial, which took place on November 12. Prosecutors presented the judge with a statement by Lanners in which he admitted that Vucic had told him he was in love with a student and that they would "be together" after she turned 18. Lanners claimed that he warned Vucic the girl was "too young" and that Vucic should "be careful." More disturbingly, Lanners also admitted that he saw a video recording that showed the student touching Vucic's genitals.

Lanners argued that notwithstanding those admissions, he had no legal obligation to report the suspected abuse because he did not know either of Vucic's victims in a professional or official capacity (since he taught at a different school).

Lake County Judge Brian Hughes ruled in January 2016 that Lanners was not guilty, agreeing that the law did not impose an obligation on him to report the suspected abuse. However, Judge Hughes expressed his profound disappointment in his behavior:

> Mr. Lanners, I've made my ruling, but what you did not do violates human decency. You knew what was going on. ... You were told about the behavior [by Vucic], and you did nothing.

Meanwhile, Vucic, the teacher who set this sorry train of events in motion, was sentenced on November 5, 2015, to 50 years in Illinois state prison.

Top Three Takeaways:

- The first takeaway is the simplest and most straightforward: if one of your colleagues tells you that he is sexually assaulting or is "in love" with a student, you don't have to believe him (or her), but you **do** have to report it. Ideally, through the application of the MCEE's ethical standard of self-care, your colleague would recognize the potential problem and seek help before he or she crossed any critical professional lines. If not, however, you have an independent ethical duty to help protect the health and safety of students, even if you are not entirely sure any harm is occurring.

- Lanners's defense that he was not legally required to take action, while ultimately correct, is a perfect illustration of the distinction between law and ethics. While he may not have had a legal duty to act, he unquestionably had an ethical obligation to do so and arguably a moral one as well. Ultimately, as the judge correctly pointed out, Lanners failed to show basic human decency towards the victim. Decency, morality, and ethics should weigh even more heavily on your conscience if you are shown or even accidentally see visual evidence of your colleague's sexual abuse of a student.

- If you've ever wondered about the origins of the phrase "Don't be left holding the bag," this cautionary tale will help explain. Of the three non-reporting teachers, only Courtney served time in jail. I suspect that was due not only to her failure to report on Vucic's statements but also because she did not immediately look at the contents of the bag Vucic handed her when she heard he had fled the country. Any reasonably thoughtful person would have suspected that the bag contained material he did not want investigators to find by investigators. Seriously, don't let your colleagues put you that position.

Relevant MCEE Provisions for Chapter 28

Principle I: Responsibility to the Profession

Standards I.A.2, I.A.3, and I.B.2

Principle II: Responsibility for Professional Competence

Standard II.C.3

Principle III: Responsibility to Students

Standards III.A.8 and III.B.3

Principle IV: Responsibility to the School Community

Standard IV.B.8

Sources

The sources for the Cautionary Tales in this chapter can be viewed at the following URL:

https://link.cybertraps.com/C4E2-Sources-Chap28

Chapter 29
Failure to Properly Handle Student Sexts

The Origins of the Selfie

By now, we've all heard of (and probably have taken) the narcissistic photo known as the "selfie." All you need to take a picture of yourself these days is a camera and mirror, or merely an outstretched smartphone. There is a decent chance that the majority of the people reading this book have taken at least one selfie, if not hundreds. The practice quickly became so ubiquitous that "selfie" was designated 2013's "Word of the Year" by the Oxford University Press.

Selfies come in a vast array of categories: the banal, which most of us have on our phone; the inquisitive, "How do this outfit look on me?"; the travel diary, "Shameless Selfie at Machu Picchu"; the self-congratulatory, "Hillary Clinton and Meryl Streep at 2012 Kennedy Center Honors"; and the wildly inappropriate, "Selfies at Funerals," to name just a few.

A related phenomenon emerged in the mid-2000s, as cellphones grew steadily more sophisticated. In a 2004 article covering an alleged affair between soccer star David Beckham and his assistant Rebecca Loos, *The Globe and Mail* reporter Josey Vogels was arguably the first person to refer to the practice of sending lewd text messages as "sext messaging." By late 2008/early 2009, people everywhere had adopted the word "sext" as shorthand for sexually explicit text messages or images sent from one cellphone to another.

2004 also happened to be the same year that cellphone manufacturers began concentrating on teenagers as a previously untapped and potentially lucrative market. At the time, just about 25% of teens used a cellphone. By 2008, that percentage would double and then nearly double again over the next four years. Today, just under 95% of high school students have a cellphone, and the majority of those are smartphones. The devices allow students to take increasingly high-resolution photos and videos and instantaneously share them with their friends, classmates, and the rest of the world.

A confluence of influential social trends—computers, the internet, the initial success of the online adult industry, easy access to pornography, the rise of "porn chic," and the ready availability of cellphones—made it inevitable that children would start sexting. (For a detailed explanation of how that happened, see *Obscene Profits: Entrepreneurs of Pornography in the Cyber Age* [Routledge 2000].) By 2009, just two years after the release of the iPhone, the National Campaign to Prevent Teen and Unplanned Pregnancy was reporting that 20% of teens were taking, sending, and redistributing naked photos of themselves or other children. The phenomenon is much more widespread now.

A Growing Problem for School Districts

One of the earliest examples—a story that helped inspire *Cybertraps for the Young* [NTI Upstream 2011]—occurred in Cincinnati, Ohio in 2008. A young woman named Jessica Logan, 18, sent nude pictures of herself to her boyfriend. When they stopped going out, the boyfriend forwarded the photos to friends of his, who then forwarded them to others. One area school board member later told me that during the ensuing investigation, officers found copies of Logan's photographs on student cellphones in seven different high schools in the Cincinnati area.

As the photos spread, Logan suffered terrible abuse: other students harassed her both physically and verbally (typical epithets included "slut" and "whore"). Logan, formerly a popular and successful student, began skipping class and showing other signs of depression. To help protect other girls, Logan made an appearance on a local Cincinnati television station (with blurred image and altered voice) to warn of the dangers of sexting. Her mother, Cynthia Logan, said that she seemed to be doing better after graduation in May, but tragically, Jessica Logan hanged herself in her bedroom in July 2008. Around the United States and across the world, there have been dozens of other instances in which post-sexting bullying has played a role (often significant) in the suicide deaths of teens and even pre-teens.

The Logan case vividly illustrates why school districts should take student sexting cases seriously. Some school districts have tried to fall back on the defense that the sexting did not occur on school grounds—in fact, that's precisely the reason given by the superintendent of Sycamore Schools, where Logan was a student, as to why the district did not punish her tormenters. However, there is an emerging legal consensus that school districts should intervene even in situations that occur off-campus or purely online, where the behavior has "a direct and immediate effect on either school safety or the safety and welfare of students and staff." Not surprisingly, some of that legal consensus is being driven by litigation, as families like the Logans seek to recover damages from school districts and individual administrators for not doing enough to protect their children from bullying.

Teachers and administrators face little legal risk when investigating allegations of purely text-based cyberharassment or cyberbullying. The primary concerns are the efficacy of the investigations, respecting student privacy to the extent possible, and following established procedures to ensure due process. Of course, if a student hands a teacher a phone with offensive or abusive text messages, he or she should never copy or send those messages to anyone. As with anything that might suggest harm to a student, the device should be hand-delivered to an administrator or school resource officer as quickly as possible.

When an investigation centers around intimate or sexually explicit images of minors, however, both teachers and administrators need to be very cautious about how they proceed. With all the daily pressures educators face, including demanding parents and inadequate supervisory guidelines, what may seem like routine decisions can have dramatic and career-damaging consequences. Couple a complicated situation with a determined and unsympathetic prosecutor, and educators could find themselves facing unexpected criminal charges.

The following examples (including a particularly lengthy one describing a situation in Virginia) will offer some guidelines, but here are some essential points to keep in mind:

- Intimate or sexually explicit images of a minor almost certainly fall within the definition of "child pornography" under federal law and the laws of all fifty states;

- There is no exception for someone who takes a nude selfie—minors can be prosecuted or producing child pornography by taking photos of themselves;

- Anyone who receives a copy of a nude selfie can potentially be charged with receipt and possession of child pornography;

- Anyone who sends or forwards a nude selfie (including the person who took it) can be charged with distribution;

- If law enforcement discovers that you used a school or personal digital devices to send a nude selfie to someone else, even for advice, that will cause a lot of problems. There is an excellent chance that officers will apply for a warrant to seize and search those devices, up to and including the servers that run the school district. Be warned: It is a wildly disruptive process.

Cautionary Tales

Cautionary Tale 29-2016-KY

In early September 2016, a 20-year-old woman called the police in Elizabethtown, Kentucky, and reported that someone had found naked photos of her on an infamous image-sharing website hosted in Russia. She told the officers that she had taken the pictures of herself when she was 15 years old and had sent them to her boyfriend.

Investigators for the Kentucky State Police and the Internet Crimes Against Children task force contacted the website and obtained the IP address used to upload the images. They traced that IP address to an internet service provider account registered to Stephen Kyle Goodlett, who at the time was principal of the LaRue County High School. A judge issued a search warrant for Goodlett's home, and police officers seized a variety of electronic devices. During a preliminary forensic examination of the digital devices, analysts uncovered 60 different images of alleged child pornography.

Goodlett was arrested on October 13 and charged with "distribution of matter portraying sexual performance by a minor, first offense, and possession or viewing of matter portraying a sexual performance by a minor." Five days later, prosecutors upgraded the charges to "sixty counts of possession and three counts of distribution of matter portraying a sex performance by a minor." Goodlett was initially held on bail of $75,000. The school district fired Goodlett from his job on October 19.

At the time the search of his home was conducted, Goodlett told investigators that he had "an addiction to pornography and that he transferred images from phones confiscated from students to his personal thumb drive without their consent or knowledge." He added that "he would take the images and share them to the . . . website with the intent of trading for more images."

On top of the state charges, the U.S. Attorney for the District of Kentucky indicted Goodlett on December 19 on one count of possessing and one count of transporting child pornography. The federal charges were filed one week after the National Center for Missing and Exploited Children issued a report stating that Goodlett's Dropbox account contained images of known victims of electronic sexual assault. The individuals depicted in the stored photos, one of whom was the student who initially filed a complaint with her local police department, were between the ages of 10 and 14.

Goodlett initially pleaded not guilty to both the state and the federal charges. However, after fairly lengthy negotiations, he accepted a plea deal in the federal case (the state charges are still pending). In documents filed with the court in support of the plea agreement, his attorney Christopher Spedding said that Goodlett's addiction had destroyed his life:

Kyle is a broken man. He is also a sick man. There is no other viable explanation for the behavior that he engaged in … He knows he has betrayed the trust of his community, his students, his colleagues and his family.

On February 8, 2018, U.S. District Court Judge accepted the proposed deal and sentenced Goodlett to nine years in federal prison, ten years of supervised release, and registration as a sex offender. During the sentencing, Goodlett acknowledged his crime and apologized to the victims: "What I've done is morally reprehensible. Your Honor, I deserve to go to prison."

At the end of September 2017, five students filed a lawsuit against Goodlett and the LaRue County School District. They sought damages for the emotional distress they suffered as a result of the invasion of privacy and infringement of their constitutional rights under the Fourth Amendment of the U.S. Constitution and Article 1, section 10 of the Kentucky Constitution (both constitutional provisions prohibit unlawful search and seizure). The lawsuit also asked for punitive damages and an award of attorney's fees.

By the time of Goodlett's sentencing, however, the number of plaintiffs had risen to ten, and counsel added a new defendant: the Hardin County School District, which employed Goodlett as a teacher of English at Elizabethtown High School for nine years.

Top Three Takeaways:

- First and foremost, this cautionary tale arises from Goodlett's ethical failure to recognize the fact that he had an addiction or, at the very least, a perilous interest in contraband materials. The MCEE imposes a duty on educators to practice self-care and, when necessary, to seek help before it leads them to do something far more unethical (i.e., misappropriating and redistributing intimate images of students). Goodlett's failure to do so stemmed in part from the illicit nature of his conduct but also from our inability to adequately discuss the rapid changes in social and sexual mores that have occurred because of the internet and mobile devices.

- I have no desire to excuse what Goodlett did, but it is worth noting that this is a type of misconduct that simply did not exist fifteen years ago. It is almost impossible to imagine a student, male or female, taking nude photos of themselves using film or even Polaroids and sending them to a boyfriend or girlfriend. And it is even harder to imagine a student carrying those photos around school, where they might be seen and confiscated by educators or administrators. But of course, students today do take nude or semi-nude pictures of themselves with regularity, they store them on the mobile devices they carry regularly, and they routinely share them both with and without consent. These images are presumed to be contraband under federal and state law, which makes them legally dangerous. School districts should draft and repeatedly review strict policies and procedures with administrators, educators, and staff about how to handle student sexts and what the consequences will be if members of the school community do not correctly follow district regulations.

- Educators and administrators should also take note of the myriad investigative techniques used in this case. While it was happenstance that the young woman learned that photos of her were on a foreign website, Goodlett would likely have been caught sooner or later. The most likely scenario (which also happened in this case) is that he would get careless and upload a photo of a known victim to an online service. All of the primary online storage and email services routinely scan uploaded files and compare them to databases of identified contraband. Anytime there is a match, the services send a notice to law enforcement in the jurisdiction of the user. Officers use those notices as the basis for applications for physical search warrants, which in turn open up a suspect's electronic devices to an intensive investigation by computer forensics experts. As is typically the case, the forensics exam of Goodlett's electronic devices led to the filing of additional charges.

Cautionary Tale 29-2008-VA

The leading object lesson of what can go wrong when an educator or administrator mishandles a student sext involves Ting-Yi Oei, an assistant principal at Freedom High School in South Riding, Virginia. In the spring of 2008, a teacher alerted Oei of a rumor making the rounds of the high school that students were sending nude photos to each other, and Oei was asked by the school's principal to investigate what was happening.

Oei did not know the identity of any students involved in the alleged incident, but he thought he knew the name of a student who might know something about it. Oei called the student into his office and, in the presence of the school's safety and security specialist, asked him about the rumor. The student admitted that he had received a nude photo and showed it to the school officials; according to Oei's version of the story, the image showed the torso of a female, dressed in panties and arms crossed over her breasts. Oei took the student's cellphone to school principal Christine Forester and showed her the photo. Forester told Oei to keep a copy of the picture on his computer for safekeeping in case it was needed later in the investigation.

Although Oei was poorly instructed by his superior (disastrously, actually), everything was still okay at that point. But Oei did not know how to get the photo from the student's cellphone to his computer, and the school's IT department apparently couldn't help. Undoubtedly seeing an opportunity to be cooperative, the student volunteered to text the photo to Oei's phone and then helped Oei email the photo from Oei's cellphone to his school computer. According to Oei, all of this transpired in front of the Freedom High School safety and security specialist.

Oei continued his investigation by interviewing other students (including, it later turned out, the girl who was the subject of the photo), but no one volunteered any additional information. Oei told Forester that there was no way to identify the girl in the picture and the school dropped the matter. Since Oei did not plan to discipline the male student who showed him the photo, Oei decided not to notify his parents. It was also a particularly stressful time for Oei: his wife was facing surgery for a potentially fatal tumor, and Oei was scheduled to meet with her physician as soon as he could leave school that afternoon.

The same morning that Oei returned from leave following his wife's surgery, a new disciplinary issue arose that involved the same young man who provided the sexting photo. Oei called him into his office to discuss a claim that he had been caught "flaggin" another student. (One of the definitions of "flagging" in The Urban Dictionary is "the act of pulling another person's pants down.") This time, Oei called the boy's mother to tell her that the student would be suspended and advised her that the victim could pursue an assault charge. During the conversation, Oei mentioned the earlier sexting incident.

As Oei himself later said, "She was outraged that I hadn't reported it to her at the time." The mother was also angry that Oei was suspending her son. After Forester rejected her appeal, she threatened Oei with legal action.

A few days later, two investigators from the Loudon County Sheriff's office visited Oei and asked to see the photo he had received from the male student. The investigators told Oei they were responding to a parental complaint, which turned out to be an act of retaliation by the mother of the male student. Oei was unable to locate the photo on his computer but remembered that a copy was on his cellphone. He turned his phone over to the investigators, who examined the image and then gave Oei his phone back. There was, according to Oei, no suggestion that he was under investigation for any reason.

It came as quite a shock, then, when the Commonwealth's Attorney for Loudon County, Jim Plowman, announced that he would be charging Oei with "failure to report suspected child abuse." The charges were eventually dropped in the early summer of 2008, in part because it was not clear under Virginia law whether consensual behavior (in this case, the taking of a photo) between two minors can be construed as "abuse." Even if it could, Oei had complied with Virginia's law by reporting the picture to the school's principal. But Plowman, who based his campaign for Commonwealth's Attorney on a promise of much stricter law enforcement, told Oei that if he did not resign from his job, he would face a felony charge for possession of child pornography. Deputy Commonwealth's Attorney Nicole Wittmann told reporters that "We just feel very strongly that this is not someone who should be in the Loudoun County school system."

Oei refused to resign, believing that he had acted appropriately during his investigation and that the image on his phone did not even constitute child pornography. In an interview with Michel Martin on National Public Radio, Oei suggested that the prosecutor was looking for a high-profile case.

"I think there are other issues, too, of perhaps the prosecutor thinking that this is indeed something that his name and reputation are tied to, and this is his way of going about—to showing it."

Regardless of Plowman's precise motive—political or legal—Oei was indicted on August 11, 2008, on one count of possession of child pornography, a charge that carried a possible sentence of five years in prison. Four months later, Plowman's office added two additional misdemeanor counts for "contributing to the delinquency of a minor," each of which could have added a year to Oei's ultimate sentence. Plowman's obvious objective was to put more pressure on Oei to resign his position and accept a guilty plea.

In March 2009, Oei's attorney Steven Stone filed a motion to dismiss all of the charges, arguing that the image in question did not constitute child pornography; the motion was granted a month later by Loudoun Circuit Court Judge Thomas Horne. The judge ruled that for an image to constitute "child pornography" under Virginia law, it must be "sexually explicit" and "lewd." Mere nudity, he said, is not sufficient.

Following the court's decision, Plowman said that the case would never have gotten so far along if Oei had simply resigned when "asked" to do so. "I thought that was a just and appropriate sanction for his behavior," Plowman told Wired's Kim Zetter. "But he was unwilling to be responsible for any kind of accountability for what he did."

The ordeal left Oei with uncertain job prospects and massive legal fees, but the story had a (quasi-)happy ending. A month after the court dismissed the criminal charges, the Loudon County School Board voted 7-1 to reimburse him $168,000. Oei received a warm welcome from colleagues and staff when he returned to his position as assistant principal at Freedom High School. But not surprisingly, the experience left him wounded and upset:

And so my legal ordeal is done, but I still ask myself: Did anyone benefit from all this? I have to put the pieces of my life and career back together. My wife and I were terrorized by a baseless prosecution, lost all our savings and were forced to borrow huge sums of money to pay for my defense. The students involved probably could have put this ill-advised sexting adventure behind them a long time ago. Instead, they had to wonder for months whether they'd have to testify in court and bring attention to themselves and their families. And a meaningful discussion about sexting and what schools, parents, the community and law enforcement can do about it has been sidetracked for more than a year by a prosecutor who should never have brought charges in the first place.

Top Three Takeaways:

- This cautionary tale arose in the very early days of student sexting, so we should make some allowances for the fact that Oei's principal offered such poor advice. Forester should never have told Oei to transmit a possibly contraband image to himself or a school computing device (distribution), and she should never have instructed Oei to hold onto a copy for future use as evidence (possession). Should Oei have notified the young man's mother that her son had received a semi-nude photo of a schoolmate? Perhaps, but whether his failure to do so was sufficient justification for trying to trump up charges of child pornography against him is another matter altogether.

- U.S. Representative Tip O'Neill was well-known for the saying that "all politics is local," and it is something that educators should always keep in mind. If a local prosecutor is hell-bent on making a name for himself or herself, there's nothing quite like a student sexting case in a socially and religiously conservative district to gin up some headlines. (A not irrelevant piece of news: in 2019, Plowman was appointed to a seat on the state Circuit Court for Loudon County and the surrounding area.) When it comes to dealing with any situation at the intersection of students and sex, educators and administrators need to be particularly careful about how they proceed.

- Oei's summary echoes the plaintive question of former United States Labor Secretary Ray Donovan, who was charged in 1987 with grand larceny and fraud in connection with a construction project in New York. After being acquitted of all charges, he famously asked, "Which office do I go to get my reputation back?" But Donovan had the relative benefit of experiencing his travails before the World Wide Web came along to tattoo each of us with our successes and failures; as a result, the prosecution against him has mostly faded into historical obscurity. Oei's experience may well be an extreme example of the toxic mix of prosecutorial zeal, self-righteous parenting, and technological ignorance. The cold reality, however, is that as a result of a small misstep, any educator could find himself or herself stamped forever online with the label of "child pornographer." Educators should insist that their districts adopt clear and well-vetted procedures for handling potentially sensitive material during in-school investigations.

Relevant MCEE Provisions for Chapter 29

Principle I: Responsibility to the Profession

Standards I.A.2 and I.A.3

Principle II: Responsibility for Professional Competence

Standard II.C.3

Principle III: Responsibility to Students

Standards III.B.3, III.C.1, III.C.2, and III.C.3

Principle IV: Responsibility to the School Community

Standard IV.B.3

Principle V: Responsible and Ethical Use of Technology

Standards V.A.5, V.A.6, V.B.1, V.B.2, and V.B.3

Sources

The sources for the Cautionary Tales in this chapter can be viewed at the following URL:

https://link.cybertraps.com/C4E2-Sources-Chap29

Chapter 30

Obstruction of Justice and Spoliation of Evidence

Overview

Obstruction of justice and **spoliation of evidence** are two different types of interference with an ongoing or potential legal proceeding. Each is a serious offense that can result in significant legal consequences. Technically, only one—obstruction of justice—is a criminal offense; however, since the conduct in each instance is roughly the same, it makes sense to discuss them in the same chapter.

Obstruction of Justice

Compared to the other types of crimes discussed in this section, there are relatively few instances in which obstruction of justice is the main focus of a prosecution. It is much more common for prosecutors to treat obstruction or tampering as an additional charge to a more significant offense, such as solicitation or sexual assault of a student.

In those types of cases, what typically happens is that news of the inappropriate behavior begins to leak out, and the educator suddenly realizes that he or she has created a trail of digital evidence so clear that denials will be utterly futile. In a desperate effort to hide the crime and avoid prosecution, however, he or she may try to destroy evidence or ask a student to do so. Sometimes, a colleague or administrator may engage in obstruction or spoliation in a misguided (and criminal) effort to protect a friend or the reputation of the school or district.

Here are just a few reasons why such efforts routinely fail:

- The field of computer forensics grows more sophisticated every day. Investigators have potent tools to recover deleted data from hard drives, USB sticks and external drives, cellphones, gaming consoles, etc.

- Despite the teacher's plea, the student may not have deleted the information. If that is the case, then it's not particularly challenging for investigators to recover potential evidence. But even if the student has tried to delete information, that gives investigators yet another device to examine forensically, increasing the chance that they will recover incriminating evidence.

- Backups, stored either on a computer in the cloud, may contain copies of incriminating messages or photos.

- The student may have shared the digital information to someone else (another student, a parent, an administrator, law enforcement, etc.).

- Someone (most likely a concerned parent) may have saved a screenshot of suspicious messages or used another smartphone to take a photo.

The point should be clear: when any uses a digital device to commit a crime, it is challenging to get rid of the data. There is an old saying, particularly in politics, that the coverup is worse than the crime. That is not true, of course, when a case involves actual physical or emotional harm to a child. Nonetheless, it is almost always futile to try to destroy electronic evidence. If you attempt to do so, the chances are good that you will only increase your likelihood of conviction and lengthen your prison sentence.

U.S. law defines the crime of **obstruction of justice** as "interference with the orderly administration of law and justice." There are over 20 different acts which can constitute obstruction of justice under federal law, including:

- Influencing or injuring an officer or juror generally (18 U.S.C. § 1503);

- Obstruction of proceedings before departments, agencies, and committees (18 U.S.C. § 1505);

- Obstruction of criminal investigations (18 U.S.C. § 1510);

- Obstruction of state or local criminal investigations (18 U.S.C. § 1511);

- Tampering with a witness, victim, or an informant (18 U.S.C. § 1512); and/or Retaliating against a witness, victim, or an informant (18 U.S.C. § 1513)

Until recently, the most high-profile obstruction of justice cases in the United States occurred in 1972-1974, when at least five of President Richard Nixon's top aides and associates were convicted of (or pleaded guilty to) obstruction charges for their role in covering up the Watergate break-in. The House of Representatives also included a charge of obstruction of justice in the Articles of Impeachment filed against the President himself.

Somewhat more recently, prosecutors filed a high-profile obstruction of justice charge levied against Martha Stewart. On December 27, 2001, Stewart sold nearly 4,000 shares of stock in a company called ImClone. If she had sold them one day later, she would have lost an estimated $51,000; the price of ImClone dropped dramatically when the news broke that ImClone had failed to get approval for "a key cancer drug."

The Securities and Exchange Commission alleged that Stewart received a tip from her broker, Peter Bacanovic, that ImClone CEO Sam Waksal, was planning on dumping a large amount of the company's stock before the news was made public. By itself, that might not have been enough to get Stewart in trouble; the SEC would have had to prove that Stewart was aware that her broker had violated his ethical duty by tipping her off.

Stewart, however, was sentenced to five months in federal prison for two explicit acts of obstruction: First, when questioned by SEC investigators and the FBI, she denied any knowledge of Waksal's plans to dump his stock; instead, she told investigators that she had previously instructed Baconovic to sell her stock when the price fell to $60 per share. Bocanovic told investigators the same thing. Unfortunately for Stewart, one of Bocanovic's assistants credibly testified at trial that Bocanovic instructed him to tip off Stewart. Second, Stewart's personal assistant testified that her boss had attempted to change the record of a phone message from Bocanovic about ImClone.

Spoliation of Evidence

During every civil lawsuit, the parties engage in a process known as **discovery**. The basic concept of litigation discovery is that each side will exchange any information and documents that might be relevant to the litigation. For instance, if you slip on a banana peel in your local grocery store and break your hip, you might sue the store for the damages you suffered: lost wages, hospital expenses, home care, pain and suffering, etc. During pre-trial discovery, your attorney would probably ask the store to produce information or documentation about how it trains its employees on stocking the fruit section, how often it has employees patrol the aisles to pick up fallen fruit or wipe up spills, and so on. In turn, the attorneys for the store will ask for copies of all your medical bills, your pay stubs, and anything else needed to document your damages.

The goal of pre-trial discovery is to narrow the potential issues that need to be resolved and to facilitate a settlement between the parties. If either side negligently or purposefully destroys relevant information or fails to produce it, then the other party can file a motion in court alleging spoliation of evidence. In this day and age, not surprisingly, one of the most significant temptations for potential spoliation is social media. If you are seeking damages for a broken hip and the defendant learns that you deleted Facebook photos that document your post-accident surfing trip to Oahu, the defendant almost certainly would file a claim of spoliation.

If the judge agrees that spoliation occurred, then she or he can apply several different remedies. The most common is known as the spoliation inference, which means that the court will instruct the finder of fact to interpret the missing evidence in the strongest possible light against the person who destroyed the information or failed to produce it. In our example, the judge could instruct the jury to infer that the deleted surfing photos would prove that your pain and suffering was minimal or even non-existent.

I was born and raised in Boston, so it pains me to admit that the controversy over Tom Brady's cellphone during the so-called Deflategate controversy during the 2014-2015 National Football League (NFL) playoffs is a pretty good example of how spoliation works in legal proceedings. On January 18, 2015, the New England Patriots played the Indianapolis Colts in the championship game of the American Football Conference. Before the game, the Colts had raised concerns with NFL officials that the Patriots were using underinflated footballs (each team supplies its own footballs for each game).

At halftime, game officials measured the air pressure of the balls used by the Patriots and found several with readings below the levels proscribed by the NFL. Officials inflated the footballs to the proper pressure levels before the start of the second half, but if the Patriots enjoyed any benefit from the underinflation, it was pretty minimal. Over the final two quarters of the game, the Patriots went on to score 28 unanswered points and routed the Colts 45-11.

Notwithstanding the lopsided final score and the ongoing confusion over whether the Patriot footballs were underinflated, the NFL decided to investigate the incident. During the probe, investigators asked Patriots quarterback Tom Brady to turn over the cellphone he was using before and after the AFC Championship game. Brady refused to do so, saying that the phone contained a trove of personal and highly-confidential information (ranging from family conversations with his wife, international model Gisele Bündchen, to contract and endorsement discussions with his agents).

It is worthwhile to point out that Brady was under no legal obligation to cooperate with the NFL's investigators. However, it is also true that his refusal to cooperate damaged Brady's reputation, particularly in the court of public opinion. Further damage occurred when investigators revealed that Brady had destroyed the cellphone he used from November 2014 to March 2015 (the four months straddling the championship game) on the same day that Ted Wells, the NFL's lead investigator, was scheduled to interview him about the incident.

In his final report, Wells specifically referenced Brady's failure to produce relevant material from the missing cellphone as damaging his credibility as a witness. Based in part on Brady's behavior, Wells concluded that it was "more probable than not" that Patriot locker room personnel removed some air from the footballs either before or during the championship game. He also found that it was "more probable than not" that Brady was at least "generally aware" of what was going on. NFL Commissioner Roger Goodell cited the destruction of the cellphone when he later announced that Brady would serve a four-game suspension.

Spoliation is a nuanced concept that depends on the particular facts of a case and the state in which it occurs. However, the basic idea should be clear: If you destroy or fail to produce relevant information during the discovery phase of civil or criminal litigation, it can be highly detrimental to your legal rights and your public reputation.

Cautionary Tales

Cautionary Tale 30-2018-IN

For the better part of eight years, beginning in 2010, Aaron Lopez Saldana worked as a teacher's aide at the Lake Ridge Middle School in Gary, Indiana. In 2011, Saldana launched a photography club for middle school students and also served as one of the school's cross-country coaches. By 2015, the photography club, which catered to both middle and high school students, had about 40 members.

Saldana, who had a background in wedding and commercial photography, said his goal was to help students develop a better understanding of image and composition. "I feel like we should foster creativity in our children whenever we can," he told one reporter, "and we're so thankful to our school administrators for their support in our endeavors."

One of the meeting places for the photography club was Saldana's home, which was well-stocked with computers and other high-end electronic devices. That equipment proved too great a temptation for former club member Scott Porta and his friend Michael McGregor, who broke into Soldana's home in the early hours of December 12, 2018. The pair swiped an impressive quantity of stuff, including a laptop, an external drive, an Xbox, an iPhone, various USB drives, three rifles, and a handgun. Saldana discovered the burglary later that same day and submitted a police report listing the missing items.

What Saldana didn't know was that while he was in the house, Porta found a black photo album under Saldana's bed. He later told police that when he opened it, he saw hundreds of Polaroid photos showing young boys "in various stages of undress." He quickly returned the album to its hiding place.

After leaving Saldana's house, Porta looked at some of the USB flash drives he had stolen and discovered videos that showed Saldana in "sexual positions" with young boys. For obvious reasons, Porta was reluctant to tell the police what he had found on the flash drives, but he did describe what he had seen to a female friend. The young woman, who was still a student in the school district, met with school officials and police detectives to report what her friend had found.

After a routine traffic stop later that same week, Porta agreed to an interview with Gary police. He admitted to the break-in and described in detail what he had seen in Saldana's home and in the electronic files he stole. Following the interview, the police charged both Porta and his friend McGregor with burglary.

Law enforcement officials used the information Porta provided to obtain warrants to arrest Saldana and search his house. On December 15, when police showed up at Soldana's home to execute the warrants, they found him outside burning photographs in his grill. On the ground next to the grill, police founded partially melted photographic negatives. Assuming that the partial photos and negatives depicted scenes of a criminal nature, there's not much question that the police found a smoking grill for the crime of obstruction.

Although the police ultimately located and seized the black photo album seen by Porta, there were no longer any photos in it. However, police did recover "hundreds of photograph negative strips." Similarly, investigators located numerous computers in Saldana's home but discovered that "components [i.e., hard drives] had been removed from them." Saldana told investigators that a friend had tipped him off that the Gary Police Department had started a child pornography investigation against him.

A review of the digital files stolen by Porta made it clear that the boys depicted in the videos were unaware of the fact that someone was recording them. When the police search Saldana's home, they looked for and located a camera hidden in his bathroom, which Saldana used to record boys while they were changing, showering, or using the toilet.

In January 2019, Saldana pleaded not guilty to the charges of child pornography, voyeurism, and obstruction of justice. The state of Indiana is continuing to examine the digital evidence in the case.

Top Three Takeaways:

- "Information wants to be free." Once you create digital content of any description, it is extraordinarily difficult to keep it from spreading. You might reasonably argue that the only reason the police caught Saldana was that two teens burgled his house, which is a relatively unusual circumstance. That may be true, but it is also a foreseeable circumstance. The odds are good that if someone broke into Saldana's house, they would either see or steal some of the massive amounts of contraband he created. I think it is also fair to say, based on my research, that this information would have eventually gained its freedom somehow, in some other way. That's just the nature of the digital beast. If you really, really don't want other people seeing something your data, then don't create it in the first place.

- The only time that computer forensics experts are truly frustrated is when they don't have a device to inspect. When someone tipped Saldana off, that gave him time to remove and possibly destroy (or at least successfully hide) his computer hard drives. By removing the hard drives, Saldana avoided charges for any crimes based on what might have been on those drives.

However, prosecutors could use the act of removing the drives as evidence supporting an obstruction of justice charge.

- For school districts, this cautionary tale is a good reminder that they should closely supervise after school clubs. I don't want to cast unfair aspersions, but that is probably particularly true for clubs that involve extensive use of digital cameras or video recorders (which, of course, includes every smartphone). And I think that a district should think long and hard about allowing any educator to run a district-sanctioned after school program out of his or her home.

Cautionary Tale 30-2018-FL

An off-hand comment by a parent to a 14-year-old boy wound up sending a 27-year-old Florida teacher to prison for three years. In early 2018, a male teacher at New Smyrna Beach Middle School called the boy's house and asked one of his parents if he could mentor the boy. The parent thought the conversation was a little odd, "and jokingly asked the teen whether he [the teacher] was going to molest him." Bursting into tears, the boy said, "Anyone could molest you."

The boy then admitted to his parent that he had been sneaking out at night to meet his former 7th-grade science teacher, Stephanie Peterson Ferri, who would pick him up in her car and take him back to her house to have sex. He also said that she purchased marijuana and smoking paraphernalia for him.

In a subsequent interview with police, the student told police that the assault began when he was in the 8th grade. He said that he would visit Peterson in her classroom to talk about various topics, including Peterson's ongoing divorce (which was finalized one month after her arrest). At one point, Peterson let the boy use her smartphone to log onto Instagram. After he left, she saw that he had not logged out, and she sent him a message that "sparked the relationship." Throughout Peterson's assault of the student, she used Snapchat and text messaging to send him nude photos of herself and to request intimate pictures from him in return.

When Peterson learned that the boy had told his parent about the molestation, her messages switched from seductive to desperate. "So she's planning on doing something with it," Peterson wrote. She followed that with a plea for sympathy:

> Pleas [*sic*] tell her it was the worst decision of my life and I know it was and idk where my brain was but that I somehow fell in love with you briefly and idk why and I'll never be the same person because of it.

She finished by telling the student (futilely) to "delete everything."

Prosecutors could have used that last message as the basis for a separate obstruction of justice charge, but in this case, they elected not to do so. In October 2018, Peterson pleaded guilty "to one count of lewd or lascivious battery sex act with a child and one count of transmission of harmful material to minors by electronic means." She faced the possibility of up to 10 years in prison, but in December 2018, the judge sentenced her to just three years behind bars. Upon her release, she will serve an additional two years under house arrest and five years of sex offender probation.

Top Three Takeaways:

- Snapchat is a particularly dangerous app for educators. It traffics in the mythology of the disappearing message or image when, in reality, there are numerous ways its content can be captured and redistributed. But because people believe that the material is self-deleting and, therefore, irrecoverable, it sometimes encourages people to engage in inappropriate behavior. I suspect many might not do so if they realized that law enforcement might bring charges based on the evidence they themselves have created. Here's a reasonably bright line: if you find yourself communicating directly with a student via Snapchat, you should discuss the situation with a colleague or supervisor. If you are not willing to do so, then you have a problem.

- It is quite remarkable how often marital problems or a pending divorce contribute to these types of assaults. Privacy, of course, is highly valued in the United States, and we don't necessarily want our employers or colleagues to be too intrusive into our personal lives. But that does place a premium on each educator's ethical duties of self-awareness and self-care. The more structures a district or school can put into place to aid educators in meeting those duties, the less likely it will be that a vulnerable educator will turn to students for the emotional support he or she needs.

- Few phrases are more damning or more futile than "Delete everything." First, since we create so much digital content so quickly these days, it is almost impossible to remember where everything is stored. Second, as I've repeatedly pointed out, while you can "delete" an electronic file, that does not necessarily mean that you have destroyed it. And third, you can never know whether or not someone has made a copy or when the data might reappear. It is far, far better not to get into these types of situations in the first place since cover-ups rarely work.

Cautionary Tale 30-2017-CO

Healthy professional relationships that form amongst teachers and administrators are valuable components of a well-functioning school community. A building staff that has strong bonds of collegiality and friendship is more likely to provide a positive learning community for students. However, those same bonds of friendship can cloud personal judgment when something goes wrong.

This cautionary tale illustrates that concern. In June 2017, local television station Denver7 reported that "[a] Douglas County High School teacher faces sexual exploitation of a child and obscenity charges after his arrest earlier this month." Douglas County High School is located in Castle Rock, Colorado, about 30 miles south of Denver.

Denver7 identified the teacher as 41-year-old Brian Stebbins, who was arrested by local police on June 2. Initially, the specifics of the case were kept under seal by local officials. However, the police later revealed that a minor female had sent "several nude or partially nude photos of herself to Stebbins, and Stebbins responded by sending the student videos of his exposed genitals."

On June 7, school principal Tony Kappas sent out a letter to parents that read in part:

> One of our teachers is currently involved in an ongoing law enforcement investigation.

> According to the Douglas County Sheriff's Office (DCSO), Brian Stebbins was recently arrested on charges of sexual exploitation of a child and obscenity.

> When these concerns were shared with me, I immediately reached out to our partners at the [Douglas County Sheriff's Office]. As this is an ongoing investigation, I am unable to share further details surrounding the investigation, but I can reassure you that Mr. Stebbins is currently on leave, pending the outcome of this situation. This is difficult news to share and something I take very seriously.

Denver7 investigative reporter Tony Kovaleski was curious about why the school district did not notify parents about the charges against Stebbins until nearly a week after his arrest in June. He filed a request under the Colorado Public Records Act for relevant school communications, including any text messages sent by Principal Kappas on his school-issued phone. The released material raised some serious questions as to whether Stebbins, a good friend of Kappas, had received preferential treatment despite the seriousness of the allegations against him.

The records showed that the district placed Stebbins on administrative leave on May 24, some days following a complaint about him by a parent. (It is not clear whether that parent was connected to the minor victim.) Stebbins and Kappas remained in frequent contact by text message; on the day Stebbins was placed on leave, he texted Kappas that "This morning felt awful. To have someone tell me I couldn't be in my room hurt bad." Kappas replied: "I can only imagine. It's tearing me up also just so you know. So sorry. Stay strong buddy."

Subsequent messages indicated that Kappas and other administrators frequently contacted the sheriff's office in an attempt to gather information about the Stebbins investigation. On April 2, for instance, Kappas texted Stebbins: "I left multiple messages with the detective and played phone tag until late into Friday night. So I'm hoping something breaks tomorrow."

Three days later, Kappas wrote: "Nor Dean and I have Heard anything at this point. I know Dist. has made multiple contacts and calls to the upper levels at the Sheriffs Office. Head of district security was given no information. We are more than perplexed with the situation and the timeliness of this issue."

Denver7 showed the messages between Kappas and Stebbins to Douglas County Sheriff Tony Spurlock, who referred them to the office of 18th Judicial District Attorney George Brauchler. His concern, Sheriff Spurlock said, "was that [Kappas and Stebbins] tried to obstruct us. And the totality of the circumstances were that we didn't feel that they did ... they didn't get in the way and they didn't interfere with us gathering any information."

On April 24, 2018, Stebbins pleaded guilty to one count of promoting obscenity to a minor (the video he sent); prosecutors dropped the charge of sexual exploitation of a minor as part of the plea deal. He was sentenced to 60 days in prison, placed on the sex offender registry, and ordered to attend 20 counseling sessions and a healthy sexual boundaries class.

Top Three Takeaways:

- Although Kappas avoided any charges, this incident illustrates how easily even relatively innocuous conversations can be viewed in a negative light. When a member of a school community faces serious charges, colleagues of that individual should be cautious about what they say, particularly when communicating electronically. From an ethical perspective, the multiple relationships in which administrators and educators found themselves contributed to the issues raised by the facts of this case. It is natural for friendships to arise in the school community, but if a problem arises, administrators should honor their duty to the school community first.

- The primary purpose of state public records statutes is to capture these types of communications and to make them available to the public. Some people may try to avoid using official communication channels to prevent sunshine law scrutiny, but that's not a good idea: Purposely evading public records act requirements is itself a crime. You should also be aware that if you use a non-public communication channel for something that is, in fact, public business, that may open up all of your personal email, texts, etc. to public records act or FOIA requests.

- This cautionary tale also helps underscore the importance of prompt and transparent communication by school officials to parents. If Kappas had notified parents of Stebbins's arrest within 24-48 hours, would Kovaleski have thought to file a public records act request? The point of this is not to encourage administrators to act ethically in one area to hide unethical conduct in another but to illustrate how easily these situations can develop in unexpected ways.

Cautionary Tale 30-2016-FL

At the beginning of the new school year in 2015, the parents of a 14-year-old Florida boy first learned that he was sexually active when they found a stash of condoms in his room and a series of explicit messages on his Instagram feed. They were shocked when they realized that their son had been having sex with Sara Moore, a substitute teacher for the Osceola County schools (including the St. Cloud Middle School attended by the victim).

Ten days after the police initially arrested her, detectives re-arrested Moore on a charge of attempting to tamper with police evidence. During the investigation into Moore's assault on the teen, St. Cloud officers took possession of her cellphone, which they believed contained evidence of the assaults. The officers informed Moore that they would store the phone in the department's evidence lock-up pending issuance of a search warrant to examine the phone's contents.

On the afternoon of January 13, 2016, Moore drove to a Verizon store and asked the staff to assist her in remotely wiping the information on her phone. It is somewhat unbelievable, but she actually told the Verizon employees that she needed their help remotely wiping her phone because the police were holding it. But instead of providing Moore with the requested assistance, the Verizon staff called the police, who then came and arrested Moore for the second time in two weeks.

Even without Verizon's assistance, Moore did interfere with the police investigation. A prosecutor told a state judge that when police removed the phone from the evidence lock-up, it now required a passcode, which made it impossible for them to execute the search warrant. Moore's attorney argued that she had merely asked Verizon for assistance in activating her daughter's old phone so she would have one to use until the police returned her phone. The judge was not convinced and ordered that Moore be held in jail without bail pending trial.

In August 2017, the 37-year-old former teacher was sentenced under a plea agreement to ten years in prison for her sexual assault on the teen, less the 581 days she had already served following the suspension of her bail for the alleged phone tampering. Before agreeing to the plea deal, Moore was facing as many as 37 years in prison. She was also required to register as a sex offender.

At the sentencing, her attorney read from a letter that Moore wrote, which said in part: "I am remorseful for my actions. They were caused by a lapse in judgment that led to a huge mistake." Her attorney added that Moore is suffering from "a personality disorder, brought on or made worse by the passing of a younger sister."

The prosecutor, in turn, offered a letter from the father of the victim, who called Moore a "monster." "The accused has caused my son to hurt on a minute-by-minute basis, changing the lives of all connected."

Top Three Takeaways:

- The first law of holes is, "If you find yourself in a hole, stop digging." Many of the cautionary tales in this book illustrate what can happen when an educator makes one wrong decision and then decides to follow it up with at least one more (and sometimes many more). The impulse to try one more thing in an attempt to avoid serious legal consequences can be overwhelming, but every educator should try to avoid the temptation. Additional digging is very, very unlikely to make the situation any better.

- Do not rely on the willingness of others to help you keep digging. Most people are law-abiding and recognize that it is not a good idea to become an accessory to a criminal act. That is particularly true for employees in tech-related jobs at cellular phone companies, big-box electronics stores, computer repair shops, and so on. Such employees typically receive training specifically designed to alert them to possible criminal activity and to teach them what they should do when they see evidence of wrongdoing. Of course, if the customer explicitly says that she wants help doing something illegal, that generally removes any doubt.

- Can you be compelled to turn over the passcode to your mobile device? That's an interesting question for which there is no good answer right now. The issue has not been addressed yet by the U.S. Supreme Court or many state supreme courts, so the answer still very much depends on the local jurisdiction in which you live. Some local state courts have granted warrants that allow police to compel you to give a fingerprint or open your phone with your face but won't force you to reveal a numeric passcode. Others have ruled that if the police have a valid search warrant, they are entitled to whatever information is needed to open the phone. This issue will be the subject of considerable litigation in the years to come.

Cautionary Tale 30-2012-OH

The towns of Weirton, West Virginia and Steubenville, Ohio, sit on opposite sides of the Ohio River, just 45 miles due west of Pittsburgh. Apart from the shared waters of the Ohio, two significant things bind the communities. The first is an economy long based on coal and steel, with all the modern-day hardship that implies. The second is high school football. The iconic series "Friday Night Lights" may have been set in west-central Texas, but it just as easily could have used the rugged western Appalachian hills as its backdrop. And few towns in the area are as passionate about their team as Steubenville.

> Big Red games are played in a 10,000-seat stadium, gigantic for a high school in a town of just more than 18,000. A red stallion named Man o' War rears atop the scoreboard, ready to shoot 6-foot-high flames from its mouth when the home team scores. Games are shown on television, and the slogan "Roll Red Roll" is plastered everywhere.

As is standard across the country, Steubenville students decided to celebrate the end of the 2012 summer with a bunch of parties. On Saturday, August 11, a young woman crossed the Ohio River from Weirton to hang out with friends and party in Steubenville. Throughout the evening, she consumed too much alcohol and possibly was drugged. Around midnight, things began to go downhill quickly.

A police investigation and subsequent trial testimony revealed that she left one party with four Steubenville football players. They took her to a second party, at which she got sick and appeared "out of it." After 20 minutes or so, the players took her to the home of a fifth student. The victim was sexually assaulted during the car ride and again in the basement of the student's home. The following morning, the young woman woke up naked in the basement with no recollection of the previous evening or how she had gotten into the basement.

Sadly, the type of assault that the young woman suffered in Steubenville is not uncommon and, under normal circumstances, would not have garnered much media coverage outside the local area. What elevated this case to a national scandal was the fact that it was documented in real-time by the perpetrators and witnesses using smartphones and a variety of social media platforms. Many were shocked by the callous indifference the perpetrators, witnesses, and social media users showed towards the victim, and by the sheer speed with which images of her assault spread around the world. Overnight, we all got a crash course in the toxic and tragic possibilities of combining social media, alcohol, and adolescent behavior.

As *The New York Times* documented in excruciating detail, the investigation of the assault was complicated. There was a delay before the victim and her parents reported the crime to police, which made the recovery of physical evidence (including toxicology) difficult. Many party-goers, all potential witnesses, refused to cooperate with police or said that they couldn't remember anything about the evening. A significant percentage of the community dismissed the victim's allegations, saying that it was merely an effort to weaken the Big Red team or that the victim was responsible for making herself vulnerable.

Despite the large quantity of social media and forensic evidence (police ended up seizing and searching multiple phones, iPads, and computers), the police had a surprisingly difficult time putting together a case. Ultimately, however, they charged sophomore quarterback Trent Mays with rape and distributing child pornography (a photo of the victim lying naked on the floor) and wide receiver Ma'lik Richmond with rape. Prosecutors tried the two young men as juveniles, and both were convicted in March 2017. The judge sentenced Mays to two years in juvenile detention and Richmond to one.

Mays and Richmond were not the only ones who faced charges arising out of the sexual assault case. In October 2013, police arrested and jailed Steubenville High School IT Director William Rhinaman on charges of "tampering with evidence, obstructing justice, obstructing official business and perjury[.]"

A month later, Michael McVey, the superintendent of the Steubenville City Schools, was indicted for tampering with evidence and two counts of obstructing justice. He also faced misdemeanor charges for making a false statement and obstructing official business. When law enforcement searched Steubenville school offices and computers, they discovered that McVey had ordered Rhinaman to delete potentially relevant evidence, notwithstanding a court order requiring its preservation. Investigators also learned that McVey had created false documents and had ordered others to do so as well.

Finally, investigators discovered evidence of a second sexual assault involving members of the Big Red team that allegedly occurred four months earlier, in April 2012. The young woman involved in that case only came forward after the publicity surrounding the later assault. Fearing further damage to the district's vaunted gridiron program, McVey tried to hide any information about the second assault allegation.

In February 2015, Rhinaman pleaded guilty to one of the lesser charges brought against him—obstructing official business—in exchange for the dropping of the other counts. The court sentenced him to 90 days in jail, with 80 days suspended provided that he completed one year of community control and 40 hours of community service.

For reasons that are not entirely clear, Mays managed to avoid any jail time. He did, however, lose his administrator position: Prosecutors agreed to drop all charges against him in exchange for his resignation from the Steubenville City Schools. Following McVey's departure, the district referred him to the Office of Professional Conduct in the Ohio Department of Education. The DoE decided not to take any disciplinary action against him. Eight months later, he was hired by the Switzerland of Ohio Local School District (just 90 minutes down Ohio-7 South) to serve as the principal of River Elementary School.

Top Three Takeaways:

- The charges filed against McVey and Rhinaman offer some particularly powerful lessons for educators about the potential cybertrap of obstruction of justice. The first lesson is that these prosecutions highlight the unpredictable nature of criminal investigations.

- The second lesson is that educators and school staff need to be prepared to exercise independent judgment when confronted with ethically questionable or improper requests from superiors. IT Director Rhinaman was put in an awkward position when Superintendent McVey asked him to delete some material from his office computer. Even if Rhinaman did not know about the court order requiring preservation of data, a reasonable person would raise questions about a non-routine request to delete information, particularly given the events that had recently occurred in the community. Of course, given Rhinaman's position as IT Director, it is unlikely that he was unaware of an order for the district to preserve data. The severity of the charges strongly suggests that prosecutors had substantial evidence that Rhinaman was aware of the court's order when he complied with McVey's request.

- The third lesson is one that accompanies many if not most of the cybertraps discussed in this book: the personal and professional consequences of unethical conduct can be severe.

Relevant MCEE Provisions for Chapter 30

Principle I: Responsibility to the Profession

Standards I.A.2, I.A.3, I.A.5, I.B.3, I.B.4, and I.B.5

Sources

The sources for the Cautionary Tales in this chapter can be viewed at the following URL:

https://link.cybertraps.com/C4E2-Sources-Chap30

Conclusion

Overview

Five years ago, when I wrote and published the first version of this book, my goal was to help educators better understand the risks associated with the use of digital technology. It is clear from even a cursory view of the headlines that there is still a lot more work to do in this area. Teachers continue to stumble into avoidable cybertraps or purposely misuse technology to the detriment of their students, their careers, and their school communities.

Much of that has to do with the acceleration of long-standing technological trends: the nearly universal use of mobile devices by teachers and students, the steady increase in the number of communication and social media apps, and the relentless push to incorporate digital communication tools into virtually all aspects of K-12 education. In a world grappling with a pandemic caused by a novel virus, that last trend was perhaps inevitable. Unfortunately, however, our professional and social norms are struggling to keep up with the technological onslaught.

The Model Code of Ethics for Educators (MCEE), introduced six months after publication of the first edition of *Cybertraps for Educators*, is a potentially powerful resource for the development of effective professional and community norms for educators. As I hope this new version illustrates, the application of the MCEE to various real-world situations can provide insight into the factors, both technological and personal, that contribute to acts of misconduct and malfeasance.

Much of the conclusory advice that I offered in the initial version, I'm pleased to report, is just as relevant five years later as it was back then. Here are the main points, with appropriate edits and updates.

Click in Haste, Repent at Leisure

Five-plus years of research and writing on this topic have convinced me of the following: the single most powerful step you can take to avoid most if not all cybertraps is to **slow down**.

That can be extremely difficult to do. If you look back, every new communication technology has ratcheted up the speed of our lives, but none compare to the internet. The acceleration caused by the World Wide Web, mobile devices, and social media has been breathtaking. The impact of these technologies on our lives is not merely accidental. Engineers and programmers have made specific choices in the design of devices and software to intensify our emotional responses and heighten our engagement.

As a result, mindfulness and reflection are no longer just guru-led exercises at some hippy-dippy retreat; they are valuable professional skills that every educator should cultivate.

If you think there is a chance that an email, a Facebook post, a tweet, or even a text message will get you in trouble, then ask another adult for their opinion before clicking send." (Of course, if you don't want another adult to see what you are writing, then that is a bright red flag right there.) If another adult is not handy at the moment, then make this your mantra: **Write. Pause. Reflect. Send.**

Take a short walk. Feed the dog or cat. Read what you wrote out loud. Water the plants. Call your mother. It doesn't matter what exactly you do, just put some time between the drafting and transmission of any significant or sensitive communication.

"Educator, Google Thyself!"

Thanks to the long memory of social media services and the data storage capacity of search engines like Google, Bing, Duck Duck Go, *etc.*, we are all in the business of reputation management these days. How people perceive us is often as much about how we appear online as we do in person.

Since school communities expect educators to serve as role models, you have a powerful incentive to monitor and maintain your brand. Fair warning: it's not easy to do. But the more effort you put into it, the better off you and your career will be.

First, take responsibility for what you can control, which includes the content you share with the world. Make intelligent decisions about what you post and where. What may have seemed hysterically funny when you were a sophomore in college is probably not as funny now that you are educating other people's children. That's an adult responsibility, and your social media presence should inspire confidence that you are prepared to meet it maturely.

Second, monitor what people post about you. Have you been tagged in unflattering or embarrassing photos? Ask the poster to pull them down. Has someone said something untrue or unfair? Again, ask if they will take it down or, at the very least, reword it. There are not many effective legal remedies in situations like these, but often, a polite request and a brief explanation can accomplish a lot.

Third, spend some time thinking about your digital past. Is there content that *you* put online that should come down? We all change as we age, and posts that we wrote 5, 10, even 15 years ago may no longer reflect who we are or what we believe. Those old posts, however, have a nasty habit of resurfacing, as any number of celebrities can attest.

You don't have to hand-curate every Facebook post, tweet, or Instagram photo; there are a variety of software solutions available that will bulk-delete social media content based on specific criteria, including the age of the post. I know of some celebrities and public figures, for instance, who by default, delete everything older than three months. Another alternative is to hire a reputation-management firm that can not only help you remove unflattering internet content but can also assist you in creating and posting more positive content.

Fourth, make an honest assessment of whether there is any off-line activity that might resurface online. The risk of this is highest, unfortunately, if your past work has anything to do with sex in general or adult entertainment in particular. Of course, controversial political activism or online fights are also fair game. You obviously can't erase history, but you can prepare yourself to explain what happened and to provide context to anyone who wants more information.

The Future Is Always Waiting

Given the inherent impossibility of the project, it's pretty amazing how much time people spend trying to predict the future. Most of the time, we can't successfully predict next year's iPhone features, let alone anything more substantive. But trends are somewhat easier to spot, and there are two on which all educators should keep a close eye.

First, the infiltration of the internet into our daily lives will steadily accelerate, by which I mean the collection of data, the ubiquity of social media, the indexing of information, *etc.* Every minute of the day, we leach a staggering amount of personal data into our individual data spheres. A daunting array of harvesters—government agencies, corporations both online and off, and the myriad devices that we carry with us—are poised eagerly to collect it.

For good reason, many of us question whether our ability to control the information we generate, the core concept of personal privacy, has been irrevocably lost. The jury may still be out on that question, but the future is not promising. For educators (and other public figures like politicians, celebrities, and so on), our already tiny zone of privacy will continue to shrink even further.

Second, the technology that leads to many of the cybertraps discussed earlier will only get smaller, faster, and cheaper. Educators will need to be continually vigilant against the temptations that these new technologies present. As we've seen, shrinking camera sizes have already induced some educators into acts of voyeurism that they might never otherwise have attempted with larger or louder cameras.

Similar to global warming or airline consolidation, these are not developments that can be reversed by a single individual. But you can make individual decisions that improve or worsen your position relative to these trends.

Choose Your Friends Carefully

Repeat after me: Facebook is not your friend. Mark Zuckerberg and Sheryl Sandberg are not your friends. No social media service or social media executive is your friend. Their job is not to be your friend, but instead, to figure out how to make their companies profitable so that financial analysts on CNBC (who are not their friends either) won't savage them and trash their stock price.

Social media sites are busily trying to figure out exactly how to be profitable. There is one thing that is an essential part of every conceivably viable social media business plan: your information—all of the information that you post online, how often and with whom you share, the identity of your friends, the information they share with you, the information of yours that they share with THEIR friends, and so on, and so on, *ad infinitum*. What this means in practical terms is that social media companies want you to have an extensive friend/follower list and want you to share as much information as possible with all of them. But if you're an educator, that's not in your best interest.

Here's just one piece of the problem: Facebook, chief among the social media services, has persuaded over one-seventh of the world's entire population that its social media service is the equivalent of an electronic diary for its users, a place where we can record our thoughts, dreams, political opinions, *etc.* But it's not a diary; instead, it's a personal newspaper that can be read by our friends, their friends, or the entire world, depending on privacy settings (which, of course, screen capture and other easy-to-use techniques can easily breach). Facebook wants to make the act of updating our "status" so automatic (you can even do it with your cellphone!) that we don't engage whatever internal filters we might have to determine whether we SHOULD update our status.

Given the corporate and social pressures associated with social media, accidents will happen, and educators will post things that they should not. But you don't have to be one of those educators. If you take the time to make some structural changes in your social media habits, you can reduce the chances that the *Daily Mail* or the *New York Post* will bestow immortal internet infamy upon you.

The Empathy Quagmire

As you read the Cautionary Tales in this book, you likely reassured yourself that you would never stumble into the most severe types of educator misconduct. I am sure that many of the teachers I've discussed in this book had precisely the same thought. But many adults go through phases of their lives during which they are more vulnerable and needy, and more at risk of doing something they will later regret.

The first step in avoiding the various cybertraps that I've described is to know what they are and how easily they can happen.

The second step is to pay attention to your own mental and emotional state. Assuming for the moment that you're not an innate predator, the challenge is to know when you might potentially be vulnerable to a breach of professional standards. A little earlier, I talked about the importance of periodically searching to see what information has been posted about you online. It is equally essential for you routinely to evaluate your mental and emotional health. How are you coping with the various stresses in your life, both in and out of the classroom? If you feel your professional and personal boundaries beginning to erode, it is your professional and ethical responsibility to seek help.

But here's the catch. Most of the educators that I've met over the years (including various family members) chose to enter the profession because they have a genuine, even passionate desire to teach kids and help them achieve their potential. A significant part of being a good teacher, particularly during high school, is the ability to communicate with sometimes surly and hormonally volatile children and to empathize with them about the challenges they face as they transition to adulthood.

My friend and colleague Troy Hutchings often points out in his lectures that all too often, the teachers who are the most empathetic and the most successful in communicating with students are the ones most at risk for the boundary violations. Their overwhelming desire to mentor and to help can all too easily create an emotional bond that, in turn, can lead to inappropriate communication and even an inappropriate relationship.

One of the critical warning signs of the empathy quagmire is a growing desire to keep your communication with the student secret. Unfortunately, the technological tools available today make it much easier and more tempting to engage in seemingly private conversations with students.

Make no mistake -- if you are going to communicate with a student electronically, then it should be through a mediated service, one that others can access in real-time or through a subsequent review of archives. Best practices include:

- The school email system, which stores copies of all emails on the school servers;

- A Facebook or other social media group set up for an entire class, with access by school administrators or parents.

Here are some obvious pitfalls to avoid: one-to-one text messages; private chats on Facebook or other messenger services; direct messages on Twitter, Instagram or any other social media service; surreptitious email accounts; and so on. If you find yourself doing any of these things (or some variant that pops up in the future), then you should be questioning your motivations and your commitment to remaining an educator. If these are impulses that you don't feel you can restrain, a new career may be your smartest choice.

I've had numerous discussions about this with educators around the country, and I know that some people passionately believe that it is essential to communicate with kids on the channels and platforms kids are most comfortable using. It's hard enough, they argue, to reach kids without requiring them to use communication tools that they feel are hopelessly outdated (like email).

I understand that argument; I know, for instance, that my odds of getting a response from one of my sons rise dramatically if I just send them a text message. But there are two reasons for school boards and administrators to draw a line in the sand on this issue.

First, the risks for educators far outweigh the rewards. In today's climate, it is much too easy for parents or colleagues to draw the wrong conclusion if they discover that you are engaging in private or secretive communication with a particular student. You may have the best of intentions, but it still looks terrible.

Second, transparent communication is much more likely to be professional communication. If you are aware that other people can read what you've written and that they know you wrote it, then you are much less likely to start discussing the more personal areas of a student's life.

Let me reiterate: I know that many teachers naturally feel a desire to give students emotional support when they are having a difficult time. The reality, however, is that educators do not receive training in social work, counseling, or therapy when they get their teacher certification. There will always be a little overlap between teaching and advice, and it is undoubtedly better to have friendly teachers than not. But everyone in a school community will be better off and safer if educators maintain strict boundaries and call in trained experts to take over when students need help with personal or emotional difficulties.

Be a Role Model for Good Online Behavior

The expectation that teachers will serve as positive role models for their students is long-established and not likely to diminish any time soon. Frankly, that's not the worst thing in the world. Students can always benefit from additional positive role models, particularly as our society navigates the rocky transition to an increasingly digital world.

Educators have the twin advantages of authority and a captive audience. Given the amount of time that students spend with teachers, it's not unreasonable to expect that school districts and educators should play an active role in raising good citizens and cybercitizens. Here are a few suggestions on how you can best do that.

The starting place for being a positive digital role model is in your overall demeanor and your online and real-life communications. Educators have spent decades working to establish that teaching is a **profession** (which, of course, is one of the reasons for the development of the MCEE). You should honor that work by professionally conducting yourself both online or off. Students will notice when you don't (as will their parents).

There's no question that most educators understand the basics of dealing professionally with parents and students in real life. One of the challenges, however, is that we are all still in the early stages of developing norms for online communications. One of the many risks of engaging students through unmediated, non-transparent, one-to-one communication channels is that it intrinsically weakens your aura of professionalism, wholly apart from what you say or do.

That same impulse, however, implicitly undercuts vital elements of professionalism: not only authority and respect, but the more intangible distance and objectivity that are a natural (and deserved) by-product of training in a particular field. If you hang out with a student on social media in the late afternoon (or worse, in the middle of the night), it's much more challenging to maintain an appropriate teacher-student relationship in the classroom.

The internet has created numerous profound benefits for educators: every day, teachers can tap into a rapidly-expanding universe of information and knowledge to help enrich their lesson plans. At the same time, however, teachers face the same risks as everyone else: distraction, wasted time, and sheer inappropriateness.

That's one of the benefits of only using mediated channels to communicate with students and their parents: The presence of a broader audience is a natural check to inappropriate behavior. Given how easy it is to stumble into improper conduct on the internet, we need all the help we can get.

Be an Advocate for Good District Policies, Procedures, and Practices

Beyond being a good digital role model for students, the next best thing that any educator can do is to advocate for good district policies, procedures, and practices. Such advocacy, among other things, can help to affirm educator professionalism, protect your due process rights, and promote confidence in the public schools and the people who teach in them. It is not easy to find the time to do all this, obviously, but it is essential work.

Policy advocacy is particularly vital concerning how educators should use technology in and out of the classroom. The standards and best practices for such use are continually evolving, as new hardware and software follow relentless upgrade cycles. Educators should be at the forefront of discussions regarding how various technologies can enhance the learning process and aid their students without crossing important boundaries and damaging educator professionalism.

It's often tricky for newly-minted or inexperienced teachers to find ways to influence district policies. Technology, however, is a field in which even the most fresh-faced educators can have a significant impact on policy debates. Younger educators bring many essential advantages to the table: They tend to have a much greater familiarity with recent and emerging technologies; they are generally more familiar with how students are using those technologies; and they can talk about and apply their personal experience of being educated in a post-World Wide Web world.

Here are two specific places to start to become an active advocate for good cyber policies in your school district.

First, research your district's policies or procedures relating to the use of technology, and familiarize yourself with them. Even now, two and a half decades into the World Wide Web, it is still possible that you work in a district that has not adopted formal policies regarding the use of technology. The more likely scenario, however, is that you will discover that your school district does have policies and procedures in place. It is equally possible, however, that those policies and procedures may have been rendered obsolete by changes in technology, ranging from upgrades to hardware to the introduction of new apps and websites.

If your research reveals that your district's policies and procedures are non-existent, inadequate, or simply outdated, then do yourself and your colleagues a favor and start the ball rolling to discuss and update the rules of the cyber road for your students and colleagues.

The vast majority of public school districts, charter schools, and private schools have at least some rudimentary policies relating to acceptable use, integration of technology in the classroom, incident response, *etc.* Perhaps the gold standard in this regard, predictably enough, is the Palo Alto Unified School District in the heart of California's Silicon Valley. On its website, there is a link to the PAUSD Policies and Regulations (stored on the BoardDocs service), which contain comprehensive documents and resources relating to the use of technology in the district.

Not every district needs to take such a thorough approach to technology management and supervision (at least right now). But every school district needs to have some conversation about these issues and adopt guidelines to govern the use and prevent the misuse of digital technology.

Second, you should educate yourself about how best to accomplish change in your district. If you initially conclude that "No change ever occurs in my district," then perhaps you should consider whether you need to change school districts instead of trying to change the district. But if moving to another school district is simply not an option, you can still work to make your community more tech-friendly and tech-savvy.

Unfortunately, advocating for better district technology policies is hardly a guarantee against stumbling into one or more of the cybertraps I've discussed in this book. Very few people get through an entire professional career without a stumble of one sort or another.

However, if you understand your district's policies well enough to advocate for change and improvement, you will make things better for your colleagues and your students. Your work will also serve as a frequent reminder of the standards of cyberethical behavior that you should be following daily.

Parting Thoughts

Often, parents and educators leave my lectures shaking their heads and muttering that they're going to lock up every piece of digital technology in their house. But that's not a realistic option for parents, let alone for entire school districts that are charged, among other things, with helping to prepare students to work in a digital world.

At the same time, we can't ignore the fact that technology has assisted people in causing real harm to others, and that our responsibility is to do everything we can to prevent that harm from occurring (or at least minimize its incidence). No single solution will achieve that goal, but there are a variety of steps that we can and should take. These include (but are not limited to):

- Develop and implement a comprehensive K-12 digital citizenship curriculum to educate students about the unique risks they face from the use and misuse of electronic devices;

- Implement the Model Code of Ethics for Educators at all levels of teacher education, certification, and professional development, with a particular focus on the unique risks posed by technology;

- Require annual professional development programs to remind educators of the cybertraps posed by technology, to educate them about new types of hardware and software, and to alert them to new ways students are using technology;

- Help inform parents about the role that students play in creating cybertraps for educators and remind them that they may be liable for their child's malicious acts;

- Develop a national clearinghouse to help catalog cases in which educators misuse technology, to understand better the extent to which these problems are occurring, the types of technology used, and the impact on victims; and

- Hold school districts and administrators accountable when they cover up instances of educator misconduct and "pass the trash" to other unsuspecting school districts.

Many of these initiatives, fortunately, are already underway in programs large and small around the world. I am pleased *that Cybertraps for Educators 2.0* (and future editions) will contribute to this work.

Appendix
Model Code of Ethics for Educators

[**N.B.**: The Model Code of Ethics for Educators is reproduced below with the kind consent of the National Association of State Directors of Teacher Education and Certification (NASDTEC), which has been spearheading the initiative to draft and promote the adoption of a national code of ethics for the teaching profession. I am proud to be a small part of this ongoing effort.]

Principle I: Responsibility to the Profession

The professional educator is aware that trust in the profession depends upon a level of professional conduct and responsibility that may be higher than required by law. This entails holding one and other educators to the same ethical standards.

A. The professional educator demonstrates responsibility to oneself as an ethical professional by:

1. Acknowledging that lack of awareness, knowledge, or understanding of the Code is not, in itself, a defense to a charge of unethical conduct;

2. Knowing and upholding the procedures, policies, laws and regulations relevant to professional practice regardless of personal views;

3. Holding oneself responsible for ethical conduct;

4. Monitoring and maintaining sound mental, physical, and emotional health necessary to perform duties and services of any professional assignment; and taking appropriate measures when personal or health-related issues may interfere with work-related duties;

5. Refraining from professional or personal activity that may lead to reducing one's effectiveness within the school community;

6. Avoiding the use of one's position for personal gain and avoiding the appearance of impropriety;

7. Taking responsibility and credit only for work actually performed or produced, and acknowledging the work and contributions made by others.

B. The professional educator fulfills the obligation to address and attempt to resolve ethical issues by:

1. Confronting and taking reasonable steps to resolve conflicts between the Code and the implicit or explicit demands of a person or organization;

2. Maintaining fidelity to the Code by taking proactive steps when having reason to believe that another educator may be approaching or involved in an ethically compromising situation;

3. Neither discriminating nor retaliating against a person on the basis of having made an ethical complaint;

4. Neither filing nor encouraging frivolous ethical complaints solely to harm or retaliate; and

5. Cooperating fully during ethics investigations and proceedings.

C. The professional educator promotes and advances the profession within and beyond the school community by:

1. Influencing and supporting decisions and actions that positively impact teaching and learning, educational leadership and student services;

2. Engaging in respectful discourse regarding issues that impact the profession;

3. Enhancing one's professional effectiveness by staying current with ethical principles and decisions from relevant sources including professional organizations;

4. Actively participating in educational and professional organizations and associations; and

5. Advocating for adequate resources and facilities to ensure equitable opportunities for all students.

Principle II: Responsibility for Professional Competence

The professional educator is committed to the highest levels of professional and ethical practice, including demonstration of the knowledge, skills and dispositions required for professional competence.

A. The professional educator demonstrates commitment to high standards of practice through:

1. Incorporating into one's practice state and national standards, including those specific to one's discipline;

2. Using the Model Code of Educator Ethics and other ethics codes unique to one's discipline to guide and frame educational decision-making;

3. Advocating for equitable educational opportunities for all students;

4. Accepting the responsibilities, performing duties and providing services corresponding to the area of certification, licensure, and training of one's position;

5. Reflecting upon and assessing one's professional skills, content knowledge, and competency on an ongoing basis; and

6. Committing to ongoing professional learning.

B. The professional educator demonstrates responsible use of data, materials, research and assessment by:

1. Appropriately recognizing others' work by citing data or materials from published, unpublished, or electronic sources when disseminating information;

2. Using developmentally appropriate assessments for the purposes for which they are intended and for which they have been validated to guide educational decisions;

3. Conducting research in an ethical and responsible manner with appropriate permission and supervision;

4. Seeking and using evidence, instructional data, research, and professional knowledge to inform practice;

5. Creating, maintaining, disseminating, storing, retaining and disposing of records and data relating to one's research and practice, in accordance with district policy, state and federal laws; and

6. Using data, data sources, or findings accurately and reliably.

C. The professional educator acts in the best interest of all students by:

1. Increasing students' access to the curriculum, activities, and resources in order to provide a quality and equitable educational experience.

2. Working to engage the school community to close achievement, opportunity, and attainment gaps; and

3. Protecting students from any practice that harms or has the potential to harm students.

Principle III: Responsibility to Students

The professional educator has a primary obligation to treat students with dignity and respect. The professional educator promotes the health, safety and well being of students by establishing and maintaining appropriate verbal, physical, emotional and social boundaries.

A. The professional educator respects the rights and dignity of students by:

1. Respecting students by taking into account their age, gender, culture, setting and socioeconomic context;

2. Interacting with students with transparency and in appropriate settings;

3. Communicating with students in a clear, respectful, and culturally sensitive manner;

4. Taking into account how appearance and dress can affect one's interactions and relationships with students;

5. Considering the implication of accepting gifts from or giving gifts to students;

6. Engaging in physical contact with students only when there is a clearly defined purpose that benefits the student and continually keeps the safety and well-being of the student in mind;

7. Avoiding multiple relationship with students which might impair objectivity and increase the risk of harm to student learning or well-being or decrease educator effectiveness;

8. Acknowledging that there are no circumstances that allow for educators to engage in romantic or sexual relationships with students; and

9. Considering the ramifications of entering into an adult relationship of any kind with a former student, including but not limited to, any potential harm to the former student, public perception, and the possible impact on the educator's career. The professional educator ensures that the adult relationship was not started while the former student was in school.

B. The professional educator demonstrates an ethic of care through:

1. Seeking to understand students' educational, academic, personal and social needs as well as students' values, beliefs, and cultural background;

2. Respecting the dignity, worth, and uniqueness of each individual student including, but not limited to, actual and perceived gender, gender expression, gender identity, civil status, family status, sexual orientation, religion, age, disability, race, ethnicity, socio-economic status, and culture; and

3. Establishing and maintaining an environment that promotes the emotional, intellectual, physical, and sexual safety of all students.

C. The professional educator maintains student trust and confidentiality when interacting with students in a developmentally appropriate manner and within appropriate limits by:

1. Respecting the privacy of students and the need to hold in confidence certain forms of student communication, documents, or information obtained in the course of professional practice;

2. Upholding parents'/guardians' legal rights, as well as any legal requirements to reveal information related to legitimate concerns for the well-being of a student; and

3. Protecting the confidentiality of student records and releasing personal data in accordance with prescribed state and federal laws and local policies.

Principle IV: Responsibility to the School Community

The professional educator promotes positive relationships and effective interactions, with members of the school community, while maintaining professional boundaries.

A. The professional educator promotes effective and appropriate relationships with parents/guardians by:

1. Communicating with parents/guardians in a timely and respectful manner that represents the students' best interests;

2. Demonstrating a commitment to equality, equity, and inclusion as well as respecting and accommodating diversity among members of the school community;

3. Considering the implication of accepting gifts from or giving gifts to parents/guardians; and

4. Maintaining appropriate confidentiality with respect to student information disclosed by or to parents/guardians unless required by law.

B. The professional educator promotes effective and appropriate relationships with colleagues by:

1. Respecting colleagues as fellow professionals and maintaining civility when differences arise;

2. Resolving conflicts, whenever possible, privately and respectfully and in accordance with district policy;

3. Keeping student safety, education, and health paramount by maintaining and sharing educational records appropriately and objectively in accordance with local policies and state and federal laws;

4. Collaborating with colleagues in a manner that supports academic achievement and related goals that promote the best interests of students;

5. Enhancing the professional growth and development of new educators by supporting effective field experiences, mentoring or induction activities across the career continuum;

6. Ensuring that educators who are assigned to participate as mentors for new educators, cooperating teachers, or other teacher leadership positions are prepared and supervised to assume these roles;

7. Ensuring that educators are assigned to positions in accordance with their educational credentials, preparation, and experience in order to maximize students' opportunities and achievement; and

8. Working to ensure a workplace environment that is free from harassment.

C. The professional educator promotes effective and appropriate relationships with the community and other stakeholders by:

1. Advocating for policies and laws that the educator supports as promoting the education and well-being of students and families;

2. Collaborating with community agencies, organizations, and individuals in order to advance students' best interests without regard to personal reward or remuneration; and

3. Maintaining the highest professional standards of accuracy, honesty, and appropriate disclosure of information when representing the school or district within the community and in public communications.

D. The professional educator promotes effective and appropriate relationships with employers by:

1. Using property, facilities, materials, and resources in accordance with local policies and state and federal laws;

2. Respecting intellectual property ownership rights (e.g. original lesson plans, district level curricula, syllabi, gradebooks, etc.) when sharing materials;

3. Exhibiting personal and professional conduct that is in the best interest of the organization, learning community, school community, and profession; and

4. Considering the implications of offering or accepting gifts and/or preferential treatment by vendors or an individual in a position of professional influence or power.

E. The professional educator understands the problematic nature of multiple relationships by:

1. Considering the risks that multiple relationships might impair objectivity and increase the likelihood of harm to students' learning and well-being or diminish educator effectiveness;

2. Considering the risks and benefits of a professional relationship with someone with whom the educator has had a past personal relationship and vice versa;

3. Considering the implications and possible ramifications of engaging in a personal or professional relationship with parents and guardians, student teachers, colleagues, and supervisors; and

4. Ensuring that professional responsibilities to paraprofessionals, student teachers or interns do not interfere with responsibilities to students, their learning, and well-being.

Principle V: Responsible and Ethical Use of Technology

The professional educator considers the impact of consuming, creating, distributing and communicating information through all technologies. The ethical educator is vigilant to ensure appropriate boundaries of time, place and role are maintained when using electronic communication.

A. The professional educator uses technology in a responsible manner by:

1. Using social media responsibly, transparently, and primarily for purposes of teaching and learning per school and district policy. The professional educator

considers the ramifications of using social media and direct communication via technology on one's interactions with students, colleagues, and the general public;

2. Staying abreast of current trends and uses of school technology;

3. Promoting the benefits of and clarifying the limitations of various appropriate technological applications with colleagues, appropriate school personnel, parents, and community members;

4. Knowing how to access, document and use proprietary materials and understanding how to recognize and prevent plagiarism by students and educators;

5. Understanding and abiding by the district's policy on the use of technology and communication;

6. Recognizing that some electronic communications are records under the Freedom of Information Act (FOIA) and state public access laws and should consider the implications of sharing sensitive information electronically either via professional or personal devices/accounts; and

7. Exercising prudence in maintaining separate and professional virtual profiles, keeping personal and professional lives distinct.

B. The professional educator ensures students' safety and well-being when using technology by:

1. Being vigilant in identifying, addressing and reporting (when appropriate and in accordance with local district, state, and federal policy) inappropriate and illegal materials/images in electronic or other forms;

2. Respecting the privacy of students' presence on social media unless given consent to view such information or if there is a possibility of evidence of a risk of harm to the student or others; and

3. Monitoring to the extent practical and appropriately reporting information concerning possible cyber bullying incidents and their potential impact on the student learning environment.

C. The professional educator maintains confidentiality in the use of technology by:

1. Taking appropriate and reasonable measures to maintain confidentiality of student information and educational records stored or transmitted through the use of electronic or computer technology;

2. Understanding the intent of Federal Educational Rights to Privacy Act (FERPA) and how it applies to sharing electronic student records; and

3. Ensuring that the rights of third parties, including the right of privacy, are not violated via the use of technologies.

D. The professional educator promotes the appropriate use of technology in educational settings by:

1. Advocating for equal access to technology for all students, especially those historically underserved;

2. Promoting the benefits of and clarifying the limitations of various appropriate technological applications with colleagues, appropriate school personnel, parents, and community members; and

3. Promoting technological applications (a) that are appropriate for students' individual needs, (b) that students understand how to use and (c) that assist and enhance the teaching and learning process.

Glossary

Boundaries

The verbal, physical, emotional and social distances that an educator must maintain in order to ensure structure, security, and predictability in an educational environment. Most often, the boundaries that are transgressed relate to role, time and place. By respecting contracted roles, appropriate working hours, and the location of the learning environment, secure boundaries are in place for all members of the schooling community.

Culture

The customary beliefs, social forms, and material traits of a racial, religious, or social group, including the characteristic features of everyday existence shared by people in a place or time. [1]

District/School District

This is often referred to as a "local education agency." A "district" in this document is defined as a public board of education or other public authority legally constituted within a State for either administrative control or direction of, or to perform a service function for, public elementary schools or secondary schools in a city, county, township, school district, or other political subdivision of a State, or for a combination of school districts or counties that is recognized in a State as an administrative agency for its public elementary schools or secondary schools. This can include charter schools, magnet schools, virtual magnet schools, regional educational school districts, or other entities falling under the definition above.

Educator

Educators are the target audience for the MCEE, and are defined as licensed educators. These include paraprofessionals, teachers, teacher leaders, student support personnel and administrators. However, others who interact with students who are not under the auspices of an education-related licensing organization such as coaches, school secretaries, custodians or other school staff are encouraged to adopt or adapt this Model Code of Educator Ethics. See a separate definition for "professional educator."

Ethic of Care

Responding with compassion to the needs of students.

Ethical Decision-Making Model

A framework utilized by educators to guide decision-making which includes professional dispositions; applicable laws, statutes, and policies; the *Model Code of Educator Ethics*; and other guidelines that have been adopted and endorsed by educational organizations.

Fiduciary Relationship

A fiduciary relationship is one in which a person justifiably places confidence in another whose aid, advice, or protection is assumed. Inherent in such fiduciary relationships is an imbalance of power. Educators have a unique responsibility, as the relationship between student and teacher differs from other professional/client relationships (e.g., attorneys, physicians, clergy). Educators are entrusted with the safety and welfare of students during and after school hours and serve "in loco parentis."

Implicit or Explicit Demands of an Organization

Implicit demands are often subjective or implied and reflect the culture of the schooling environment. Explicit demands are clearly articulated through mandates, policies, or statutes.

Harm

The impairment of learning or any potential action which may lead to physical, emotional, psychological, sexual, or intellectual damage to a student or a member of the school community.

Learning Community

A group of educators who work with one another to achieve the shared goals of their school and engage in collaborative professional learning to strengthen practice and increase student results. [2]

Multiple Relationships

Multiple relationships occur when the educator is in a professional role with one or more members of the school community and also has a personal relationship with that person or a member of that person's family. Multiple relationships have the potential to impair objectivity, competence, or effectiveness in performing his or her functions as an educator.

New Educators

New educators include individuals in an educator preparation program or newly employed in the education profession, including paraprofessionals, teachers, administrators, and student support personnel.

Professional Educator

A licensed educator who demonstrates the highest standards of ethical and professionally competent practice and is committed to advancing the interests, achievement and well-being of students. The professional educator is also committed to supporting the school community and the education profession.

Proprietary Materials

Materials that protected from unauthorized use by copyright or other forms of intellectual property rights.

Safe Environments/Safety and Well-Being

A school setting which promotes the well-being of all members of the school community and is characterized by the absence of physical, psychological, sexual or emotional harm.

School Community

This term usually refers to those stakeholders invested in the welfare of a school and its community. A school community includes school administrators, teachers, school staff members, students, their parents and families, school board members and other community members. [3]

Sensitive Information

This includes but is not limited to student information and educational records, including medical or counseling records.

Student

A learner attending a P-12 school.

Technology

Tools, systems, applications and processes that can include, but are not limited to, electronic communications networks such as the Internet and electronic devices such as computers, laptops, phones and other hardware/software that deliver text, audio, images, animation, and streaming video.

Transparency

Openness and accountability with respect to one's behaviors, actions and communications as an educator.

Footnotes

1. http://www.merriam-webster.com/dictionary/culture

2. http://learningforward.org/standards/learning-communities#.VTVerkv7Q3Y

3. http://edglossary.org/school-community/

© NASDTEC 2015

Acknowledgments

Five years ago, when I wrote and published the first version of this book, my goal was to help educators better understand the risks associated with the use of digital technology. It is clear from even a cursory view of the headlines that there is still a lot more work to do in this area. Teachers continue to stumble into avoidable cybertraps or purposely misuse technology to the detriment of their students, their careers, and their school communities.

Much of that has to do with the acceleration of long-standing technological trends: the nearly universal use of mobile devices by teachers and students, the steady increase in the number of communication and social media apps, and the relentless push to incorporate digital communication tools into virtually all aspects of K-12 education. In a world grappling with a pandemic caused by a novel virus, that last trend was perhaps inevitable. Unfortunately, however, our professional and social norms are struggling to keep up with the technological onslaught.

One of the solutions, of course, is to delineate professional norms and ethical expectations and use them for training up and coming generations of educators. The first edition of *Cybertraps for Educators* was released shortly before the introduction of the Model Code of Ethics for Educators, so there was no opportunity to address that critical development. In the years since, however, I have had a chance to study the MCEE and consider its application to educator technology use.

My many conversations with my good friend and colleague, Dr. Troy Hutchings, have immeasurably improved my understanding of the MCEE and its application to my work. As the lead subject matter expert in the development of the Model Code, Troy is uniquely qualified to offer that guidance, and it has been a great gift to have his input on this project.

As I noted in my original acknowledgments, Troy introduced me to two outstanding educator certification and licensing organizations: the National Association of State Directors of Teacher Education and Certification (NASDTEC) and its subsidiary group, the Professional Practices Institute (PPI). Although the pandemic forced the postponement of the 2020 annual conference for each group, I've enjoyed a series of Zoom conversations with a close group of colleagues: Dr. Glenn Lipson, Catherine Slagle, Carolyn Angelo, Joe Jamieson, and Troy. Their friendship and collegiality have been particularly important to me, since my planned nine-month stay in York, England wound up lasting five months longer than expected.

Since becoming involved in NASDTEC and PPI, I have had the privilege of working with many outstanding education professionals from around the country. I am highly grateful to Phil Rogers, Mike Carr, and Linda Stowers, who keep NASDTEC and PPI running and pull together great conferences year in and year out. They have been gracious in welcoming me to the fold and for allowing me to contribute to the work that they are doing.

In large part, because of my work with NASDTEC and PPI, I have had the opportunity over the last several years to visit school communities around the country. Along the way, I have met hundreds of dedicated educators, administrators, school board members, and parents. All of them are committed to providing quality education to the children in their communities. They share a powerfully optimistic view of the role education can play in a child's life, and I believe it is one of the best things we do as a country. I hope that at least some of the travel returns post-pandemic.

There is one group of people that deserve special mention. During my research and writing, I have had the honor of meeting and working with a loose-knit coalition of survivors of educator sexual abuse. Many now provide counseling services to other victims or have shared their stories in powerful memoirs. It is remarkable to watch their efforts to make something positive out of an experience that should never have happened in the first place. Their work is an endless inspiration.

My wife Amy Werbel and I have collaborated in raising four young men – Ben, Graham, Peter, and Emmett. All of them are well past K-12 age, but my siblings—Jonathan Lane, Elizabeth Murdock, and Kate Van Sleet—are all parents of school-age children. I hope that my nieces and nephews are taught by educators who fully understand the cybertraps that can damage their careers and harm the students they teach.

In addition to nearly two decades of co-parenting, Amy is my partner in fascinating travel, a terrific editor and sounding board, and my best friend. After the ninth or tenth acknowledgment, it can be challenging to come up with a fresh version of how much she means to me. But the times have inspired me: I now can honestly say there is no one with whom I would rather spend six months in pandemic lockdown.

About the Author

I am an author, attorney, expert witness, and professional speaker on the legal and cultural implications of emerging technology. My main areas of concentration are educator cyberethics, digital safety, privacy, cybersecurity, ethics, and law.

Following my graduation from Amherst College (1985) and Boston College Law School (1988), I clerked for two years for the Honorable Frank H. Freedman, Chief Judge of the U.S. District Court in Massachusetts. After practicing law for five years and writing my first book, *Vermont Jury Instructions—Civil and Criminal* [with John Dinse and Ritchie Berger] (Butterworths 1993), I launched a computer consulting business that in turn led to my current work as an author, lecturer, and computer forensics expert.

In response to the passage of the Communications Decency Act in 1996, I began researching the legislative and media response to the rise of the online adult industry. The resulting book, *Obscene Profits: The Entrepreneurs of Pornography in the Cyber Age* (Routledge, 2000), was the first of what are now ten mainstream non-fiction books. The others are:

- *The Naked Employee: How Technology Is Compromising Workplace Privacy* (Amazon, 2003);

- *The Decency Wars: The Campaign to Cleanse American Culture* (Prometheus Books, 2006);

- *The Court and the Cross: The Religious Right's Crusade to Reshape the Supreme Court* (Beacon Press, 2008);

- *American Privacy: The 400-Year History of Our Most Contested Right* (Beacon Press, 2010);

- *Cybertraps for the Young* (NTI Upstream, 2011);

- *Cybertraps for Educators* (Mathom Press, 2015);

- *Cybertraps for Expecting Moms & Dads* (Mathom Press, 2018);

- *Raising Cyberethical Kids: How a Family Acceptable Use Policy Can Make Your Young Digital Citizens Smarter, Safer, Kinder, and More Empathetic* (Mathom Press, 2020); and most recently,

- *Cybertraps for Educators 2.0* (Mathom Press, 2020).

I have also written numerous magazine and newspaper articles on a wide variety of topics, including constitutional rights (particularly freedom of speech), privacy online and in the workplace, the impact of technology on our rights and liberties, and the separation of church and state.

On August 23, 2006, I had the honor of appearing on "The Daily Show with Jon Stewart" to discuss *The Decency Wars: The Campaign to Cleanse American Culture.* I have also appeared as a guest on a variety of other national television programs, including ABC's "Good Morning America Weekend," NBC's "Weekend Today," ABC's "Nightline," CBS's "60 Minutes," and various BBC documentaries. In addition to those televised appearances, I have been interviewed by numerous radio shows, magazines, and newspapers around the world on topics relating to my books.

Over the last fifteen years, I have frequently lectured to college, university, and professional audiences across the United States and in Canada and China on topics related to my books, including educator misconduct, student online safety, internet technology, workplace and personal privacy, computer forensics, free speech, and censorship.

For my information about my lectures and professional services, please free to contact me through one of the following channels.

Connect with Frederick Lane Online

Thank you for purchasing this e-book and for taking the time to read it. If you found this book to be engaging, useful, shocking, alarming, accessible, charming, and witty—please leave a review for me on Amazon.

If you'd like to keep up to date on my latest books, news, and the latest Cybertraps, please drop me a line at **FSLane3@FrederickLane.com** and ask to be added to my mailing list.

If you have any suggestions for ways it can be improved or additional resources that I should add, or if you just want to reach out, you can find me online through the following services:

- LinkedIn: http://www.linkedin.com/in/fredericklane
- Facebook: https://www.facebook.com/Cybertraps
- Twitter: @Cybertraps and @FSL3
- Web: FrederickLane.com and Cybertraps.com

Word of mouth is an enormous help in promoting any book or product. If you found this book useful and informative, please tell your friends and acquaintances about it on your various social networks or by email.

CPSIA information can be obtained
at www.ICGtesting.com
Printed in the USA
LVHW100717260821
696138LV00013B/686

9 798684 352362